PRE-CAROLINGIAN LATIN COMPUTUS AND ITS REGIONAL CONTEXTS

STUDIA TRADITIONIS THEOLOGIAE
EXPLORATIONS IN EARLY AND MEDIEVAL THEOLOGY

VOLUME 54

Series Editor
Thomas O'Loughlin, *Professor of Historical Theology*
in the University of Nottingham

EDITORIAL BOARD

Director
Prof. Thomas O'Loughlin

Board Members
Dr Andreas Andreopoulos
Dr Nicholas Baker-Brian
Dr Augustine Casiday
Dr Mary B. Cunningham
Dr Juliette Day
Prof. Johannesn Hoff
Prof. Paul Middleton
Prof. Simon Oliver
Prof. Andrew Prescott
Dr Patricia Rumsey
Prof. Jonathan Wooding
Dr Holger Zellentin

Pre-Carolingian Latin Computus and its Regional Contexts

Texts, Tables, and Debates

Edited by

IMMO WARNTJES, TOBIT LOEVENICH, AND
DÁIBHÍ Ó CRÓINÍN

BREPOLS

Cover illustration: *Tabula Peutingeriana* © ÖNB Vienna Cod. 324, Segm. VIII + IX

© 2023, Brepols Publishers n.v., Turnhout, Belgium.

All rights reserved. No part of this publication may be reproduced, stored in a retrieval system, or transmitted, in any form or by any means, electronic, mechanical, photocopying, recording, or otherwise without the prior permission of the publisher.

D/2023/0095/59
ISBN 978-2-503-60556-2
eISBN 978-2-503-60557-9
DOI 10.1484/M.STT-EB.5.133434
ISSN 2294-3617
eISSN 2566-0160

Printed in the EU on acid-free paper.

Brendan Halligan (1936-2020), supporter and benefactor of the *Galway Computus Conference* from the beginning.

Table of Contents

Abbreviations 9

Foreword
Immo WARNTJES, Tobit LOEVENICH, Dáibhí Ó CRÓINÍN 11

The Zeitz Paschal Table of AD 447
Daniel MC CARTHY 17

How King Oswiu Made Northumbria Orthodox. The Social and Political Background of the 'Synod' of Whitby (AD 664)
Colin IRELAND 87

'If you find it, give thanks'. A Problematic Chapter of Bede's
De temporum ratione
Leofranc HOLFORD-STREVENS 121

A Visigothic Computus of AD 722 (Leiden, Universiteitsbibliotheek, VMI 11, 26r–27r)
Immo WARNTJES 141

Irish Computistical Texts of the Seventh Century. Three Dating Passages
David HOWLETT 159

An Eighth-Century Irish Computus in Lombardy
James T. PALMER 177

Victorian Survival in High Medieval Chronography. The Strange Case of the Angevin Paschal Chronicle
C. Philipp E. NOTHAFT 201

Bibliography 223

Index of Biblical Citations 241

8   TABLE OF CONTENTS

Index of Sources 242

Index of Manuscripts 250

Abbreviations

CCCM	*Corpus Christianorum, Continuatio Mediaevalis*
CCSL	*Corpus Christianorum, Series Latina*
CLA	*Codices Latini Antiquiores*
CSEL	*Corpus Scriptorum Ecclesiasticorum Latinorum*
FGrH	*Fragmente der griechischen Historiker*
GCS	*Die griechischen christlichen Schriftsteller der ersten Jahrhunderte*
MGH	*Monumenta Germaniae Historica*

Auct. ant.	*Auctores antiquissimi*
SS	*Scriptores (in Folio)*
SS rer. Germ.	*Scriptores rerum Germanicarum in usum scholarum separatim editi*
SS rer. Merov.	*Scriptores rerum Merovingicarum*

PL	*Patrologia Latina*

IMMO WARNTJES, TOBIT LOEVENICH,
DÁIBHÍ Ó CRÓINÍN

Foreword

The *International Conference on the Science of Computus in Ireland and Europe in Late Antiquity and the Middle Ages* was established in Galway in 2006. What turned out to be its first iteration marked the end of the Project *Foundations of Irish Culture, AD 500–850*, funded by the Irish government as part of the *Programme for Research in Third Level Institutions [PRTLI]*. The first conference in 2006 proved surprisingly successful, so much so that it was decided to hold follow-up events on a biannual basis, which saw a further six conferences take place in Galway (the agreed permanent venue) between 2008 and 2018. The 2020 event, scheduled for June of that year, was postponed by a year due to the Covid pandemic, which brought a halt to all international travel. By 2021 the situation had not improved to any substantial degree, which meant that this 8th conference was the first to be held virtually. The personal interactions in coffee breaks, conference dinner, and pub evenings of previous Galway events were sorely missed, but at the same time the virtual format allowed for many more people to engage around the globe, which saw a record of almost 200 participants.

The principal idea of organising these conferences from the outset was to bring a neglected field of early medieval studies more into the academic mainstream. 2006 saw the publication of Arno Borst's great three-volume *Schriften zur Komputistik im Frankenreich, 721–818* (which was officially launched at that first Galway conference), but it is probably fair to say that even this monumental effort has not yet established computus as a viable field of research among Carolingianists, certainly not in the same way that historiography, hagiography, or exegesis has been for decades. More worrying still, Borst's study of the early medieval calendar tradition, which led to two monographs (1998; 2004; full titles for these and the following publications can be found in the bibliography) and an almost 2000-page edition based on more than 270 calendars (2001), should have opened up numerous avenues of pioneering research, but this monumental study is hardly ever cited, especially in anglophone publications on the subject.

Still, more broadly speaking, the study of late antique and early medieval computus has gathered some momentum over the past fifteen years, as we tried to outline in the introduction to the previous conference volume of 2017. This trend is certainly evidenced by the progress made between the last two conferences of 2018 and 2021, in monographs and projects (and obviously articles too numerous to be mentioned here). Leofranc Holford-Strevens published in 2019 an *editio princeps*, translation, and commentary of excerpts from Macrobius' *Saturnalia* outlining the origin of the Julian calendar, a text that circulated especially among seventh- and eighth-century insular scholars (most prominently Bede) as the *Disputatio Chori et Praetextati*; this monograph grew out of a Galway conference talk. Bede's view on the cosmos was reassessed in 2020 by Eoghan Ahern, and in the same year Máirín MacCarron provided a fundamental study on Bede's conception of time, which systematically analyses the Northumbrian monk's reliance on Irish ideas. The Irish contribution to early medieval computus and its influence on Carolingian Europe is currently studied in an *Irish Research Council Laureate Project* based at Trinity College Dublin, which will lead to an *editio princeps* and translation of one of the most important seventh- and eighth-century Irish texts, the *Computus Einsidlensis* by Tobit Loevenich, and of a fundamental and highly original ninth-century text by the Irish scholar Dicuil, his *Liber de astronomia* by Christian Schweizer (now more appropriately called *De cursu solis lunaeque*); this text was also the subject of a recent study by Werner Bergmann in the second Galway conference proceedings of 2011. The Dublin project will also include a database of all computistical manuscripts, texts and, eventually, ideas pre-AD 900 designed by Judith ter Horst and Jean-Paul Rehr (https://computus.huma-num.fr/). For the 2019 Kathleen Hughes Lecture in Cambridge (published in 2020) Jacopo Bisagni studied the origin and transmission history of the Irish *De divisionibus temporum* and its numerous recensions. He is now heading another *Irish Research Council Laureate Project*, based in Galway, which is researching Irish influence on early medieval Breton intellectual culture, with a strong focus on computus; this project will also provide a first edition of the highly important *Computus Hibernicus Parisinus* of AD 754.

The Carolingian period has been the life-long focus of research by Wesley Stevens, whose 2018 study of St Gall, Stiftsbibliothek, 878 illustrates how much more careful analysis is needed for the hundreds of substantial computistical codices of the early medieval period. For the eleventh century, a new edition of Notker of St Gall's and Hermann of Reichenau's computistical works and related texts, started by Arno Borst in the mid-1970s and brought to completion by Immo Warntjes, is currently in the press. Without a doubt the most substantial progress in the field of computistics in recent years has been made by the combined efforts of Philipp Nothaft und Alfred Lohr on twelfth- and thirteenth-century computistics, through Nothaft's 2017 edition of Walcher of Malvern's writings on the subject, their co-authored 2019 edition of Robert Grosseteste's Computus, and Nothaft's brilliant 2018 monograph on the pre-history of the Gregorian calendar reform. Much more is to be expected from their pens, as Nothaft is currently leading a two-year project based in Dublin on *The Transformation of Latin Astronomy, 1050–1250*, and Lohr is preparing a corpus of *editiones principes* of no fewer than sixteen unpublished computistical texts of the twelfth and thirteenth centuries.

Another indicator of the renewed interest in matters scientific and calendrical for the late antique and early medieval period may be illustrated by the fact that the 67th iteration of the *Settimana di studi sull'alto medioevo* in Spoleto dealt with *La cognoscenza scientifica nell'alto medioevo* (2019, published 2020), and the 70th iteration in 2023 will focus on *Il tempo nell'alto medioevo*. Also worth noting, and representative of the increased number of conferences in fields adjacent to computus, are the numerous collected volumes on apocalypticism in the past few years, edited by Matthew Gabriele and James Palmer in 2019, by Veronika Wieser et al. in 2020, and by Hans-Christian Lehner in 2021.

When we first started out organizing the Galway conference and publishing its proceedings, we were acutely aware that there was hardly any space in existing journals for specialists to publish highly technical articles on late antique and early medieval computus (with the luminous exception of *Peritia*, Journal of the Medieval Academy of Ireland, which, from its inception, has always had a section devoted to computistics); such studies were and are essential for meaningful progress in the field, and we wanted to provide a platform for this research. The first three volumes of Galway conference proceedings were produced in that spirit. Since then, and since the fourth iteration of our conference in particular, we felt it essential to substantially broaden our scope to include studies of computus from various different perspectives, such as the underlying intellectual cultures, the theological frameworks, or the political and institution settings in which these computists operated. This we tried to encourage through special themes, such as prognostics, computus and the vernacular, etc., hoping that this would lead to more focused volumes. Of the submissions that reached us over the past few years, three main themes emerged that we felt deserved special attention. Borst's path-breaking *Schriften* contained the inherent risk of overemphasizing the Carolingian endeavour as the crucial period of early medieval calendrical science, at the risk of eclipsing the pre-Carolingian era that saw the formation of computus into a central pillar of Christian learning; this is addressed in the present volume. At the same time, Borst's publication of twenty key Carolingian texts on computus created the problematic sense of a clearly defined corpus of Carolingian computistical literature; Borst's texts are only the tip of the iceberg, and his notion of master texts informing Carolingian intellectual circles seems to misrepresent how schoolmasters and librarians in this age picked and chose from rather fluid compilations of computistical items; this time-period will be dealt with in a second volume on Carolingian computus. Finally, over the years the Galway conference has highlighted that notable progress has been made in certain fields, such as late antique, Bedan, Irish, Frankish, and high medieval computus, but that other areas too are in desperate need of systematic analysis; one of these is Iberian computus (despite the efforts of Alfred Cordoliani and Joan Gomez Pallarès, and Brigitte Englisch's contributions in the second and third Galway conference proceedings of 2011 and 2017 respectively), and this will be addressed in a third and final volume.

Computus was not a Carolingian invention, it emerged as a monastic discipline in the century before the coronation of the first Carolingian king in AD 751/754. It had its roots in the debates about the correct date of Easter, which became particularly vibrant with Christianity becoming state religion in the late Roman Empire and its subsequent split into East and West in the late fourth century. With the emergence of a Christian elite in the successor kingdoms to the Roman Empire in what developed into the Latin West, learning was monopolized by this elite and therewith turned decidedly Christian. But the lack of an overarching authority, either political or ecclesiastical, meant that in each of those successor kingdoms strong regional customs of Christian knowledge developed. This volume seeks to highlight the potential of studying these regional manifestations of Christian learning in pre-Carolingian Europe, with their unique and characteristic ideas and debates, in the hope that future scholars will apply this more systematically to the regions of their own particular interest, and beyond the discipline of computus.

In Late Antiquity, the best window into the Easter controversy is provided by the incumbency of Pope Leo I, not only through his correspondence on the controversial Easters of AD 444 and 455, but also and particularly because of his attempts to reform the Roman Easter calculation as evidenced by the Zeitz table of AD 447 and Victorius of Aquitaine's 532-year paschal cycle of AD 457. Of the Zeitz table, new fragments have come to light in recent years that have provided a stimulus for a new assessment of this Easter reckoning by Dan Mc Carthy in the present volume, which stands here as representative of the debates in mid-fifth-century Rome.

But it is obviously imperative to also look beyond the papal see. Articles by Max Lejbowicz and Leofranc Holford-Strevens in the first two volumes of the Galway computus conference proceedings of 2010 and 2011 highlighted the disputes in Milan under Bishop Ambrose in AD 387, and much more work needs to be done on Byzantine influence on the Apennine peninsula in the transition period from Late Antiquity to the early Middle Ages. It is no coincidence that one of Leo's chief advisors in paschal matters and his chief chronicler, Prosper, and his most skilled computist, Victorius, hailed from Aquitaine. As has been stressed many times since Dan Mc Carthy's fundamental articles of 1993/1994 on the *latercus* (the dominant Easter reckoning in Britain and Ireland from the fifth to the seventh centuries), this was invented by another Aquitanian, Sulpicius Severus, early in the fifth century (see also Mc Carthy's article in the second conference proceedings of 2011). A thorough study of the intellectual milieu in Aquitaine that produced this almost unrivalled chronological, calendrical, and mathematical knowledge in the first half of the fifth century certainly would be a fruitful study.

Another highly understudied region in this context is northern Africa, where in St Augustine's time the writings of Quintus Iulius Hilarianus prove a certain expertise and certainly considerable interest in matters chronological and calendrical. It appears that the Vandals managed to instrumentalise this expertise to anchor themselves in salvation history as the chosen people; the key document, the Carthaginian computus of AD 455 to which Alden Mosshammer drew renewed attention in the second Galway conference proceedings of 2011, remains hopelessly understudied, especially concerning its cultural background.

FOREWORD   15

From Leo's time to the seventh century, more work needs to be done on the processes of introducing the Alexandrian Easter reckoning in the Latin West, either through translation by Dionysius Exiguus (AD 525) as in Italy, or independently as in the Iberian peninsula. Rome itself conformed with the Eastern practice as late as the AD 640s, and the role played in this by Eastern exiles after the Arab conquest of Jerusalem and the theological debates between the papacy and the emperor in Constantinople is not yet fully appreciated. By this time, the Easter controversy was in full swing in Ireland, which led to Irish scholars acquiring an expertise in computus unrivalled by their seventh-century contemporaries. It was arguably here that computus became a fully developed discipline of Christian learning in its own right, evidenced by the invention of a new genre, the computistical textbook. In the present volume, David Howlett engages with some of the key Irish texts, while James Palmer stresses the legacy of Irish knowledge on the Continent a few decades later. Such second-generation texts merging imported Irish knowledge with local customs create a new characteristic regional imprint — in Palmer's case Lombard Italy –, which need to be more closely studied in the future (as is currently the case in the *Irish Research Council* projects for the Carolingian Empire and Brittany).

Irish thought also influenced northern Northumbria, which was traditionally divided between the Irish-influenced northern kingdom of Bernicia, and the Continental- and Roman-oriented southern kingdom of Deira. Famously, the two outlooks clashed over the correct date of Easter at the Synod of Whitby, at least if Bede is to be believed. Besides Leo's incumbency, this is the best documented debate of the Western Easter controversy, and it does not surprise, therefore, that it has been the subject of studies by Leofranc Holford-Strevens and David Pelteret in the first two conference proceedings of 2010 and 2011, and that it is also analysed by Colin Ireland in the present volume. The emerging Northumbrian computus can not only be best, but exclusively accessed through Bede's shorter and longer textbooks on this discipline, and Leofranc Holford-Strevens provides in the present volume a thorough commentary of one of the most controversial chapters of the longer *De temporum ratione*, a chapter that led high-medieval computists from Abbo of Fleury († AD 1004) to Heimo of Bamberg († AD 1139) to recalculate the incarnation era. Important as Bede's works became, especially in and from the ninth century, it remains an interesting fact that we do not know of any other computistical text produced in the Angli, Saxon, and Jutish kingdoms of Britain in pre-Carolingian times. In particular, what exactly may have been taught in Theodore's Canterbury school in the last third of the seventh century still remains an unanswered question.

Besides Ireland and Britain, the only other western European region with a substantial corpus of surviving literature dealing with the Easter question and the intricacies of computus in the pre-Carolingian age was the Iberian peninsula (though this is obviously not to say that the more limited Frankish and Italian evidence does not deserve thorough investigation). In fact, the presentations at the Galway conference demonstrated that this region needs much closer attention than had previously been thought, and deserves a full volume in its own right. The process of compiling that volume led to more background research, which unearthed a Visigothic text of AD 722 that will be key in the future endeavour of defining characteristic Visigothic computistical features. It was therefore decided to include a preliminary study of this text here, so that this prominent region will also be represented in a volume on pre-Carolingian computus.

The debates, texts, and tables of late antique and early medieval computus had a long afterlife, right into the high Middle Ages. One need only think of how (as mentioned above) Bede's chapter on the problem of where to locate the historic *annus passionis* in the Dionysiac Easter table triggered recalculations of the incarnation era from the late tenth to the early twelfth centuries. Likewise, there was a renewed interest, by Marianus Scotus († AD 1082) and others, in late antique texts like the *Acta Synodi Caesareae*, a work that was frequently discussed at the Galway conferences and which will receive a thorough treatment by Leofranc Holford-Strevens shortly. Another interesting example from an Irish perspective is how the late seventh-/early-eighth-century pseudo-Columbanian tract *De saltu lunae* provoked the computistical studies of Notker of St Gall († AD 1022) and Hermann of Reichenau († AD 1054). Dáibhí Ó Cróinín drew attention to this phenomenon of lasting legacy in the first Galway conference proceedings of 2010, and much more work needs to be done in this field, especially for lesser-known texts or tables. It is therefore fitting that the present volume is concluded by an excellent study by Philipp Nothaft on the use of the long-outdated Victorian Easter table by high medieval chronologers.

It remains only to thank those institutions and repositories that granted permission to reproduce images from manuscripts in their care: the Vereinigte Domstifter zu Merseburg und Naumburg und des Kollegiatstifts Zeitz; the Universiteitsbibliotheek, Leiden; and the Bodleian Library, Oxford. We are grateful also to Thomas O'Loughlin, who has continued to offer us a home in his series of *Studia Traditionis Theologiae*, and to Bart Janssens at Brepols, who, by his steadfast support for the publication of these volumes, has encouraged us to believe in the value of what we have been doing.

Cortegaça – Bonn – Galway
January 2022

DANIEL MC CARTHY

The Zeitz Paschal Table of AD 447

▼ *ABSTRACT* In 1816 Andreas Cramer identified that the two bifolia in late antique Latin script lining the covers of Zeitz, Stiftsbibliothek, fol. 33 preserved fragments of the preface and its associated paschal table, and in 1826 he published a transcription of all the legible text. The preface fragment showed that the table had been compiled in AD 447 and it commenced in AD 29 and employed an 84-year lunar table, all suggestive of a Roman context. In the ensuing century Gustav Hänel, Theodor Mommsen, and Bruno Krusch published increasingly accurate editions of the preface and table fragments. However, a major obstacle to the reconstruction of the paschal table was that the available preface provided no indication of the compiler's paschal principles, the *termini* to be imposed on the Julian calendar date of Pasch and age of the paschal moon. Remarkably, in 2005 three further small fragments were identified in Zeitz which were published by Eef Overgaauw and Frank-Joachim Stewing, and these revealed that the compiler intended to tabulate paschal dates and moons according to both Roman and Alexandrian *termini*. This article provides a full transcription of all the known manuscript fragments, a reconstruction of the paschal table based upon these, and a discussion of the historical context of the table's compilation.

▼ *KEYWORDS* Pasch, paschal tables, Roman paschal history, Roman consuls, computus, 84-year lunar cycles, 12-year *saltus*, epacts, ferials; Bruno Krusch, Pope Leo I, Bishop Paschasinus of Lilybaeum, Prosper of Aquitaine, Victorius of Aquitaine

Pre-Carolingian Latin Computus and its Regional Contexts, ed. by Immo Warntjes, Tobit Loevenich, and Dáibhí Ó Cróinín, Studia Traditionis Theologiae, 54 (Turnhout: Brepols, 2023), pp. 17–86

BREPOLS ❧ PUBLISHERS   10.1484/M.STT-EB.5.133485

Introduction

The two vellum bifolia pasted down to line the inside back and front covers of Zeitz, Stiftsbibliothek, fol. 33, were recognised by Andreas Cramer in 1816 from their uncial script to date from Late Antiquity. By 1826 he had transcribed and published the text legible on the visible pages of these bifolia, from which it became apparent that they were fragments of a compilation dealing with celebration of the Pasch that had consisted of a preface followed by tabular material. The visible part of the preface published by Cramer indicated that the compilation had been made in AD 447, and that five 84-year lunar cycles, or 420 years, would bring it to the following year, AD 448. This implied that these five lunar cycles had extended from AD 29 to 448, and these were to be followed by a sixth cycle for which the date of Pasch of its first year is given as *VI kal April* (27 March), stated to be the date of Jesus' Resurrection. This is followed by the statement that to these paschal days would be attached the sequence of the consuls with the years of the primates of the Apostolic See and reigns of the emperors carefully noted. These references to the apostolic primates and emperors clearly implied that the compilation had been made in a Roman context.[1]

In these circumstances the compilation had been made just three years after the bishop of Rome, Pope Leo I (incumbency AD 440–461), had agreed in AD 444 to celebrate Pasch in Rome on 23 April, and so to synchronize with the Alexandrian date.[2] Subsequently, in AD 455, he would make further adjustments in order to accommodate Alexandrian tradition, and in AD 457 Victorius of Aquitaine would, at the request of Leo's archdeacon, Hilarus, compile a 532-year paschal table incorporating both Roman and Alexandrian paschal principles. From these events it was clear that the work identified by Cramer was compiled at a time of very significant developments regarding the papal determination of the celebration of their Pasch. For this reason alone the work has attracted the attention of scholars ever since Cramer published his account of the manuscript and his edition of the then visible pages, as will be further discussed below.

There are, however, some major obstacles to both examining and understanding the compilation. First, the surviving manuscript represents only a small part of the original compilation; just four folios plus three small fragments of another two folios discovered in Zeitz in 2005 survive from an estimated total of about twenty-four folios (cf. Table 1).[3] Second, the published transcriptions from the manuscript are distributed in six articles published between 1826 and 2005, and they are all incomplete.[4] Third, the three small fragments discovered in Zeitz in 2005 have not been transcribed or considered. Fourth, the analyses

---

1 Cramer (1826), 3–16: 13 for the preface, 14–16 for tabular material.
2 Mosshammer (2008), 169 (Leo and Pasch of AD 444).
3 Overgaauw and Stewing (2005), 9 (discovery of three Zeitz fragments).
4 Transcriptions: Cramer (1826), 13–16; Hänel (1837), 957–59; Mommsen (1863), 541–45; MGH Auct. ant. 9, 507–10; Krusch (1933), 996; Overgaauw and Stewing (2005), 8.

and reconstructions of the tabular material published by Mommsen (1863) and Krusch (1880) exhibit some significant differences. For all these reasons it seems worthwhile to prepare a comprehensive transcription of all the available manuscript fragments, and to reconsider the reconstruction that may be derived from these fragments, and that is the purpose of this article.

Finally, regarding nomenclature, although the bifolia identified by Cramer have been in Berlin since 1861 I shall identify them by the place of their discovery, Zeitz, as has been customary. Also, since it is clear that the tabular material in this Zeitz manuscript was the result of a Roman computation made in AD 447, I shall refer to this computation and its table with the siglum RS-447.

The scholarship

In 1826 Cramer published an account of his discovery of the two bifolia still glued to the inside covers of MS Zeitz, Stiftsbibliothek, fol. 33, and he gave a careful transcription of all the text legible to him. He identified that the three visible sections of the table extended over AD 41–52, 183–198, and 365–376, and that the bifolia came from separate gatherings, but assigned incongruent bifolium and folio numbers to the third page.[5] Subsequently the two bifolia were detached from MS Zeitz, Stiftsbibliothek, fol. 33 and reagent applied to much of the text. Consequently in his 1837 publication Gustav Hänel was able to correct some of Cramer's readings, and to provide an edition of all the text that was legible on the previously glued pages, and in his transcription of the table he dated the first year of each tabular page by both *Ab Urbe Condita* (a.u.c.), and *Anno Domini* (AD). He discussed the make-up of the bifolia in some detail assigning them to two successive quaternions; that with the preface and start of the table to 'Quat. I Bl 3 & 6', and that with the remaining table to 'Quat. II Bl. 1 & 8'.[6] Neither Cramer nor Hänel made any endeavour to analyse the tabular material.

In 1861 Giovanni de Rossi, as part of his examination of the history of the Roman 84-year paschal table, was the first to place the Zeitz compilation explicitly within that Roman tradition. Working from Cramer and Hänel's editions, de Rossi stated that the tract was composed in AD 447, that the table commenced in AD 29 and had extended originally to AD 448. He reviewed the literary evidence for, and the reconstructions of, the Roman 84-year paschal table with a 12-year *saltus* published by Enrico Noris, Ludovico Muratori, Johannes van der Hagen, and Ludwig Ideler. Then, pointing to the ambiguity in its 63rd year which would arise in deciding the paschal date for AD 444, de Rossi repeated a hypothesis published by van der Hagen: he proposed that Prosper of Aquitaine, serving as

---

5 Cramer (1826), 14–16 n. 1, for his AD ranges; 14–15, where headings assign 'Plagulae 1ᵐᵃᵉ Folii 2ᵈⁱ' to both the second and third pages; it appears likely that on p. 15 the numbers '1' and '2' have been transposed.

6 Hänel (1837), 757 (corrections), 757–59 (transcription), 759–60 (quaternion make-up).

20 DANIEL MC CARTHY

secretary to Pope Leo, had revised the Roman 84-year table by changing the *saltus* interval from 12-years to 14-years in order to reduce the epacts and so eliminate that paschal ambiguity. Nevertheless, de Rossi concluded that Leo had not accepted Prosper's revision, but had instead instigated the compilation of the table found at Zeitz. Thus de Rossi was the first scholar to place the compilation of Zeitz explicitly in Rome and to associate it closely with Leo.[7] The Roman 84-year paschal cycle with a 12-year *saltus* discussed by de Rossi was designated by him as *Romana supputatio*, and, since the earliest witness to its lunar cycle is the Chronography of AD 354, I shall refer to it by the siglum RS-354.[8]

Also in 1861, Georg Pertz, at Theodor Mommsen's instigation, arranged for the Königliche Bibliothek of Berlin to acquire the two Zeitz bifolia, where they now bear the shelf-mark Berlin, Staatsbibliothek Preußischer Kulturbesitz, Lat. qu. 298, henceforth MS B.[9] There, following a careful examination of these with the assistance of Philipp Jaffé, Mommsen prepared an edition of them based principally on the editions of Cramer and Hänel, since much of the text had by then been rendered illegible by the reagent. In this edition Mommsen undertook to reproduce a facsimile of the eight pages, using an uncial typeface and preserving the spacing and position of the text on these pages, as well as representing accurately the occasional non-literate inscriptions. He added only folio and line numbers, and marginal *Anno Domini* years to the tabular material, and confined his occasional suggested restorations to his apparatus. Consequently this edition gives an excellent sense of the presentation and content of the two bifolia.[10]

---

7 de Rossi (1861), LIX–LX, on the composition and extent of Zeitz, citing Cramer and Hänel; LXXXII–LXXXIII, on the reconstructions of the Roman 84-year table and differences with the Alexandrian; LXXXIX–XCI, on Prosper's revision; XCI–XCII, on Leo's role in compiling Zeitz: 'Tabulam paschalem editam anno 447, cujus jam saepe mentionem celebravi, Romano certe pontifici oblatam ab auctore esse verba e superstite prologi fragmento a me recitata pag. LXXXVII dubitare minime sinunt', and, 'Novae tabulae auctor Leoni Magno cyclum quidem proposuit LXXXIV annorum, at eundem Prosperianae et Romanae *supputationi* plane difformem'.

8 Reconstructions of the *Romana supputatio* referenced by de Rossi (1861), LXXXII nn. 4–5, LXXXIII nn. 1–3: Noris (1691), where his reconstruction table, Tessaradecaeteris I–VI, is on six un-paginated pages prefixed to his 'Dissertatio de paschali Latinorum cyclo ann. LXXXIV'; Muratori (1697–1713), iii 204–07; van der Hagen (1733), 227–38, 247–92; Ideler (1825–1826), ii 247–81. Mommsen in Auct. ant. 9, 13–148 (edition of the Chronography of AD 354); Mosshammer (2008), 206, for the correspondence of the lunar cycle of the *Romana supputatio* and the Chronography of AD 354. Modern published reconstructions of the *Romana supputatio* are by: Krusch (1880), 62–64; Schwartz (1905), 46–49; Mosshammer (2008), 210–11. Krusch gives ambiguous dates for seven years; Schwartz accepts cyclic 6 and 55 as ambiguous, resolving the remainder, but his resolution of cyclic 63 at p. 49 n. 2, misrepresents both manuscript witnesses; Mosshammer accepts cyclic 6, 55, and 63 as ambiguous. All three reconstructions will be cited below.

9 Overgaauw and Stewing (2005), 11 (bifolia acquisition).

10 Mommsen (1863), 539: 'so dass in diesem Abdruck der Text nach sorgfältiger und wiederholter Prüfung des Originals durch mich und Hrn. Jaffé hat gegeben werden können. [...] auch bei der Anwendung chemischer Reagentien nicht mit gehöriger Sorgfalt verfahren und daher auf diesen das Meiste unlesbar geworden ist'.

THE ZEITZ PASCHAL TABLE OF AD 447   21

As well, Mommsen presented a detailed reconstruction of the make-up of the quaternions, based principally on the observation that the consuls and ferial and lunar criteria of the first and fifth 84-year cycles were tabulated at twelve years per page, whereas the preface and the second and third 84-year cycles tabulated just the names of the two consuls for each year at 25 lines per page. Mommsen placed the conclusion of the preface and start of the table at AD 29–52 on fols 4–5 of the first quaternion, and the years AD 159–198, 365–388 of the continuation on fols 2, 7 of the second quaternion, and proposed that the last 36 years of the fifth cycle, AD 413–448, had occupied fols 1–2 of a third, completely lost, quaternion.[11] He then presented a full 84-year reconstruction of the January kalends ferials and lunar epacts, and, with some reconstruction, the paschal new-moon dates, identifying all his manuscript readings with italic font. This presented clearly for the first time the evidence that the Zeitz 84-year lunar cycle inserted the *saltus* at 12-year intervals, and thus corresponded in this respect with the *Romana supputatio* discussed by de Rossi, RS-354. Mommsen tabulated his reconstruction of ferials, epacts, paschal new-moons, and eleven paschal dates beside Ideler's reconstruction of RS-354, which Mommsen designated simply as 'im gewöhnlichen'. Some of Mommsen's new-moon dates for Zeitz are inconsistent, and where inconsistent his dates correlate with those of Ideler.[12] Following this reconstruction Mommsen gave a brief discussion of the Zeitz consular list, and then turned to paschal matters writing:[13]

> Wichtiger ist die eigentliche Paschaltafel, hinsichtlich derer folgendes zu bemerken ist. 1. Im Allgemeinen liegt das lateinische vierundachtzigjährige, nicht das alexandrinische neunzehn — oder fünfundneunzigjährige Schema der Tafel zu Grunde. Auch im Übrigen schließt sie sich im Ganzen genommen, so viel wir sehen, der lateinischen Observanz an und giebt, wo Divergenzen namhaft gemacht werden, derselben die erste Stelle.

Thus Mommsen here identified the Zeitz paschal table with the 'Latin observance', which appears to mean the paschal principles of RS-354, and he asserted that these were given priority. However, the manuscript as Mommsen had it contained no statement concerning the paschal principles used to determine the date of Pasch. This would appear to explain the rather vague character of his assertion. His ensuing discussion, points 2–5, focusses upon the matter that the Zeitz epacts are regularly either two or three less than the 'ältere Schema' (older scheme, i.e. RS-354), and so would sometimes result in different paschal

---

11 Mommsen (1863), 550 (quaternion reconstruction).

12 Mommsen (1863), 554: 'Bringt man in unserer Tafel den *saltus lunae*, wie im gewöhnlichen Cyclus, in Rechnung vom je zwölften zum folgenden Jahr'; 553–54, his reconstruction, where the following new-moon dates are inconsistent: epact 4 (no. 13 has 29M, nos 32, 78 have **28M**); epact 26 (nos 15, 34 have 4A, nos 61, 80 have **6M**); epact 27 (no. 53 has **5M**, nos 7, 72 have 3A); epact 29 (nos 18, 64 have **1A**, no. 83 has 2A), where in each case the date shown here in bold corresponds with Ideler's new-moon date for that epact; cf. Ideler (1825–1826), ii 249–51; cf. Figure 1 and Table 4 below.

13 Mommsen (1863), 556.

dates. These epactal reductions Mommsen interpreted as an endeavour to bring the tabular moon closer to the real moon, and he considered whether a change from a 14-year *saltus* to a 12-year *saltus* might have played some role in the modification, as had been suggested earlier by van der Hagen, Ideler, and de Rossi. He concluded this discussion with his examination of the paschal dates of the nine years AD 387, 397, 414, 417, 427, 444, 453–455, which are witnessed by various early sources, comparing these with paschal dates that he reconstructed from the Zeitz new-moon table.[14]

Mommsen's publication represented by far the most substantial attempt to understand the structure of the Zeitz table and to place it in an appropriate Roman historical context, and his numerous scholarly achievements have rightly ensured that it has been accorded great respect. However, his extensive account does not address the question of the paschal lunar *termini*, and he gave no paschal lunars for the eleven paschal dates in his reconstructed table. When paschal lunars are computed from his new-moon dates it is found that two paschal dates fall on *luna* 15 (nos 7 and 34), the Alexandrian early lunar *terminus*, and the remaining nine dates fall in the range *luna* 17–22 inclusive. These two instances of paschal *luna* 15 are incongruent with Mommsen's assertion that the table 'adheres to the Latin observance as a whole'.

In 1880 Bruno Krusch published his monumental study of 84-year paschal cycles, including his own editions of twelve of the primary sources. In this he made an extensive study of the early witnesses for these cycles but unfortunately he conflated the paschal principles of the Roman cycle with a 12-year *saltus* with the paschal principles of the cycle with a 14-year *saltus* used in Britain and Ireland.[15] As a consequence he proposed a two-stage evolution for the *Romana supputatio* as follows:

1   For AD 312–342 an 'ältere' *Romana supputatio* with Pasch falling between *luna* 14–20 and 25 March–21 April inclusive.

2   For AD 343–354 a 'jüngere' *Romana supputatio* with Pasch falling between *luna* 16–22 and 22 March–21 April inclusive.

Then, since the paschal table of Vatican, Biblioteca Apostolica Vaticana, Reg. lat. 2077 gives dates for AD 354–427 observing the principles of his 'jüngere' *supputatio* Krusch concluded that this had prevailed subsequently.[16] Consequently, when he turned to reconstruct the Zeitz table of AD 447 these

---

14 Mommsen (1863), 560–62, for his discussion of the paschal dates of the years AD 387, 397, 414, 417, 427, 444, 453–455; 553–554, for Mommsen's reconstructed paschal dates for the eleven years AD 387, 391, 398, 414, 417, 444, 448–449 (from Zeitz preface), 453–455.

15 Warntjes (2010), XVII: 'Most unfortunately [...] he [Krusch] connected the *latercus* information of the Munich Computus with the *laterculus* of Augustalis as transmitted in the *Computus Carthaginiensis*'.

16 Krusch (1880), 64–75 for his 'ältere' and 'jüngere' *Romana supputatio* for AD 312–354; 75–90 for Vatican, Biblioteca Apostolica Vaticana, Reg. lat. 2077 and AD 354–427; cf. Mosshammer (2008), 217. See n. 57 below for the MS.

were the paschal principles that he assumed for it.[17] In his reconstruction Krusch reproduced Mommsen's ferial and epactal series identically, and regarding new-moons, except for Krusch's ambivalences at nos 42, 53, and 80, and for epact 30 (nos 10, 37, and 56), and his corrections of Mommsen's inconsistencies, his new-moon dates agreed with those of Mommsen. For epact 30 Krusch's date of 31 March conflicts with the manuscript evidence at no. 10 of 1 April which Mommsen had accepted. However, when Krusch turned to the question of paschal dates, in contrast to Mommsen, he addressed in detail the matter of the paschal lunar and Julian *termini*. The principles Krusch assumed in computing his paschal dates were those established by him for his 'jüngere' *Romana supputatio* as follows:[18]

a) The Sunday falling, where possible, within *termini luna* 16–22 and 22 March–21 April, both inclusive;

b) Paschal *luna* 1 falling not earlier than 7 March.

However, Krusch was not always able to simultaneously fulfil constraints a) and b), as in the following instances:

1. For nos 7, 34 and 64 he chose April paschal dates with *luna* 15 in order to accommodate constraint b), thereby violating the *luna* 16 terminus of constraint a);

2. For nos 53 and 80 he ambivalently accepted paschal new-moons on 5 and 6 March respectively, in order to accommodate constraint a), thereby violating b);

3. For no. 42 he ambivalently accepted the paschal date of 22 April, thereby violating the 21 April Julian *terminus* of constraint a).

In the commentary to the reconstruction of the Zeitz paschal table given in Table 4 below these ambivalences of Krusch will be examined in more detail (cf. p. 65).

In 1892 Mommsen published a second edition of the Zeitz bifolia in which he sought to make the text more accessible for the reader by using a standard typeface and introducing punctuation, capitalization, some reconstruction of the preface, and tabulated spacing for the new-moon table. To this he prefixed a reconstruction of three successive quaternions closely resembling that of 1863, but now ambivalently suggesting the addition of a sixth 84-year cycle together with indices to the Roman popes and emperors ('Inscriptio cyclo sexti? – indices paparum et imperatorum'). He did not undertake any further analysis of the

---

17 Krusch (1880), 116–23 (reconstruction of Zeitz).
18 Krusch (1880), 118: 'Der letztere Fall ist insofern lehrreich, als wir daraus ersehen, dass der Verfasser den 6. März als Neumond bestimmt verschmähte'; 121: 'Bei der Voraussetzung, dass der Verfasser die Osterregeln des alten römischen Cyclus über die Ostersonntage (22 März – 21 April) und die Mondalter derselben (Luna 16–22) beibehalten habe, würde die Zeitzer Tafel in folgender Weise herzustellen sein'.

table, but his commentary included a number of criticisms of Krusch's 1880 reconstruction.[19]

In 1901 Bartholomew Mac Carthy published the first substantial account of the 84-year paschal cycle in English, reconstructing a cycle with a 14-year *saltus*, and another with a 12-year *saltus* evidently cognate with Krusch's 'jüngere' *Romana supputatio*. He did not discuss Zeitz, but simply referred to the publications of Mommsen and Krusch.[20]

In 1905 Eduard Schwartz, as part of his comprehensive examination of Christian and Jewish paschal tables, carefully considered the evidence for the Roman 84-year paschal cycle and rejected Krusch's hypothesis of an 'ältere' *Romana supputatio*. Schwartz rightly judged the paschal principles assumed here by Krusch to belong to the 84-year cycle with a 14-year *saltus* followed in Britain and Ireland, and the deviations that had prompted Krusch's misjudgement to have been actually the result of Roman concessions to Alexandria.[21] Schwartz's own detailed reconstruction of RS-354 confirmed by his collation with the dates of Pasch actually celebrated in Rome that the Roman paschal principles were *luna* 16–22 and 22 March–21 April, except at nos 6 and 63 where no solution existed, and so he accepted paschal *luna* 15.[22]

Schwartz then discussed the Zeitz epacts and new-moons, and their implied full-moons, and compared these for AD 377–388 with the equivalent cyclic years of his reconstruction of the RS-354, and with the Alexandrian paschal cycle for AD 461–472, showing that the Zeitz new-moons implied paschal *luna* 14 dates that corresponded closely with the Alexandrian *luna* 14 dates, whereas the *luna* 14 dates of RS-354 were mostly two days in advance.[23] Schwartz inferred from the Zeitz new-moons for epacts *luna* 26 and 29 that, whereas for these epacts RS-354 made the April lunation the paschal month, the Zeitz author had moved his paschal month to the May lunation. He wrote that 'the Zeitz Easter table considers not only the full-moon of 18 March but also that of 19 March incorrect', implying rejection of a paschal *luna* 1 falling earlier than 7 March (cf. Figure 1).[24] Schwartz considered these epactal modifications of the Zeitz paschal table to have

---

19 MGH Auct. ant. 9, 504 (reconstruction of the quaternions); 507–10 (edition); 504–05 nn. 1–4 (criticisms of Krusch).

20 Mac Carthy (1901), LXV–LXXXI, for his reconstruction of '84 (14)'; LXXXII–III, for his reconstruction of '84 (12)', where he cites Krusch (1880) thrice but does not acknowledge his reconstruction; LXXXIII n. ∴: 'For the Zeitz paschal Table, a modification of the 84 (12), see Mommsen: *Abhndlngn. der Kön. Akad. ... J. 1862*, pp. 539–66; id. *M.G.H. SS. Antiqss* IX. 503–10 (a second and less satisfactory edition by the same editor); Krusch, *ubi sup.*, pp. 116–29'.

21 Schwartz (1905), 57: 'Die Schwierigkeit löst sich sofort, wenn jene Daten nicht als Zeugnisse für eine ältere *supputatio Romana* — die es nie gegeben hat — sondern als Concessionen an die Alexandriner aufgefasst werden'.

22 Schwartz (1905), 46–49 (his reconstruction of the *Romana supputatio*); 50–58 (showing that the occasional derogations represent accommodation of the Alexandrian principles).

23 Schwartz (1905), 71.

24 Schwartz (1905), 72: 'die Zeitzer Ostertafel hält nicht nur den Vollmond des 18., sondern auch den des 19. März für incorrect'.

been an attempt to reduce the discrepancies between the Roman 84-year cycle and the Alexandrian paschal table of Theophilus, but that it was apparently not considered by the curia because Victorius, who was commissioned by the curia, ignored it.[25] Schwartz did not engage with the questions of the paschal lunar and calendrical *termini*, considering there to be insufficient evidence available.[26]

In 1933 Krusch published the results from an examination that he had apparently made circa 1890 of the covers of MS Zeitz, Stiftsbibliothek, fol. 33, where, as a result of applying reagent to these, he was able to recover most of the tabulated criteria for AD 29–40. Krusch saw these additional readings as further confirmation of his reconstruction of 1880.[27]

Next, and most remarkably, in 2005 three small further fragments of the manuscript were identified in the library at Zeitz and a photographically illustrated account of these and the two bifolia was published by Eef Overgaauw and Frank-Joachim Stewing. These three fragments had all been cut from the upper part of a third bifolium and they preserved further text from the preface, as well as table entries for the years AD 54–57, 66–69 (cf. Plates 1a,1b). In this publication Overgaauw discussed the content and make-up of the manuscript and adapted Mommsen's 1892 reconstruction to include the new-found fragments in the first quaternion, and he expanded the third quaternion to show a full sixth paschal cycle and a register of the popes and emperors ('Verzeichnis der Päpste und Kaiser'). However, only the verso of one preface fragment was transcribed, and no analysis of the new tabular material was presented except to identify AD years. No shelf-mark was assigned to these three fragments, but they were arranged in reading order and labelled a, b, c, and located on fols 3, 6 of the first quaternion. Consequently I shall reference them as Zeitz, Stiftsbibliothek, fols 3, 6 a–c (henceforth MS Z), where fol. 3 is a preface folio, and fol. 6 a tabular folio; cf. Table 1 below. For his part Stewing discussed the history, codicology, and provenance of MS Zeitz, Stiftsbibliothek, fol. 33 in detail, and concluded that it had been bound and its covers lined using MSS B and Z in Bologna in the 1420s.

---

25 Schwartz (1905), 72: 'Der Versuch der Zeitzer Tafel durch eine leichte Verschiebung des 84-jährigen Cyclus die Discrepanzen, die immer häufiger zwischen diesem und dem Pinax des Theophilus eintraten, zu beseitigen, scheint von der Curie keiner besonderen Beachtung wert gehalten zu sein: denn Victorius ignorirt ihn, und dieser schrieb wirklich in officiösem Auftrag'.

26 Schwartz (1905), 72: 'Es ist von der Zeitzer Ostertafel zu wenig erhalten um sicher feststellen zu können, welche Ostergrenzen sie innegehalten hat'.

27 Krusch (1933), 996 (transcription of the tabular criteria for AD 29–40); 997: 'Für die Osterberechnung bringt der neugewonnene Text keine Überraschung. Er bestätigt lediglich die Richtigkeit meiner vor so langen Jahren aufgestellten Tafel'.

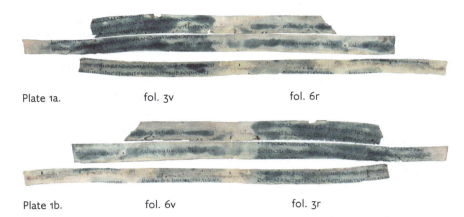

Plates 1a–1b: Re-assembly of the three fragments a–c of fols 3, 6, to illustrate their approximate original horizontal and vertical relative positions. From the differing curvatures of the lines of text it can be seen that the fragments have become distorted, most likely as a result of their use as binding for MS fol. 33. Above fols 3v, 6r, and below fols 6v, 3r.

This then suggested an Italian provenance for MSS B and Z.[28] Subsequently, Overgaauw published a very brief summary of this account.[29]

In 2007 Immo Warntjes emphasized the unique character of the differences between the Zeitz table and RS-354, noting in particular the alignment of its epacts with the Alexandrian epacts, and that the Zeitz paschal date for AD 29, 27 March *luna* 17, is 'in agreement with the Synoptic Gospels and contemporary theology'.[30] Finally, in 2008 Alden Mosshammer briefly and lucidly described the

---

28 Overgaauw and Stewing (2005), 5–24 (Overgaauw is designated author of this section headed 'Die Zeitzer Ostertafel – Enstehung, Inhalt und Erforschung'); 25–30 (Stewing is designated author of this section headed 'Die Zeitzer Ostertafel – Von Bologna nach Zeitz'); 8 fig. 2, reproduces and transcribes fragment fol. 3v c; 9, reconstruction of the make-up; 18–19, figs 10–11, reproduce photographically both sides of the three fragments labelling them '1 a–c', and identify the preface on fol. 3, and assign AD years to the tabular data on fol. 6; 25: 'Gebunden wurde die Handschrift Ende der zwanziger Jahre des 15. Jahrhunderts in Bologna in einen Halbledereinband, wobei die Aussenseiten der beiden Buchdeckel teilweise roh blieben (Abb. 4). Anders verfuhr der Buchbinder mit den Innendeckeln. Als Bezug verwendete er hierfür zwei Doppelblätter des spätantiken Codex sowie die Streifen, die im Juni 2005 neu aufgefunden wurden'.

29 Overgaauw (2009).

30 Warntjes (2007), 71, where his n. 118 identifies four further published discussions of Zeitz: O'Connell (1936), 74–75, gives a brief account of the table; Declercq (2000), 79, asserts that the Zeitz table was 'dedicated to pope Leo the Great', and that the epacts were 'corrected by two days', and p. 84, that Zeitz's date for AD 29 was 'in perfect accordance with the synoptic chronology'; I have not examined Ginzel (1914), iii 244–45, or Strobel (1977), 270–71.

content and date of MS B and asserted it to be the earliest source to connect the first year of a paschal cycle with the year of the Passion, but did not consider its paschal principles.[31]

In summary, de Rossi, Mommsen (1863), Krusch (1880), and Schwartz all inferred from Zeitz's evident Roman provenance and its 84-year lunar table with a 12-year *saltus* that it was a development from the earlier Roman 84-year paschal table, RS-354, and all except Schwartz inferred that it employed the same paschal principles. But only Krusch stated these principles explicitly and explored the consequent paschal dates and paschal lunars, thereby demonstrating that in six instances the Zeitz lunar table could not accommodate the principles of RS-354.[32]

The manuscript

The surviving manuscript comprises two complete vellum bifolia measuring approximately 44 × 30 cm, and three fragmentary strips approximately 2–2.5 × 27–40 cm, all cut from adjacent areas of a third bifolium (cf. Plate 1).[33] In order to discuss these unambiguously it is necessary to establish an appropriate nomenclature, for with the recovery of these fragments from a third bifolium in 2005 the fols 1–4 used hitherto for MS B is inadequate. Hänel was the first to identify that MS B's two complete bifolia came from two successive quaternions that he labelled 'I' and 'II', and he assigned the first bifolium to quaternion I fols 3, 6 and the second to quaternion II, fols 1, 8. In 1863 Mommsen published a much more detailed reconstruction of MS B, re-assigning the first bifolium to quaternion I fols 4*, 5*, and the second bifolium to quaternion II fols 2*, 7*. He placed the preface on the first four folios and the tables of cycles 1–5 on the following fourteen folios, so that the concluding 36 years of the fifth cycle required two folios of a third quaternion. Strangely, even though he entitled his edition 'Zeitzer Ostertafel' and included a reconstruction of the ferial, epactal, and new-moon criteria and some paschal dates for AD 449–532, his reconstruction of the make-up did not include provision for a sixth paschal cycle. In 1892 Mommsen again reconstructed the make-up of MS B, now re-foliated as quaternion I, fols 1–8, quaternion II, fols 9–16, quaternion III, fols 17–18, and so he assigned MS B's second bifolium to fols 10, 15. In this reconstruction he again did not include a sixth paschal cycle, though the last item he gave for fol. 18 was an ambivalent 'Inscriptio cycli sexti?'.[34]

---

31 Mosshammer (2008), 227; since the Pasch of the first year of Sulpicius Severus' 84-year table preserved in Padua, Biblioteca Antoniana, I 27, 76r–77v, is 27 March, *luna* 16, it synchronizes Johannine Passion chronology with the traditional Roman date, i.e. Passion on 25 March, *luna* 14. Sulpicius compiled this table *c.* AD 410, so about 37 years before Zeitz; cf. Mc Carthy (2022), 151–52.

32 Krusch (1880), 121–23 (nos 7, 34, 42, 53, 64, 80, all breach the principles of RS-354).

33 Overgaauw (2009), 14 (manuscript dimensions).

34 Mommsen (1863), 550, and MGH Auct. ant. 9, 504 (reconstructing the make-up of MS B).

In 2005 Overgaauw essentially summarized Mommsen's 1892 reconstruction, assigning the recently recovered fragments to quaternion I, fols 3, 6, but now also including the sixth cycle for AD 449–532 on quaternion III, fols 19–22, followed by a register of Roman bishops and emperors on fols 23–24.[35] Since cycles 1–5 do not include paschal dates but the preface anticipates presenting alternative dates whenever the Roman and Alexandrian principles conflict it seems certain that the compilation had incorporated a paschal table for the forthcoming 84 years AD 449–532. The logical position for this chronologically would follow cycle five, and this is indeed in accordance with the preface's reference to a sixth cycle and statement of the paschal date of *VI kal. Apr.* (27 March) for the first year of this cycle. This reference in the preface to the sixth cycle is immediately followed by the statement: 'But to this collection of paschal days we have attached not only the sequence of consuls but also added with most careful annotation the years of the primates of the Apostolic See and the regnal period of Roman emperors.'[36] Since no paschal dates were provided for cycles 1–5 this reference to the 'collection of paschal days' (*collectio paschalium dierum*) must be to the sixth cycle, and it is explicitly stated that this is to be followed by a chronological register of the years of the apostolic primates and reigns of the Roman emperors. The reference here to the 'primates of the Apostolic See' (*apostolicae sedis antistitum*), I take to refer to the most senior ecclesiastical figures of that See, the bishops of Rome. Furthermore, the combination of chronological criteria cited here, consuls, years, and regnal periods, associated with the bishop of Rome and the Roman emperors would suggest a register resembling the Liberian Catalogue of the Chronography of AD 354, which lists the bishops of Rome in chronological order from Peter († *c.* AD 64) to Liberius († AD 366).[37] For each bishop this catalogue includes the name of the bishop and length of his episcopate in years, months, and days; the name of the emperor at the time, and the names of the consuls at the beginning and end of each episcopate. The details of the organisation of this register in Zeitz must remain conjectural, and likewise its physical extent in folios, but nevertheless its existence following the sixth cycle is not in doubt. Consequently, my reconstruction of the make-up of the manuscript in Table 1 is based principally upon fols 1–18 of Mommsen's account in MGH Auct. ant. 9, 504, followed by fols 19–24 of Overgaauw and Stewing (2005), 9, to include the sixth cycle and register of bishops of Rome and Roman emperors.

---

35 Overgaauw and Stewing (2005), 9 (reconstructing the make-up of MSS B and Z).
36 Preface, fol. 4r; see pp. 35 and 44 below.
37 MGH Auct. ant. 9, 73–76 (edition of the 'Liberian Catalogue').

THE ZEITZ PASCHAL TABLE OF AD 447 29

Table 1. The reconstruction of three Zeitz quaternions by Mommsen based upon his analysis of MS B, and extended by Overgaauw to include the sixth cycle and register of Roman bishops and emperors on fols 19–24.[38] In each case the 'criteria' are the *feria* and lunar epact of 1 January, and the Julian calendar date of the paschal new-moon, while the 'paschal date(s)' of AD 449–532 are either one or two Julian calendar dates of Pasch. The locations in these quaternions of MS B fols 1–4, and the fragments a–c of MS Z fols 3, 6, have been indicated.

Q.	FOL.	AD	CONTENT	MS
I	1	–	Preface	–
I	2	–	Preface	–
I	3	–	Preface	Z fol. 3 a–c
I	4	–	Preface conclusion; cycle 1 heading	B fol. 1
I	5	29–52	24 × consuls + criteria	B fol. 2
I	6	53–76	24 × consuls + criteria	Z fol. 6 a–c
I	7	77–100	24 × consuls + criteria	–
I	8	101–112	12 × consuls + criteria; cycle 2 heading	–
II	9	113–158	46 × consuls only	–
II	10	159–198	33 × consuls only; cycle 3 heading; 7 × consuls only	B fol. 3
II	11	199–248	50 × consuls only	–
II	12	249–280	32 × consuls only; cycle 4 heading	–
II	13	281–330	50 × consuls only	–
II	14	331–364	34 × consuls only; cycle 5 heading	–
II	15	365–388	24 × consuls + criteria	B fol. 4
II	16	389–412	24 × consuls + criteria	–
III	17	413–436	24 × consuls + criteria	–
III	18	437–448	11 × consuls + 12 × criteria; cycle 6 heading	–
III	19	449–472	24 × criteria + paschal date(s)	–
III	20	473–496	24 × criteria + paschal date(s)	–
III	21	497–520	24 × criteria + paschal date(s)	–
III	22	521–532	12 × criteria + paschal date(s)	–
III	23	–	Register of bishops of Rome and Roman emperors	–
III	24	–	Register of bishops of Rome and Roman emperors	–

I turn next to consider the various inscriptions added to MS B.

Bifolia – At the top centre of fol. 4r 'I' is inscribed, and similarly at fol. 10r is 'II', and these are likely to have been written by Hänel since his edition was the first to use these numerals to identify the quaternions of the bifolia.

Foliation – At the top right-hand corners of fols 4r, 5r, 10r, 15r are inscribed the numerals 1–4 respectively, which, to judge by the ink and their appearance, are also likely to have been written by Hänel.

a.u.c. and AD – A series of a.u.c. and AD equations in Arabic numerals have been inscribed, usually at the beginning, and sometimes at the end, of the different tabular sections which may be clearly seen in Overgaauw and Stewing's reproductions.[39] These Arabic digits are in Mommsen's hand and he appears to have transcribed most of them from Hänel (1837), 757–60, and it would appear that he wrote the a.u.c. data first and then subsequently added the AD.

'Blätter' and 'quaternio' – Instances of these words appear in inscriptions written on the bottom margin of fol. 4r and the top margin of fol. 5r, apparently in the same but unidentified hand. On the bottom margin of fol. 10v in a different hand are references to '6 Blätter' and '3 Lagen', and the ink, digits, and content all suggest this to be the hand of Hänel.[40]

Shelf-marks – On the top left margin of fol. 4r in brown ink is the inscription 'Access. 6807' which is the Berlin Staatsbibliothek's accession number for MS B. On the top right-hand margin of fol. 10r in black ink is the inscription 'MS Lat. Quarto N°. 298', which is the shelf-mark of MS B at the Berlin Staatsbibliothek, and so both were likely added c. 1861.

Reagent – While reagent would not normally be considered an 'inscription', in this manuscript it is by far the most conspicuous intrusion, substantially obscuring the majority of the lines of uncial script and complicating endeavours to read the content of the manuscript, so that it is worth examining the situation. The application of this reagent had the effect of staining the vellum blue, varying from a pale blue where text may be easily read, to deep blue, almost black, apparently completely obscuring the text. The mechanism behind this wide variation in discolouration may be understood by comparing the lines of text at fol. 10r ll. 14–16, all three of which are discoloured by reagent, with l. 15 of fol. 10v, which is likewise discoloured (cf. the colour reproductions given by Overgaauw and Stewing (2005), 21–22). From these can be seen that where reagent was applied congruently to both sides of a folio the text on both sides has been substantially obscured. In some places also the reagent has been applied more liberally, with the same consequence. Overall it is apparent that this reagent was applied clumsily,

---

38 MGH Auct. ant. 9, 504, where Mommsen's figures for the number of consuls and AD years for fols 9, 10, 11, 13 differ from Mommsen (1863), 550, and are slightly inconsistent, so in Figure 1 these have been restored to his earlier edition, except at fol. 18 where in both editions he presumes consuls were known for AD 448.

39 Overgaauw and Stewing (2005), 14–17, 20–23.

40 Cf. Hänel (1837), 759: 'Das erhaltene 2te Bl. der dritten Lage oder das 6ste Bl.'

often straying away from the actual text itself, and sometimes even into the margin (cf. fol. 10v and fol. 15v[41]). Regarding the question of who applied this reagent, Overgaauw considered that Hänel was likely responsible, writing that 'vermutlich war es Hänel, der versucht hat, die nicht leserlichen Textteile mit einem blauen Reagens leserlich zu machen'.[42] Mommsen's statement that 'f.2 pagina recta tota fere evanuit. Haenel, qui eam vidit minus corruptam, in ea legit haec' would likewise suggest he was of the same opinion.[43] That it was indeed Hänel who applied this reagent, rather than somebody before him, is supported by the fact that Hänel gave a full listing of the twenty-five consul pairs from fol. 10r, which transcription would have been virtually impossible for many lines once the text had been deeply obscured by the reagent.[44] In addition, the correspondence in appearance between the reagent applied to the bifolia fols 4, 5, 10, 15 and the three fragments from fols 3, 6 suggests that it was Hänel who also treated these fragments, but he chose not to reference them in his 1837 publication.

These observations further suggest, however, that reagent had not been applied in Hänel's time to the inside covers of MS Zeitz, Stiftsbibliothek, fol. 33, because Hänel wrote of the lines fol. 5v ll. 1–12, which folio had been previously glued to the inside back cover of MS Zeitz, Stiftsbibliothek, fol. 33: 'Zeile 1–5 sind nicht zu lesen, weil bei dem Ablösen des Blattes vom Deckel das Pergament mit abgelöst worden ist. Auch das Uebrige mit Puncten angezeigte ist nicht lesbar'.[45] As Overgaauw's reproduction of the inside back cover illustrates, most of the text from fol. 5v had transferred to the cover of MS Zeitz, Stiftsbibliothek, fol. 33 and has been rendered easily legible there by the application of a light blue reagent. Clearly Hänel had not seen this, and neither subsequently had Mommsen in 1863 or 1892.

The text from fol. 5v was not substantially known until Krusch published his transcription in 1933, and in his discussion of this he acknowledged that he had been sent material from the Zeitz Stiftsbibliothek and given permission to treat it with 'Tinktur', writing:[46]

> Ich schrieb also nach Zeitz und fand auch bei Hrn. Studienrat Dr Schamberger, dem staatlichen Stiftsbibliothekar, volles Verständnis. Er schickte die betreffenden Bände an das Staatsarchiv in Hannover und gestattete auch die Behandlung mit Tinktur, ohne die nichts zu machen gewesen wäre.

---

41 Overgaauw and Stewing (2005), 20, 22.
42 Overgaauw and Stewing (2005), 10.
43 MGH Auct. ant. 9, 508.
44 Cf. Overgaauw and Stewing (2005), 21, and Hänel (1837), 758.
45 Hänel (1837), 758.
46 Krusch (1933), 985.

It appears from this, therefore, that Krusch was responsible for the application of the reagent to the inside covers, and a comparison of these covers with the folios shows that Krusch handled the reagent far more skillfully than did Hänel.

Regarding the question of reading text that has been severely obscured by reagent, my experience using good scanned images of the two bifolia and the three fragments from fols 3, 6 has been that enlargement and simple graphic editing techniques often allow one to read much of the text on them (cf. the edition of fols 3, 6 below and Overgaauw and Stewing (2005), 8 figure 2, 18–19 figures 10–11). However, there are places where even sophisticated graphic editing has not been able to resolve what was written by the scribe.

Edition

This edition is substantially based upon MGH Auct. ant. 9, 507–10, supplemented from Krusch (1933), 996, and by my own transcriptions from fols 3–6, 10, 15.

The following editorial conventions have been adopted for all the folios:

1. Following Mommsen in MGH Auct. ant. 9, a modern font, word spacing, and capitalization have been introduced, but the relative horizontal positions of the lines of text have been approximately preserved;
2. Each '.' represents approximately one illegible letter;
3. Restorations and interpolated comments are shown in square brackets '[…]'; deletions are shown in parentheses '(…)'.
4. Mommsen's capitalized representation of Roman numbers and his use of 'V' for the numeral five have been adopted.
5. The scribe wrote the preface and tables of consuls of cycles 2–3 at 25 lines per page, whereas he wrote the tables of consuls and criteria of cycles 1 and 5 at 12 double-spaced lines per page, and so the textual lines of these folios have been numbered accordingly.

The following observations are relevant to the three fragments of fols 3, 6 of the edition:

6. It is clear from the preserved script and the sequence of the criteria on fol. 6 that fragments a and b almost share a common boundary, whereas there is some vellum missing between fragments b and c. Consequently the wide vertical separation of the three fragments shown in Overgaauw and Stewing (2005), 18–19, figures 10–11, misrepresents their relative vertical positions. Fragments a and b should be shown almost touching each other, and fragments b and c should be separated vertically by approximately half the height of a fragment (cf. Plate 1).
7. Consequently we have significant parts of seven consecutive lines of the preface from fol. 3r ll. 3–9, and similarly significant parts of eight further consecutive lines from fol. 3v ll. 3–10, but only vestiges of fol. 3r l. 7 and fol. 3v l. 8 because of the missing vellum between fragments b and c.

THE ZEITZ PASCHAL TABLE OF AD 447   33

8. Since the first tabular line has been lost from fol. 6r–v, and about two lines of preface were written for one tabular line, this suggests that two lines of the preface have been lost from the top of fol. 3r–v, hence these transcriptions commence at l. 3.

LINE	FOL. 3R, FRAGMENTS A–C: PREFACE
1–2	[*lost*]
3	prehendere stiloque explicare [..]
4	non est auctoritatem alexandrinae ecclesiae prae
5	minere cui iudicio sanctorum patrum [...]ac proprie
6	sollicitudo commissa est ut quia uerum [......]
7	dodiuesa[..]t[....] ... [.........]
8	quem praedictae ecclesiae pronunti[.]nt et a[.]
9	de pertractatis de hac re plurimorum oru
10–25	[*lost*]

Cf. Overgaauw and Stewing (2005), 18 figure 10, which shows that fragments a–c preserve the beginnings of each line 3–9, and fragment b preserves the ends of lines 4–5, but the ends of lines 3, 6–9 are all truncated. Fragment a extends over lines 3–5, fragment b over lines 4–7, and fragment c over lines 7–9; cf. Plate 1.

l. 3: Immo Warntjes points out the occurrence of *stiloque explicare* in Victorius, *Prologus* 6 (Krusch (1938), 21 ll. 15–16): *ingenti tamen studio condere **stiloque explicare** conati sunt*. However, as Victorius' context refers to Creation, not to Alexandrian paschal authority, it is difficult to see how the two texts could relate semantically.

LINE	FOL. 3V, FRAGMENTS A–C: PREFACE
1–2	[lost]
3	[re]gulariter seruatu[.]
4	plenilunium id est quartam decimam
5	lunam non[..]f[.]iat neque in primo mense illut sed
6	in duo^{de}cimo censeat numerandum unde apparet
7	[pri]mam lunam primi mensis ab octauo idus martias
8	cou[....] ui[.]tinh[.]me[...]m
9	[plenilunium] id est quarta decima·luna·quaeratur ac si
10	[pl]enilunio dies fuerit sabbati in subsequenti
11–25	[lost]

Cf. Overgaauw and Stewing (2005), 8 figure 2, fragment c and its transcription; 19 figure 11, showing that fragments a–c preserve the ends of each line 4–10, and fragment b preserves the start of lines 5–6, but the lines 3–4, 7–10 are all acephalous. Fragment a extends over lines 3–6, fragment b over lines 5–8, and fragment c over lines 8–10; cf. Plate 1.

ll. 3–6: Immo Warntjes points out the parallel textual and semantic elements of Victorius, *Prologus* 4 (Krusch (1938), 20 ll. 11–14): *hoc **regulariter** cauteque custodiens, ne ante duodecim kalendarum aprilium **plenilunium, id est luna XIIII**, huic definiendo sacramento patiatur adponi. **Neque hoc in primo menso sed in duodecimo** aestimat conputandum.*

ll. 7–10: Immo Warntjes points out the parallel textual and semantic elements of Victorius, *Prologus* 4 (Krusch (1938), 20 ll. 6–11): *conditum paschale direxit, in quo **ab VIII. idus martias** usque in diem nonarum aprilium, quolibet in medio eiusdem temporis spatio natam perhibet lunam, facere primi mensis exordium, a duodecimo vero kalendarum aprilium usque in quartum decimum kalendarum maiarum **lunam quartam decimam** sollerter inquiri, etiamsi diae inciderit **sabbatorum**, post quam sequente dominico luna quinta decima celebrandum pascha sine dubitatione conscribit.*

Victorius is in both these passages likewise specifying the Alexandrian criteria defining the first month and the paschal lunar *termini*, and he explicitly attributes this to Theophilus' epistle to Theodosius, writing (Krusch (1938), 20 ll. 4–6): *Sancte memoriae contra Theophilus quondam Alexandrinus antestis ad Theodosium imperatorem datis epistolis, ex primo ipsius et Gratiani quinto consulato, conditum paschale direxit, in quo ab VIII. idus martias usque in diem nonarum aprilium.* However, the very intermittent textual correspondences between Zeitz and Victorius would suggest that the two accounts have drawn independently on Theophilus' epistle.

LINE	FOL. 4R: PREFACE

ut dixi, accidit, quia et in regulis festi et in cursu luna[e]
pars utraque non consonat.

Unde cum ex iudicio venerabilium patrum Aegyp-
tiae ad haec scientiae emineret auctoritas, ita

5   paschalis revolutionis ordinem credidimus dige-
rendum, ut, ubi duplicem denuntiationem opinio-
num diversitas facit, subnotatio nostra non de-
sit et quid [d]electatione tua, ad quam cuncta respici-
unt, dignius videatur, ostendat.

10   Initium autem totius decursionis ab illo pascha du-
ximus inchoandum, quod sua passione dominus conse-
cravit. Cuius octogensimus et quartus annus ita omnes
lunares cursus in sua mutabilitate concludit, ut in id
unde coeperat redeat adque ad eundem finem pari

15   lege decurrat. Quae renovatio quinquiens octoge-
nos quaternos annos peragens quadrigentos et
viginti eo anno completura est, qui Calepii et Artaburis consulatum sequetur, ut post illud pascha, quod
III·idus·April· celebrandum est, sexti cycli exordium

20   faciat resurrectio salvatoris, cuius dies est ·VI·kal·April·
Huic autem collectioni paschalium dierum non so-
lum seriem consulum conexuimus, sed
etiam annos apostolicae sedis antistitum et
aetates regni principium Romanorum diligen-

25   tissima adnotatione subdidimus, ut quum

Cf. MGH Auct. ant. 9, 507 ll. 1–25; Cramer (1826), 13; Hänel (1837), 757; Mommsen (1863), 541; Overgaauw and Stewing (2005), 15 figure 7.

l. 8: Cramer (1826), 13: 'Aut ope geminationis legendum DELECTATIONE, aut ELECTIONE', and Mommsen in MGH Auct. ant. 9, 507, writes 'electione *malim*', but Cramer's former suggestion seems the more likely scribal error.

LINE	FOL. 4V: PREFACE AND CYCLE 1 HEADING

[o]mnia sibi et in temporibus et in lunae recursib-
[us con]son ar[...]d testimonium quodammodo per
[.]on constitu[tum] nullo de paschali successio-
[ne] d[ubi]tetur [modo].

5

———————/ \ \ \ \ \ \ \ \ \ \ \ /———————

10

cyclus

15

20

\ \ \ \ \ \ \ \ \

25

Cf. MGH Auct. ant. 9, 507 ll. 26–32; Hänel (1837), 757; Mommsen (1863), 542; Overgaauw and Stewing (2005), 13 figure 5, 16 figure 8.

ll. 1–3: Mommsen in MGH Auct. ant. 9, 507 l. 26, wrote 'deficiunt litt. c. 14', from which it is clear that he had not seen the text on the inside back cover of MS Zeitz, Stiftsbibliothek, fol. 33 which preserves about fifteen letters fully or partially from line 1, about six letters fully or partially from line 2, and traces of some letters from line 3; cf. Overgaauw and Stewing (2005), 13 figure 5.

l. 7: These strokes appear to mark the boundary between the preface and the tabular material.

ll. 13–15: Mommsen in MGH Auct. ant. 9, 507 ll. 30–32, has '[incipit] | cyclus | [primus]', and while 'cyclus' is certain it appears not to have been written by the first hand, and I can find no evidence for either 'incipit' or 'primus'.

l. 24: Cf. the similar strokes at fol. 10v l. 11.

THE ZEITZ PASCHAL TABLE OF AD 447   37

LINE	AD	FOL. 5R: CONSULS AND CRITERIA FOR AD 29–40
	[29] Duobus Geminis consš	kal·Ian d·VII·lun·XXI·m̄n·V·īd·M̄ar·
	[30] Vinicio et Longino	kal·Ian·d·I·lun·II·m̄en·III·k·Apr·
	[31] Tiberio Caesare·IIII·[sol]o	kal·Ian·d·II·lun·XIII·m̄n·XIIII·k·Apr·
	[32] Arrontio et Aenoba[r]bo	kal·Ian·d·II[I] ·lun·XXIIII·m̄n·VIII·id·M·
5	[33] Galba et Sylla	kal·Ian·d·V·lun·V·m̄n·VI·k·Apr·
	[34] Vitellio et Persico	kal·Ian·d·VI·[lun]·XVI·m̄n·XVII·k·[Apr·]
	[35] Camerino et Nonniano	kal·Ian·d·VII·lun·XXVII·m̄n·III·non·A[pr·]
	[36] Aemiliano et Plauto	[k]al·Ian·d·I·lun·[.......................]·Apr·
	[37] Proculo et Nigrino	[ka]l Ian·d III·lun·XVIIII·m̄n·III·id·[Mar·]
10	[38] [Iu]liano et Asprenate	kal·Ian·d IIII·[lun] XXX·m̄n·k·[Apr·]
	[39] G·Caesare et Caesiano	kal·Ian·d·V·lun·XI·m̄n·XII·k·A[pr·]
	[40] G·Caesare II solo	kal·Ian·d·VI·lun·XX[..]·m̄n·VI·[..........]

Cf. Krusch (1933), 996; Hänel (1837), 758; Mommsen (1863), 543; MGH Auct. ant. 9, 508; Overgaauw and Stewing (2005), 13 figure 5, 17 figure 9.

Krusch's editing of this text is erratic: always reading 'Jan' against the manuscript 'Ian'; randomly ending numbers with or without '·'; supplying a comma after 'Apr' in [31]; writing capital 'K' in [30] but lower-case 'k' elsewhere; restoring [ka] in [37] but nothing in [36]; using both '(...)' and '[...]' to delimit restored text; restoring a consul's name in [32] but in [31], [36], [38–39] just supplying ellipses.

I have collated Krusch's edition with the Zeitz scan of the back cover of MS Zeitz, Stiftsbibliothek, fol. 33 and corrected a number of Krusch's readings, and then edited this to conform with the other tabular pages by: showing restored text in '[...]'; showing illegible text as '[...]'; inserting raised points '·' between criteria; replacing 'Jan' with 'Ian'; restoring incomplete but identifiable consuls' names from the *Descriptio consulum* (ed. Theodor Mommsen in MGH Auct. ant. 9, 220).

LINE	AD	FOL. 5V: CONSULS AND CRITERIA FOR AD 41–52	
		[41] G·Caesare III et Saturnino	kal·Ian·d·I·lun·IIII·m̄n̄·(IIII)[V]·k·Apr
		[42] Tib·Claudio et Largo	kal·Ian·d·II·lun·XV·m̄n̄·XVI·k·Apr·
		[43] Tib·Claudio II et Vitellio II	kal·Ian·d·III·lun·XXVI·meni II·non·Apr·
		[44] Prispo et Tauro	kal·Ian·d·IIII·lun·VII·men·VIII·k·Apr·
5		[45] Vinicio II et Corvino	kal·Ian·d·VI·lun·XVIII·m̄n̄ II id·Mart·
		[46] Asiatico II et Silano	kal·Ian·d·VII·lun·XXVIIII·mn·k·Apr·
		[47] Tib·Claudio IIII et Vitellio	kal·Ian·d·I·lun·X·mn·XI·k·Apr·
		[48] Vitellio IIII et Publicola	kal·Ian·d·II·lun·XXI·m̄n̄·V·id·Mart·
		[49] Q·Veranio et Gallo	kal·Ian·d·IIII·lun·II·mn·III·k·Apr·
10		[50] Vetere et Nerviliano	kal·Ian·d·V·lun·XIII·m̄n̄·XIIII·k·Apr·
		[51] Tib·Claudio V et Orphito	kal·Ian·d·VI·lun·XXIIII·m̄n̄·VIII·id·Mart·
		[52] Sylla et Othone Theophilus pasc·in XIIII kal·Mai pro nuntiavit quod forte sit melius tan tum ut XII kal· Apriles quod Latini elege rant refu tetur	kal·Ian·d·VII·lun·V(II) mn VI k·April·

Cf. MGH Auct. ant. 9, 508; Cramer (1826), 14; Hänel (1837), 757; Mommsen (1863), 544; Overgaauw and Stewing (2005), 14 figure 6.

Mommsen in MGH Auct. ant. 9 has systematically inserted a tab before 'lun', and another between the lunar epact and 'mn', but the manuscript normally just delimits the criteria with raised points '·', and I have reproduced this. Sometimes the scribe omitted the raised point and Mommsen represents these omissions as spaces.

l. 3: The first minim of 'II·non·Apr' has been subsequently interpolated.

l. 11: The interpolation 'Theophilus … refutetur' under 'Orphito' is written by the first hand with smaller script and line-spacing down into the lower margin, see further discussion following Table 4 below.

LINE	AD	FOL. 6R, FRAGMENTS A-C: CONSULS AND CRITERIA FOR AD 54–57	
1	[53]		[all lost]
2	[54] Marcello et Auiol[a]		[criteria lost]
3	[55] Saturnino et Scipione		kal·Ian·d·IIII·lun·VI[III]
4	[56] [consuls lost]		kal·Ian·d·V·lun·XX mn IIII·id·Mar
5	[57] Nerone II et Messala		kal·Ian·d·VII·l[un]
6–12	[58–64]		[all lost]

Cf. Overgaauw and Stewing (2005), 19 figure 11, showing that fragments a–c preserve the start of lines 2–3, 5, and fragment c preserves the end of line 4, but lines 2–3 and 5 in fragments a–c are truncated. See also Plate 1 above.

Overgaauw's caption to figure 11 states: 'Tafel für die Jahre 54 und 56 bis 58', but the criteria and line spacing require that lines 2–5 represent AD 54–57.

The omission of *Nerone et Vetere* at [55] results in *Saturnino et Scipione* and *Nerone II et Messala* located at AD 55 and 57 respectively, rather than AD 56 and 58 as in Mommsen's editions of the *Consularia Constantinopolita* and the Chronography of AD 354. For further discussion see the section 'Zeitz Consuls' below.

LINE	AD	FOL. 6V, FRAGMENTS A-C: CONSULS AND CRITERIA FOR AD 66–69	
1	[65]		[all lost]
2	[66] [consuls lost]		[kal·Ia]n·d·IIII·lun·XI mn·XII kl·Apr
3	[67] Tracalo et Talico		kal·Ian·d·V lun·XXII mn·VI·id·Mar
4	[68] Galba II et Ruf[i]n[o]		[criteria lost]
5	[69] [Ves]pasiano II et Tito		kal·Ian·d·I lun·XIII[I] mn·XV k·Apr
6–12	[70–76]		[all lost]

Cf. Overgaauw and Stewing (2005), 18 figure 10, showing that fragments a–c preserve the ends of lines 2–3 and 5, and fragments b–c preserve the beginnings of lines 3–4, but line 2 in fragment a, and line 5 in fragment c are acephalous. See also Plate 1.

Overgaauw's caption to figure 10 states: 'Tafel für die Jahre 66 und 68 bis 70', but the consuls, criteria, and line spacing all show that lines 2–5 are synchronized to AD 66–69, and hence confirm that the omission of consuls *Nerone et Vetere* at AD 55 had retarded the subsequent consuls at least as far as AD 69, see the discussion in 'Zeitz Consuls' below.

DANIEL MC CARTHY

LINE	AD	FOL. 10R: CONSULS FOR AD 159–182	
	[159]	Quintillo	et Prisco
	[160]	Bradua	et Varo
	[161ª]	Antonino IIII	et Aurelio Caesare
	[161ᵇ]	duobus	Agostis
5	[162]	Rustico	et Aquilino
	[163]	Laeliano	et Pastore
	[164]	Macrino	et Celso
	[165]	Orphito	et Pudente
	[166]	Pudente II	et Polione
10	[167]	Varo III	et Quadrato
	[168]	Aproniano	et Paulo
	[169]	Prisco	et Apollonari
	[170]	Cethego	et Claro
	[171]	Severo	et Herenniano
15	[172]	Orphito II	et Maximo
	[173]	Severo II	et Pompeiano
	[174]	Gallo	et Flacco
	[175]	Pisone	et Iuliano
	[176]	Polione	et Apro
20	[177]	Commodo III	et Quintillo
	[178]	Orphito III	et Rufo
	[179]	Commodo	et Vero
	[180]	Praesente	et Cordiano
	[181]	Com[.]	et Rufo
25	[182]	Mamertino	et Rufo

Cf. MGH Auct. ant. 9, 508–09; Hänel (1837), 758; Mommsen (1863), 545; Overgaauw and Stewing (2005), 21 figure 13, 24 figure 16, which show the two consuls' names to be written on each line with a tabulated space preceding the 'et'.

Without ferial and epactal criteria we have no means of assessing the Zeitz AD chronology of the consuls here from lines 1–25. However, as there are good grounds to synchronize lines 3–4 with AD 161, and in order to simplify collation with other consular lists, I have here reproduced Mommsen's AD chronology.

ll. 3–4: At [161ᵇ] Mommsen has not enumerated the year of the 'duobus Agostis', entering simply '–' in both editions. However, Burgess (2000), 273, 286–87, shows that 'Antonino IIII et Aurilio Caesare' and 'duobus Agostis' refer to the same two individuals who served as consuls in AD 161. Consequently, I locate these four names at AD 161.

l. 24: At [181] Mommsen in MGH Auct. ant 9, 509 wrote 'Comm//// et Rufo II', however, I can find no evidence for the second 'm' or remainder of 'Commodo', nor the concluding 'II', and it appears to me that the first hand left 'Commodo' incomplete.

THE ZEITZ PASCHAL TABLE OF AD 447   41

LINE	AD	FOL. 10V: CONSULS FOR AD 183–191, CYCLE 3 HEADING, CONSULS FOR AD 192–198	
	[183]	[..] Commodo VI	et Victorino
	[184]	Marullo	et Aeliano
	[185]	Materno	et Bradua
	[186]	Commodo VII	et Glabrione
5	[187]	Crispino	et Aeliano
	[188]	Fusciano	et Silano
	[189]	duobus	Silanis
	[190]	Commodo VIII	et Septimiano
	[191]	Aproniano	et Bradua
10		[blank line]	
		\\\	
		[blank line]	
		[blank line]	
		[blank line]	
15		Incipiunt consules cycli tertii	
		[blank line]	
		[blank line]	
		[blank line]	
	[192]	Commodo VIIII	et Pertinace
20	[193]	Falcone	et Claro
	[194]	Severo	et Albino
	[195]	Tertullo	et Clemente
	[196]	Dextro	et Prisco
	[197]	Laterano	et Rufino
25	[198]	Saturnino	et Gallo

Cf. MGH Auct. ant. 9, 509; Cramer (1826), 15; Hänel (1837), 757; Mommsen (1863), 546; Overgaauw and Stewing (2005), 22 figure 14.

l. 1: At [183] Mommsen in MGH Auct. ant. 9, 509, has '|||Commodo VI', without any further comment. There are one or two faint illegible characters written before the 'C' of 'Commodo', but they are in a different hand with different ink, and the 'C' of 'Commodo' aligns with the initial letters of the names below, so the preceding characters appear to be a subsequent addition.

l. 11: The oblique strokes '\ \' extend across the full width of the folio and were evidently intended by the scribe to mark the end of cycle 2 (cf. similar strokes at fol. 4v ll. 7, 24).

| LINE | AD | FOL. 15R: CONSULS AND CRITERIA FOR AD 365–376 |

[365] Valentiniano et Valente conss·kal Ian d

[366] Gratiano et Dagalaifo ·kal·Ian·d·I·lun·II

[367] Lupicino et Iovino ·kal·Ian·d·II·lun·XII[I]

[368] Valentiniano II et Valente II·kal·Ian·d·III·lun·XXI[III]

5 [369] Valentiniano·np·et Victore ·kal·Ian·d·V·lun·V

[370] Valentiniano ·III ·et Valente·kal·Ian·d·VI·lun·XVI

[371] Gratiano II et Probo ·kal·Ian·d·VII·lun·XX[VII]

[372] Modesto et Arintheo ·kal·Ian·d·I·lun·VIII

[373] Valentiniano·IIII·et Valente IIII·kal·Ian·d·III·lun·X[VIIII]

10 [374] Gratiano III· et Equitio ·kal·Ian·d·IIII·lun·XX[X]

[375] post conss·Gratiano III et Equitii·kal·Ian·d·V·lun·XI

[376] Valente ·V ·et Valentiniano V·kal·Ian·d·VI·lun·XX[II]

Cf. Mommsen in Auct. ant. 9, 510; Cramer (1826), 16; Hänel (1837), 757; Mommsen (1863), 547; Overgaauw and Stewing (2005), 23 figure 15.

It is apparent from the manuscript that on commencing this page the scribe maintained the same substantial left-hand indentation for the consuls that he had used for cycles 2–3, suggesting thereby that for cycle 4 he had likewise only tabulated the consuls for each year. This indentation had the consequence that at line 1 he had insufficient space to write the ferial, epact, and new-moon criteria for this year. For lines 2–12 he maintained this same indentation but, by controlling his script size and omitting the space before 'kal' in most lines, he provided sufficient space to write the feria and epact, but not the new-moon date; however, the least significant digits of the larger epacts are frequently missing. Instead of spacing the criteria from the consuls he regularly introduced a ':' before each 'kal' in order to separate them. The edition above approximately reproduces these features. On fol. 15v he took care to avoid these problems by commencing the consuls at the left-most position of each line; cf. the reproductions at Overgaauw and Stewing (2005), 20 figure 12, 23 figure 15.

LINE	AD	FOL. 15V: CONSULS AND CRITERIA FOR AD 377–388
	[377] Gratiano IIII et Merobaude	kal·Ian·d·I·lun·IIII·m̄n̄·(IIII)[V]·k·Apr
	[378] Valente ·VI· et Valentiniano V	kal·Ian·d·II·lun·XV·m̄n̄·XVI·kal·Apr·
	[379] Ausonio et Olybrio	kal·Ian·d·III·lun·XXVI·m̄n̄ II non·Apr·
	[380] Gratiano ·V·et Theodosio	kal·Ian·d·IIII·lun·VII·m̄n̄·VIII·kal·Apr·
5	[381] Syagrio et Eucaerio	kal·Ian·d·VI·lun·XVIII·mn·II·id·Mar
	[382] Antonino et Syagrio	kal·Ian·d·VII·lun·XXVIIII·mn·k·Apr
	[383] Merobaude II et Saturnino	kal·Ian·d·I·lun·X·mn·[XI] k·Apr·
	[384] Ricomere et Clearcho	kal·Ian·d·II·lun·XXI·mn·V·id·Mar
	[385] Arcadio·et Bautone	kal·Ian·d·IIII·lun·II·m̄n̄·[III] k·Apr
10	[386] Honorio n̄p̄·et Euodio	kal·Ian·d·V·lun·XIII·m̄n̄·XIIII·k·Apr·
	[387] Valentiniano III·et Eutropio	kal·Ian·d·VI·lun·XXIIII·m̄n̄·VIII·id·Mar
	[388] Theodosio II et Cynegio	kal·Ian·d·VII·lun·V(I)·m̄n̄·VI k·Apr·

Cf. MGH Auct. ant. 9, 510; Hänel (1837), 758–59; Mommsen (1863), 548; Overgaauw and Stewing (2005), 20 figure 12, 24 figure 16.

ll. 1, 7, 9, 12: For the emendations to the new-moon dates and the lunar epact see the discussion in the section 'A reconstruction of the Zeitz paschal table' below.

Translation of the Preface

LINE(S)	FOL. 3R, FRAGMENTS A-C: PREFACE – A PARAPHRASE ONLY OF COHERENT PASSAGES
1–2	[lost]
3	…
4–5	… that the authority of the Alexandrian church is preeminent, to which by the judgement of the holy fathers the question has been properly entrusted [paraphrasing *auctoritatem … comissa est*]
6–9	…
10–25	[lost]

LINE(S)	FOL. 3V, FRAGMENTS A-C: PREFACE – A PARAPHRASE ONLY OF COHERENT PASSAGES
1–2	[lost]
3	…
4–7	… the full-moon, that is *luna* 14, … that it should be reckoned not in the first month but in the twelfth, whence it is clear that the *luna* 1 of the first month is from 8 March … [paraphrasing *plenilunium … idus martias*]
8	…
9	…, that is *luna* 14 is to be sought and if the full moon falls on Saturday then on the following … [paraphrasing *id est … subsequenti*; identifying Alexandrian paschal *termini*]
11–25	[lost]

LINE(S)	FOL. 4R: PREFACE
1–25	… happens, as I said, because both in the rules of the Feast and in the course of the moon the two parts do not agree.

Since by the judgement of the venerable fathers the authority of Egyptian science was supreme for these matters, we have thought that the scheme of the Easter cycle should be so arranged in such a way that, where a difference of opinions produces a twofold designation, our annotation shall not be wanting, but displays whichever seems worthier of your choice, to which all turn.

We have considered that the beginning of the entire sequence must start from that Easter which the Lord made holy by his Passion. Its eighty-fourth year puts a conclusion to all the lunar revolutions in their changeability, so that it reverts to the point from which it began and runs down to the same end by a like rule. This renewal, running the course of eighty-four years five times, is going to complete four hundred and twenty years in the year that will follow the consulate of Calepius and Artabur, so that after the Easter that is to be celebrated on 11 April, the Saviour's resurrection, which is 27 March, makes the beginning of the sixth cycle.

But to this collection of paschal days we have attached not only the sequence of consuls but also added with most careful annotation the years of the primates of the Apostolic See and the regnal period of Roman emperors, so that since.

LINE(S)	FOL. 4V: PREFACE
1–4	all things, both in the seasons and in the moon's revolutions, are in agreement, ... evidence somehow ... established, there may be no doubt of any kind about the sequence of Easters.

Zeitz consuls

It appears certain that each year of cycles 1–5 was identified by first naming the Roman consuls for that year. For these are the first tabulated data given for the available sections of cycles 1 and 5, the only data given for the available sections of cycles 2 and 3, and both the make-up of quaternion II and the scribe's substantial indentation of fol. 15r suggest that this was also the case for cycle 4 (cf. Table 1 fols 10–15). Consequently it represented a formidable consular list and it is, therefore, of interest to examine how the surviving consular series compares with other Christian series. In 2000, from a comprehensive examination of consular lists, Richard Burgess demonstrated that a consular list compiled in AD 161 had provided the common source for the Chronography of AD 354, Suetonius, Zeitz (Burgess' *Liber Paschalis*), the *Descriptio consulum*, Prosper's *Epitoma Chronicon*, and the *Fasti Vindobonenses*. He identified that the last four of these together share a common heritage and consequently these four will be collated here.[47]

1. The *Descriptio consulum*, Mommsen's *Consularia Constantinopolitana*, is a list from the end of the third century that was put into its final form in Constantinople in AD 389, and subsequently continued elsewhere to 468.[48]
2. The *Fasti Vindobonenses priores et posteriores* are two recensions of the same list which extend from 44 BC, the *priores* to AD 493, and the *posteriores* to AD 539.[49]
3. The *Epitoma Chronicon* was compiled by Prosper of Aquitaine as a continuation of the chronicle of Jerome, first in AD 433, then two later editions extended it to 445 and 455 respectively.[50] In AD 457 Victorius of Aquitaine

---

47 Burgess (2000), 260–65, for a detailed account of consular lists; 284–86, for the edition of AD 161; 289 Table 1, for the stemma of descendants of this edition where the four collated lists are all shown descending from '78/92–161 (*Fasti* of 161)'. Mosshammer (2008), 12–13, discusses consular sources.

48 *Descriptio consulum* (ed. Theodor Mommsen in MGH Auct. ant. 9, 220–47); cf. Burgess (2000), 260.

49 *Fasti Vindonenses priores et posteriors* (ed. Theodor Mommsen in MGH Auct. ant. 9, 274–98); cf. Burgess (2000), 260.

50 Prosper of Aquitaine, *Epitoma Chronicon* (ed. Theodor Mommsen in MGH Auct. ant. 9, 341–485); Brooks (2014), 26–35, provides a comparison of Prosper's editions of AD 445 and 455, and on 50–80 a critical edition and English translation of the years AD 378–445 of the AD 445 edition; Becker and Kötter (2016), 61–141, provide a critical edition and German translation of the years AD 378–455

employed Prosper's consular list as chronological criteria for the first 428 years of his paschal table.[51]

Collation of the consular sequences of these sources over AD 29–161 indeed confirms that Zeitz exhibits a close textual relationship with the other three sources, especially the *Descriptio*, as the sample in Table 2 demonstrates.

---

of the AD 455 edition; cf. Burgess (2000), 260. In his edition Mommsen systematically enumerated as I–CCCCXXVIII each consular pair from the Passion to AD 455, but Brooks, 45, asserts that 'the *anni a passione* were only ever intended to appear every ten years from 29', and expresses some doubt whether they originated with Prosper. The relationship between Mommsen's enumeration of consuls and his editorial AD is erratic, for examples: at p. 421 consuls LXXXVII are assigned AD '?'; at p. 427 consuls CXVII are assigned AD '?'; at p. 428 consuls CXXXII–CXXXIV are aligned with AD 161; at p. 436 consuls CC are assigned AD '?'; at p. 443 between consuls CCXLVIIII–CCL AD 276 is omitted.

51 Mosshammer (2008), 12–13, and Nothaft (2012), 74, for Victorius' use of Prosper.

Table 2. Collating consuls from the *Descriptio*, Zeitz, Prosper's *Chronicon*, and *Fasti Vindobonenses*. The first column gives Mommsen's editorial AD year of the *Descriptio*, and in the other columns consuls are cited strictly in the sequence of their source with '[none]' indicating any absence, and ':' marking any introduced lacunae.

AD	DESCRIPTIO	ZEITZ	PROSPER CHRONICON	FASTI VINDON.
29	Rufo et Rubellione	Duobus Geminis conss	F. Gemino et R. Gemino	Duobus Geminis
30	Vinicio et Longino Cassio	Vinicio et Longino.	Vicinio et Longino	Tiberio III et Silio
31	Tiberiano Caes. IIII solo	Tiberio Caesare IIII [sol]o	Sulpicio et Sylla	Sulpicia et Sila
32	Aruntillo et Ahenobarbo	Arrontio et Aenobar[b]o	Prisco et Vitellio	Persico et Vitello
:	:	:	:	:
44	Crispo II et Tauro	Prispo et Tauro	Crispino et Tauro	Crispino et Tauro
:	:	:	:	:
54	Marcello et Aviola	Marcello et Auiol[a]	Marcellino et Aviola	Marcellino et Aviola
55	Nerone et Vetere	[none]	Nerone et Vetere	Nerone et Vetere
56	Saturnino et Scipione	Saturnino et Scipione	[none]	Saturnino et Scipione
57	Nerone II et Pisone	[criteria only]	Nerone II et Pisone	Nerone II et Pisone
58	Nerone III et Messala Corvino	Nerone II et Messala	Nerone III et Messala	Nerone III et Messala
:	:	:	:	:
68	Italo et Trahalo	Tracalo et Talico	Italico et Turpiliano	Italico et Turpilione
69	Galba II et Tito Rufino	Galba I et Ruf[i]n[o]	Silvano et Othone	Silviniano et Othone
70	Vespasiano II solo	[Ves]pasiano II et Tito	Vespasiano et Tito	Vespasiano et Tito

AD	DESCRIPTIO	ZEITZ	PROSPER CHRONICON	FASTI VINDON.
..	..	..	..	..
159	Quintillo et Prisco	Quintillo et Prisco	Quintillo et Prisco	Quintillo et Prisco
160	Bradua et Varo	Bradua et Varo	Vero II et Bradua	Vero II et Bradua
161[a]	Antonino V et Aurelio Caes.	Antonino IIII et Aurelio Caesare	Antonino III et Aurelio III	Antonino IIII et Aurelio
–	[none]	[none]	p.c. Antonino III et Aurelio III	[none]
161[b]	duobus Augustis	duobus Agostis	Duobus Augustus	duobus Augustus

As may be seen in Table 2 textually the consuls in Zeitz between AD 30 and 161 correspond most closely with those of the *Descriptio*. However, at AD 55 their chronological structure differs, for here Zeitz omits *Nerone et Vetere* found in the other three sources. That this was a deliberate rearrangement and not a scribal omission is clear from the ferial criteria given in Zeitz for the following three years. These give the ferials 4, 5, and 7 respectively, which are indeed the ferials of the kalends of January for the years AD 55–57, whereas in the *Descriptio* these consuls are located in the years AD 56–58, as shown. This omission is also reflected in Zeitz' enumeration of *Nerone II* at AD 58, where the other three enumerate this as *Nerone III*. Thus, the omission of *Nerone et Vetere* was a deliberate choice either by the compiler of Zeitz or his source.

Turning to consider the other sources at AD 55–56 we find that, while all three have *Nerone et Vetere* at AD 55, Prosper alone has omitted *Saturno et Scipione* from AD 56, which sequence Victorius subsequently reproduced. Thus Zeitz and Prosper show a closely synchronized revision of their common source at AD 55–56, and since Prosper compiled the first edition of his *Chronicon* in AD 433 it seems clear that the revision of consular chronology at this point predates the compilation of Zeitz. However, that the compiler of Zeitz did not draw directly on Prosper is suggested both by their difference of one year, and by their differing orthography and names of consuls for AD 29–44.

A second chronological divergence between Prosper and the other three sources occurs at AD 161 where Prosper alone inserted an additional year *p.c. Antonino III et Aurelio III*. The absence of this particular consular year from Zeitz is a further indication that its compiler did not draw on Prosper's *Chronicon*. Regarding the two other consular entries in Zeitz at this year, *Antonino IIII et Aurelio Caesare*, and *duobus Agostis*, found in all four sources, scholarship has long accepted that these represent a duplication, and so in the edition of fol. 1or above both are located at AD 161.[52]

For the consuls of the years after AD 161 Burgess has shown that Zeitz relates most closely to Prosper's *Chronicon* and the *Fasti Vindobonenses*, and collation of the consuls for the available years AD 162–198, 365–388, confirms his conclusion.[53] Leaving aside the variations in the numerations of consulships, the Zeitz readings for consular names usually correspond more closely to those of Prosper than to the *Fasti Vindobonenses*. Table 3 tabulates all the orthographical differences found between the three sources over AD 162–198; for the years AD 365–388 there are far fewer differences, with none between Zeitz and Prosper, and just six between Zeitz and the *Fasti Vindobonenses*.

---

52 Burgess (2000), 260 n. 7.
53 Burgess (2000), 290 Table 2.

Table 3. Collation of the consuls for AD 162–187 of Zeitz versus Prosper's *Chronicon* and the *Fasti Vindobonenses* with the orthographical variants in the consular names of the latter two underlined.

AD	ZEITZ	PROSPER *CHRONICON*	*FASTI VINDONENSES*
[162]	Rustico et Aquilino	Rustico et Aqui_lo_	Rustico et Aquilino
[164]	Macrino et Celso	Macrino et Celso	Ma_ri_no et Celso
[165]	Orphito et Pudente	Or_fi_to et Pudente	Or_fi_to et Pudente
[166]	Pudente II et Polione	Pudente II et Po_ll_ione	Pudente II et P_ull_ione
[167]	Varo III et Quadrato	V_e_ro IIII et Quadrato	V_e_ro V et Quadrato
[168]	Aproniano et Paulo	Aproniano et Paulo	_P_roniano et Paulo
[169]	Prisco et Apollonari	Prisco et Apo_ll_inar_e_	Prisco et Apo_l_onar_o_
[171]	Severo et Herenniano	Severo et Herenniano	_V_ero et _E_renniano
[172]	Orphito II et Maximo	Or_fi_to et Maximo	Or_fi_to et Maximo
[173]	Severo II et Pompeiano	Severo II et Pompeiano	Severo II et Pompei_o_
[175]	Pisone et Iuliano	Pisone et Iuliano	Pisone et _T_u_ll_iano
[176]	Polione et Apro	P_ull_ione et Apro	P_ull_ione et Apro
[178]	Orphito III et Rufo	Or_fi_to et Rufo	Or_fi_to et Rufo
[180]	Praesente et Cordiano	Praesente et _G_ordiano	Pr_e_sente et _G_ordiano
[181]	Com[.] et Rufo	Commodo II et _Byrro_	Commodo III et _Birro_
[187]	Crispino et Aeliano	Crispino et Aeliano	Crisp_o_ et Aeliano II

In summary, up to AD 161 the compiler of Zeitz appears to have drawn primarily upon a source descended from the *Descriptio* for his consular series. However, he or this source omitted one year at AD 55, which revision correlates chronologically closely with Prosper's omission at AD 56. After AD 161 the Zeitz consuls correlate identically chronologically, and closely orthographically, with those of Prosper's *Chronicon* and the *Fasti Vindobonenses*.

Paschal principles observed in fifth-century Rome

Before considering the structure of the paschal table implied by the Zeitz manuscript it is helpful to first examine its historical context. Regarding the time of the compilation, it is remarkably well dated by stating in the preface that the fifth 84-year cycle will complete in the year following the consulship of Calepius and Artaburis, AD 447. That Rome was the place is suggested by the author's undertaking to catalogue the years of the bishops of Rome and the reigns of the Roman emperors. That it was an episcopal context in Rome is further suggested by the author's pledge, when ambivalent paschal dates arise, that he will display 'which seems worthier of your choice, to which all things look.'[54] These Roman associations are consistent with the use of an 84-year lunar cycle with a 12-year *saltus*, for the earliest known attestation of this lunar cycle is in the Chronography of 354, a Christian celebration of Roman history and chronology compiled about that year by Furius Dionysius Philocalus.[55]

The Roman use of the 84-year lunar cycle of the Chronography of AD 354 to determine the date of the Pasch is attested by two full 84-year paschal tabulations. In Milan, Biblioteca Ambrosiana, H 150 inf., 135v–137v (MS A) (France?, *c.* AD 810), the preface to the table refers to three such cycles commencing in years AD 298, 383 and 467, and the table proper enumerates the years as I–LXXXIIII.[56] In Vatican, Biblioteca Apostolica, Reg. lat. 2077, 79r–81r (MS V) (Italy, saec. VII), the table is synchronized to the consuls for AD 354–437.[57] These sources have been extensively analysed by modern scholarship and their underlying paschal table reconstructed, which reconstruction is normally identified either as the *Romana Supputatio* or *Supputatio Romana*.[58] However, as is clear from the compilation of Zeitz in AD 447, in fifth-century Rome there was more than one version of the 84-year paschal table employing a 12-year *saltus*.[59] Consequently, I have identified this 84-year paschal table witnessed by MSS A and V with the siglum 'RS-354', in order to indicate that the earliest datable witness to its distinctive lunar cycle is the Chronography of AD 354. While the actual date of compilation of RS-354 has not been precisely established, the tabulated range of MS V, AD 354–437, clearly suggests the fourth century. Further, by collating the full-moons of this table with the astronomical full-moons for AD 296, 382, and 446, Schwartz demonstrated that the lunar cycle of RS-354 was synchronized with the real moon at about the beginning of the fourth century.[60] Consequently, since the epacts of an 84-year lunar cycle gain one day on the average astronomical

---

54 Preface, fol. 4r; see pp. 35 and 44, and also pp. 60–61 and 83.

55 Chronography of AD 354 (ed. Theodor Mommensen in Auct. ant. 9, 13–148). See Burgess (2000), 282, and Mosshammer (2008), 206, 213–17, for discussion.

56 Milan, Biblioteca Ambrosiana, H 150 inf. is available online at: https://ambrosiana.comperio.it/opac/detail/view/ambro:catalog:58504; see Bischoff (1998–2017), ii 156 (no. 2621). See Krusch (1880), 236–40, for an edition of the Ambrosian text and table; description in Mosshammer (2008), 206–07.

57 Vatican, Biblioteca Apostolica, Reg. lat. 2077 is available online at: http://digi.vatlib.it/view/MSS_Reg.lat.2077; see CLA 1, 35 (no. 114). See Mommsen's edition of the Vatican table in MGH Auct. ant. 9, 739–43; description in Mosshammer (2008), 208.

58 Krusch (1880), 32 ('Die Theorie der Romana Supputatio'), 62–64 (reconstruction). Schwartz (1905), 41: 'Dieser *Romana supputatio* entspricht am genausten die Ostertafel, die in dem Prolog des im Cod. Regin. 2077 erhaltenen Paschalcyclus [Chron. min. 1, 740] beschrieben wird', 46–49 (reconstruction). Mosshammer (2008), 209 ('Reconstruction of the *Supputatio Romana*'), 210–01 (reconstruction).

59 Warntjes (2007), 69, identifies four '[a]lterations to the Supputatio Romana', namely the *laterculus* of Augustalis, two cycles described by the Carthaginian computist of 455, and the Zeitz table, the first three of which are associated with North Africa.

60 Schwartz (1905), 44: 'im Gegenteil, es spricht alles dafür dass 298 oder vielmehr etwas später, vielleicht erst 312, der Cyclus neu eingestellt wurde'.

52 DANIEL MC CARTHY

moon in about 65 years, at the time that the Zeitz table was compiled in AD 447 the epacts of RS-354 were about two days in advance of the astronomical moon.

The structure of the paschal table of RS-354 was first analysed in detail by van der Hagen in 1733, where he documented the following features:

1. In 82 years the table provides one or more paschal dates falling simultaneously between the Julian *termini* 22 March–21 April, and lunar *termini* 16–22, both inclusive, so that both paschal date and lunar are coordinated to their *termini*. These lunar *termini* and the later Julian *terminus* of 21 April are attested by the third century paschal table attributed to Hippolytus. These Julian *termini* were stated by Leo, bishop of Rome, when writing to the Emperor Marcian in AD 453, and the prologue to MS V makes a similar assertion.[61]

2. In two years, cyclic nos 6 and 63, no dates simultaneously satisfying these *termini* exist, and here the manuscript tables typically provide corrupt paschal dates, whereas modern reconstructions of RS-354 provide paschal dates that transgress either the *luna* 16–22 or the 22 March – 21 April *termini*; I shall designate such paschal date and lunar pairs as uncoordinated.[62]

3. For some years there exists more than one date simultaneously satisfying the Julian and lunar *termini*, and van der Hagen listed six such instances.[63]

Clearly the non-existence of paschal dates simultaneously satisfying both lunar and Julian *termini* in the cyclic years nos 6 and 63, offered a vulnerability that could be exploited by anyone wishing to challenge this paschal table. Indeed, as shall be discussed below, the deficiency at no. 6 resulted in the gloss at fol. 5v l. 11 unfavourably comparing the paschal date *quod Latini elegerant* with that of Theophilus. Likewise, it was the problematic dates at no. 63 that would prompt a major reform in the Roman Julian and lunar *termini*, as will now be reviewed.

The ferial and epactal criteria for AD 444 synchronize with those of the 63rd year of RS-354, so that table presented paschal dates with uncoordinated lunars for that year. Two years beforehand, in AD 442, Pope Leo wrote to Paschasinus, bishop of Lilybaeum in Sicily, requesting his advice on the forthcoming

---

61 Mosshammer (2008), 123–24 (paschal table of Hippolytus where the earlier Julian terminus was 20 March), 208 (for MS V). Jones (1943), 57 n. 4, and Krusch (1880), 259, for Leo's *Epistola ad Marcianum* (Ball. no. 121); see also below p. 56 [n. 75].

62 At no. 6 MS V has 27 March *luna* 21, which fell on a Saturday, while at no. 63 it has 9 April *luna* 16, which did fall on Sunday but with *luna* 8. At no. 63 MS A has 17 April *luna* 16, which fell on a Monday. At no. 6 Krusch (1880), 62, Schwartz (1905), 46, and Mosshammer (2008), 210, give 21 March *luna* 16 or 18 April *luna* 15, both dates transgressing one or other *terminus*. At no. 63 Krusch (1880), 64, and Mosshammer (2008), 210–11, give the alternatives 26 March *luna* 23 or 16 April *luna* 15, while Schwartz (1905), 49, tabulates only 16 April *luna* 15, all transgressing the *termini luna* 16–22.

63 van der Hagen (1733), 236–38, cyclic nos 9, 17, 44, 55, 71, 82, all have ambivalent coordinated paschal dates.

Pasch.[64] Leo's letter is lost but Paschasinus' reply has survived and in this he wrote:[65]

Diutino itaque tractatu vel ratiotinatione id verum invenimus, quod ab Alexandrine ecclesiae antestite beatitudine vestrae rescriptum est. Nam cum Romana suppotatio quae cyclo concluditur, cuius ipse, de quo agitur, erit annus sexagesimus tertius, qui coepit consulatu Antonii et Siagri, nobis dubietatem afferet, eo quod septimo kalendarum aprilium dies dominica et luna XXI incurreret et iterum none kalendarum maiarum die, ut rei veritas habet, dominica dies et luna XVIIII, obveniret, in hoc ambiguo fluctantes, ad Hebreorum, hoc est legalem supputationem, nos convertimus, quae cum a Romanis ignoratur, facile errorem incurrunt.

> And so in a long-lasting discussion and reasoning we have found that true which has been written in response to your blessedness by the bishop of the Alexandrian church. For since the Roman reckoning which is completed in a cycle which began with the consulates of Antonius and Siagrus, of which that which is now being considered will be the sixty-third year, would bring doubt to us, for the reason that on the 26th of March the Lord's day and *luna* 21 would occur and again on the 23rd of April, on a day, as the truth of the case has [it] the Lord's day and *luna* 19 would come together, wavering in this uncertainty we turn ourselves back to the legal reckoning, that is, of the Hebrews, which, since it is not known by the Romans, they easily incur error.

Paschasinus' statement here concerning the *Romana supputatio* and its alternative paschal dates and lunars presents a unique glimpse of Roman paschal principles in the midst of their evolution. However, scholars have published conflicting interpretations of the paschal data in this letter.

Krusch, referring in the singular to the 'paschal day of the *Romana supputatio*', represented that Paschasinus considered it very questionable and so he turned instead to the 'Alexandrian reckoning'. Then, paraphrasing Paschasinus, Krusch stated that in the 19-year cycle AD 444 was an embolismic year, and, should a choice of two dates arise then the later one had always to be taken. Next, characterizing the 26 March date as 'Roman', Krusch paraphrased Paschasinus' statement that if this date had been chosen the whole calculation of years would be distorted. Finally, in support of choosing the later date in accordance with the embolismic rationale, Krusch summarized Paschasinus' account of a miracle from

---

64 For extensive discussions of the Pasch of AD 444 see Krusch (1880), 98–103, 109–15; Schmid (1907), 12–14; Jones (1943), 55–56; Mosshammer (2008), 62–63, 204. Krusch (1880), 100 n. 1, for the date of Leo's letter and Paschasinus' reply.

65 *Epistola Paschasini* 1 (ed. Krusch (1880), 248). I am grateful to David Howlett for kindly providing his translation of Paschasinus; Mosshammer (2008), 62–63, gives an English paraphrase of much of this citation.

AD 417.[66] Thus Krusch represented that the *Romana supputatio* provided only the paschal date 26 March, and that Paschasinus had taken both the later date, 23 April, and *luna* 19, from an Alexandrian source. He further asserted, without any justification, that the paschal *luna* 21 accompanying 26 March had also been taken by Paschasinus from an Alexandrian source.[67] Thus Krusch considered that the *Romana supputatio* sent by Leo provided only the paschal date 26 March, and that the later date of 23 April and both paschal lunars had all been taken by Paschasinus from an Alexandrian source. Subsequently, Schwartz repeated Krusch's assertion that Paschasinus' *luna* 21 was derived from the Alexandrian source, in 1907 Schmid published a cogent summary of Krusch's interpretation, and in 1943 Jones' brief reference suggests that he too accepted this interpretation.[68]

Mosshammer, on the other hand, considered that the *Romana supputatio* provided both paschal dates and their lunars, writing: 'The Roman calculation, he [Paschasinus] says, provided either Sunday, 26 March, the 21st day of the moon, or Sunday 23 April, the 19th day of the moon, leaving the matter ambiguous'.[69] Thus Mosshammer explictly identifies the two Julian and lunar dates with the 'Roman calculation'; which interpretation, Krusch's or Mosshammer's, should we accept?

I would observe firstly that Paschasinus explicitly associates both paschal dates and lunars with the *Romana supputatio*, the two coupled together with *et iterum*, and he immediately states that it was their ambiguity that had prompted consideration of the Hebrew or legal reckoning. Then his subsequent reference to the 26 March date acknowledges his earlier reference, writing: *si voluerimus illud, quod superius diximus, id est quod primum incurrit, septimo kalendarium aprilium die*

---

66 Krusch (1880), 100: 'Der Ostertag der Romana Supputatio erschien ihm sehr bedenklich, und er nahm daher zu der alexandrinischen Berechnungsweise, die er als "legalis Hebreorum supputatio" bezeichnet, seine Zuflucht [...]. Nach dem 19jährigen Cyclus war aber das Jahr 444 ein Mondschaltjahr, in welchem, wenn die Wahl zwischen zwei Ostertagen war, stets der entferntere genommen werden musste. Hätte man nun den 26. März in Uebereinstimmung mit den Römern ausgewählt, so wäre dadurch der "annus embolismus" zum "communis" geworden, und somit die ganze Berechnung der folgenden Jahre erschüttert worden. [...] Schliesslich führt er für die alexandrinische Berechnung noch ein Wunder aus der Zeit des Pabstes Zosimus (417) an, welches sich in einem kleinen, armseligen Flecken, Meltinas, zugetragen hatte'; 101, similarly designating 23 April as 'Alexandrian': 'Nachdem so der Bischof von Lilybaeum die alexandrinische Ansicht gebilligt und die Bedenken welche die Römer gegen dieselbe gehabt hatten, in befriedigender Weise beseitigt hatte, liess sich Leo dazu bewegen, gegen die alte Satzung der römischen Kirche Ostern am 23. April zu feiern'.

67 Krusch (1880), 107: 'In derselben Weise hatte Pascasinus früher dem römischen Ostertage die alexandrinische Luna beigefügt'.

68 Schwartz (1905), 49 n. 1: 'Paschasinus notirt in seinem Brief am Papst Leo [Krusch, Studien p. 248, vgl. p. 107] Sonntag den 26. März *lunae XXI*; das Mondalter ist aus der alexandrinischen ιδ für das Jahr 444, dem 18. April, zurückgerechnet. Das correcte römische Datum war der 19. März'. Schmid (1907), 12–14. Jones (1943), 55: 'a letter from Leo [...] asking him [Paschasinus] to give his opinion on the differences between the Alexandrian and Roman reckoning', reflects Krusch, whom he cites.

69 Mosshammer (2008), 62, cf. 204. *Luna* 21 on 26 March implies *luna* 20 on 23 April.

caelebrare ('if we choose that of which we have spoken above, that is which first occurs, to celebrate on the 26th day of March'), and his *primum* here implictly affirms that the *Romana supputatio* provided two dates.[70] Secondly, it must be noted that Paschasinus' conclusion that the later date should be celebrated does not depend in any way upon the two paschal lunars that he cites. The basis for his conclusion is that the year in question, AD 444, will be the eighth year of the ogdoad of the Alexandrian 19-year cycle commencing in AD 437, and so will be an embolismic year, and then that an embolismic year requires celebration on the later date.[71] In support of this he compares the lengths of common versus embolismic years, and this analysis and conclusion is likely to have been the response from the Alexandrian bishop that he earlier mentions.

Krusch's interpretation requires that Paschasinus, while writing an affectionate and fraternal reply to Leo's enquiry, silently interpolated an Alexandrian paschal date and lunar data while associating them with Leo's *Romana supputatio*, and then that Paschasinus made no use of these interpolated lunar data. Krusch's own reconstruction of RS-354 for AD 444 likewise gave ambiguous dates and lunars, three of which differed from those cited by Paschasinus, and it was these that Krusch assumed to be Paschasinus' interpolations. He evidently presumed that the *Romana supputatio* sent by Leo had to correspond with his own reconstruction of RS-354, and did not appreciate that in 442 Leo was seeking to reconcile Roman and Alexandrian paschal principles.

I conclude that Mosshammer's interpretation is correct, so that Paschasinus' letter preserves some significant implications regarding the *Romana supputatio* that was before him. Namely, neither of the data for the two paschal dates that Paschasinus cites from the 63rd year of this compilation, 26 March *luna* 21, and 23 April *luna* 19, correspond with those of RS-354 for this year. The possible data for RS-354 are 26 March *luna* 23, 16 April *luna* 15, and 23 April *luna* 22, so that the paschal lunars cited by Paschasinus are two and three days younger respectively than those of the RS-354.[72] As was remarked above, Schwartz demonstrated that in the mid-fifth century the epacts of RS-354 were about two days in advance of the astronomical moon, and likewise the Alexandrian epacts. It emerges, therefore, that the *Romana supputatio* sent by Leo to Paschasinus in AD 442 had its epacts closely synchronized with both the real moon and the Alexandrian epacts. Thus its lunar data did not correspond with RS-354 as reconstructed by modern scholarship, or as witnessed by MSS A or V. At the same time Paschasinus' identification of the ambiguity at the tabular 63rd year, and the table commencing with consuls Antonius and Siagrus, the consuls for AD 382,

---

70 *Epistola Paschasini* 1 (Krusch (1880), 248).

71 *Epistola Paschasini* 1–2 (Krusch (1880), 248–49), for Paschasinus' embolismic rationalization; see especially ch. 1 p. 248: *Coepit ergo ogdoas consulatu virorum clarissimorum Aetii iterum et Segisfulti* [AD 437] [...] *ne a vero deviare videamur.*

72 Only van der Hagen (1733), 238, has 23 April; Krusch (1880), 64, and Mosshammer (2008), 210–11, both have the first two dates.

show that the initial year and consular sequencing of this table corresponded with that of RS-354. Thus the *Romana supputatio* sent by Leo appears to have been a revision of RS-354 with its epacts updated to correspond closely with the Alexandrian epacts. Consequently, I shall identify this revision with the siglum 'RS-442' in order to indicate the year of Leo's despatch of the table to Paschasinus.

Furthermore, the alternative date favoured by Paschasinus of 23 April is two days after the later *terminus* of 21 April assumed for RS-354. Thus the RS-442 sent by Leo to Paschasinus not only had its lunar epacts advanced to correspond closely with the Alexandrian epacts, but it also included an alternative paschal date beyond the 21 April *terminus* of RS-354. These details, and the fact that Prosper's chronicle records that the Roman church celebrated Pasch on 23 April in AD 444, all imply that well before that year Leo was actively engaged in re-considering and upgrading the RS-354 that he had inherited on becoming bishop of Rome in AD 440.[73] His exchange with Paschasinus and its outcome demonstrate a commitment on Leo's part to bring the Roman 84-year paschal table's lunar dates and its later Julian *terminus* into closer coordination with the Alexandrian paschal principles.

Three years after the celebration in Rome of Pasch on 23 April 444 the Zeitz table, RS-447, was compiled there, and I shall examine the details of its construction below. Shortly after this Leo, who also possessed a copy of the 100-year paschal table of Theophilus (+ AD 412), bishop of Alexandria, was confronted with further conflict because for AD 455 Theophilus' table scheduled Pasch on 24 April. In June 451 Leo prepared to challenge this date, writing again to Paschasinus, citing Theophilus' date of 24 April and objecting that 'in our cycles, which you know well, it is written that Easter shall be April 17'.[74] While no response from Paschasinus has survived, in AD 453–454 Leo pursued the matter further with three letters written to the Emperor Marcian, and three more to Julian, bishop of Constantinople. In his first letter to Marcian Leo explained why he could accept the dates of 22–23 April, but not 24 April, writing:[75]

---

73 Prosper of Aquitaine, *Epitoma Chronicon* § 1352 (MGH Auct. ant. 9, 479): *Hoc anno pascha domini VIIII kal. Maias celebratum est, nec erratum est, quia in die XI kal. Mai. dies passionis fuit. ob cuius reverentiam natalis urbis sine circensibus transiit.* However, in her edition of Prosper's 445 recension, Deanna Brooks (2014), 67, has simply *Hoc anno pascha domini VIIII kalendas Maias celebratum est.* The longer version appeared in Prosper's AD 455 recension and it echoes Leo's rationalization of AD 453 written to the Emperor Marcian; cf. Becker and Kötter (2016), 124 (Prosper's AD 455 edition); 297–98 (commentary).

74 Pope Leo I, *Epistola ad Paschasinum* of AD 451 c. 4 (ed. Krusch (1880), 257): *in nostris autem paschalibus cyclis, quod bene nosse dignaris, xv. kl maias eius anni pascha celebrandum esse sit scribtum.* The translation is Jones's (1943), 57. At AD 455 RS-354 has epact 30 and Pasch on 17 April *luna* 18 (cf. Krusch (1880), 64, and Schwartz (1905), 49), and if RS-442 had decremented this to epact 28 then its paschal date would remain 17 April but with *luna* 16.

75 Pope Leo I, *Epistola ad Marcianum* 2 (ed. Krusch (1880), 259; Ball. no. 121). The English translation kindly provided by Immo Warntjes; cf. Jones (1943), 57 n. 4, paraphrase; see also below at n. 91. Leo's rationale here for accepting Pasch on 22–23 April echoes that of *Epistola Paschasini* 2 (Krusch (1880), 249): *Nec nobis [...] incurramus errorem.*

siquidem ab XI. kl ap usque in XI. kl maias legitimum spatium sit praefixum, intro quod omnium varietatum necessitas concludatur, ut pascha dominicum nec prius possimus habere nec tardius. Quod enim in decimum et in nonum kl maias videtur nonnumquam pervenisse festivitas, quadam ratione defenditur, quia etsi dies resurrectionis ultra terminum videtur exisse, dies tamen passionis limitem positum non invenietur egressus. Ad octavum autem kl mai paschalem observantiam perducere nimis insolens et aperta transgressio est.

> If indeed the legitimate period would be set from 22 March to 21 April, the constraints (*necessitas*) of all variations should be covered by this, so that we could not have Easter Sunday either earlier or later. But should the festivity sometimes come up on 22 and 23 April, it can be justified by a certain logic, because though the day of the resurrection appears to have transgressed the *terminum*, the day of the passion will not be found to exceed the set limit. However, it is too much of an open and insolent transgression to prolong observing Easter to 24 April.

Thus Leo was able to accept Pasch on 22–23 April because then the Passion, Good Friday, fell on 20–21 April, the rationalization given by Paschasinus, but Leo considered it an insolent transgression to celebrate Good Friday after 21 April.

In AD 454 Marcian referred the question to Proterius, bishop of Alexandria, who in May AD 454 responded to Leo with a vigorous justification for celebration on 24 April, citing Theophilus' 100-year table, and giving and an aggressive assertion of Alexandria's pre-eminent authority in paschal matters. Proterius wrote:[76]

Celebretur autem ita potius, ut centinarius annorum cursus eiusdem beatissimi patris nostri et episcopi Theophili continet, qui antiquorum paginis omnino concordat, id est XXVIIII. die mensis parmuthi iuxta Aegyptius, qui est VIII. kl mai. Et nos enim et tota Aegyptia regio atque oriens universus sic ipsum diem caelebraturi sumus, deo praestante. Ut autem non arbitremur absolute, quod nobis videtur, scribere seu velle firmare, inseruimus etiam causas huic epistule, quibus tua sanctitas forte estimet, non se debere reprehendere Aegyptiorum ecclesiae veritatem, quae mater huiuscemodi laboris existit diligenterque conscripsit.

> It is better celebrated in the way as outlined by the 100-year table of the very same and most revered bishop Theophilus, our father, which agrees wholeheartedly with the scriptures of the ancients, i.e. the 29th day of the month Pharmuti according to the Egyptians, which is 24 April. And surely we and all Egypt and the entire East shall celebrate it on that very same day, God willing! However, so that we are not considered stubborn in what occurs to us to write and to postulate, we also included in this letter the reasons, through which your Holiness can thoroughly verify that the truth

---

76 *Epistola Proterii* 1–2 (ed. Krusch (1880), 270–71). The translation is by Immo Warntjes; cf. Jones (1943), 58.

of the Church of the Egyptians, which emerges as the mother of this sort of work (*laboris*) and thoroughly put this into writing, is not to be refuted.

In the event Leo reluctantly accepted celebration on 24 April, and notified this date to the churches of Gaul and Spain, but beforehand he wrote to Marcian in May AD 454, explaining his motive for conforming, but registering his own strong disapproval. He wrote:[77]

> *Sed cum Aegyptiis alia ratio placeat, consensum meum, ne qua discrepantia per provincias de observantia tam venerabilis festi fieret* [...] *non quia hoc ratio manifesta docuerit, sed quia unitatis, quam maxime custodimus, cura persuaserit.*

> Since another calculation appealed to the Egyptians, I have given my consent so that there might be no discrepancy throughout the provinces in the observance of so venerable a holiday [...] not because the calculation is manifestly correct, but because the desire for unity, which I hold as my greatest desire, persuades me.

It is clear from this sequence that in the years AD 442–455 Leo, while endeavouring to maintain the Roman 84-year paschal tradition was obliged by his desire for unity to extend the later *terminus* of Rome's paschal celebration three days beyond the 21 April *terminus* of RS-354.

Shortly after AD 455, Leo's archdeacon, Hilarus, wrote to the mathematician Victorius of Aquitaine, asking him to examine the causes behind the differences between the Roman and Alexandrian tables. By AD 457 Victorius had responded with a 532-year paschal table which tabulated paschal dates between 22 March and 24 April inclusive, and accommodated both the Roman *luna* 16–22 *termini* and the Alexandrian *luna* 15–21 *termini*. He made, however, two significant omissions: when epact 27 occurred with *feria* 6 in a common year, or *feria* 5 in a bissextile year, Victorius tabulated only the Alexandrian *luna* 15 date on 18 April, but omitted the Roman *luna* 22 date on 25 April. Further, when epact 25 occurred with *feria* 6 in a common year, or *feria* 5 in a bissextile year, Victorius sometimes tabulated only the Roman date on 28 March *luna* 22; he could not include the Alexandrian date on 21 March *luna* 15 because it fell on the day of the equinox.[78] Indeed, all Victorius' paschal dates for epact 25 depend upon *luna* 14 on 20 March, and consequently all violate the Alexandrian principle that paschal *luna* 14 cannot precede the equinox on 21 March. Thus Victorius, having compiled a 19-year lunar cycle whose epacts better approximated those of the Alexandrian 19-year cycle than did those of RS-354, imposed the Julian

---

77 Pope Leo I, *Epistola ad Marcianum* 1 (ed. Krusch (1880), 264; Ball. no. 137); the translation is Jones's (1943), 59.

78 Victorius of Aquitaine, *Cyclus* AP 18, 113, 360, 455 for epact 27 and *feria* 5 or 6, where AP 360 and 455 have marginal *luna* 22 dates incongruently designated *Graeci* (ed. Krusch (1938), 27, 32, 43, 48); AP 7, 102, 349, 444 for epact 25 and *feria* 5 or 6 (Krusch (1938), 27, 32, 44, 49). Cf. Warntjes (2020), 657–63, for Victorius' epacts 25 and 27.

termini that Leo had accepted in AD 455, 22 March–24 April, and, where possible, accommodated both the Roman *luna* 16–22 and the Alexandrian *luna* 15–21 *termini*, leaving the decision to the pope.

In his prologue to this table Victorius gave brief accounts of the Roman and Alexandrian paschal *termini*. He stated that the Roman tradition celebrated Pasch on a Sunday falling within *luna* 16–22, and that the new-moon, *luna* 1, of the paschal lunation should fall between *III non. Mar.* (5 March) and *IIII non. Apr.* (2 April), so that the paschal full-moon, *luna* 14, fell between *XV kal. Apr.* (18 March) and *XVII kal. Mai.* (15 April).[79] Further, Victorius indicated that the Roman paschal moons were one to two days in advance of the Alexandrian moons, so it is clear that he was not referring to either RS-442 or RS-447.[80] Moreover, his assertion that the earliest date for the Roman new-moon is 5 March is correct for all but one year of RS-354, as Mosshammer's reconstruction demonstrates.[81] Regarding the Alexandrian principles, Victorius explicitly attributed these to Theophilus' epistle to Theodosius, which had accompanied his 100-year list of paschal dates commencing in AD 380. It seems, therefore, that Victorius took RS-354 to represent the paschal tradition of the *Latini*, and Theophilus to represent that of the *Aegypti*.[82]

Thus the fifteen years of Leo's international negotiation concerning the celebration of Pasch exceeding 21 April resulted in the compilation of at least three new paschal tables, two 84-year tables, and one 532-year table. RS-442 and RS-447, as we shall see, both sought to bring the epacts of the Roman 84-year lunar cycle closer to the Alexandrian epacts, and also to extend the Julian *terminus* beyond 21 April. For his part Victorius endeavoured to accommodate both Roman and Alexandrian paschal lunar *termini* within 22 March–24 April. Not only were all these compilations closely contemporaneous, all were undertaken within the papacy of Leo.

A reconstruction of the Zeitz paschal table

I next consider the question of reconstructing the 84-year paschal table that is anticipated by the Zeitz preface, and, because the ferial, epactal, and Julian calendar data provide the most substantial preserved corpus of chronological criteria, I begin with them. The penultimate paragraph of the preface anticipates

---

79 Victorius of Aquitaine, *Prologus* 4 (ed. Krusch (1938), 19–20) for Victorius' account of the Roman and Alexandrian *termini*.

80 Victorius of Aquitaine, *Prologus* 5 (Krusch (1938), 20): *Cumque eam Aegyptii sextam decimam in diae paschae verbi gratia numerarent, nostri eandem XVII. vel etiam XVIII. calculantur.*

81 Mosshammer (2008), 208–11, where he accepts only for no. 36 Pasch on 25 March *luna* 22, implying *luna* 1 on 4 March; for nos 55 and 63 he ambivalently accepts an April paschal date, thereby providing a possible alternative to paschal *luna* 1 on 3–4 March; cf. Krusch (1880), 63–64.

82 Victorius of Aquitaine, *Prologus* 4–5 (Krusch (1938), 19–21), for Victorius' references to *Latini*, *Aegypti*, Theophilus.

the presentation of a series extending for five 84-year cycles for 420 years.[83] Of this it explicitly states that the final year of this series will follow the year of the consuls Calepius and Artabur, the consuls for AD 447, implying that the series would commence in AD 29, which is stated to be the year of the Passion. The surviving preface gives no indication as to how the criteria for these 420 years would be presented, but the ensuing table does preserve 32 years from the first cycle, 33 years from the second cycle, 7 years from the third cycle, and 24 years from the fifth cycle. While consuls are cited for each of these years, chronological criteria are given only for the first and fifth cycles, and it is only from these that the 84-year lunar cycle can be reconstructed. Therefore, I commence by making an assessment of the nature and quality of these criteria.

The chronological criteria provided for the surviving sections of the first and fifth cycles are the ferial and epact of the kalends of January (1 January) followed by a Julian calendar date regularly prefixed by 'mn', or a variant, usually over-scored. I shall first examine only the ferials and the epacts, and will then consider the Julian calendar dates below.

Regarding the ferials, because a common Julian calendar year of 365 days contains 52 weeks plus one day ($365 = 52 \times 7 + 1$), the ferial of the kalends of January following a common year increments by 1. Following a bissextile year of 366 days the ferial of the following year increments by 2; in both instances, should the result exceed 7, then the ferial of the following year is given by seven subtracted from this result. In his calendar reform of 46 BC Julius Caesar ordained that every fourth year should be bissextile, and, while this was misinterpreted following Caesar's murder, a restoration was instituted by Augustus in AD 8.[84] Consequently, since AD 8 the AD years exactly divisible by four have been bissextile, and so the ferial of the kalends of January follows a 28-year cycle, usually referred to as the solar cycle.[85] The preface implies that tabulation commenced at AD 29, and the years AD 29–31 are common years with kalends ferials of 7, 1, 2, respectively, AD 32 is bissextile with ferial 3, and AD 33 follows with ferial 5. This is exactly the ferial sequence presented by the manuscript, and this is then sustained across the numerous *lacunae* in the criteria to AD 388. Thus the ferial data of the manuscript present no scribal errors, and this was the series reconstructed by Mommsen (1863), 553–54, and accepted by Krusch (1880), 121–23, and this is reproduced in Table 4.

Turning to the epactal data, because both common and bissextile Julian years normally exceed 12 lunar months by 11 days, the epact or age of the moon on the kalends of the following January will usually be 11 greater than that of the preceding year; should this increase by 11 exceed 30, then 30 is subtracted. However, in order to maintain better synchronism between the calendar and real moons, at regular intervals one of the 12 lunar months is reduced by 1 day resulting in

---

83 Preface, fol. 4r ll. 15–20; cf. above pp. 35 and 44.

84 Blackburn and Holford-Strevens (1999), 670–71 (the inception of regular bissextile years).

85 Mc Carthy (2008), 345 (tabulation of the 28-year solar cycle of the ferials of the kalends of January).

an increase of the epact by 12. This was effected by reducing one 30-day lunar month to a 29-day month, a reduction designated as the *saltus lunae*. Examination of the instances of successive epacts in our manuscript shows that in most cases the difference is indeed 11 modulo 30; for example, AD 29–35 have epacts 21, 2, 13, 24, 5, 16, 27, all with differences of 11 modulo 30. There is no instance in the surviving epacts of a difference of 12 modulo 30. However, the preface makes explicit that the lunar cycle extended for 84 years, for which two different *saltus* intervals are known, a 12-year and a 14-year.[86] At AD 29–52 and 365–388 we have two copies of the first 24 years of this cycle, but unfortunately both epactal sequences are incomplete at their twelfth year of AD 40 and 376 respectively. However, in both instances their epact 11 at AD 39 and 375 is followed two years later by epact 4 at AD 41 and 377, showing that a *saltus* has been inserted between these years. That it was at the twelfth rather than the eleventh year is shown in both cases by the increments of 11 at the years AD 50–51 and 386–387, and so this 12-year *saltus* accords with the interval in the earlier Roman 84-year cycle, RS-354. This then was the epactal series reconstructed for Zeitz by Mommsen (1863), 553–54, and accepted by Krusch (1880), 121–23, and this is reproduced in Table 4. From this it emerges that the only actual epactal errors in the surviving data are the 'VII' at AD 52 and the 'VI' at AD 388, which both require emendation to 'V', and it is curious that both errors should occur at the 24th year of the lunar cycle, suggesting that both may be the result of later interpolation.

Turning now to consider the question of paschal dates, there is nothing recorded in the Zeitz preface preserved in fol. 4r–v, or in the table in fols 5, 10, 15, that allowed earlier scholars to identify reliably the paschal principles employed by the compiler for his table. While the preface gives the date of Pasch for AD 448 as 11 April, and anticipates the date 27 March for AD 449, it gives no lunar data for either. Even though the manuscript supplies intermittent Julian calendar dates for AD 29–388 that the preface and other details would suggest to be the dates of the paschal new-moons, there is no indication given of either the lunar or the Julian *termini* to be imposed on the paschal dates. However, as already noted above the preface's undertaking to catalogue the years of the primates of the Apostolic See and the reigns of the Roman emperors both suggest a Roman context for the compilation. It seems likely that it was this, together with the 84-year lunar cycle with a 12-year *saltus* that prompted de Rossi, Mommsen, and Krusch all to assume that the paschal principles of its table would resemble

---

86 Victorius of Aquitaine, *Prologus* 3 (Krusch (1938), 18–19), adverts to 84-year paschal tables as having either a 12-year or, implicitly, a 14-year *saltus*. For descriptions of the sources and reconstructions of a Roman 84-year table with a 12-year *saltus*, cf. Krusch (1880), 32–64, and Schwartz (1905), 40–58. For a description of the 84-year table with a 14-year *saltus* used in Britain and Ireland preserved in Padua, Biblioteca Antoniana, I 27, 76r–77v, and its reconstruction, cf. Mc Carthy (1993).

62   DANIEL MC CARTHY

those of the RS-354. For his part Schwartz frankly acknowledged that there was insufficient evidence.[87]

However, the manuscript fragments recovered in Zeitz in 2005 preserve some brief and incomplete statements from the preface that show that the compiler was giving serious consideration to the paschal principles of the Alexandrian church. His references at fol. 3r to that church as *auctoritatem alexandrina[e] ecclesiae praeminere cui iudicio sanctorum patrum* ('that the authority of the Alexandrian church is preeminent, to which by the judgement of the holy fathers'), and *quem praedictae ecclesia pronuntiare* ('on which the aforesaid churches pronounce'), suggest that he was according both respect and consideration to that church and its paschal principles. Then his statement on fol. 3v *neque in primo mense illut sed in duo^{de}cimo censeat numerandum unde apparet [...] [pri]mam lunam primi mensis ab octauo idus martias* ('that it should be reckoned not in the first month but in the twelfth, whence it is clear that the *luna* 1 of the first month is from 8 March') appears to identify *VIII id. Mar.* (8 March) as the earliest date for the paschal new-moon. This date corresponds with the earliest new-moon permitted by Alexandrian paschal principles, but not with that of RS-354.[88] Further, the final surviving lines of the preface on fol. 3v state *id est quarta decima·luna·quaeratur ac si [pleni]lunio dies fuerit sabbati in subsequenti* ('that is *luna* 14 is to be sought and if the full moon falls on Saturday then on the following'), which appears to be part of the Alexandrian specification that, should paschal *luna* 14 fall on Saturday, then Pasch falls on the following Sunday, *luna* 15. Furthermore, the intermittent textual correlation of some details of fol. 3v with Victorius' account of the Alexandrian paschal principles taken from Theophilus epistle to Theodosius suggest that here the Zeitz preface drew on this source. It is clear from these fragmented references that the compiler was considering very closely the details of the Alexandrian church's paschal principles.

Then, just seventeen lines later, on fol. 4r, he states the following:

> *Unde cum ex iudicio venerabilium patrum Aegyptiae ad haec scientiae emineret auctoritas, ita paschalis revolutionis ordinem credidimus digerendum, ut, ubi duplicem denuntiationem opinionum diversitas facit, subnotatio nostra non desit et quid [d]electatione tua, ad quam cuncta respiciunt, dignius videatur, ostendat.*
>
> Since by the judgement of the venerable fathers the authority of Egyptian science was supreme for these matters, we have thought that the scheme of the Easter cycle should be so arranged in such a way that, where a difference of opinions produces a twofold designation, our annotation

---

87 Schwartz (1905), 72: 'Es ist von der Zeitzer Ostertafel zu wenig erhalten um sicher feststellen zu können, welche Ostergrenzen sie innegehalten hat'.

88 The earliest paschal full-moon allowed by Alexandrian principles is on 21 March, the spring equinox, implying the earliest new-moon on 21 – 13 = 8 March; cf. Schwartz (1905), 24 s.a. 338. The earliest paschal new-moon definitely employed by the RS-354 is that implied by its Pasch on 25 March *luna* 22, implying new-moon on 25 – 21 = 4 March; cf. Krusch (1880), 63 cyclus no. 36.

shall not be wanting, but displays whichever seems worthier of your choice, to which all turn.

Here the compiler acknowledges that 'by the judgement of the venerable fathers the authority of Egyptian science was supreme for these matters', which in a Roman context can only reasonably be understood to refer to the judgement of the Roman episcopacy on Alexandrian paschal principles. It is effectively a reiteration of the attitude towards Alexandrian authority expressed by Paschasinus in his letter of AD 442, which attitude was clearly reciprocated by Leo I.[89] Then the compiler undertakes to document instances of conflicting opinions, leaving the decision to 'your choice', which likewise can only credibly reference the bishop of Rome. Consequently, it appears that the compiler was committed to computing paschal dates according to both Roman and Alexandrian paschal principles, and to leave to the bishop of Rome the decision as to which should be used when these differed. Moreover, we recall that Paschasinus' statement that the 63rd year of RS-442 presented a choice between 26 March *luna* 21, an acceptable Roman date, and 23 April *luna* 19, a date considered Alexandrian, indicating that RS-442 likewise had tabulated both traditions. As discussed above, about ten years after the compilation of Zeitz Victorius would likewise tabulate paschal dates according both Roman and Alexandrian principles, and similarly leave the choice to the papacy. From all of these instances it is clear that from at least AD 442 Leo was seeking to adjust the later Julian *terminus* of the Roman Pasch in order to accommodate Alexandrian paschal principles.

I now turn to consider the Julian dates in the manuscript tabulated after the lunar epact and preceded by 'mn' or 'men', representing probably the word 'mensis'. This prefix suggests that the Julian date refers to a lunar month, and to examine this I consider the lunar epact and the date together, and follow the progress of the lunar months between 1 January and that date. I first note that in the Roman lunar calendar the lunar months are named from the Julian solar months in which they end, and they alternate in length between full months of 30 days, and hollow months of 29 days. Thus lunar *January*, *March*, and *May* are full, and lunar *February*, *April*, and *June* are hollow, and I shall use italic font to distinguish lunar months from Julian months. For example, at AD 51 is tabulated *lun·XXIIII·m̄n·VIII·id·Mart*, that is *January luna* 24 on 1 January, and *mensis* on *VIII id. Mar.* (8 March). Consequently, 1 January has *January luna* 24, 7 January has *January luna* 30, 8 January has *February luna* 1, 5 February has *February luna* 29, 6 February has *March luna* 1, 7 March has *March luna* 30, 8 March has *April luna* 1. Thus the tabulated date, *VIII id. Mar.*, identifies the new-moon (*luna* 1) of the lunar month of *April*, falling on 8 March. At AD 67 the epact 22 is two days less than epact 24, and correspondingly the tabulated date *VI id. Mar.* (10 March) identifies the new-moon of lunar *April*, two days later. Examination of all the

---

89 *Epistola Paschasini* 1 (Krusch (1880), 248): *Diutino itaque tractatu vel ratiotinatione id verum invenimus, quod ab Alexandrine ecclesiae antestite beatitudine vestrae rescriptum est.*

64 DANIEL MC CARTHY

tabulated dates for epacts 2–24 shows that all identify the date of new-moon for lunar *April* (cf. Figure 1).

I next consider the epacts greater than 24, commencing at AD 379 where is tabulated *lun·XXVI·mn̄ II non·Apr*, so *January luna* 26 on 1 January and *mensis* on *II non. Apr.* (4 April). Consequently, 1 January has *January luna* 26, 5 January has *January luna* 30, 6 January has *February luna* 1, 3 February has *February luna* 29, 4 February has *March luna* 1, 5 March has *March luna* 30, 6 March has *April luna* 1, 3 April has *April luna* 29, 4 April has *May luna* 1. Thus the tabulated date, *II non. Apr.*, identifies the new-moon (*luna* 1) of the lunar month of *May*, falling on 4 April. Examination of all the tabulated dates for epacts 26–30 shows that most identify the date of new-moon for lunar *May* (cf. Figure 1).

In order to examine the consistency of these dates I tabulate all of them graphically in Figure 1, plotting each manuscript date as a square positioned a distance above its date equal to its associated epact. For example, at both AD 39 and 66 we have *lun·XI·mn̄·XII·k·Apr*, which identifies a year with epact 11, and the new-moon date *XII kal. Apr.* (21 March). Thus in Figure 1 the square is placed a distance of eleven units directly above the date 21 March, and an '11' is inscribed into the square to identify clearly that it is associated with epact 11. Similar squares are inscribed for all the other new-moon dates preserved in the manuscript, and where there are two or three instances in the manuscript of the same date, as for epacts 11 and 13, the square has been outlined with a heavy border. This graphic representation allows us to examine the consistency, or otherwise, of all these dates, from which it emerges that a small number do not correspond with the new-moon of either *April* or *May*.

From Figure 1 it can be seen that in most instances the manuscript new-moon date advances by one day for each one day increment of the epact, with the following exceptions:

1. For epacts 2 and 10, the manuscript gives two different dates, and in each instance the earlier date is in accordance with the new-moon date calculated from the epact; the later date in each case represents a typical scribal omission.
2. For epact 4 the manuscript gives the date of *IIII kl. Apr.* (29 March) twice, but this date is one day later than the new moon for *April* on *V kl. Apr.* (28 March). This is not a typical scribal error and the repetition suggests that it was either an error in the original compilation, or a subsequent mis-correction.
3. For epact 30 the new-moon date of 1 April is the same as that for epact 29. This will indeed occur if a 30-day embolismic month was inserted before lunar *May* for epact 30, and since the manuscript date at AD 38, though incomplete, does imply the date *kl. Apr.* I accept this date.[90]

---

90 Mommsen (1863), 553–54, at nos 10, 37, 56, gave new-moon at 1 April for epact 30. Krusch (1880), 121–23, gave new-moon on 31 March for nos 10, 37, 56, against the manuscript; 123, where his 'Anmerkung' lists the new-moon dates for the *January* to *May* lunations, omitting an embolism before the *May* lunation.

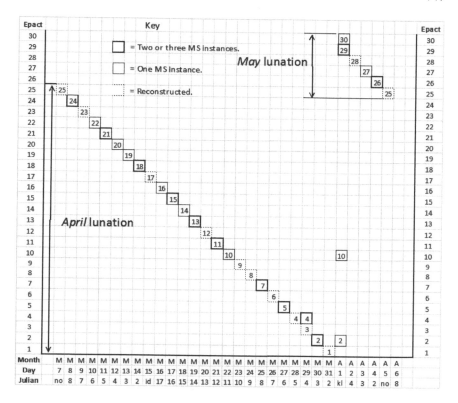

Figure 1. All of the Zeitz manuscript epact and new-moon dates are plotted in squares with continuous borders, and when a date is recorded twice or thrice the square has a heavy border, while reconstructed dates are plotted in squares with dashed borders. The number within each square identifies the epact, while on the left the lunation which they initiate, *April* or *May*, is indicated.

With these observations we reconstruct the *April* new-moon dates for epacts 1, 3, 4, 6, 8, 9, 12, 17, 23, and 25, and the *May* new-moon dates for epact 25 and 28, which epacts are all lost from the manuscript. In Figure 1 all the manuscript dates have been plotted in squares with continuous borders, while all reconstructed dates have dashed borders.

An important observation arising from this is that, since the new-moon for epact 24 on 8 March implies *luna* 14 on 21 March, this full-moon falls on the date of the spring equinox, so that all full-moons for epacts 1–24, and 26–30 fall on or after this crucial date. I consider that this property identifies that these tabulated new-moon dates represent for each year the first day of the compiler's paschal month. Since epact 25 is lost from the manuscript, for the present its paschal new-moon date must be left as ambivalent, and thus both its *April* and *May* new-moons shall be considered possible and hence both are plotted.

Next, in order to examine both Roman and Alexandrian lunar *termini* we need to identify for each epact the dates of *luna* 15–22 falling within its paschal month. Consequently, in Figure 2 these are represented by eight squares positioned precisely 14–21 days later than the *luna* 1 square locating its paschal new-moon. For example, for epact 1, with new-moon on 31 March, these eight squares are placed directly above the dates 14–21 April. For each epact these eight squares identify the ages *luna* 15–22, as is indicated explicitly in Figure 2 for epacts 1, 25, and 30.

Following this we need to establish when any of these eight days with *luna* 15–22 may fall on *feria* 1, Sunday, and so potentially may serve as the date of Pasch. Since the Zeitz table provides the *feria* of 1 January we seek to identify for any given feria N on 1 January where in the eight days of *luna* 15–22 Sunday will fall. For example, for epact 1 the *luna* 15 of its paschal moon falls on 14 April, and this date is the $31 + 28 + 31 + 14 = 104$th day of a Julian common year. Thus, if 1 January falls on *feria* N then 14 April will fall on:

$$(N + 104 - 1) \bmod 7 = (N + 103) \bmod 7 = (N + 14 \times 7 + 5) \bmod 7 = (N + 5) \bmod 7$$

Hence to obtain $(N + 5) \bmod 7 = 1$ requires that $N = 3$, i.e. $(3 + 5) \bmod 7 = 8 \bmod 7 = 1$. Consequently, for 14 April to fall on Sunday, 1 January must fall on *feria* 3, a Tuesday, so to record this relationship we inscribe a '3' into this square positioned above 14 April. If, however, 1 January falls one day earlier, *feria* 2, then the Sunday must fall one day later on 15 April, and so forth. Hence we inscribe '2', '1', '7', '6', '5', '4', '3' into the subsequent seven squares. This process is then repeated for the epacts 2–30.

Finally, we need to consider the 84 combinations of the epact and *feria* of 1 January implied by the Zeitz table. Of these 84 years, $3 \times 21 = 63$ years are common and 21 years are bissextile, and so we identify all instances of these 63 common years by colouring the appropriate squares yellow. For example, the first year of this table refers to AD 29, which is a common Julian calendar year, and it has epact 21 and *feria* 7, and consequently we colour yellow the square with the inscribed *feria* 7, which is directly above the date 27 March, in accordance with the statement in the preface. Since this is the third square for epact 21 it identifies *luna* 17, so that in this year Pasch should fall on Sunday, 27 March *luna* 17; this date and its Julian equivalent are shown directly below this square. However, since bissextile years have an additional day in February this will cause a one day advance in the date of the paschal Sunday, relative to a common year with the same epact and feria. Consequently, in order to correctly identify the paschal date for bissextile years in Figure 2 we first increment the manuscript *feria* for 1 January by 1 mod 7. For example, the fourth year of this table, AD 32, is a bissextile year with epact 24 and *feria* 3, so to locate its paschal Sunday we first increment the *feria* 3 as $(3 + 1) \bmod 7 = 4$ and then colour the square with the inscribed '4' above 23 March green. Since this green square is in the second position it shows that in AD 32 Pasch should fall on Sunday, 23 March *luna* 16. In this way we identify all 21 bissextile years with squares that are coloured green.

Figure 2 identifies in a compact way all the paschal dates that can arise accommodating both Alexandrian and Roman paschal principles in the 84 years determined by the Zeitz table. The advantage of this graphic representation is that it clearly shows those combinations of epacts and ferials that fall close to the Julian and lunar *termini* proposed by the Roman and Alexandrian paschal principles. From this figure we may readily identify those epact and ferial combinations that will yield paschal dates conforming to either of these paschal principles.

To consider first the Alexandrian paschal principles which require Pasch to fall on *luna* 15–21, and paschal *luna* 14 to fall no earlier than 21 March. The *luna* 15–21 *termini* constrain the Alexandrian dates to the coloured squares within the seven left-most squares for each epact. The Alexandrian constraint that paschal *luna* 14 fall no earlier than 21 March excludes the *April* lunation for epact 25 since its *luna* 14 falls on 20 March. Consequently, the Alexandrian Pasch arising from epact 25 will fall in the *May* lunation on 22 April *luna* 18. The Julian *termini* arising from these observations are: the earlier *terminus* is 22 March *luna* 15, arising from epact 24 and *feria* 5 in a common year, and the later *terminus* is 23 April *luna* 20, arising from epact 26 and *feria* 7 in a bissextile year.

Turning to consider the paschal principles adopted by the compiler as Roman, a more complex situation presents itself because we have no statement from him concerning these particular lunar and Julian *termini*. Regarding the lunar *termini*, since both the Hippolytan paschal table and RS-354 observed *luna* 16–22, and subsequently Victorius repeated this, I assume these to have been maintained by the compiler.[91] Regarding the Julian *termini*, inspection of Figure 2 shows that the earliest *luna* 16 paschal date is 23 March at epact 24 *feria* 3 in a bissextile year; the latest *luna* 22 paschal date is 25 April at epact 26 *feria* 6 in a common year. Thus the Julian *termini* for coordinated Roman paschal lunar dates of *luna* 16–22 is 23 March–25 April. While this may be considered a disproportionate modification of the Julian *termini* of RS-354, 22 March–21 April, it should be recalled firstly that its celebration on 22 March could only be made possible by the acceptance of the paschal full-moon falling before the equinox. Secondly, as mentioned above, in the two years, cyclic nos 6 and 63 of RS-354, no dates simultaneously satisfying these *termini* exist. In these two years either a March date relying on a paschal full-moon falling before the equinox, or an April date with *luna* 15 must be accepted. While the Zeitz new-moons appear to preclude the paschal full-moon falling before the equinox, but if the freedom to choose April dates with *luna* 15 was accepted with this table then the epact 26 *feria* 6 celebration on 17 April *luna* 15, and the epact 27 *feria* 7 celebration on 16 April

---

91 Mosshammer (2008), 124 (Hippolytan *luna* 16–22); Krusch (1938), 19 (Victorius on *luna* 16–22).

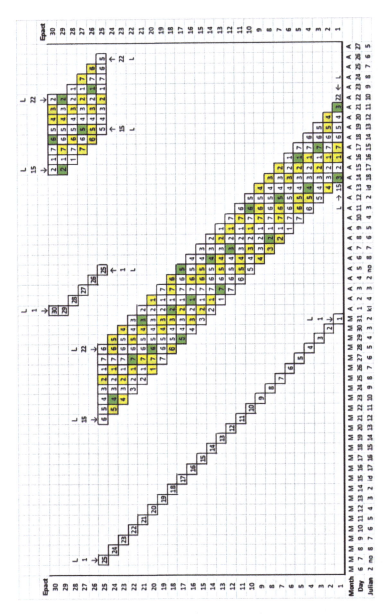

Figure 2. Identifying for each epact 1–30 the date of its paschal *luna* 1 and *luna* 15–22; for each *luna* 15–22 the inscribed number identifies the *feria* on 1 January that will result in that day falling on Sunday; squares coloured yellow identify the common years in the Zeitz table, while green squares identify the bissextile years, and to obtain the actual *feria* on 1 January for these bissextile years the inscribed number must be decremented by 1 mod 7.

luna 15 may be adopted, and the later Julian *terminus* would then become 23 April, determined by epact 26 *feria* 7 in a bissextile year.

Regarding this later Julian *terminus* of 23 April, the weakness of the Roman position with respect to 21 April, inherited by RS-354 from the Hippolytan paschal table, was tacitly acknowledged by Leo when he wrote to Marcian in AD 453:[92]

> *siquidem ab XI. kl ap usque in XI. kl maias legitimum spatium sit praefixum, intro quod omnium varietatum necessitas concludatur, ut pascha dominicum nec prius possimus habere nec tardius. Quod enim in decimum et in nonum kl maias videtur nonnumquam pervenisse festivitas, quadam ratione defenditur, quia etsi dies resurrectionis ultra terminum videtur exisse, dies tamen passionis limitem positum non invenietur egressus.*

> If indeed the legitimate period would be set from 22 March to 21 April, the constraints (*necessitas*) of all variations should be covered by this, so that we could not have Easter Sunday either earlier or later. But should the festivity sometimes come up on 22 and 23 April, it can be justified by a certain logic, because though the day of the resurrection appears to have transgressed the *terminum*, the day of the passion will not be found to exceed the set limit.

Leo's conjecture regarding of the adequacy of 22 March–21 April is immediately undermined by his ready acceptance of 22–23 April. Furthermore, immediately before this, in his rejection of Theophilus' date of 24 April for AD 455, Leo wrote:[93]

> *Sed sanctae memoriae Theophilus Alexandrine urbis episcopus cum huius observationis annos centum numero colligisset, septuagensimi sexti anni paschale festum longe aliter, quam alii decreverant, tenendum esse constituit. [...] Sed in anno, qui erit septuagensimus sextus, is paschae dies invenitur adscribtus, quem a passione domini nullius exempli, nullius constitutionis admittit auctoritas. Nam diem octavum kalendarum maiarum ab eo cognoscimus praefinitum, qui nimiae limitem antiquae contitutionis excedit, cum alii XV. kl maias huic festivitati deputaverint diem.*

> But Theophilus of holy memory, bishop of the city of Alexandria, when considering 100 years of his observation in one count, constituted that the Easter festival of the 76th year was to be held a long way out than others had otherwise decreed. [...] But in the year, which is the 76th, this day of Easter is found noted (on a date), which for the passion of the Lord no

---

92 Pope Leo I, *Epistola ad Marcianum* 2 (Krusch (1880), 259; Ball. no. 121); see n. 75 above. Mosshammer (2008), 121–22 (Hippolytus).

93 Pope Leo I, *Epistola ad Marcianum* 2 (Krusch (1880), 258–59; Ball. no. 121); cf. Jones (1943), 57 n. 4.

> authority of example or constitution allowed. For we know that 24 April set by him by far exceeds the limit of the ancient constitution, while others considered 17 April for this festival.

Leo's rejection of 24 April relies on his reference to anonymous 'limits set by a powerful ancient convention' (*nimiae limitem antiquae constitutionis*), and this anonymity further undermines Leo's weak authority for a *terminus* of 23 April. The source to which Leo is referring is possibly the paschal tract of Anatolius, bishop of Laodicea († *c.* AD 282), where the later *terminus* of his paschal table is indeed 23 April. This 23 April *terminus* was successfully maintained by Sulpicius Severus in *c.* AD 410 when he adapted Anatolius' 19-year lunar cycle to an 84-year cycle with a 14-year *saltus*.[94] In these circumstances of collapsing authority in Rome for the later limit of 21 April, and given the esteem accorded by the compiler's preface towards Alexandrian authority, and his adoption of 8 March as the early *terminus* for his paschal new-moon, and that Alexandrian principles permit Pasch on 25 April, I conclude that he likewise accepted into his table dates beyond the traditional 21 April Roman *terminus*.

Thus, referring to Figure 2, the *luna* 16–22 *termini* will constrain the Roman dates to the coloured squares within the seven right-most squares for each epact, and it is apparent that six instances exceed the 21 April limit. Four of these fall on 22–23 April and thus within the limits accepted by Leo. However, in two instances for epacts 26–27 their *luna* 22 dates fall on 25 April and 24 April respectively. Here it must be noted that for each instance neither alternative date for the *April* lunation provides a paschal date coordinated with the Roman *termini*.[95] Moreover, since the manuscript reading at AD 35 for epact 27, *feria* 7 in a common year, gives *III non. Apr.* (3 April) as the paschal new-moon, the compiler here has explicitly identified the *May* lunation as his paschal month for this critical combination of epact and ferial (cf. Figure 2). If Leo wished to avoid these 24–25 April paschal dates the choice was presented to him to choose the *luna* 15 dates on 17–18 April. By including these two *luna* 15 dates the Zeitz table would provide Leo with the paschal *termini* 23 March to 23 April (nos 4 and 80).

Regarding the compiler's choice for epact 25, Figure 2 shows that the two possible paschal dates for the single instance of this epact have no implications for the paschal *termini*. Then, since Figure 1 shows that the paschal new-moons for all the other epacts fell on or after 8 March I infer that for epact 25 the compiler chose the *May* lunation with new-moon on 5 April, and paschal date 22 April *luna* 18.

---

94 Mc Carthy and Breen (2003), 51, 68, for Anatolius' 23 April *terminus*; 118 it is argued that the Latin translation of Anatolius' tract was available in Italy by *c.* AD 400 when it was cited by Rufinus of Aquileia in his *Ecclesiastical History* V 24 and VII 32. Mc Carthy (1994), 38–44, for Sulpicius Severus' 84-year paschal cycle and *c.* AD 410.

95 For epact 26, *feria* 6 in a common year the *April* lunation has Sunday on either 21 March *luna* 16, or 28 March *luna* 23; for epact 27, *feria* 7 in a common year, the *April* lunation has Sunday on either 20 March *luna* 16, or 27 March *luna* 23, and all possibilities are uncoordinated with the Roman *termini*.

In summary, since the compiler undertook to tabulate both Roman and Alexandrian paschal traditions, leaving the choice to the bishop of Rome, I conclude that he tabulated all paschal dates for *luna* 15–22 falling between 22 March and 25 April inclusive, and that has been done in Table 4.

Table 4. A reconstruction of the sixth Zeitz cycle for the years AD 449–532, tabulating the cyclic number, the *feria* and epact of 1 January, the paschal new-moon, and the Alexandrian *luna* 15 and Roman *luna* 16–22 paschal dates and moons.

AD	CYCLE NO.	FERIA	EPACT	LUNA 1	ALEXANDRIAN LUNA 15		ROMAN LUNA 16–22		REMARKS
449	1	7	21	11 M			27 M	17	
450	2	1	2	30 M			16 A	18	
451	3	2	13	19 M			8 A	21	
452	4	3	24	8 M			23 M	16	Earliest Roman
453	5	5	5	27 M			12 A	17	
454	6	6	16	16 M			4 A	20	
455	7	7	27	3 A	17 A	15	24 A	22	
456	8	1	8	24 M			8 A	16	
457	9	3	19	13 M			31 M	19	
458	10	4	30	1 A			20 A	20	
459	11	5	11	21 M			5 A	16	
460	12	6	22	10 M			27 M	18	
461	13	1	4	28 M			16 A	20	
462	14	2	15	17 M			1 A	16	
463	15	3	26	4 A			21 A	18	
464	16	4	7	25 M			12 A	19	
465	17	6	18	14 M	28 M	15	4 A	22	
466	18	7	29	1 A			17 A	17	

AD	CYCLE NO.	FERIA	EPACT	LUNA 1	ALEXANDRIAN LUNA 15	ROMAN LUNA 16–22		REMARKS
467	19	1	10	22 M		9 A	19	
468	20	2	21	11 M		31 M	21	
469	21	4	2	30 M	13 A 15	20 A	22	
470	22	5	13	19 M		5 A	18	
471	23	6	24	8 M		28 M	21	
472	24	7	5	27 M		16 A	21	
473	25	2	17	15 M		1 A	18	
474	26	3	28	2 A		21 A	20	
475	27	4	9	23 M	6 A 15	13 A	22	
476	28	5	20	12 M		28 M	17	
477	29	7	1	31 M		17 A	18	
478	30	1	12	20 M		9 A	21	
479	31	2	23	9 M		25 M	17	
480	32	3	4	28 M		13 A	17	
481	33	5	15	17 M		5 A	20	
482	34	6	26	4 A	18 A 15	25 A	22	L. 15 avoids 25 A
483	35	7	7	25 M		10 A	17	
484	36	1	18	14 M		1 A	19	
485	37	3	30	1 A		21 A	21	
486	38	4	11	21 M		6 A	17	

AD	CYCLE NO.	FERIA	EPACT	LUNA 1	ALEXANDRIAN LUNA 15		ROMAN LUNA 16–22		REMARKS
487	39	5	22	10 M			29 M	20	
488	40	6	3	29 M			17 A	20	
489	41	1	14	18 M			2 A	16	
490	42	2	25	5 A			22 A	18	
491	43	3	6	26 M			14 A	20	
492	44	4	17	15 M	29 M	15	5 A	22	
493	45	6	28	2 A			18 A	17	
494	46	7	9	23 M			10 A	19	
495	47	1	20	12 M	26 M	15	2 A	22	
496	48	2	1	31 M	14 A	15	21 A	22	
497	49	4	13	19 M			6 A	19	
498	50	5	24	8 M	22 M	15	29 M	22	
499	51	6	5	27 M			11 A	16	
500	52	7	16	16 M			2 A	18	
501	53	2	27	3 A			22 A	20	
502	54	3	8	24 M	7 A	15	14 A	22	
503	55	4	19	13 M			30 M	18	
504	56	5	30	1 A			18 A	18	
505	57	7	11	21 M			10 A	21	
506	58	1	22	10 M			26 M	17	

AD	CYCLE NO.	FERIA	EPACT	LUNA 1	ALEXANDRIAN LUNA 15		ROMAN LUNA 16–22		REMARKS
507	59	2	3	29 M			15 A	18	
508	60	3	14	18 M			6 A	20	
509	61	5	26	4 A			19 A	16	
510	62	6	7	25 M			11 A	18	
511	63	7	18	14 M			3 A	21	
512	64	1	29	1 A	15 A	15	22 A	22	
513	65	3	10	22 M			7 A	17	
514	66	4	21	11 M			30 M	20	
515	67	5	2	30 M			19 A	21	
516	68	6	13	19 M			3 A	16	
517	69	1	24	8 M			26 M	19	
518	70	2	5	27 M			15 A	20	
519	71	3	16	16 M			31 M	16	
520	72	4	27	3 A			19 A	17	
521	73	6	9	23 M			11 A	20	
522	74	7	20	12 M			27 M	16	
523	75	1	1	31 M			16 A	17	
524	76	2	12	20 M			7 A	19	
525	77	4	23	9 M	23 M	15	30 M	22	
526	78	5	4	28 M			12 A	16	

AD	CYCLE NO.	FERIA	EPACT	LUNA 1	ALEXANDRIAN LUNA 15		ROMAN LUNA 16–22		REMARKS
527	79	6	15	17 M			4 A	19	
528	80	7	26	4 A			23 A	20	Latest Roman
529	81	2	7	25 M	8 A	15	15 A	22	
530	82	3	18	14 M			31 M	18	
531	83	4	29	1 A			20 A	20	
532	84	5	10	22 M			11 A	21	

Since the only other published reconstruction of this sixth Zeitz cycle with comprehensive paschal dates is that by Krusch (1880), 121–23, it will be helpful to indicate how the reconstruction in Table 4 differs from his, and below these differences are listed in order of their frequency:

1. *Table 4* registers all thirteen instances of the Alexandrian *luna* 15 and Roman *luna* 22 paschal divergences, whereas for ten of these Krusch provided only the Roman *luna* 22 date, while for nos 7, 34, 64, he provided only the Alexandrian *luna* 15 date, all thirteen without comment.

2. *Table 4* includes six Roman *luna* 22 dates between 22–25 April, nos 7, 34, 42, 53, 64, 80, whereas Krusch presented nos 42, 53, 80, falling on 22–23 April parenthetically with a '?', while for nos 7, 34, 64, he cited just the Alexandrian *luna* 15 date without comment.

3. *Table 4* has no instances of ambivalent Roman paschal dates, whereas Krusch gives ambivalent dates for cyclic nos 42, 53, 80, and his use of the *April* lunation dates for nos 53 and 80, with epacts 27 and 26 respectively, conflict with the manuscript *May* lunation dates (cf. Figure 1).

4. *Table 4* places the new-moon for epact 30 on 1 April in accordance with the reading at AD 38, whereas Krusch nos 10, 37, 56, place it on 31 March, so that in each case for this epact his paschal moon is one day older than that given in this table.

5. *Table 4*'s earliest new-moon is 8 March (epact 24), so its earliest paschal full-moon is 21 March, whereas Krusch nos 42, 53, 80 have paschal new-moons on 7, 5, 6 March respectively, with full-moons on 20, 18, 19 March, all before the spring equinox.

6. *Table 4* assigns the paschal new-moon for epact 25, no. 42, to the *May* lunation, whereas Krusch ambivalently assigns it to both *April* and *May* lunations.

From these features can be discerned that Krusch, with no indication from the then available manuscript of the compiler's paschal preferences, understandably assumed that the Zeitz paschal table should reflect the same paschal tradition as RS-354. He did not appreciate that Zeitz was compiled at a time when the paschal attitudes of the Roman episcopacy were evolving towards accommodation of Alexandrian paschal principles into the Roman tradition, in particular the adoption of the constraint that the paschal full-moon should not be allowed to fall more than one day before the spring equinox on 21 March.[96] Krusch, not realising this, allowed his paschal full-moon to fall as early as 18 March, and then sought unsuccessfully to maintain 21 April as the later Julian *terminus*.

I next consider the gloss written in eleven short lines extending into the bottom margin, directly underneath the name of the consul Orphito at AD 51. This is neatly written by the first hand but with a script size and line spacing of about one third of his other text on this page. That this originated as a gloss

---

96 The *Romana supputatio* allowed paschal *luna* 14 to fall as early as 16 March, whereas the earliest *luna* 14 allowed by Victorius was 20 March.

78   DANIEL MC CARTHY

added to the archetype is indicated by its interlinear presentation, and a number of other considerations. First, its stern rejection of the paschal date of the *Latini*, 21 March, in favour of the 18 April attributed to Theophilus, bishop of Alexandria, stands in stark contrast to the relaxed attitude to paschal ambiguity expressed in the Zeitz preface. Second, since Theophilus compiled his 100-year paschal table between AD 385 and 395, and it began at 380, the reference to him here at AD 51 is profoundly anachronistic.[97] Third, the paschal date of 21 March ascribed to the *Latini* is not that of Zeitz which here places paschal *luna* 1 on 8 March, and hence Pasch on 28 March *luna* 21 (cf. no. 23 in Table 4). Moreover, as has been demonstrated above, the early Roman *terminus* of RS-447 is 23 March. All of these details show that this gloss is both anachronistic and incongruent with the Zeitz criteria at AD 51.

However, if we ask to which year of Theophilus' table could this gloss refer, then the first possible year after Theophilus' start at AD 380 is 387, because 387 = 51 + 4 × 84, so that in the Zeitz 84-year cycle AD 51 and 387 have the same *feria*, epact, and new-moon. The year AD 387 is synchronized with cyclic no. 6 of RS-354, which, like no. 63, has no coordinated paschal date.[98] Moreover, at this year the Ambrosian manuscript and all modern reconstructions of RS-354 have the two uncoordinated dates, 21 March *luna* 16, and 18 April *luna* 15.[99] Since both Julian dates of the gloss correspond with these it appears likely that the author of this gloss was comparing a copy of RS-354 with Zeitz and observed that their ferial criteria at this year synchronized precisely, and their epacts approximately. Since the RS-354 date of 21 March coincides with the spring equinox the glossator dismissed it, mistakenly attributing it to the *Latini*, whereas, as Schwartz demonstrated, in AD 387 Rome actually celebrated Pasch on 18 April. Regarding the glossator's attribution of the 18 April to Theophilus it seems certain he did not consult Theophilus' table, for, as Krusch and Schwartz pointed out, in AD 387 Alexandria celebrated Pasch on 25 April.[100] We also note that Victorius repeatedly uses the term *Latini* to identify the Roman paschal tradition in his epistle to Hilarus (i.e. his prologue) and his 532-year paschal table.[101] Thus it seems that this

---

97 Mosshammer (2008), 190–91 (Theophilus' table and dates of compilation).

98 Mommsen (1863), 560; Krusch (1880), 111; Schwartz (1905), 53–54; all likewise identify that the gloss refers to the year AD 387.

99 Krusch (1880), 237 (Ambrosian no. 6); Krusch (1880), 62, Schwartz (1905), 46, Mosshammer (2008), 210 (reconstruction of RS-354 no. 6).

100 Krusch (1880), 111: 'im Jahre 387 [...] das Osterfest der Alexandriner auf den 25. April fiel [...] der 18. April und 21. März waren die in der Ostertafel der Supputatio notirten Ostertage, und der abendländische Verfasser der Zeitzer Tafel übertrug in irrthümlicher Weise den späteren auf die Alexandriner'. Schwartz (1905), 54: 'Denn dass der Chronograph von 354 [für 387] das historisch richtige Datum [in Rom], den 18. April, giebt, wird im höchsten Grade wahrscheinlich gemacht [...] Dieses Compromissdatum ist von der Zeitzer Ostertafel dem Theophilus zugeschrieben, mit Unrecht: denn dass 387 in Alexandrien, ja im Orient überhaupt Ostern am 25. April gefeiert ist, steht [...] unbedingt fest'.

101 Victorius of Aquitaine, *Prologus* 4, 5, 12 (Krusch (1938), 19, 20, 26); *Cyclus*, for various years (Krusch (1880), 27–52) (Victorius' references to *Latini*).

gloss is the result of a clumsy collation of RS-354 with Zeitz, and the glossator's attribution to Theophilus is simply a mistaken assumption.

Finally, regarding the identity of the compiler of the preface and table of Zeitz the most that can be inferred from the text is that for him to leave the decision in instances of ambiguity to whichever 'seems worthier of your choice, to which all turn', would suggest that the compiler was in contact with Leo.[102] As well, he clearly was a skilled computist with access to and knowledge of a substantial range of paschal and historical sources. However, while his compilation exhibits Leo's inclination to accommodate Alexandrian paschal principles, he takes the process of accommodation much further, accepting both the 8 March as the early *terminus* for the paschal new-moon, and 25 April as a possible later *terminus* of Pasch. From the complete subsequent papal silence regarding this compilation it appears that these features went further than Leo was prepared to accept. Rather it was Victorius' 532-year compilation that achieved papal recognition.

The compilation of RS-442

Before concluding I wish to briefly consider the circumstances of the compilation of RS-442 because its compilation closely precedes RS-447, and Paschasinus' references show that they shared some significant features. Namely, their epacts had been updated to closely approximate those of Alexandria, and they had extended the later Julian *terminus* beyond 21 April so as to include 23 April as a possible paschal date. This extension of the later Julian *terminus* represented an important change in the Roman paschal principles, and since Leo was elected pope only in AD 440, this would suggest that both the decision and the compilation of RS-442 were recent developments.

N. W. James reviewed the scholarship and textual evidence that in the first years of his episcopacy Leo repeatedly drew upon Prosper's anti-Pelagian writings in order to express his own opposition to Pelagius. James wrote that 'Antelmy was correct in seeing Prosper's hand behind the Pope's anti-Pelagian letters dating from 440–442'. This was the beginning of a long relationship between Leo and Prosper, and James concluded that there can 'be little doubt that Prosper was used during the 440s and 450s to draft a number of important papal letters'.[103]

Prosper was a well-educated layman from Aquitaine born c. AD 390 who by the AD 430s had compiled polemic works in favour of the doctrines of Augustine of Hippo, and opposing those of Pelagius. He visited Rome in AD 431 and from c. AD 435 he was resident in Rome for an uncertain period. In AD 433 he had compiled the first edition of his *Epitoma Chronicon*, a continuation of the chronicle of Jerome extending to that year. In this, he abandoned most of Jerome's elaborate chronological apparatus between Adam and the fifteenth

---

102 Preface, fol. 4r; see pp. 35 and 44, and also pp. 60–61 and 83.

103 James (1993), 565–67, for the textual evidence; 574, for the citation.

year of Tiberius, which imperial year Prosper synchronized with Jesus' Passion. Then from the Passion to AD 433 he synchronized each year with the Roman consuls.[104] This feature of his chronicle demonstrates that Prosper was concerned to place the chronology of the elapsed years between the Passion and his own time in a specifically Roman consular context.[105] That Prosper also took a critical interest in the theology and chronological details of the celebration of the Passion and Resurrection is demonstrated by his account of the Pasch of AD 444 in the 455 edition of his chronicle:[106]

> *Hoc anno pascha domini VIIII kal. Maias celebratum est, nec erratum est, quia in die XI kal. Mai. dies passionis fuit. ob cuius, reverentiam natalis urbis sine circensibus transiit.*

> This year the Lord's Pasch is celebrated on 23 April, nor has a mistake been made because 21 April was the day of the Passion. On account of this the veneration of the birth of the City passed without the circuses.

This implicitly acknowledges that celebration on 23 April represented a departure from Roman tradition, causing cancellation of the customary circuses, and Prosper rationalizes it, just as did Leo and Paschasinus, with the defence that the Passion (Good Friday) fell on 21 April, and thus within the later *terminus* of RS-354.[107] This acceptance of paschal celebration on 23 April in AD 444 is a singular feature of RS-442 which Prosper explicitly asserts not to be in error.

On the other hand, Prosper's account of the Pasch of AD 455 expresses his deep disapproval of the rejection of Leo's date of 17 April, and of Leo's own acceptance of the Alexandrian date of 24 April. Prosper stated explicitly that the date of 17 April did not err in either its full-moon or its limit for the first (paschal) month, showing thereby his understanding of the computational basis for the date of 17 April.[108] He gave details of Leo's correspondence with Marcian, and expressed his apprehension at the consequences of Leo's acceptance

---

104 Prosper of Aquitaine, *Epitoma chronicon* § 390 (MGH Auct. ant. 9, 410): *Incipit adnotatio consulum a passione domini nostri Iesu Christi cum historia.*

105 Prosper of Aquitaine, *Epitoma chronicon* (MGH Auct. ant. 9, 410–85) systematically enumerates the years as *I–CCCCXXVIII*, but Brooks (2014), 45, wrote that 'the *anni a passione* were only ever intended to appear every ten years from 29, the year of the Passion, not for every consular pair as Mommsen presented them'. Cf. Becker and Kötter (2016), 64–136, editing the years AD 378–455 and systematically enumerating them as *CCCLI–CCCCXXVIII*.

106 Prosper of Aquitaine, *Epitoma chronicon* § 1352 (MGH Auct. ant. 9, 479).

107 *Epistola Paschasini* 2 (Krusch (1880), 249): *Nec nobis aut novum aut erratum, cum dies passionis XI. die kalendarum maiarum occurrat.*

108 The reconstructions of RS-354 for AD 455, no. 74, by Krusch (1880), 64, and Schwartz (1905), 49, both give 17 April *luna* 18; Mosshammer (2008), 210–11, tabulates only AD 298–381, but his 74th year likewise gives 17 April *luna* 18. These dates would, with the two-day reduction in the epacts estimated for RS-442, result in Pasch on 17 April *luna* 16.

of 24 April for his ecclesiastical authority.[109] Prosper here demonstrates both a detailed understanding of the computational aspects of the paschal celebration, and a knowledge of Leo's diplomatic endeavour seeking a paschal unity, which Prosper considered a failure.

By AD 457 Victorius implicitly relied on Prosper's chronology when he reproduced his consular list from the Passion to AD 455 as the primary chronological apparatus for his paschal table. Furthermore, in his prologue he explicitly acknowledged this debt to Prosper, and also reproduced parts of Prosper's Biblical chronological conspectus.[110]

All of these contemporaneous references suggest a close association during Leo's episcopacy between Prosper and the Roman celebration of the Pasch. This, and Leo's reliance upon his anti-Pelagian scholarship for the years AD 440–442, make Prosper the most likely compiler of RS-442. Moreover, this conclusion is supported by Gennadius' *De viris illustribus*, where having praised Victorius as a *calculator scrupulosus*, he names Prosper as the last of four predecessor compilers of paschal tables.[111] From all of this evidence I conclude that by AD 442 Prosper had indeed compiled a paschal cycle, namely RS-442, updating the epacts of RS-354 and extending the Julian *terminus* to 23 April. This then was the *Romana supputatio* that Leo sent to Paschasinus, requesting his judgement on the alternative dates 26 March or 23 April.

Gennadius' assertion that Prosper had composed a paschal cycle has prompted earlier hypotheses. In 1733 van der Hagen, seeking to explain Leo's paschal date of 4 April in AD 454, whereas RS-354 has 28 March, proposed that Prosper had reduced the epact 19 of no. 73 of RS-354 to epact 18 by switching the *saltus* from a 12-year interval to a 14-year interval, and hence effected the change in paschal date.[112] We note that Prosper's reduction of the epacts in RS-442 would achieve just this outcome. Van der Hagen's hypothesis, which was possible only

---

109 Prosper of Aquitaine, *Epitoma chronicon* § 1396 (MGH Auct. ant. 9, 484–85): *Eodem anno pascha dominicum die VIII kal. Maias celebratum est pertinaci intentione Alexandrini episcopi, cui omnes Orientales consentiendum putarent, cum sanctus papa Leo XV. kal. Mai. potius observandum protestaretur, in quo nec in ratione plenilunii nec in primi mensis limite fuisset erratum. extant eiusdem papae epistolae ad clementissimum principem Marcianum datae, quibus ratio veritatis sollicite evidenterque patefacta est et quibus ecclesia catholica instrui potest, quod haec persuasio studio unitatis et pacis tolerata sit potius quam probata, numquam deinceps imitanda, ut, quae exitialem attulit offensionem, omnem in perpetuum perdat auctoritatem.* Cf. Brooks (2014), 17; and Becker and Kötter (2016), 138–40 (Prosper's AD 455 edition); 329–31 (commentary).

110 Victorius of Aquitaine, *Prologus* 7 (Krusch (1938), 22): *hisque etiam quae a sancto et venerabili viro Prospero usque in consulatum Valentiniani august VIII. et Anthemi constat fuisse suppleta, repperi a mundi principio usque ad diluviium* [...] *eadam monumenta testantur*'; cf. Prosper of Aquitaine, *Epitoma chronicon* § 383–85 (MGH Auct. ant. 9, 409) (conspectus).

111 Gennadius, *De viris illustribus* 89 (ed. Richardson (1896), 92): *Victorius, homo natione Aquitanicus, calculator scrupulosus, invitatus a saneto Hilario, urbis Romae episcopo, conposuit Paschale recursum indagatione cautissima post quattuor priores qui conposuerunt, id est Hippolytum, Eusebium, Theophilum et Prosperum.*

112 van der Hagen (1733), 221–26 (*saltus* switch hypothesis).

because of the very limited information available to him concerning the use of the 14-year *saltus*, was subsequently repeated by Ideler, the Ballerini brothers, and de Rossi.[113] Mommsen, while acknowledging van der Hagen's hypothesis, was more circumspect, saying only that modifications to RS-354 were introduced between 437 and 444.[114] Krusch, while explicitly rejecting van der Hagen's hypothesis, essentially modified it to develop his own hypothesis of an 'ältere Supputatio', with the paschal *termini* of *luna* 14–20 and 25 March–19 April.[115] Both hypotheses are the result of mistaken conflations of the Roman 84-year cycle with a 12-year *saltus*, with the 84-year paschal table with a 14-year *saltus* and *termini* of *luna* 14–20 and 26 March–23 April used by the early churches of Britain and Ireland. The significance of the cryptic medieval references to this cycle remained obscure until the identification by Dáibhí Ó Cróinín in 1985 of a full copy of this table in Padua, Biblioteca Antoniana, I 27, 76r–77v. Subsequent studies have revealed that this table, known in Ireland as the *latercus*, was compiled in first decade of the fifth century by Sulpicius Severus, a devotee of St Martin of Tours in southern Gaul, basing its paschal principles upon *De ratione paschali*, the Latin translation of the Greek paschal tract of Anatolius of Laodicea († *c.* AD 282).[116] This cycle provided 84 paschal dates all coordinated with the *termini luna* 14–20 and 26 March–23 April, a range of only 29 days. It would seem very likely from Leo's assertion that the *termini* 22 March–21 April, a range of 31 days, would 'surely be enough time to include all the necessary variations', that he was aware of the unique achievement of Sulpicius' 84-year cycle.[117]

Twentieth-century scholarship has generally not accepted either van der Hagen's Prosper hypothesis or Krusch's 'ältere Supputatio' hypothesis. Schwartz considered it unlikely that the Roman church had varied its *luna* 16–22 *termini*,

---

113 Ideler (1825–1826), ii 270–71, where his tabulated 'Epakte des 1. Jan.' is systematically lower than the epacts of RS-354. De Rossi (1861), XC: 'Prosperianae emendationis veritatem ac rationem sagaci quodammodo divinatione feliciter explicavit ille, quem toties laudo, harum rerum consultissimus auctor Van der Hagen, cujus inventum et Ballerinii fratres et Idelerus comprobarunt'.

114 Mommsen (1863), 562: 'Damit soll natürlich behauptet werden, dass diese Modification des 84jährigen Cyclus zuerst durch unsere Tafel 447 eingeführt ist; vielmehr ergiebt sich aus dem Gesagten, dass die römische Kirche dies Modification zwischen 437 und 444, also vor Abfassung unserer Tafel, [...] recipirt hat'; 566: 'Schon van der Hagen hat die Modificiation des 84jährigen Cyclus, die unter Leo I. in Geltung war, auf Prosper von Aquitanien zurückgeführt'.

115 Krusch (1880), 129: 'Das Resultat ist demnach folgendes: Die Ansicht, dass die römische Kurie bei der Ansetzung der Osterfeste von 444 und 454 einen 84jährigen Cyclus mit 14jähr. Saltus, dessen Urheber Prosper war, befolgte, ist unhaltbar'; 64–67, for the 'ältere Supputatio'.

116 For discovery of the *latercus*, Mc Carthy and Ó Cróinín (1987–1988), 227–28. For the *latercus* construction, Mc Carthy (1993); Blackburn and Holford-Strevens (1999), 870–75; Holford-Strevens (2008), 178–87; Mc Carthy (2022), 142–50. For Sulpicius Severus and *c.* AD 410, Mc Carthy (1994), 38–44; Blackburn and Holford-Strevens (1999), 872; Ó Cróinín (2003), 211; Warntjes (2007), 34–37; Warntjes (2010), XXXVII; Mc Carthy (2011), 60–63, 69, 71, 74. For Sulpicius' inclusion of the traditional Roman Passion date of 25 March, with both Synoptic and Johannine chronology, Mc Carthy (2022), 152–53. For Anatolius, Mc Carthy (1996); Mc Carthy and Breen (2003), 17, 114–22; Mc Carthy (2012).

117 See above p. 69.

or its 12-year *saltus*. Consequently he rejected the 'ältere Supputatio' hypothesis, and he correctly associated the *luna* 14–20 *termini* and the 14-year *saltus* with the paschal traditions of Ireland and Britain.[118] Jones dismissed Krusch's 'older Supputatio Romana' as an instance of 'rather isolated examples of tables created in various provincial sees according to local beliefs'.[119] Mosshammer concluded his extensive review of Roman 84-year Paschal computation with a lucid summary of Schwartz's conclusions, and in 2010 Warntjes was definite: 'only the discussion of what Krusch calls the younger *Supputatio Romana* is valid'.[120] In place of these diverse hypotheses I submit that RS-442, compiled by Prosper in coordination with Pope Leo, supplied alternative Roman paschal dates in the middle decades of the fifth century.

Conclusions

The papacy of Leo I is considered remarkable by modern scholarship for the extent to which he succeeded to advance and consolidate the influence of the Roman See in the Western Church.[121] His role in the development of the Roman celebration of the Pasch is one important aspect of this. He inherited a fourth-century compilation of an 84-year paschal cycle, RS-354, with lunar and Julian *termini* that resulted in both ambiguous and uncoordinated paschal dates. When Leo became pope in AD 440 the lunar epacts of this cycle were two days in advance of both the real moon and the Alexandrian epacts. By AD 442 Prosper had updated the epacts of this cycle and had extended the later Julian *terminus* to accept Pasch on 23 April for AD 444. By this means Leo was able to reconcile the Roman and the Alexandrian paschal date for that year. Shortly after this someone close to Leo compiled a much more ambitious 84-year cycle, RS-447, which likewise updated the epacts but also reset the first year of the cycle to synchronize with AD 29 and to give the paschal date of 27 March *luna* 17 for that year. This then accorded both with Synoptic chronology and the traditional Roman date for the Passion maintained since at least the early third century.[122] The paschal new-moon table of RS-447 explicitly demonstrated this synchronism by commencing its first cycle at the year of the consulship of the two Gemini, AD 29, with the criteria of *feria* 7 *luna* 21 and new-moon on 11 March, thereby implying Pasch on 27 March *luna* 17. The preface to this table indicated that it would provide both Roman and Alexandrian paschal dates, and the surviving

---

118 Schwartz (1905), 50–58, on Krusch; 89–100, on the insular tradition.
119 Jones (1943), 16–17, on the 'older Supputatio Romana'.
120 Mosshammer (2008), 204–22, Roman paschal computation with Schwartz's conclusions; Warntjes (2010), XX n. 75.
121 Cross and Livingstone (1974), 811, on the papacy of Leo I.
122 Nothaft (2012), 50–51, on the earliest evidence for Roman dating of the Passion to 25 March, AD 29; cf. Mosshammer (2008), 48–49.

new-moon dates show that the compiler had accepted the Alexandrian principle that the paschal *luna* 14 should not fall before 21 March, so the paschal new-moon does not fall before 8 March. The resultant Alexandrian paschal dates with *luna* 15–21 fall between 22 March and 23 April, while the Roman paschal dates with *luna* 16–22 fall between 23 March and 25 April. While the compiler accepted for the Roman paschal dates the possible later *terminus* of 25 April, his table left open the possibility of advancing the later Roman *terminus* to 23 April by choosing the Alexandrian *luna* 15 dates for nos 7 and 34.

It is clear that RS-447 did not receive Leo's approval for by AD 457, at the instigation of Leo's archdeacon, Hilarus, Victorius of Aquitaine had compiled a further paschal table similarly commencing at the supposed year of Jesus' Passion. This likewise tabulated both Roman and Alexandrian paschal dates, but these extended only to 24 April, and Victorius' compilation conflicted with RS-447 in other important respects. Namely, while Victorius commenced his paschal table at the Passion he set this at AD 28, and he employed Prosper's consular list which differed textually and chronologically with that of RS-447. These contrasts would suggest that the adoption by the compiler of RS-447 of Alexandrian paschal principles went too far for Leo, Prosper, or Victorius to accept. Nevertheless, between AD 440 and 457 Leo oversaw the progressive extension of the later Roman Julian *terminus* from the 21 April of Hippolytus and RS-354 to the 24 April of Victorius, and the introduction of the 19-year lunar cycle for the scheduling of Roman paschal celebration. These were crucial steps towards the eventual adoption in the seventh century by the Roman church of the Alexandrian paschal tradition in the form of the paschal cycle of Dionysius Exiguus.

Acknowledgements

This article originated in a visit organised by Immo Warntjes to the Berlin Staatsbibliothek in August 2011, in order to examine some computistical manuscripts, one of which was MS B. This was the first manuscript of an 84-year lunar cycle with a 12-year *saltus* that I had an opportunity to inspect, and my curiosity was stirred. Consequently, in July 2012 I presented a paper to the Galway Computus Conference discussing the Zeitz paschal table. In this I concluded that the ferial and epactal combinations of the Zeitz table accommodated the Alexandrian paschal termini of *luna* 15–21 and 22 March–25 April, but did not accommodate the Roman *termini* of RS-354 considered as *luna* 16–22 and 22 March–21 April. Subsequently I enjoyed numerous conversations with Immo concerning the table, and crucially his assistance in obtaining high-grade scans of the two Berlin bifolia and the three Zeitz fragments, which revealed more of the text of the preface. As well, he repeatedly assisted my access to important German publications and my own preference would be that this edition should appear under our joint names, but Immo has modestly declined this.

I also wish to acknowledge invaluable assistance from the following: Dr Robert Giel at the Berlin Staatsbibliothek and Cordula Strehl at the Domstiftsbibliothek und Domstiftsarchiv Naumburg who made available excellent scans of the two Zeitz bifolia, the three fragments, and the inside back and front covers of MS Zeitz, Stiftsbibliothek, fol. 33; Dr Leofranc Holford-Strevens of Christ Church College, Oxford, for his constructive suggestions concerning the Latin of the three fragments; Dr David Howlett, Editor emeritus, *Dictionary of Medieval Latin from British Sources*, Oxford, for his kindness in providing the English translation of Paschasinus' letter to Leo; Dr Steven Collins of *Frontline Ventures*, for his expert advice with the graphical editing and assistance with reading some of the severely obscured passages in the manuscript.

COLIN IRELAND

How King Oswiu Made Northumbria Orthodox

The Social and Political Background of the 'Synod' of Whitby (AD 664)

▼ **ABSTRACT** The reported topics at the 'synod' of Whitby (AD 664) involved the dating of Easter and the promotion of the method favoured by Rome. The issues were debated by named clerics, but the process was controlled, and the final decision reached, by the secular ruler King Oswiu (AD 642–670). A survey of the participants and analysis of the outcome suggest that political and social agendas were as important as ecclesiastical ones. Oswiu's background and experience as Gaelic-speaking ruler of an *imperium* who understood the polities of Ireland and northern Britain; who had three multi-ethnic marital liaisons that each produced a son who became a king; who admired Gaelic learning and ruled at a time when Anglo-Saxons availed themselves of free tuition at Gaelic monastic schools; and whose regular personal contacts involved him with supporters of opposing Easter practices; was perfectly suited to assess the issues and arrive at a decision that was appropriate for both him and his kingdom into the future.

▼ **KEYWORDS** 'Synod' of Whitby; Alhfrith, Agilberht, Cedd, Abbess Hild, King Oswiu, Wilfrid; Gaelic influence

---

Pre-Carolingian Latin Computus and its Regional Contexts, ed. by Immo Warntjes, Tobit Loevenich, and Dáibhí Ó Cróinín, Studia Traditionis Theologiae, 54 (Turnhout: Brepols, 2023), pp. 87–120
BREPOLS ❧ PUBLISHERS   10.1484/M.STT-EB.5.133486

Introduction[1]

The 'synod'[2] of Whitby of 664 was a pivotal event in the cultural, social, political, and religious history of Anglo-Saxon Britain. The decision taken there by King Oswiu ended the rule of Ionan bishops over the Northumbrian churches. Iona had successfully evangelized Northumbria but followed older Easter traditions that differed from those trained in Kent, Gaul, or the orthodox regions of Ireland.[3] Underlying the issues of paschal observance and tonsure[4] in surviving accounts was the question of apostolic authority.[5] The contentious issues at the 'synod' were complex. But politics drove the agenda.

Through the personal histories of the named participants at the 'synod' this paper will highlight the social and political, over the ecclesiastical, character of the contention.[6] The incipient seventh-century Anglo-Saxon Church relied on foreign influence for its inchoate intellectual development.[7] The debt to the Gaels[8] is prominent for both parties in the controversy. This article will emphasise the rôles

---

1 I dedicate this essay to the memory of Dr Aidan Breen, who died unexpectedly 9 June 2013. *Go ndéana Dia trócaire ar a anam.*

2 The term 'synod' implies an assembly of clergy, but King Oswiu oversaw this meeting at Whitby in 664. The early Gaelic synods held at Mag Léne and Mag nAilbe (*c.* AD 630) were decided by attending clerics and not by secular rulers: Byrne (2001), 34. For brief surveys of Gaelic synods, see Ó Cróinín (1995), 151–54; Dumville (1997), 19–20. The implementation of *Cáin Adomnáin* (*Lex Innocentium*) in AD 697 combined secular and ecclesiastical authorities to decide issues that were primarily ecclesiastical: Dumville (1997), 29–31; Charles-Edwards (2000), 276–81; and Ní Dhonnchadha (1982) for the list of ecclesiastical and secular guarantors. For evidence that kings might be involved at synods, see Etchingham (1999), 150–52, 206–08. At Whitby three bishops attended while clerics argued the issues, but King Oswiu controlled the outcome: Dumville (1997), 24; Ohashi (2011), 138; Dailey (2015), 61–64.

3 For general overviews of the Easter controversy in the early Christian world up to and including the insular world in the seventh century, see Wallis (1999), XXXIV–LXIII; Warntjes (2010), XXX–XLI. For discussions of the controversy in its insular context, see Charles-Edwards (2000), 391–415; Corning (2006). For examples of early paschal controversies in their political contexts, see Holford-Strevens (2011).

4 For a discussion of the tonsure against the background of paschal observance, see James (1984); and for arguments about the shape and appearance of the 'Celtic' tonsure, see Mc Carthy (2003). The differing tonsures provided a visible contrast for both parties.

5 This issue involved the eventual primacy of the Apostle Peter over the Apostle John. Followers of the *latercus*, many British, Pictish, and Ionan churches saw John (known as *Eoin bruinne* 'John of the Breast') as the disciple most beloved of Jesus. This ensured a scripturally based conflict with the orthodox party who privileged the apostle Peter as the 'rock' upon which the Church of Rome was built: Walsh and Ó Cróinín (1988), 69–70 n. 89; Pelteret (2011). For John's treatment in subsequent Gaelic tradition, see Monge Allen (2017).

6 Bede named participants and the sides they represented at the 'synod': Bede, *Historia ecclesiastica gentis Anglorum* 3.25 (ed. and trans. Colgrave and Mynors (1969), 298–99), hereafter as Bede, *HE*.

7 For example, for contacts between Northumbria and Francia, particularly as reflected in the works of Stephen of Ripon and Bede, see Wood (1995); Fouracre (2013); Wood (2013).

8 I prefer the terms Gael and Gaelic as deriving from the one vernacular language represented prominently on both major islands, Ireland and Britain, of the archipelago. Gael is paralleled by Latin *Scottus*.

of Hild, Abbess of Whitby and, especially, of King Oswiu as key operatives in the proceedings and their aftermath.

Much of Bede's *Historia ecclesiastica gentis Anglorum* (*HE*) is devoted to chronicling the successful mission to Northumbria, and beyond, established at Lindisfarne from Iona, beginning with the arrival of Bishop Aidan [Áedán] in King Oswald's reign (AD 634–642) to the 'synod' at Whitby (AD 664) in the reign of Oswiu (AD 642–670). Bede outlined the thirty-year period of three Gaelic bishops, Aidan, Fínán, and Colmán, established at Lindisfarne from AD 634 to 664.[9] The mission from Iona was made possible by the fact that the sons of the Bernician King Æthelfrith (*c.* AD 592–617), including Oswald and Oswiu, lived in political exile among the Gaels of northern Britain during the reign of King Edwin [Eadwine] (AD 617–633).[10] They were educated, baptized and became fluent in Gaelic during their extended exiles.[11]

However, an earlier evangelization of Northumbria by Bishop Paulinus from the Gregorian mission at Canterbury is first described in records produced at Whitby in the early eighth century.[12] The *Vita Gregorii* was produced by an anonymous monk of Whitby and succinctly describes the conversion of King Edwin by Paulinus *c.* AD 627.[13] These records from Whitby show that Northumbria had been evangelized by the 'orthodox' Gregorian mission for six or seven years before the arrival of the Ionan mission. Bede, it must be noted, portrayed a reluctant Edwin whom Paulinus had to persuade persistently in order for him to accept the faith.[14]

Furthermore, Bede provides evidence that Edwin's infant daughter, Eanflæd, was baptized by Paulinus a year before her father.[15] Eanflæd would eventually become Oswiu's queen shortly after he became king of Northumbria in AD 642.[16] Hild was also baptized as a youngster of twelve or thirteen, as part of Edwin's retinue, along with Eanflæd.[17] The scenario is complicated by the tradition that Edwin had been exiled, or fostered, among Christian Britons, probably at Angle-

---

9 Bede, *HE* 3.26 (Colgrave and Mynors (1969), 308–09). See n. 119 below.

10 Some sources name seven brothers: *Historia Brittonum* 57 (ed. Morris (1980), 37, 77); Anglo-Saxon Chronicle, manuscript E [Peterborough Chronicle] s.a. 617 (ed. Swanton (2000), 24). These two sources do not agree in all of the names, but include Oswald and Oswiu.

11 Bede, *HE* 3.1 (Colgrave and Mynors (1969), 212–13): *apud Scottos siue Pictos exulabant*. See Moisl (1983). Aldfrith's maternal background shows that Oswiu spent time in northern Ireland among the Cenél nÉogain: Ireland (1991a), 68–69, 72–73.

12 The traditional dates for the anonymous *Vita Gregorii* are from AD 704 to 714 during the time of Abbess Ælfflæd: Colgrave (1968), 48–49 (dating).

13 Anonymous of Whitby, *Vita Gregorii* 16 (ed. Colgrave (1968), 98–101). The text stresses the Gregorian mission but is full of Gaelic characteristics: Ireland (2015a), 143–73.

14 Bede, *HE* 2.9, 2.12–13 (Colgrave and Mynors (1969), 162–67, 174–87).

15 Bede, *HE* 2.9, 3.15 (Colgrave and Mynors (1969), 164–67, 260–61).

16 Bede, *HE* 3.15 (Colgrave and Mynors (1969), 260–61).

17 Bede, *HE* 4.23 (Colgrave and Mynors (1969), 406–07).

sey before he became king.[18] Brittonic traditions also conflated the identities of Paulinus and a certain Rhun mab Urien.[19]

The two retrospective accounts of the 'synod' at Whitby both portray Oswiu as the person responsible for the final decision. The earliest and shortest account is found in chapter 10 of the *Vita Wilfridi* (*VW*)[20] by Stephen of Ripon written sometime between AD 712 and 714.[21] The fuller version is found in Bede's *Historia ecclesiastica gentis Anglorum* (AD 731).[22] Bede knew Stephen's work without specifically acknowledging it, but it should not be assumed that the two agreed on all details of the controversy.[23] Both of these accounts were written from the perspective of ecclesiastical authority and orthodox practice. But for the participants, the immediacy of political control and dynastic rivalries would have been at the forefront.[24]

King Oswiu deserves credit for his decision to change to catholic observance. A survey of his personal history will reveal his political astuteness as an overlord;[25] his cross-cultural connections in his multi-ethnic *imperium*; his appreciation for, and likely promotion of, Gaelic learning; his efforts at conversion of pagans under his *imperium*; his awareness of the issues for both parties prior to the 'synod'; his

---

18 The Welsh triads of perhaps the twelfth century, while not necessarily accurate as history, reflect traditional Welsh lore as used by the bards. One triad within a triad names 'one of the three chief oppressions of Môn (Anglesey) nurtured therein' (*vn o Deir Prif Ormes Mon a uagwyt yndi*) as being Edwin, king of England (*Lloegr*): *Trioedd Ynys Prydein* 26W.30–32 (ed. and trans. Bromwich (1978), 47–48). Anglesey was the royal seat of King Cadfan whose son, Cadwallon, became an implacable foe of Edwin and the Anglo-Saxons generally: Bede, *HE* 2.20 (Colgrave and Mynors (1969), 202–05). Bromwich remarked that Geoffrey of Monmouth accurately reflected Welsh tradition when he stated that Edwin and Cadwallon were foster-brothers and that Cadwallon was forced into exile in Ireland by Edwin: Bromwich (1978), XCVII–XCVIII. See also Rowland (1990), 123; Charles-Edwards (2013), 345.
19 *Historia Brittonum* 63 (Morris (1980), 38, 79); *Annales Cambriae* s.a. 626 (ed. Morris (1980), 46, 86); but see Rowland (1990), 86, 92; and Koch (1997), XXXIII n. 4. The *Historia Brittonum* equates the two identities and applies the name Rhun mab Urien to Paulinus of York: Lot (1934), 203–04. Welsh genealogies attest to King Urien of Rheged having a son named Rhun: Williams (1978), 137 n. 39c. The name Paulinus occurs commonly in Welsh ecclesiastical tradition, for example, as the name of Dewi Sant's teacher: *Buched Dewi* (ed. Evans (1965), 5); see other examples of Paulinus in early Welsh tradition at Howlett (2003–2004), 66–67.
20 Stephen of Ripon, *Vita Wilfridi* (ed. and trans. Colgrave (1927), 20–23). For the identification of Stephen, see Kirby (1983), 102–04.
21 Stancliffe (2013), 22–25.
22 Bede, *HE* 3.25 (Colgrave and Mynors (1969), 294–309). Jones (1943), 103, had pointed out that neither account is derived from formal transcripts of the proceedings and that such transcripts probably never existed.
23 For example, see Pelteret (2011), 150–51; Goffart (1988), 307–24, argued that a major purpose of Bede's *HE* was as a response to, and correction of, Stephen's *VW*. Some critics now consider that Goffart overstated his case, while others continue to support it: Stancliffe (2012), 9–20; Higham (2006), 58–69; Higham (2013b), 64–66 (conclusion).
24 For an interpretation that takes this view, see Abels (1983); Dailey (2015), 56–63.
25 See Fanning (1991).

personal control of proceedings at the 'synod'; and the acknowledgement by Pope Vitalian of his efforts to promote catholic observance in his *imperium*.[26]

The issues at the 'synod' had already been subjects of study and debate in Ireland before either Wilfrid or Bede had been born.[27] Sometime in the seventh century Dionysiac traditions were promoted by Rome.[28] Nevertheless, the *latercus* continued in use by Iona and its establishments, among the Picts and many of the Britons into the eighth century.[29] The *latercus* had been introduced into the insular world in the fifth century, and those who supported its use saw themselves as upholding long-standing tradition.[30]

Unfortunately, both Bede and Gaelic records are equally vague about the timing and locations of the changes in insular paschal traditions.[31] Bede

---

26 Higham (2013a), 492, has argued that Bede's reform agenda in *HE* Book 4 (Colgrave and Mynors (1969), 324–449) was intended to serve, in essence, as a *speculum principum* for King Ceolwulf, to whom *HE* was dedicated, although Higham does not use that specific term. In the context of reform, he argues that Bede was disparaging of the quality of Oswiu's early reign, but that Oswiu had achieved the 'high moral ground' by the beginning of Book 4: Higham (2013a), 485. I thank Prof. Mary Clayton for calling this article to my attention. In contrast, Gunn (2009), 31, noted that Ceolwulf may not have been able to read the Latin of the text.

27 See the paschal letter (AD 632) of Cummian, most thoroughly discussed by Walsh and Ó Cróinín (1988), 3–97.

28 The methods of paschal reckoning favoured by Rome had gone through various changes in the decades leading up to the 'synod' of Whitby. The Dionysiac reckoning favoured by Bede had largely derived from Alexandrian tables and tracts and had been adopted by Rome by the AD 640s or soon after: Warntjes (2010), XXXIX. Victorian Easter tables were commonly used in the insular world by those who considered themselves orthodox: Ohashi (2011); Warntjes (2015), 40–63; Dailey (2015).

29 In discussing Ecgberht's conversion of Iona practices in AD 716 Bede, *HE* 5.22 (Colgrave and Mynors (1969), 552–53), says 'those monks of Irish [Gaelic] extraction who lived in Iona, together with the monasteries under their rule' (*qui insulam Hii incolebant, monachi Scotticae nationis, cum his quae sibi erant subdita monasteriis*) were converted. At the beginning of the Ionan mission to Northumbria Bede, *HE* 3.3 (Colgrave and Mynors (1969), 218–19), stated that 'The northern province of the Irish [Gaels] and the whole nation of the Picts' (*Hoc etenim ordine septentrionalis Scottorum prouincia et omnis natio Pictorum*) were not following orthodox practices. See also Ceolfrith's letter to King Nechtan of the Picts (Bede, *HE* 5.21 (Colgrave and Mynors (1969), 532–53).

30 The *latercus* had been composed by Sulpicius Severus, relying on earlier works by Anatolius. It used an 84-year lunar cycle with paschal limits of *luna* 14 to 20, with Easter Sunday falling between 26 March to 23 April on the Julian calendar. The *latercus* was introduced into the insular world in the first quarter of the fifth century: Mc Carthy (1994), 25–30, 39–42; Mc Carthy (2008), 132–33; Warntjes (2010), XXXVI–XXXVIII; Mc Carthy (2011). The lunar terms of the *latercus* accord with John's Gospel but disagree with the Synoptic Gospels: Mc Carthy (1994), 27–28. This underlies the defence of John by the Ionan party and the championing of Peter by the Wilfridian party in both accounts of the 'synod': Pelteret (2011).

31 Bede, *HE* 5.15, 5.21 (Colgrave and Mynors (1969), 504–09, 550–51), reported that Abbot Adomnán of Iona had conformed to orthodox practice during a visit to Northumbria, *c.* AD 687, but that he had no luck converting his own monastery although, apparently, continuing to work productively with its members: Stancliffe (2010); see also Ireland (2020). The careers of Adomnán and the three Lindisfarne bishops from Iona suggest that the Gaels held more tolerant attitudes toward divergent practices than their Anglo-Saxon contemporaries. Hunter Blair (1970), 100–01, pointed out the eclectic mix of ecclesiastical practice, and presumed tolerance, in Northumbria prior to the 'synod'.

acknowledged that the Gaels in 'the southern parts of the island of Ireland' followed canonical paschal practices.[32] Rather than take Bede too literally, it should be noted that the entire island of Ireland is 'south' of Iona and the 'northern province of the Irish [Gaels]' in Britain as described by Bede.[33] The eventual domination of paschal practices promoted from Rome was to prove an ineluctable historical process for all insular peoples.

Daniel Mc Carthy and Aidan Breen have shown that a solar eclipse and a plague in AD 664 may have contributed to a sense of urgency among the participants of the Whitby 'synod', with the eclipse being seen as an omen portending the plague.[34] The solar eclipse would have been total at Whitby on 1 May 664[35] although Bede reported the eclipse for 3 May.[36] The eclipse is a likely reason for Whitby, having experienced the maximum duration of darkness, being chosen as the site for the 'synod'. As the royal patron of Whitby, and a dozen ecclesiastical sites in Deira and Bernicia that fell within the eclipse's path of totality,[37] Oswiu may have felt obligated to submit to demands to hold the 'synod'.[38] The plague took a heavy toll in both Britain and Ireland that year.[39] Unfortunately, we have no precise dates or time of year for the 'synod' and, therefore, no firm sense of the sequence of events. Based on available evidence, supported by the syntax of

---

32 Bede, *HE* 3.3 (Colgrave and Mynors (1969), 218–19): *Porro gentes Scottorum, quae in australibus Hiberniae insulae partibus morabantur, iamdudum ad admonitionem apostolicae sedis antistitis pascha canonico ritu obseruare didicerunt.* Mayr-Harting (1991), 109–10, had suggested that Bangor, Co. Down, was orthodox as early as Abbot Sillán in the first decade of the seventh century; but for the correction of that view, see Ó Cróinín (1982a).

33 Bede, *HE* 3.3 (Colgrave and Mynors (1969), 218–19): *septentrionalis Scottorum prouincia.* Most commentators have kept their statements on the growth of orthodoxy in Ireland vague. See, for example, Dumville (1997), 22–24.

34 Both of these events are recorded in Gaelic annals for AD 664, the eclipse given on 1 May at the correct hour, and the plague described as reaching Ireland by August: Annals of Ulster s.a. 663 (ed. and trans. Mac Airt and Mac Niocaill (1983), 143–45). Note that the plague induced apostasy among the East Saxons under King Sigehere, although his co-regent Sebbi remained true to the faith; Bede, *HE* 3.30 (Colgrave and Mynors (1969), 322–23).

35 Mc Carthy and Breen (1997), 12, 24–30, 43 (with map showing Whitby in the middle of the path of totality of the eclipse); Moreton (1998), 50–52.

36 Bede, *HE* 3.27 (Colgrave and Mynors (1969), 310–13). This discrepancy may have been instituted in an attempt to show the superiority of the Dionysiac reckoning. For a discussion of how and why this eclipse is recorded in Bede's *HE*, in his *Chronica minora* and his *Chronica maiora* on the wrong day, a date that Bede seems eventually to have realized was incorrect, see Mc Carthy and Breen (1997), 24–25; Moreton (1998), 50–65; Ohashi (2011), 139–44.

37 Bede, *HE* 3.24 (Colgrave and Mynors (1969), 292–93).

38 Mc Carthy and Breen (1997), 27.

39 Bede, *HE* 3.27 (Colgrave and Mynors (1969), 310–13). The plague, noted in Gaelic annals as beginning in August (cf. n. 34), seems to have taken its greatest toll after the 'synod'. Cedd, one of the participants, died of plague on 26 October: Bede, *HE* 3.23 (Colgrave and Mynors (1969), 286–89); see Plummer (1896), ii 194–96. But Bishop Deusdedit died of plague on 14 July, apparently after the 'synod' as well: Bede, *HE* 3.28, 4.1 (Colgrave and Mynors (1969), 316–17, 328–29). For one approach to solving the problem of the sequence of events, see Abels (1983), 20–25.

Bede's description, it has been plausibly proposed that the sequence of events was: 1) solar eclipse, 2) plague, 3) 'synod', 4) Colmán's departure.[40]

Tensions at Oswiu's court may have been enough to bring the controversy to a head. As Bede noted, 'it sometimes happened that Easter was celebrated twice in the same year, so that the king had finished the fast and was keeping Easter Sunday, while the queen and her people were still in Lent and observing Palm Sunday'.[41] The potential for ritual discord and marital strife with his Queen Eanflæd, who was raised in Kent, is obvious.[42] The two had been married for at least twenty years by AD 664. Oswiu had ample opportunity to grasp the implications of the differing practices and good reason to conform.

The issues at the 'synod' were complex and may be interpreted as a political confrontation between a dominant father and an ambitious son.[43] Oswiu, one of seven *imperatores* named by Bede,[44] directed proceedings. He saw his son Alhfrith, sub-king of Deira,[45] as responsible, along with the priest Wilfrid, for pushing an agenda designed to overturn established political order through an alternative ecclesiastical authority. Oswiu had been educated and baptized in an older tradition whose paschal observance was being challenged now that Rome had consolidated its own stance on Easter.

The remainder of this article will examine brief biographies of the participants to fill in the social and political background of the 'synod' and to show the contribution of the Gaels to members of both parties.

---

40 Mc Carthy and Breen (1997), 27–28. But for different dates, see Stancliffe (2013), 19–20; Fouracre (2013), 193.

41 Bede, *HE* 3.25 (Colgrave and Mynors (1969), 296–97): *ut bis in anno uno pascha celebraretur, et cum rex pascha dominicum solutis ieiuniis faceret, tum regina cum suis persistens adhuc in ieiunio diem palmarum celebraret.*

42 The situation is more complicated than Bede indicated and opportunities for discord more frequent: Holford-Strevens (2010); Corning (2006), 120–21.

43 See, for example, Mayr-Harting (1991), 107–08. Richard Abels (1983), 7–8, argued that Alhfrith, son of Rhiainfellt, felt pressure from his younger half-brother Ecgfrith, son of Eanflæd (married to Oswiu c. AD 643), who had, therefore, a claim to both Deiran and Bernician ancestry. Ecgfrith would have been about 19 years old at the time of the 'synod': Abels (1983), 7; Higham (2015), 89.

44 Bede, *HE* 2.5 (Colgrave and Mynors (1969), 150–51).

45 Edwin had descended from the Deiran royal line but his death (AD 633) marked its effective end: Yorke (1990), 169, 76 table 9. Oswiu ensured the lack of rivalry from the Deiran line with the elimination of Oswine in AD 651 (Bede, *HE* 3.14; Colgrave and Mynors (1969), 254–61). Oswiu's nephew, Œthelwald, son of Oswald, ruled as sub-king of Deira for a time but he chose to fight on the Mercian side at the battle of Winwæd (AD 655) and so was eliminated from future participation (Bede, *HE* 3.24 (Colgrave and Mynors (1969), 288–95)). Alhfrith, Oswiu's son by Rhiainfellt, subsequently became sub-king of Deira.

The Wilfridian party

The named proponents at the 'synod' who, as Bede said, 'came from Kent or Gaul',[46] included King Alhfrith (son of Oswiu) of Deira; Wilfrid the newly ordained priest; Bishop Agilberht originally from Francia but formerly of Wessex and Ireland; Agatho, a companion of Agilberht; the priest Romanus from Queen Eanflæd's household; and James who had been a deacon with Bishop Paulinus. Wilfrid acted as spokesman for the party and so those named above are referred to as the Wilfridian party.

Alhfrith [Ealhfrith/Alchfrith]

Alhfrith, son of Oswiu, was the sub-king of Deira. He was almost certainly Oswiu's son by Rhiainfellt [Rieinmelth], granddaughter of Rhun of Rheged.[47] The latter is the man associated with Bishop Paulinus in the *Historia Brittonum* and *Annales Cambriae*.[48] Rhiainfellt reflects the Brittonic rôle in Northumbrian affairs.[49] Alhfrith assisted his father Oswiu in the conversion of the Mercians in the period leading up to and after the defeat and death of King Penda (AD 655).[50] Bede portrayed Penda's son Peada as having converted to the faith in order to marry Alhfrith's sister Alhflæd (daughter of Rhiainfellt), and Alhfrith married Cyneburh (sister of Peada).[51] Penda and the Mercians were allied with Britons under Cadwallon [Caedualla/Cædwalla], son of Cadfan of Anglesey.[52] It is likely, therefore, that Alhfrith's and Alhflæd's maternal backgrounds were an advantage to Oswiu in forming relations with Penda and his Brittonic allies.

---

46 Bede, *HE* 3.25 (Colgrave and Mynors (1969), 294): *qui de Cantia uel de Gallis aduenerant.*

47 *Historia Brittonum* 57 (Morris (1980), 36, 77), stated that Oswiu had two wives (*uxores*), the first was Rhiainfellt [Rieinmelth], daughter of Royth, son of Rhun; the second was Eanflæd, daughter of Edwin, son of Ælle. Alhfrith was old enough *c.* AD 653 to marry Cyneburh, daughter of the Mercian King Penda (Bede, *HE* 3.21 (Colgrave and Mynors (1969), 278–79)), and so must have been born in the early AD 630s: Kirby (1991), 90; Higham (2015), 80.

48 *Historia Brittonum* 63 (Morris (1980), 38, 79); *Annales Cambriae* s.a. 626 (Morris (1980), 46, 86); see the genealogical chart in Stancliffe and Cambridge (1995), 13. Jackson (1963), 71, suggested that Oswiu acquired the Brittonic kingdom of Rheged through marriage and not through conquest.

49 It has been suggested that runic inscriptions on the Bewcastle monument refer to secular rather than ecclesiastical figures. The name Cyneburh appears on the north face, and a certain [A]lcfri[th] (Alhfrith?) has been attested on the west face: Orton (2003), 78–83. See Wood (2003) and Tyler (2007) for evidence of timelines and ethnic diversity.

50 Bede, *HE* 3.21 (Colgrave and Mynors (1969), 278–81): Peada's conversion, and the marriages between the children of Oswiu and Penda, took place two years before Penda's death in AD 655 (Bede, *HE* 5.24 (Colgrave and Mynors (1969), 564–65)).

51 Bede, *HE* 3.21 (Colgrave and Mynors (1969), 278–79).

52 Bede, *HE* 2.20 (Colgrave and Mynors (1969), 202–05). For more on Cadwallon and Cadfan, see n. 18.

Bede described Alhfrith and Wilfrid as friends, Wilfrid having instructed him in the faith.[53] It is possible that Rhiainfellt's household was orthodox, so that Alhfrith may have been exposed to orthodoxy before meeting Wilfrid.[54] Subsequently Alhfrith requested that Bishop Agilberht ordain Wilfrid priest.[55] James Campbell suggested that Alhfrith's support of Wilfrid against Gaelic influence reflects his rivalry with his half-brother Aldfrith.[56] The *sapiens* Aldfrith was most likely living and working at the time at Bangor or at a Bangor-affiliated institution in Ireland.[57]

In the *Historia Abbatum* Bede had noted that Alhfrith proposed to visit the tombs of the apostles with Benedict Biscop on what would have been Benedict's second visit to Rome *c.* AD 665, but that Oswiu made Alhfrith stay at home.[58] Bede related that Oswiu was attacked (*inpugnatus*) by his son Alhfrith.[59] Both Stephen and Bede are silent about Alhfrith after the 'synod'. It has been assumed that Alhfrith had lost his life in open conflict or rebellion.[60]

Wilfrid

Wilfrid acted as spokesman for the group, ostensibly because the senior cleric Agilberht did not speak Old English well enough.[61] Wilfrid was born *c.* AD 634 of a well-off Northumbrian family.[62] He was introduced to religious life *c.* AD 648 at Lindisfarne during the bishopric of Aidan, where he met Oswiu's Queen Eanflæd and 'found grace in her sight'.[63] From an early age Wilfrid had been exposed to Ionan and orthodox practices. Wilfrid had been to Kent, Rome, and Gaul by the early AD 660s and instructed Alhfrith in the faith. Alhfrith, apparently

---

53 Bede, *HE* 3.25 (Colgrave and Mynors (1969), 296–97).

54 Miller (1979), 47 n. 3, had suggested, based on the equation of Rhun and Paulinus, and on Bede's statement that Ninian of Whithorn was orthodox, that Rhun and Rhiainfellt may also have been orthodox: Bede, *HE* 3.4 (Colgrave and Mynors (1969), 222–23). The territory around Whithorn may have been part of Rheged.

55 Bede, *HE* 3.25 (Colgrave and Mynors (1969), 298–99).

56 Campbell (1987), 336–37. It is more likely that Alhfrith's main rival was Ecgfrith: Abels (1983), 7–8.

57 Ireland (2015b), 63–72.

58 Bede, *Historia abbatum* 2 (ed. Plummer (1896), i 365; ed. and trans. Grocock and Wood (2013), 24–27); Stancliffe (1983), 156, 170.

59 Bede, *HE* 3.14 (Colgrave and Mynors (1969), 254–55).

60 Mayr-Harting (1991), 107–08; Yorke (1990), 79. Or, as Abels (1983), 20, succinctly put it, 'Alhfrith had destroyed himself at Whitby'.

61 Goffart (1988), 312, argued that by having Wilfrid speak for the more senior Agilberht, Bede belittled Wilfrid's contribution to the debate. Stephen of Ripon, *VW* 10 (Colgrave (1927), 20–21), had Agilberht and his priest Agatho request of Wilfrid that 'with his persuasive eloquence explain in his own tongue the system of the Roman Church' (*suaviloqua eloquentia in sua lingua Romanae ecclesiae* [...] *dare rationem*).

62 Stephen of Ripon, *VW* 1, 2 (Colgrave (1927), 4–7).

63 Stephen of Ripon, *VW* 2 (Colgrave (1927), 6): *invenit gratiam in conspectu illius*, quoting Esther 2:9.

in opposition to his father, preferred Wilfrid's teachings to those of the Ionan clerics.[64]

Ripon was originally offered by Alhfrith to Eata and Cuthbert who followed the practices of Melrose, a daughter-house of Iona.[65] Since they refused to alter their traditions Alhfrith presented Ripon to Wilfrid instead sometime before the 'synod'.[66]

Both Stephen and Bede are vague about the chronology of events after the 'synod'. Bede reported that the replacement for Bishop Colmán was a certain Tuda who 'had been educated among the southern Irish [Gaels] and there consecrated bishop'.[67] In addition 'he had the ecclesiastical tonsure in the form of a crown, according to the custom of that kingdom, and also observed the catholic rules for the date of Easter'.[68] Unfortunately, soon after his appointment Tuda died of the plague.[69] Stephen's account in his *Vita Wilfridi* ignored the presence of Tuda. Bede's description of Tuda implies that Wilfrid had the option of orthodox consecration in Ireland, had he so chosen.[70]

Subsequently Alhfrith organized to have Wilfrid consecrated in Gaul.[71] Stephen described how the kings consulted with counsellors to choose Wilfrid as next bishop.[72] Wilfrid, at 30 years of age, had risen rapidly through the ecclesiastical ranks. The ostensible reason for consecration in Gaul was to avoid any taint of 'schism' through bishops who were not 'catholic and apostolic'.[73] Chapter 12 of *Vita Wilfridi* describes how Wilfrid was consecrated in Gaul in pomp and grandeur by a host of twelve bishops, among whom was Agilberht, although he

---

64 Bede, *HE* 3.25 (Colgrave and Mynors (1969), 296–99).

65 Bede, *Vita Cuthberti* 7 (ed. Colgrave (1940), 174–75). Bede, *HE* 3.25 (Colgrave and Mynors (1969), 298–99), said that Wilfrid received Ripon and forty hides of land, but Stephen of Ripon, *VW* 8 (Colgrave (1927), 16–19), said that Wilfrid previously had received from Alhfrith ten hides at *Stanforda* and then thirty hides at Ripon when Eata and Cuthbert refused to change their practices.

66 Stephen of Ripon, *VW* 8 (Colgrave (1927), 16–19); Bede, *HE* 3.25 (Colgrave and Mynors (1969), 298–99). Most critics suggest that this took place *c.* AD 661, but Abels (1983), 9, argued for a date nearer *c.* AD 663. Catherine Cubitt (2013), 342, left the time open, AD 660×663.

67 Bede, *HE* 3.26 (Colgrave and Mynors (1969), 308–09): *qui erat apud Scottos austrinos eruditus atque ordinatus episcopus.*

68 Bede, *HE* 3.26 (Colgrave and Mynors (1969), 308–09): *habens iuxta morem prouinciae illius coronam tonsurae ecclesiasticae, et catholicam temporis paschalis regulam obseruans.*

69 Bede, *HE* 3.27 (Colgrave and Mynors (1969), 312–13).

70 Bede sometimes seems to have accepted Victorian and Dionysiac traditions as orthodox. If Tuda had been educated and consecrated in the Victorian tradition, is it likely that Wilfrid would not have accepted that as an option? For discussions of the Victorian tradition in the insular world, see Ohashi (2011); Warntjes (2015), 38–40, 57–59.

71 Stephen of Ripon, *VW* 11 (Colgrave (1927), 22–23); Bede, *HE* 3.28 (Colgrave and Mynors (1969), 314–17); Cubitt (1989), 18.

72 Stephen of Ripon, *VW* 11 (Colgrave (1927), 22–25). It should be noted that several passages from Stephen's *Vita Wilfridi* are lifted nearly word for word from the Anonymous *Vita Cuthberti*; compare Stephen of Ripon, *VW Praef.* and 11 (Colgrave (1927), 2–3, 24–25, and nn. 150, 159) with Anonymous, *Vita Cuthberti* prologue and 4.1 (ed. Colgrave (1940), 60–62, 110–13).

73 For a discussion of these events and the rôle of Agilberht, see Wood (2013), 202–03.

was not yet serving as bishop of Paris.[74] However, Wilfrid was gone so long that Oswiu, 'imitating the activities of his son', pre-empted him and installed Chad, abbot of Lastingham, as bishop of York.[75] Wilfrid's delay in returning from Gaul must reflect his loss of secular patronage with Alhfrith now out of the picture.[76]

Bede described Oswiu's 28-year reign as 'troublesome' (*laboriosissime*).[77] The same could be said for Wilfrid's time as bishop, from his consecration c. AD 665 to his death in AD 710,[78] a total of 45 years. But he served officially as bishop of Northumbria for only about 20 years.[79] His experience with each Northumbrian king was a series of co-operations followed by confrontations and occasional reconciliations, whether we speak of Oswiu (AD 642–670), Ecgfrith (AD 670–685), or Aldfrith (AD 685–704).[80] He had similarly contentious relationships with the archbishops of Canterbury, Theodore (AD 668–690) and Beorhtwald (AD 692–731), and with Benedict Biscop c. AD 653, and with Abbess Hild c. AD 678.[81] Some of his confrontations resulted in expulsions from Northumbria, and on two occasions he sought redress from the pope in Rome (AD 678×680; AD 703×704).[82]

Stephen of Ripon portrayed Wilfrid as declaring that, after the death of the missionaries sent by Pope Gregory, among his [Wilfrid's] personal successes were

---

74 Stephen of Ripon, *VW* 12 (Colgrave (1927), 24–27); Bede, *HE* 3.28 (Colgrave and Mynors (1969), 314–15); Wood (2013), 202–03. Wilfrid's work methods and search for patronage have been discussed by Pelteret (1998); see also Jones (1995) for a discussion of some of the estates that Wilfrid received from his patrons. This latter work highlights the Brittonic background of several of these newly acquired estates.

75 Bede, *HE* 3.28 (Colgrave and Mynors (1969), 316–17): *imitatus industriam filii*. This phrase has not been satisfactorily explained, but may imply that Oswiu decided to act contrary to a previously agreed course of action and moved to block Wilfrid by appointing Chad.

76 Wood (2013), 203–04.

77 Bede, *HE* 3.14 (Colgrave and Mynors (1969), 254–55).

78 Stancliffe (2013), 20–21.

79 Goffart (1988), 258 n. 115, for an overview.

80 After the 'synod' of Whitby Oswiu acted on his own against the wishes of Wilfrid: Bede, *HE* 3.28 (Colgrave and Mynors (1969), 314–17); Stephen of Ripon, *VW* 14 (Colgrave (1927), 30–31). Ecgfrith turned against Wilfrid c. AD 678: Stephen of Ripon, *VW* 24 (Colgrave (1927), 48–51); Bede, *HE* 5.24 (Colgrave and Mynors (1969), 564–65); Aldfrith banished Wilfrid (c. AD 703) and then refused to meet with him and obey the papal judgements when Wilfrid returned from Rome c. AD 704: Stephen of Ripon, *VW* 45, 58 (Colgrave (1927), 90–93, 124–27).

81 In the dispute of c. AD 678 Archbishop Theodore and Abbess Hild were said to be among Wilfrid's accusers: Stephen of Ripon, *VW* 54 (Colgrave (1927), 116–17). Wilfrid and Benedict Biscop set out for Rome from Kent together c. AD 653, but separated before reaching their destination and never cooperated again: Stephen of Ripon, *VW* 3 (Colgrave (1927), 8–9); Bede, *HE* 5.19 (Colgrave and Mynors (1969), 518–19); see further Wood (2013), 200, 208–09; Ó Carragáin and Thacker (2013), 216–17. Archbishop Beorhtwald was among Wilfrid's accusers c. AD 703: Stephen of Ripon, *VW* 50 (Colgrave (1927), 102–03).

82 Wilfrid's first appeal to the pope in Rome is related in Stephen of Ripon, *VW* 25, 29 (Colgrave (1927), 50–51, 56–61). Wilfrid's trip to Rome c. AD 703 is related in Stephen of Ripon, *VW* 50 (Colgrave (1927), 102–03), and his order by the pope to return home in Stephen of Ripon, *VW* 55 (Colgrave (1927), 120–21).

'to root out the poisonous weeds planted by the Scots [Gaels]' and to 'change and convert the whole of the Northumbrian *gens* to the true Easter'.[83] Careful examination shows that these 'accomplishments' were not achieved by Wilfrid in any meaningful way.[84]

Wilfrid emphasized his relationships with the Continent, Francia specifically, but he maintained important connections with Ireland as well. Wilfrid's rôle in the return of Dagobert II to Austrasia from Ireland in AD 676 is an example. Dagobert was brought to Ireland as a child for protection after a court coup sometime in AD 656/7. He had spent roughly 20 years in Ireland when Wilfrid was requested to help with his return to Francia.[85] Wilfrid was able to call on Gaelic contacts to locate Dagobert and have him escorted back to the Continent.[86] It has been suggested that Dagobert had been at Ráth Máelsigi,[87] and Wilfrid's relations with Willibrord support this. However, there is also an oral tradition that Dagobert had been in exile at Slane (Sláine) in Mag Breg.[88] These events show Wilfrid involved in continental politics while also familiar with Ireland, its institutions and their personnel.

Wilfrid's claimed protégé, Willibrord, the successful missionary to Frisia, trained for twelve years (*c.* AD 678–690) at Ráth Máelsigi.[89] Stephen described

---

83 Stephen of Ripon, *VW* 47 (Colgrave (1927), 98–99): *Scotticae virulenta plantationis germina eradicarem* [...] *ad verumque pascha* [...] *totam Ultrahumbrensium gentem permutando converterem.* See Goffart (1988), 307–24, for fuller discussion and contrast between Stephen's and Bede's treatments.

84 Other achievements claimed for Wilfrid include the introduction of the Benedictine Rule, but see López (2013); and the introduction of double choir singing, but see Billett (2013). Neither study can support the claim made for Wilfrid by Stephen.

85 Stephen was familiar with Jonas's Life of Columbanus, and Columbanus's mission had left its mark in Meaux which implies that Wilfrid was familiar with Gaelic missions on the Continent and their relationships with royal houses in the region: Wood (1990), 12–17. For more on Wilfrid and Dagobert II, see Ó Cróinín (1983b), 245; Ó Cróinín (1987); Picard (1991), 37, 42–43, 49; Richter (1999), 154–56.

86 Stephen of Ripon, *VW* 28, 33 (Colgrave (1927), 54–57, 68–69).

87 Ó Cróinín (1987), 41. For a sense of the wider rôle Ráth Máelsigi played in the interplay between the early Gaels and Anglo-Saxons, see Ó Cróinín (1984) and Ireland (1991b), 3–4, 9–10; Ireland (2015b), 34–35, 59–63, 72.

88 Picard (1991), 43–46. It may not be productive to search for a single place of exile in Ireland for someone like Dagobert. Based on the records of people like Wilfrid himself, travel from place to place with sojourns for study of varying lengths in each is not an uncommon pattern. Bede, *HE* 3.27 (Colgrave and Mynors (1969), 312–13), says as much of the Anglo-Saxons who came to Ireland to study. If the exile was purely political, and not for study, then the example of Edwin's exile during Æthelfrith's reign shows him moving from place to place; Bede, *HE* 2.12 (Colgrave and Mynors (1969), 176–79). Stephen of Ripon, *VW* 28 (Colgrave (1927), 54–55), implies as much when he states that authorities in Francia asked Wilfrid to invite Dagobert 'from Scotland and Ireland' (*de Scottia et Hibernia*) to send him back to the Continent. The wording implies that they did not know Dagobert's whereabouts, or they expected him to be on the move from place to place, or both. See Fouracre (2008) for an overview of how later, sometimes fabulous, stories developed around the figure of Dagobert.

89 Bede, *HE* 5.10 (Colgrave and Mynors (1969), 480–85).

Willibrord as Wilfrid's son, brought up at Ripon (*filius eius, Inhripis nutritus*),[90] but did not refer to Willibrord's sojourn and relationships in Ireland. Willibrord's training in Ireland began when Wilfrid was having problems with King Ecgfrith, Archbishop Theodore and Abbess Hild which resulted in his diocese's division and his expulsion from Northumbria.[91] In the same year (AD 678) Archbishop Theodore of Canterbury consecrated Bosa of Whitby as bishop of York presiding over Deira, and Abbot Eata of Lindisfarne became bishop over Bernicia.[92] This helps explain why Willibrord should go to Ráth Máelsigi for advanced training rather than to Theodore's school at Canterbury.[93] Willibrord's successful career was based on his training at Ráth Máelsigi. He achieved the archbishopric of the Frisians by AD 696 and worked productively at Echternach until his death in AD 739.[94]

Bede portrayed Wilfrid working in the context of Gaels. When Wilfrid returned to Britain after his expulsion in AD 678, he evangelized the South Saxons (*c.* AD 680). Bede stated that a certain Dícuill and five or six brothers had preceded him at a place called Bosham but that Wilfrid had the greater success converting the pagans.[95] In addition, Bede repeated an anecdote told by Willibrord to Wilfrid and Bishop Acca, when they were visiting Willibrord in Frisia on their way to Rome (*c.* AD 703), about the efficacy of King Oswald's relics in healing a Gaelic scholar at Ráth Máelsigi.[96]

Agilberht

Bishop Agilberht was the senior ecclesiastic in the Wilfridian group, originally from Gaul (Francia) and about to return to become, *c.* AD 668, bishop of

---

90 Stephen of Ripon, *VW* 26 (Colgrave (1927), 52). It should be noted, however, that despite Stephen's claims for Wilfrid's and Willibrord's relationship, Wilfrid does not appear in Willibrord's *Calendar*: Wilson (1918); Paris, Bibliothèque nationale de France, Lat. 10837, 34v–40r (https://gallica.bnf.fr/ark:/12148/btv1b6001113z/f.81.item.r=10837).

91 Bede, *HE* 4.12 (Colgrave and Mynors (1969), 370–71); Cubitt (1995), 250–51.

92 Bede, *HE* 4.12 (Colgrave and Mynors (1969), 370–71), is vague about where Eata set up his see in Bernicia, saying 'at Hexham or else at Lindisfarne' (*in Hagustaldensi siue in Lindisfarnensi*). See Cubitt (1989), 19, 22.

93 After the synod of Hatfield Wilfrid would hardly have encouraged his protégé to study at Canterbury with Theodore: Cubitt (1995), 250–51; see further Bischoff and Lapidge (1994), 140–46.

94 In order to trace some of Willibrord's debt to orthodox foundations in Ireland and his success in Frisia, see Ó Cróinín (1982b); Ó Cróinín (1984); Warntjes (2011); Pelteret (2011–2012).

95 Bede, *HE* 4.13 (Colgrave and Mynors (1969), 372–73).

96 Bede, *HE* 3.13 (Colgrave and Mynors (1969), 252–55). The anecdote is important at two levels. Firstly, it relates that relics of the saintly King Oswald, who had introduced the 'schismatics' from Iona into Northumbria, had efficacy for healing purposes as believed by Willibrord. Secondly, it was a Gael who had requested Willibrord's personal help and advice, thus reminding us that the school at Ráth Máelsigi would have taught Gaelic and Anglo-Saxon students together. For further connections between Willibrord and Ráth Máelsigi, see Ó Cróinín (1982b); Warntjes (2011).

Paris. Bede described Agilberht as a friend of King Alhfrith and Wilfrid.[97] Just previous to the 'synod' Agilberht had ordained Wilfrid priest at Alhfrith's request. Agilberht is an enigmatic character whose career can be divided into three stages: 1) a period of study in Ireland; 2) roughly a decade as bishop of the West Saxons; and 3) the conclusion of his career as bishop of Paris.[98] His presence at Whitby seems to have been between the bishoprics of the West Saxons and of Paris. But no sources clarify why he was present in Deira to attend the 'synod' between those two phases of his career.

Bede stated that Agilberht 'had spent a long time in Ireland for the purpose of studying the Scriptures',[99] before coming to the West Saxons. But beyond Bede's statement we have little corroborating evidence.[100] Where he studied in Ireland is not mentioned, but Ráth Máelsigi is a possible location.[101] Ian Wood has argued that Agilberht would have supported Columbanian monasticism on the Continent because of contacts between Agilberht's family and Columbanus's mission.[102] Therefore, Bangor may be a location where Agilberht had studied in Ireland.[103] Whatever about Agilberht's time spent in Ireland, it apparently did not taint Wilfrid's opinion of him.

In Bede's account, Agilberht had served as bishop to the West Saxons in the AD 650s and had been removed, sometime c. AD 661×663, at the request of King Cenwealh and replaced by Wine (who had trained in Gaul), because the king was not satisfied with Agilberht's ability to speak Old English.[104] Agilberht's poor linguistic ability is used in Bede's account, though not in Stephen's,[105] as the excuse for Wilfrid to act as spokesman rather than the senior cleric.[106] Agilberht's presence at Whitby during the transition between two bishoprics has yet to be adequately explained.[107]

---

97 Bede, *HE* 3.25 (Colgrave and Mynors (1969), 298–99).

98 Hammer (2011–2012). For an earlier summary of his career, see Hunter Blair (1970), 111–12.

99 Bede, *HE* 3.7 (Colgrave and Mynors (1969), 234–35): *sed tunc legendarum gratia scripturarum in Hibernia non paruo tempore demoratus.*

100 Hammer (2011–2012), 61–66.

101 Unfortunately, we have no idea when this important foundation which trained so many foreigners was first established. See Ó Cróinín (1987) for plausible connections with other Continentals.

102 Wood (1990), 11; Wood (2013), 203.

103 Hammer (2011–2012), 62. Given the peripatetic nature of Agilberht's career there may be no reason to have to choose between locations: Hammer (2011–2012), 55–60, 62. For connections between Bangor and Leinster, including the region around Ráth Máelsigi, see Bhreathnach (2001), 261–64; Ireland (2015b), 59–63, 71–72.

104 *HE* 3.7 (Colgrave and Mynors (1969), 234–35).

105 Bede, *HE* 3.25 (Colgrave and Mynors (1969), 300–01); Stephen of Ripon, *VW* 10 (Colgrave (1927), 20–23). It has been suggested that this was Bede's way of belittling Wilfrid's contribution to the debate since Agilberht was senior and, presumably, more knowledgeable: Goffart (1988), 312.

106 The language issue is an important subtext here. It seems odd that Agilberht could have been bishop in Wessex for more than a decade, then removed because he had not learned Old English well enough to satisfy King Cenwealh, only to be asked by the king to return later as bishop: see Hammer (2011–2012), 61, 66, 67.

107 Wood (2013), 202–03.

Agilberht was present in AD 665 at Compiègne for Wilfrid's consecration, but not in his capacity as a local bishop.[108] Agilberht apparently did not become bishop of Paris until AD 668.[109] He is buried among family members at Jouarre in an elaborate tomb.[110]

Agatho

The priest Agatho accompanied Agilberht but no further details are known about him.[111] We have no indication of how long Agatho and Agilberht had been together, and whether or not they had been together in Ireland and during Agilberht's tenure as bishop of the West Saxons.

Romanus

Romanus was a priest who accompanied Oswiu's Queen Eanflæd to the Northumbrian court from Kent. As daughter of King Edwin, Eanflæd had been baptized by Bishop Paulinus as an infant (AD 626) and raised in Kent after the death of her father.[112] Oswiu's and Eanflæd's wedding took place soon after he became king c. AD 643,[113] so Romanus had spent two decades in Northumbria before the 'synod' and would have been familiar with any contentions arising at Oswiu's court over the differing Easter practices.

James

The priest James had been deacon to Bishop Paulinus and survived into Bede's own time.[114] When King Edwin was killed by Cadwallon (AD 633), Paulinus fled back to Kent and left James in charge of the region around York. Paulinus took up the bishopric at Rochester, not far from Canterbury, and remained there until his death in AD 644.[115] Since Paulinus is credited with converting Edwin and the child Hild, James must have been present at their ceremonies, implying that

---

108 Bede, *HE* 3.28 (Colgrave and Mynors (1969), 314–15); Stephen of Ripon, *VW* 12 (Colgrave (1927), 24–27).

109 Hammer (2011–2012), 69–70.

110 Hammer (2011–2012), 68–77.

111 Bede, *HE* 3.25 (Colgrave and Mynors (1969), 298–99); Stephen of Ripon, *VW* 10 (Colgrave (1927), 20–21).

112 Bede, *HE* 3.15 (Colgrave and Mynors (1969), 260–61).

113 Bede, *HE* 3.15 (Colgrave and Mynors (1969), 260–61).

114 Bede, *HE* 2.16 (Colgrave and Mynors (1969), 192): *qui ad nostra usque tempora permansit*. This would have made James very advanced in years to have survived into Bede's *floruit*; see Hunter Blair (1970), 98.

115 Bede, *HE* 2.20 (Colgrave and Mynors (1969), 202–05).

James knew Hild from her teenage years. Bede speaks highly of James's successful teaching and baptizing in the region of York and his skill in church music.[116] There was a village near Catterick that bore his name.[117]

Pro-Iona participants

Those who supported the Iona mission centred at Lindisfarne were termed 'Irish' (*Scotti*; Gaels) by Bede in Colgrave's translation.[118] His habit of not distinguishing between orthodox Gaels and those who followed the practices of Iona obfuscates the dynamics of cultural and ecclesiastical interaction in Anglo-Saxon Britain. Iona's supporters included Bishop Colmán of Lindisfarne, who acted as spokesman; Bishop Cedd of Essex, who served as interpreter; and Abbess Hild of Whitby and her community, who hosted the gathering. There is no reason to assume that those who supported the Ionan party at the 'synod' did so because they were sympathetic to the older traditions of the *latercus*. They would have been aware of the political agenda as well.

Colmán

Colmán was accompanied by clergy from Lindisfarne but we have no idea how large his retinue may have been. Colmán was the third Ionan bishop of Lindisfarne (*c.* AD 661–664) having been preceded by Aidan (AD 634–651) and Fínán (AD 651–*c.* 661),[119] both of whom had worked with Hild. Colmán acted as principal spokesman for the Ionan party.[120]

Among the outcomes of the 'synod' was the departure from Lindisfarne of Colmán with many Gaels and thirty Anglo-Saxon monks who left Northumbria for Iona before resettling in Ireland, first on the western island of Inishboffin (*Inis bó finne*)[121] and then on the mainland at Mayo of the Saxons (*Mag nÉo na*

---

116 Bede's (*HE* 2.20 (Colgrave and Mynors (1969), 206–07)) claim for James's skill at church music must be contrasted with the reputed claim by Wilfrid to have instructed in musical matters (Stephen of Ripon, *VW* 47 (Colgrave (1927), 98–99). For an assessment of Wilfrid's musical contribution, see Billett (2013).

117 Bede, *HE* 2.20 (Colgrave and Mynors (1969), 206–07).

118 Bede, *HE* 3.25 (Colgrave and Mynors (1969), 294–309).

119 These episcopal dates are based on Bede's account: *HE* 3.26 (Colgrave and Mynors (1969), 308–09). Gaelic annals tend to put Fínán's death before AD 661: Annals of Ulster s.a. 660 (Mac Airt and Mac Niocaill (1983), 132–33; for the synchronised dating, see Mc Carthy (2005) s.a. 659); the Frankish Annals of Lindisfarne and Kent put his death s.a. 658 (ed. Story (2005), 65–67, 108).

120 Bede, *HE* 3.25 (Colgrave and Mynors (1969), 298–309); *VW* 10 (Colgrave (1927), 20–23). Bede, *HE* 3.25 (Colgrave and Mynors (1969), 296), described Colmán as having been sent from 'Scottia' (*missus a Scottia*).

121 Bede used an acceptably accurate Gaelic form of the name and its meaning in Latin, *insula uitulae albae*, *HE* 4.4 (Colgrave and Mynors (1969), 346–47).

Saxan).[122] Alcuin, a century later, corresponded with the Anglo-Saxon monks at this western monastery.[123]

Bede described Colmán, the Ionan clergy, and their pastoral practices in sympathetic terms, stating that they had few possessions and no grand structures. If they received money, they dispersed it to the poor, for they had no desire to entertain powerful men. Their sole purpose was to serve God and not the world, to satisfy the soul and not the body. They were free of avarice and had no desire to receive lands or possessions from the wealthy. For these reasons the religious habit was held in high esteem among the people.[124]

The pastoral practices of Bishops Colmán, Aidan, and Abbess Hild consistently contrast with Wilfrid's acceptance of gifts of land and riches from wealthy patrons.[125] By contrast Stephen's account is categorical: 'Bishop Colmán was told what he must do [...] he must retire and leave his see to be taken by another and a better man'.[126] Although Colmán departed Northumbria with those who wished to accompany him,[127] Bede said that Oswiu 'greatly loved Bishop Colmán on account of his innate prudence'.[128] Oswiu's attitude toward Colmán was one of respect and appreciation.

Tuda replaced Colmán at Lindisfarne. Tuda, according to Bede, observed the 'catholic' Easter and wore the coronal tonsure. Unfortunately, Tuda died of the plague soon after.[129] Tuda is not mentioned in *Vita Wilfridi*.

Eata, formerly of Melrose, was appointed abbot of Lindisfarne when Tuda was made bishop.[130] Eata, one of twelve Anglo-Saxon boys trained by Bishop Aidan, would be appointed bishop of Lindisfarne by Archbishop Theodore in AD 678 when Wilfrid's diocese was split. Eata, clearly, had made a smooth transition from Ionan to orthodox practice.

---

122 Bede, *HE* 4.4 (Colgrave and Mynors (1969), 346–49); Orschel (2001).

123 Alcuin, *Epistola ad monachos Mugensis ecclesiae* (no. 287) (ed. Ernst Dümmler in MGH Epp. 4, 445–46; trans. Allott (1974), 44–45).

124 Bede, *HE* 3.26 (Colgrave and Mynors (1969), 310–11).

125 Kirby suggests that Bede may be deliberately contrasting an idealized pastoral past with a contemporary problem that he wrote about in his letter to Ecgberht: Kirby (1992), 13; referring to comments by Sims-Williams (1990), 126–27.

126 Stephen of Ripon, *VW* 10 (Colgrave (1927), 22–23): *Colmanus vero episcopus audiens, quid esset faciendum, [...] ut secederet et alii meliori sedem suam occupandam relinqueret.*

127 Bede, *HE* 3.26, 4.4 (Colgrave and Mynors (1969), 308–09, 346–47).

128 Bede, *HE* 3.26 (Colgrave and Mynors (1969), 308–09): *Multum namque eundem episcopum Colmanum rex pro insita illi prudentia diligebat.*

129 Bede, *HE* 3.27 (Colgrave and Mynors (1969), 312–13).

130 Bede, *HE* 3.26 (Colgrave and Mynors (1969), 308–09).

Cedd

Bishop Cedd of Essex, consecrated by the Gaels, sided with the Ionan party and 'acted as a most careful interpreter for both parties at the council'.[131] It is not known if a retinue accompanied him to the 'synod'. Cedd is another person never mentioned in the *Vita Wilfridi*, in any context.

Cedd was instrumental in Oswiu's campaign to convert King Sigeberht and the East Saxons and eventually was consecrated their bishop by Bishop Fínán due to his successes there.[132] Cedd also established the monastery at Lastingham on land given to him by Œthelwald, son of King Oswald.[133] His brother Chad took over Lastingham from him.[134] Chad had trained at the orthodox monastery of Ráth Máelsigi with Ecgberht[135] but his brother Cedd supported the Ionan party at the 'synod', which suggests the complexity of the issues at Whitby, with ecclesiastical politics alongside doctrinal issues. As a result, 'Cedd left the practices of the Irish [Gaels] [...] having accepted the catholic method of keeping Easter'.[136] Cedd died shortly afterwards, as did Tuda, in the plague that ravaged parts of Britain and Ireland.[137]

Hild and her background

A frequently overlooked statement by Bede about the 'synod' is that 'Abbess Hild and her followers were on the side of the Irish [Gaels]'.[138] This statement implies that personnel at Whitby were sympathetic to the Ionan party and its Lindisfarne representatives. Bede does not elaborate so we cannot know if Whitby personnel favoured the *latercus* specifically or were sympathetic generally to the ethos and

---

131 Bede, *HE* 3.25 (Colgrave and Mynors (1969), 298–99): *qui et interpres in eo concilio uigilantissimus utriusque partis extitit.* Cedd's rôle as interpreter raises questions about the linguistic dynamic at the synod. Agilberht had excused himself from oral presentation evidently based on his weak command of Old English despite his many years as bishop of Wessex. Agilberht had also studied scripture in Ireland and could be assumed to have spoken Gaelic. But Agilberht's deferral to Wilfrid implies that all arguments were made in Old English. We are given no indication of whether or not Bishop Colmán spoke Old English, but it is hard to believe that he could hold a bishopric at Lindisfarne without it. Oswiu, who oversaw proceedings, spoke both Gaelic and Old English as, apparently based on Bede's statement, did Cedd. Despite the ecclesiastical topic of the debate and the churchmen who argued each side, as Michael Herren (1998), 38, concluded, 'Latin, apparently, was not one of the official languages of the synod!'.

132 Bede, *HE* 3.22 (Colgrave and Mynors (1969), 280–85).

133 Bede, *HE* 3.23 (Colgrave and Mynors (1969), 286–89).

134 Bede, *HE* 3.23 (Colgrave and Mynors (1969), 288–89).

135 Bede, *HE* 4.3 (Colgrave and Mynors (1969), 344–45).

136 Bede, *HE* 3.26 (Colgrave and Mynors (1969), 308–09): *Cedd, relictis Scottorum uestigiis,* [...] *utpote agnita obseruatione catholici paschae.*

137 Bede, *HE* 3.23 (Colgrave and Mynors (1969), 288–89); Plummer (1896), ii 194–96.

138 Bede, *HE* 3.25 (Colgrave and Mynors (1969), 298–99): *Hild abbatissa cum suis in parte Scottorum.*

modus operandi of the Gaelic missionaries in Northumbria.[139] From what can be reconstructed of Hild's career it would seem that she and her community favoured the pastoral ethos of the Gaels, whether orthodox or Ionan, as opposed to the Wilfridians.

Anglo-Saxonists have portrayed Abbess Hild as Bede's ideal teaching nun.[140] Bede devoted a chapter to a recapitulation of her life.[141] For example, he related how Hild's death was revealed to other nuns in visions.[142] The first recorded poetry in the Old English vernacular, along with a description of how Cædmon composed his verse, occurred at Whitby during Hild's abbacy or soon after.[143] The anonymous *Vita Gregorii*, written early in the eighth century, is a product of Whitby.[144] Interestingly, the *Vita* eschews all mention of Hild herself, or any mission from Iona, or references to Wilfrid's campaign.

Among Whitby's achievements, which imply Hild's educational ethos, are the five men from Whitby who became bishops in various parts of Anglo-Saxon Britain.[145] Among the five, Bosa was ordained bishop of York (AD 678–706) when Wilfrid's see was divided and he was expelled from Northumbria in AD 678.[146] John of Beverley, who succeeded Bosa at York, ordained Bede as deacon (AD 691×692) and priest (AD 702×703).[147] John is, therefore, likely to have been Bede's primary witness for events at Whitby and its personnel. John's

---

139 Gunn (2009), 179–81, argued that Bede was deliberately ambiguous about the loyalties of Hild and her community leading up to the 'synod' and during its aftermath.

140 See, for example, Fell (1981), 95–98; Hunter Blair (1985), 22–29; Ward (1993), 107–08; Wormald (1993), 272–74; Lees and Overing (1994); Bauer (1996), 21, 23–25; Gunn (2009), 176–77. For a more critical view, see Hollis (1992), 243–70.

141 Bede, *HE* 4.23 (Colgrave and Mynors (1969), 404–15).

142 Bede, *HE* 4.23 (Colgrave and Mynors (1969), 412–15).

143 Bede, *HE* 4.24 (Colgrave and Mynors (1969), 414–21). For an extensive study, see O'Donnell (2005). For comparative studies, see Ireland (2005); Ireland (2016b).

144 The *Vita* devotes several chapters to the reign of King Edwin including his conversion by Paulinus of the Gregorian mission: *Vita Gregorii* 12–19 (Colgrave (1968), 94–105). For a discussion of Gaelic characteristics in this work, see Ireland (2015a), 143–71.

145 Bede, *HE* 4.23 (Colgrave and Mynors (1969), 408–11). The five bishops are Oftfor, Bosa, John of Beverly, Wilfrid (II), and Ætla. Oftfor started with Hild at Heruteu, went to Canterbury and the school of Theodore (Bede, *HE* 4.2, 5.8 (Colgrave and Mynors (1969), 408–11)), then to Rome. He went to assist Bosel, bishop of Hwicce and was consecrated bishop, to replace Bosel, by Wilfrid *c.* AD 690×692. Bosa was consecrated bishop of York by Theodore in AD 678 (Bede, *HE* 5.3, 24 (Colgrave and Mynors (1969), 458–61, 564–65 s.a. 678). Bosa died *c.* AD 706 (Bede, *HE* 5.3 (Colgrave and Mynors (1969), 458–61; Anglo-Saxon Chronicle, manuscript E [Peterborough Chronicle] s.a. 685 (Swanton (2000), 39). John of Beverly became bishop of Hexham *c.* AD 688, then succeeded Bosa at York *c.* AD 706 (Bede, *HE* 5.2–6, 5.24 (Colgrave and Mynors (1969), 456–69, 566–67)). Wilfrid (II) succeeded John of Beverly as last bishop of York and resigned in AD 732 (Bede, *HE* 5.6, 5.23 (Colgrave and Mynors (1969), 464–69, 558–59)). Ætla became bishop of Dorchester-on-Thames (Bede, *HE* 4.23 (Colgrave and Mynors (1969), 408–09)), but little is known of him.

146 Bede, *HE* 4.12 (Colgrave and Mynors (1969), 370–71).

147 Bede, *HE* 5.24 (Colgrave and Mynors (1969), 566–67).

106   COLIN IRELAND

successor at York was Wilfrid II (AD 718–732) who could also have served as a source for Bede's history of Whitby.[148]

Hild was born *c*. AD 614, probably while her father, Hereric, a nephew of King Edwin, lived in exile in the Brittonic kingdom of Elmet (near Leeds) under the protection of King Ceredig.[149] Edwin occupied Elmet and expelled Ceredig according to *Historia Brittonum*.[150] Bede noted that Hereric was poisoned but does not indicate by whom.[151] Hild would have been 2 or 3 years old when her father was poisoned and Ceredig was expelled. Hild was baptized at approximately 13 years of age *c*. AD 627, along with Edwin, by Paulinus. Hild was apparently raised as part of Edwin's retinue. Since Hild was baptized by a member of the Gregorian mission to Canterbury,[152] she could be expected to be orthodox in practice. Her decision at the 'synod' seemingly contradicts this early history.

We have two decades, from *c*. AD 627 when Hild was baptized to *c*. AD 647, for which we know nothing of her activities. Christine Fell has speculated that, like most women of her time, she had married, but was widowed by her late 20s or early 30s.[153] We pick up the thread of her life *c*. AD 647 when she went to East Anglia where the local king was her sister's son.[154] She intended following her sister Hereswith to the Continent and the monastery at Chelles,[155] or, at least, somewhere nearby.[156] We have no precise dates for this East Anglian sojourn, but Fursa, whose vision Bede recorded,[157] was also there at this time.[158] Fursa and Hild may or may not have met, but his companions Fáelán (Fullanus), Gobbán

---

148 Bede, *HE* 5.6, 5.23 (Colgrave and Mynors (1969), 464–69, 556–61).
149 Hereric lived in a political exile (Bede, *HE* 4.23 (Colgrave and Mynors (1969), 410–11); Koch (1997), XXXIII–XXXIV) much as Edwin had done among the Britons on Anglesey and with Rædwald in East Anglia during the reign of Æthelfrith (Bede, *HE* 2.12 (Colgrave and Mynors (1969), 174–83)); Bromwich (1978), XCVII–XCVIII; see also Rowland (1990), 123; Charles-Edwards (2013), 345).
150 *Historia Brittonum* 63 (Morris (1980), 38, 79).
151 Bede, *HE* 4.23 (Colgrave and Mynors (1969), 410–11); Rowland (1990), 100–01. Colgrave and Mynors speculate that Edwin conquered Elmet in revenge for Hereric's being poisoned, but given the nature of dynastic rivalries, it seems as likely that Hereric had been poisoned on Edwin's orders. One need only recall the rivalry between Æthelfrith and Edwin, and how Æthelfrith tried to persuade Rædwald of the East Angles either to have Edwin killed when he sought refuge in East Anglia or hand him over: Bede, *HE* 2.12 (Colgrave and Mynors (1969), 174–83).
152 Bede, *HE* 1.29 (Colgrave and Mynors (1969), 104–07).
153 Fell (1981), 80–81.
154 Bede, *HE* 4.23 (Colgrave and Mynors (1969), 406–07).
155 Bede, *HE* 4.23 (Colgrave and Mynors (1969), 406–07).
156 Whitelock (1972), 2–3. Wallace-Hadrill (1988), 232, pointed out that Bede or his sources had to be wrong about Hild's proposed destination as being Chelles since at this time it was not likely to have been functioning, that is, if it had yet been founded.
157 Bede, *HE* 3.19 (Colgrave and Mynors (1969), 268–77), considered Fursa and his vision important enough to devote a full chapter to him.
158 Charles-Edwards (2000), 318 n. 176, argued that Fursa was in East Anglia from the late AD 630s to *c*. AD 648, before he left for France. Hild must have been in East Anglia *c*. AD 646–647 before she was called back to Northumbria by Bishop Aidan in AD 647.

(Gobbanus), Dícuil (Dicullus), and Ultán (Ultanus) would have been active in East Anglia at the same time.[159]

Hild's visit to East Anglia, and the presence of Fursa and his companions, would have occurred during the tenure of Bishop Felix (c. AD 631–c. AD 648).[160] Felix had been born and educated in Burgundy and may have been influenced by the Columbanian foundation at Luxeuil.[161] It is likely that Aidan, Felix, and Honorius of Canterbury cooperated throughout their overlapping bishoprics.[162] In this context of episcopal cooperation Bede did not mention Paulinus, who had retired to Rochester from AD 633 to 644.[163]

Bishop Aidan called Hild back (reuocata) to Northumbria from East Anglia before AD 647.[164] Bede's wording implies that Aidan and Hild already had a working relationship before she departed for East Anglia. Aidan gave her land on the River Wear where she lived a monastic life with a small group for a year.[165] By AD 647 Aidan put Hild in charge of Heruteu (Hartlepool). Aidan 'and other devout men who knew her visited her frequently, instructed her assiduously, and loved her heartily for her innate wisdom and her devotion to the service of God'.[166] Aidan died in AD 651, but Hild maintained working relationships with Bishops Fínán and Colmán. Around AD 655 Oswiu submitted his daughter Ælfflæd to be raised by Hild in gratitude for his victory over the pagan Mercian Penda at Winwæd.[167] Ælfflæd remained with Hild all her life and succeeded her as abbess of Whitby from AD 680–714. The anonymous Vita Gregorii is a product of Ælfflæd's Whitby.[168]

In AD 657, during Fínán's bishopric, Hild founded, or 'set in order',[169] a monastery at Strēanæshalh, better known by its Norse-derived name Whitby, which she oversaw until her death in AD 680.[170] Bede stated that:[171]

> quibus prius monasterium, etiam hoc disciplinis uitae regularis institui, et quidem multam ibi quoque iustitiae pietatis et castimoniae ceterarumque uirtutum, [...] nullus ibi diues, nullus esset egens, omnibus essent omnia communia, cum nihil cuiusquam esse uideretur proprium.

---

159 Bede, HE 3.19 (Colgrave and Mynors (1969), 274–77); Whitelock (1972), 2–6.
160 It has been suggested that Felix and Fursa, working in conjunction, may have influenced King Sigeberht's desire to go on pilgrimage to Rome: Stancliffe (1983), 169–70.
161 Bede, HE 2.15 (Colgrave and Mynors (1969), 190–91); Stancliffe (1983), 169 n. 61.
162 Bede, HE 3.25 (Colgrave and Mynors (1969), 296–97); Whitelock (1972), 2–6.
163 Bede, HE 2.20 (Colgrave and Mynors (1969), 204–05).
164 Bede, HE 4.23 (Colgrave and Mynors (1969), 406–07).
165 Bede, HE 4.23 (Colgrave and Mynors (1969), 406–07).
166 Bede, HE 4.23 (Colgrave and Mynors (1969), 408–09): et quique nouerant eam religiosi, pro insita ei sapientia et amore diuini famulatus, sedulo eam uisitare, obnixe amare, diligenter erudire solebant.
167 Bede, HE 3.24 (Colgrave and Mynors (1969), 290–93).
168 Colgrave (1968), 48; Ireland (2015a), 140–41.
169 Bede, HE 4.23 (Colgrave and Mynors (1969), 408): construendum siue ordinandum monasterium.
170 Bede, HE 4.23 (Colgrave and Mynors (1969), 408–09).
171 Bede, HE 4.23 (Colgrave and Mynors (1969), 408–09).

> She established the same Rule of life as in the other monastery [i.e.
> Heruteu], teaching them to observe strictly the virtues of justice, devotion,
> and chastity and other virtues too, [...] no one was rich, no one was
> in need, for they had all things in common and none had any private
> property.

Hild's *modus vivendi* is paralleled by Bede's descriptions of the Ionan bishops at
Lindisfarne and contrasts with Wilfrid's acceptance of gifts of land and riches from
wealthy patrons.[172]

Hild's baptism as a teenager by Paulinus (AD 627) when contrasted with her,
and her community's, support for the Ionan party at the 'synod' (AD 664) seems
an inherent contradiction. Hild had established Whitby only seven years before
(AD 657). It must have been difficult for her to have influential, powerful men
with whom she disagreed present at the 'synod'. Her baptism implies that she was
raised in the orthodox tradition. Alhfrith sub-king of Deira, her home region, had
convened the 'synod'. James, Paulinus' deacon, who had known her since she was
a teenager, was present.[173] Ælfflæd's mother, Eanflæd, whose priest Romanus also
attended, would eventually join her daughter and Hild at Whitby when Oswiu
died (AD 670).[174] Such challenges reveal a woman of strong character and deep
conviction.

Hild worked closely with all three Ionan bishops from Lindisfarne. Aidan had
been her mentor. Fínán had assigned her to oversee Whitby. The Gaelic-educated
Oswiu had left his daughter Ælfflæd, who would succeed her as abbess, perma-
nently in her care. Hild's visit to East Anglia during the bishopric of Felix, in the
time of Fursa, implies that her life in religion began already imbued with Gaelic
influence.

Hild's opposition to Wilfrid towards the end of her life indicates her convic-
tions and helps explain her support for the Ionan party. The *Vita Wilfridi* cites
a letter from Pope John VI to Æthelræd of Mercia and Aldfrith of Northumbria
in which Hild and Theodore of Canterbury are described as among Wilfrid's
accusers in the dispute of AD 678 when the diocese of York was split and Wilfrid
was expelled from Northumbria.[175]

---

172 It has been argued that Bede's description of Aidan's pastoral methods and teaching reflect that
he lived exactly as he preached and that this ideal was based on Pope Gregory's *Liber regulae
pastoris*: Thacker (1983), 144–45; McClure (1984), 79–80 n. 6. Butler (2011), 172, noted that Bede's
description of Aidan (and, by extension, of Hild, Colmán and other Gaelic or Gaelic-trained clerics),
portrays him as an 'ideal preacher in the Gregorian mould'.

173 Bede, *HE* 3.20 (Colgrave and Mynors (1969), 206–07).

174 Bede, *HE* 4.26 (Colgrave and Mynors (1969), 428–31).

175 Stephen of Ripon, *VW* 54 (Colgrave (1927), 116): *et Hyldae religiosae memoriae abbatissae ad eum
accusandum huc prius advenerat*. For details of the council at which Hild and Theodore were accusers
of Wilfrid, see Cubitt (1995), 250–51; for details of the synod attended by Aldfrith, see Cubitt
(1995), 259. Aldhelm's *Epistula ad Wilfridi abbates* (ed. Rudolf Ehwald in MGH Auct. ant. 15,
500–02; trans. Lapidge and Herren (1979), 168–70) was probably written at this time: Lapidge and
Herren (1979), 150–51.

Bede offered no justification for Hild's support of the Ionan party. It may have been that she supported the social and pastoral style of the Ionan mission, as described for Aidan and Colmán. Hild and her recently founded community were hardly loyal to the tradition of the *latercus*. Bede stated that 'as the catholic principles daily gained strength, all the Irish [Gaels] who had remained among the English either gave way or returned to their own land'.[176] Some chose to depart Northumbria, as noted of Bishop Colmán and at least thirty Anglo-Saxon monks.[177] It necessarily follows from Bede's statement that all who remained, including Hild, Cedd, and their communities, adopted 'catholic and apostolic' practices. But it seems equally likely that many who supported the Ionan party were already sympathetic to those same 'catholic and apostolic' practices.

Oswiu's background and contribution

King Oswiu's son Alhfrith, the sub-king of Deira, in consort with Wilfrid, initiated the 'synod'. Yet, as both accounts make clear, it was Oswiu who oversaw proceedings and who made the final decision. It seems likely that the coincidence of the solar eclipse over Bernicia and Deira followed by the plague throughout Britain and Ireland allowed Oswiu's rivals to force his hand and submit to the 'synod' in AD 664.[178]

Oswiu reigned for 28 years, from AD 642 to 670. He had been fostered, along with all of his brothers,[179] among the Gaels, probably in Dál Riata, during the reign of King Edwin of Northumbria. In other words, Oswiu and his brothers had undergone an enforced political exile during Edwin's seventeen-year reign (AD 616–633), much as Edwin had done during the reign of Æthelfrith (AD 593–616), Oswiu's father.

As part of their exile Oswiu and his brothers were baptized, educated, and became fluent in the Gaelic language. For example, King Oswald (AD 634–642) had acted as interpreter for Bishop Aidan because 'the king had gained a perfect knowledge of Irish [Gaelic]', and Oswiu himself was 'well versed in their [the Gaels'] language'.[180] Bede stated that Oswiu had a high regard for Gaelic learning

---

176 Bede, *HE* 3.28 (Colgrave and Mynors (1969), 316): *crescente per dies institutione catholica, Scotti omnes, qui inter Anglos morabantur, aut his manus darent aut suam redirent ad patriam.*

177 *HE* 3.26 (Colgrave and Mynors (1969), 308–09). See also p. 99 above.

178 Corning (2006), 120–23. See p. 88 above.

179 Bede, *HE* 3.1 (Colgrave and Mynors (1969), 212), said that the sons of Æthelfrith lived in exile among the Gaels or Picts (*apud Scottos siue Pictos exulabant*). There is no reason to assume that the brothers lived out their exiles at Iona itself. See p. 85 above.

180 Bede, *HE* 3.3 (Colgrave and Mynors (1969), 220–21): (Oswald) *ipse rex* [...] *linguam Scottorum iam plene didicerat*; Bede, *HE* 3.25 (Colgrave and Mynors (1969), 296–97): (Oswiu) *illorum etiam lingua optime inbutus.*

and thought there was none better.[181] Oswiu's respect for Gaelic learning should not be interpreted as a bias for or against any particular ecclesiastical practices. Bede told of the many Anglo-Saxons of every social class who exiled themselves among the Gaels for the sake of free education or to pursue an ascetic life during the time of bishops Fínán and Colmán (AD 651–664).[182] This period is in the middle of Oswiu's reign and suggests that he encouraged this process as someone who respected Gaelic learning. His relationships with Cenél nÉogain, continued by his cooperation with Bishop Fínán,[183] brought him into the ambit of Gaelic intellectual life. Two of the earliest named *sapientes*, Cenn Fáelad mac Ailello († AD 679),[184] and Oswiu's son Aldfrith *sapiens*, came from that extended family.[185] None of the early sources challenge Aldfrith's orthodoxy.[186] The reputation among the Gaels of Aldfrith *sapiens* must be considered when assessing Bede's statement about Oswiu's respect for Gaelic learning.[187]

In Bede's discussion of various Anglo-Saxon *imperia*, Oswiu is listed as the last of seven overlords.[188] He ruled over a territory roughly equal to his brother Oswald's reign, but Oswiu spread his hegemony over Picts and Gaels in northern Britain.[189] Bede described Oswiu's reign as very troublesome.[190] One contentious aspect of Oswiu's reign was that he had a rival, King Oswine of Deira, murdered in AD 651.[191] Bede described Oswine as a pious king and related how Bishop Aidan and Oswine had a close relationship.[192] Their relationship demonstrates the

---

181 Bede, *HE* 3.25 (Colgrave and Mynors (1969), 296): *Quia nimirum Osuiu a Scottis edoctus ac baptizatus, illorum etiam lingua optime inbutus, nil melius, quam quod illi docuissent autumabat*. For a survey of the literature produced at Iona, in both Gaelic and Latin, during the seventh century, see Clancy and Márkus (1995).

182 Bede, *HE* 3.27 (Colgrave and Mynors (1969), 312–13).

183 Bishop Fínán was evidently of Cenél nÉogain. He was called *mac Rimedo* 'son of Rimid' in the Annals of Ulster s.a. 660 and of Tigernach (Mac Airt and Mac Niocaill (1983), 132–33; Stokes (1896), 195), that is, son of Colmán Rimid, grandfather of Flann Fína/Aldfrith: Plummer (1896), ii 189; Ireland (1991a), 74; Higham (2015), 92–93.

184 Ireland (1996), 68–72; Ireland (2016a).

185 For genealogical information, see Ireland (1991a). For Aldfrith as *sapiens*, see Ireland (1996), 73–76; Ireland (2015b), 35–48. For a wider discussion of seventh-century Gaelic *sapientes*, see Johnston (2013), 102–05.

186 Yorke (2010), 44, 49, stated that Aldfrith was probably a *Romanus*.

187 Ireland (1996), 73–76; Ireland (1999), 52–56. If Aldfrith was orthodox then the argument that he was educated at Iona by Adomnán during the mid- to late-AD 660s along with Aldhelm must be viewed with scepticism: see Lapidge (2007), 22–26; Lapidge (2010), 148–50; and contrast Ireland (2015b), 48–52. For arguments that Bangor, Co. Down is most closely associated with Aldfrith, see Ireland (2015b), 63–69.

188 Bede, *HE* 2.5 (Colgrave and Mynors (1969), 150–51).

189 Bede, *HE* 2.5 (Colgrave and Mynors (1969), 150–51).

190 Bede, *HE* 3.14 (Colgrave and Mynors (1969), 254): *suscepit regni terrestris sedem* […] *et per annos XXVIII laboriosissime tenuit*. See p. 93 above.

191 Bede, *HE* 3.14 (Colgrave and Mynors (1969), 256–61). See n. 45 above.

192 Bede, *HE* 3.14 (Colgrave and Mynors (1969), 256–61). Kirby (1991), 92, noted that Oswine did not attempt to revive the mission from Canterbury into Deira. With the baptism of Edwin by Paulinus and the descriptions of Paulinus' success at conversion (Bede, *HE* 2.14 (Colgrave and Mynors

Ionan inroads into Deiran polity beyond the borders of Bernicia. Aidan himself, however, was to die shortly after Oswine's elimination by Oswiu.[193]

Some critics have seen Oswine's murder as an example of Bede's deprecation of Oswiu's kingship.[194] In order to atone for his crime a monastery was established at Gilling for the redemption of both kings.[195] Gilling was established at the urging of Oswiu's Queen Eanflæd.[196] Trumhere, a near relative (*propinquus*) of both Eanflæd and the murdered Oswine, was its first abbot and had trained and been consecrated among the Gaels.[197] Ceolfrith, Bede's mentor, began his monastic training there before eventually moving on to Ripon.[198] Cynefrith, Ceolfrith's brother, had been in charge of Gilling but chose to withdraw to Ireland to study the scriptures and serve the Lord.[199] Gilling would have reminded Oswiu of the contention between Ionan and orthodox parties.

The two Northumbrians with the firmest and earliest relations with Rome would have been known to Oswiu. Wilfrid, as already noted, served in the household of Oswiu's Queen Eanflæd.[200] Benedict Biscop had been a thegn in Oswiu's retinue and had received land from the king before opting for a life in religion.[201] Both left Northumbria for instruction in Kent before setting off together for Rome *c.* AD 653.[202] Although each became a leading proponent for Rome, they parted ways on this trip and never cooperated again. Both Wilfrid and Benedict Biscop developed relationships with Alhfrith into which Oswiu interceded.[203]

Oswiu had three marriages, or liaisons, that produced sons who attained kingship within Northumbria. Each liaison shows Oswiu's political astuteness and his ability, and willingness, to cross the linguistic, cultural, and political boundaries

---

(1969), 186–89)) and the successes of his deacon James in the area around York (Bede, *HE* 2.20 (Colgrave and Mynors (1969), 206–07)) one could expect that Deira would have naturally inclined towards Canterbury and not towards Iona and Lindisfarne, as in the individual case of Oswine and the general case of the community at Whitby.

193 Bede, *HE* 3.14 (Colgrave and Mynors (1969), 258–61).

194 Bede, *HE* 3.6 (Colgrave and Mynors (1969), 230–31), suggested that he was in favour of a unified Northumbria under Oswald, Oswiu's brother, and said that Bernicia and Deira 'were peacefully united and became one people' (*in unam sunt pacem et uelut unum conpaginatae in populum*); see McClure (1984), 79, and Thacker (1983), 147–48.

195 Bede, *HE* 3.14 (Colgrave and Mynors (1969), 256–57).

196 Bede, *HE* 3.24 (Colgrave and Mynors (1969), 292–93).

197 Bede, *HE* 3.24 (Colgrave and Mynors (1969), 292–93).

198 As related in *Vita Ceolfridi* 2 (ed. Plummer (1896), i 388; ed. and trans. Grocock and Wood (2013), 78–81).

199 *Vita Ceolfridi* 2 (Plummer (1896), i 388; Grocock and Wood (2013), 78–81); Hunter Blair (1970), 101. One must consider that there were orthodox establishments in Ireland as options for *peregrini* such as Cynefrith.

200 See p. 91 above.

201 Bede, *Historia abbatum* 1 (Plummer (1896), i 364–65; Grocock and Wood (2013), 21–25).

202 See n. 81 above.

203 Oswiu interceded between Alhfrith and Wilfrid at the 'synod' and after it: Bede, *HE* 3.25, 3.28 (Colgrave and Mynors (1969), 294–309, 314–17). Oswiu also prevented Alhfrith from going to Rome with Benedict Biscop after the 'synod'; see p. 91.

that formed the ethnic patchwork of his expansive, and expanding, *imperium*. Oswiu's political and social acuity must be borne in mind when discussing the 'synod'.

The sequence for the first two liaisons is not clear. The *Historia Brittonum* states that Oswiu had a wife named Rhiainfellt [Rieinmelth] daughter of Royth son of Rhun (son of Urien Rheged), conceivably a great-granddaughter of Urien Rheged.[204] Rhun has been variously associated with Bishop Paulinus in the conversion of King Edwin.[205] Rhiainfellt of Rheged was the mother of Alhfrith.

At an early stage Oswiu had a relationship with a woman of the Cenél nÉogain, the product of which was his son Aldfrith *sapiens* (king of Northumbria AD 685–704).[206] This liaison suggests that Oswiu spent time in Ireland itself, probably in Inishowen, the heart of Cenél nÉogain territory in the seventh century. The rivalry between Cenél nÉogain and Cenél Conaill in that century has been documented.[207] Iona was controlled by Cenél Conaill, so Oswiu's relationships with Cenél nÉogain may have facilitated him in going against the interests of Iona at the 'synod'.[208]

Bede recognized Eanflæd, daughter of Edwin, as Oswiu's queen.[209] Eanflæd was mother of Ecgfrith (AD 670–685),[210] who succeeded his father in the Northumbrian kingship. Oswiu's marriage to Eanflæd early in his reign meant that he had two decades to experience the discrepancies in Easter traditions between Kent and Lindisfarne.[211] Oswiu did not need to be a theologian or computist to

---

204 *Historia Brittonum* 57 (Morris (1980), 36, 77). Some have suggested that this marriage helped secure the territory of Rheged for Northumbria: Jackson (1963), 71; Mayr-Harting (1991), 119. Bede, *HE* 3.4 (Colgrave and Mynors (1969), 222–23), described Bishop Ninian as an 'orthodox' Briton, trained in Rome, whose site was at Whithorn. This area along the Solway Firth may have been in the territory of Rheged.

205 *Historia Brittonum* 63 (Morris (1980), 38, 79); *Annales Cambriae* s.a. 626 (Morris (1980), 46, 86); but see Rowland (1990), 86, 92; and Koch (1997), XXXIII and n. 4. The *Historia Brittonum* equates the two identities and applies the name Rhun mab Urien to Paulinus of York: Lot (1934), 203–04. Welsh genealogies attest to King Urien Rheged having a son named Rhun: Williams (1978), 137 n. 39c. The name Paulinus occurs commonly in Welsh ecclesiastical tradition, for example, as the name of Dewi Sant's teacher: Evans (1965), 5; see other examples of Paulinus in early Welsh tradition at Howlett (2003–2004), 66–67.

206 *Mínigud Senchais Síl Chuind inso sís* (ed. O'Brien (1962), 135, 140 a37–40); Ireland (1991a). Aldfrith's Gaelic name was Flann Fína. His reputation for learning is well known: Ireland (1996), 73–76; Ireland (1999), 10–20; Ireland (2015b), 35–48.

207 Ireland (1991a), 75–76; Lacey (2006), 227–32, 278–79.

208 Gunn (2009), 38.

209 Bede, *HE* 3.15 (Colgrave and Mynors (1969), 260–61). Oswiu's marriage to Eanflæd may have involved relations with Francia as well as helping secure the ties between Bernicia and Deira: Moisl and Hamann (2002). For Eanflæd's background, see pp. 85 and 97 above.

210 Bede, *HE* 4.26 (Colgrave and Mynors (1969), 428–29), where he relates that Ecgfrith was killed in AD 685 at the age of 40 and was, thus, born *c.* AD 645 after Oswiu had married Eanflæd; Higham (2015), 88–89.

211 See p. 89 above.

appreciate the effects of the controversy. He certainly had the political acuity to grasp the advantages of a change.

In both Stephen's and Bede's accounts of the 'synod' it was the secular figure Oswiu who presided over proceedings while it was the clerics, Bishop Colmán and the priest Wilfrid, who argued their cases. Both accounts make Oswiu responsible for the decision that confirmed the outcome.[212] In the following comments I am more concerned with the dynamics of the proceedings than with the content of the arguments.

In Bede's account Oswiu began the proceedings by declaring that 'it was fitting that those who served one God should observe one rule of life and not differ in the celebration of the heavenly sacraments, seeing that they all hoped for one kingdom in heaven'.[213] This statement in itself implies that Oswiu arrived at the 'synod' intending to reach a solution that provided conformity and unified his kingdom. He ordered Colmán[214] to go first and explain his customs. When Colmán had finished Oswiu then ordered Agilberht[215] to explain the traditions that he observed. Agilberht excused himself (ostensibly for his poor command of Old English) and asked that Wilfrid be allowed to speak in his stead.[216] Wilfrid waited to receive instructions from Oswiu to speak, then he proceeded with his explanation.[217] Bede's account greatly elaborates the exchange between Colmán and Wilfrid when compared to Stephen's account.

In Bede's account Oswiu asked Colmán if Wilfrid's arguments about the words of St Peter are true,[218] to which Colmán replied that they are. Again, the king asked Colmán and Wilfrid[219] if they both agree that Peter had been presented the keys to heaven. Upon receiving their confirmation Oswiu then concluded[220] that he would not contradict Peter who holds the keys to heaven.[221] In Stephen's *Vita*

---

212 As observed by one commentator on matters of computus, 'we can safely conclude from their [Stephen's and Bede's] narratives that it was King Oswiu who decided in favour of the 'Roman' calculation of Easter'; Ohashi (2011), 138. The same conclusion is expressed by Dumville (1997), 24; Dailey (2015), 61–64.

213 Bede, *HE* 3.25 (Colgrave and Mynors (1969), 298–99): *Primusque rex Osuiu, praemissa praefatione — quod oporteret eos qui uni Deo seruirent unam uiuendi regulam tenere, nec discrepare in celebratione sacramentorum caelestium, qui unum omnes in caelis regnum expectarent.*

214 Bede, *HE* 3.25 (Colgrave and Mynors (1969), 298): *iussit primo dicere episcopum suum Colmanum.*

215 Bede, *HE* 3.25 (Colgrave and Mynors (1969), 300): *iussit rex et Agilberctum proferre.*

216 Bede, *HE* 3.25 (Colgrave and Mynors (1969), 300): *Respondit Agilberctus: 'Loquatur, obsecro, uice mea discipulus meus Uilfrid presbyter [...] et ille melius ac manifestius ipsa lingua Anglorum, quam ego per interpretem'.*

217 Bede, *HE* 3.25 (Colgrave and Mynors (1969), 300): *Tum Uilfrid, iubente rege ut diceret.*

218 Bede, *HE* 3.25 (Colgrave and Mynors (1969), 306): *dixit rex: 'Verene, Colmane'.*

219 Bede, *HE* 3.25 (Colgrave and Mynors (1969), 306): *Rursum rex [...] inquit.*

220 Bede, *HE* 3.25 (Colgrave and Mynors (1969), 306): *At ille ita conclusit.*

221 Wallace-Hadrill pointed out that Oswiu, in these proceedings, never identified Peter as the bishop of Rome but rather as the doorkeeper of heaven. This statement appears in a reprinted article: Wallace-Hadrill (1975), 83 = Wallace-Hadrill (1976), 373; and in the introduction to his historical commentary: Wallace-Hadrill (1988), XXIII. Stephen of Ripon, *VW* 10 (Colgrave (1927), 22–23),

Wilfridi, Oswiu 'smilingly' (*subridens*)[222] asked them all, 'tell me which is greater in the kingdom of heaven, Colum Cille or the Apostle Peter?'[223] Stephen had Oswiu deliberately contrast Iona and Rome in the figures of St Columba and St Peter. Máire Herbert noted that by personalising the argument in this way reconciliation would be more difficult.[224]

In both accounts Oswiu's statements are full of first-person singular pronouns, emphasizing Oswiu's personal, active involvement. At the conclusion, in Bede's account, once the king had spoken then all present signified their agreement to the conclusion of the meeting.[225] In Bede's description Oswiu was in full control and acted as 'executive in charge'. Oswiu's rôle as overseer is confirmed in the *Vita Wilfridi* when, in a response full of first-person singular forms, Oswiu replied: 'He [Peter] is the porter and keeps the keys. With him I will have no differences, nor will I agree with those who have such, nor in any single particular will I gainsay his decisions so long as I live'.[226]

In the *Vita Wilfridi* Colmán is ordered to leave Northumbria if he will not change: 'Bishop Colmán was told what he must do [...] he must retire and leave his see to be taken by another and a better man'.[227] In contrast, Bede portrayed the good works of Colmán and his monks and, although he noted Colmán's departure with those who wished to accompany him,[228] Bede said that Oswiu 'greatly loved Bishop Colmán on account of his innate prudence'.[229] In another executive order Oswiu appointed Eata abbot of Lindisfarne at Colmán's request.[230]

---

has Oswiu say of Peter in his conclusion: *Ille est hostiarius et clavicularius* ('He is the porter and keeps the keys'). For Stephen's emphasis on the apostolic authority of Peter, see Pelteret (2011).

222 Stephen of Ripon, *VW* 10 (Colgrave (1927), 22–23). For some interpretations of the significance of *subridens* in this context, see Mayr-Harting (1991), 108; Abels (1983), 10–11.

223 Stephen of Ripon, *VW* 10 (Colgrave (1927), 22–23): *Enuntiate mihi, utrum maior est Columcillae an Petrus apostolus in regno coelorum?* Note that although Colgrave translated with the Latin name Columba, both manuscripts have the Gaelicised forms *Columcillae* and *Columhcillae* (intended for 'Columbcillae'); Colgrave (1927), XIII–XV (manuscript discussions), 22 (Latin text and variant readings). See further Herbert (1988), 44–46.

224 Herbert (1988), 44.

225 Bede, *HE* 3.25 (Colgrave and Mynors (1969), 306–08): *Haec dicente rege, fauerunt adsidentes quique siue adstantes maiores una cum mediocribus.*

226 Stephen of Ripon, *VW* 10 (Colgrave (1927), 22–23): '*Ille est hostiarius et clavicularius, contra quem conluctationem controversiae non facio nec facientibus consentio et iudiciis eius in vita mea in nullo contradicam*'.

227 Stephen of Ripon, *VW* 10 (Colgrave (1927), 22–23): *Colmanus vero episcopus audiens, quid esset faciendum,* [...] *ut secederet et alii meliori sedem suam occupandam relinqueret.*

228 Bede, *HE* 3.26, 4.4 (Colgrave and Mynors (1969), 308–11, 346–47).

229 Bede, *HE* 3.26 (Colgrave and Mynors (1969), 308–09): *Multum namque eundem episcopum Colmanum rex pro insita illi prudentia diligebat.*

230 Bede, *HE* 3.26 (Colgrave and Mynors (1969), 308): *Colmanum abiturum petisse et inpetrasse a rege Osuiu.*

In the confused chronology following the 'synod', Tuda was appointed bishop,[231] but Alhfrith sent Wilfrid to Gaul for consecration.[232] Both accounts describe Wilfrid's consecration at Compiègne.[233] Neither account mentions Alhfrith again. With the permanent absence of Alhfrith, Wilfrid's loss of secular patronage best explains his delayed return to Britain.

But as Wilfrid lingered abroad, Oswiu sent Chad to Kent to be consecrated bishop of York.[234] When Chad arrived in Kent, accompanied by Oswiu's priest Eadhæd,[235] they found that Bishop Deusdedit of Canterbury (AD 655–664) had died. Therefore, Chad had to be consecrated by Bishop Wine of Wessex, who had replaced Agilberht, and by two Brittonic bishops.[236] The participation of Brittonic bishops raised questions about the orthodoxy of Chad's consecration. When Archbishop Theodore of Canterbury pointed out the irregularity of his consecration, in contrast to Wilfrid's style, Chad expressed feelings of unworthiness and offered to resign.[237] Chad was re-consecrated by Theodore as bishop of Mercia (AD 669–672).[238]

To follow up his decision at the 'synod', Oswiu and King Ecgberht of Kent (AD 664–673) consulted together and sent a priest named Wigheard († c. AD 668) to Rome to be consecrated archbishop so as to be able to consecrate other bishops throughout Britain.[239]

Their delegation sent presents to the pope and a large number of gold and silver vessels.[240] Oswiu must have borne the greatest responsibility for this action based on the wealth of the retinue sent to Rome and the response from Pope Vitalian (AD 657–672). The pope wrote only to Oswiu and did not include Ecgberht.[241] As overlord of a large *imperium* Oswiu controlled the wealth to send this rich delegation and the power to extend the pope's influence into northern Britain. Ecgberht ruled a smaller kingdom and had only recently succeeded his

---

231 Bede, *HE* 3.26 (Colgrave and Mynors (1969), 308–09).

232 Stephen of Ripon, *VW* 11 (Colgrave (1927), 22–25); Bede, *HE* 3.28 (Colgrave and Mynors (1969), 314–17).

233 Stephen of Ripon, *VW* 12 (Colgrave (1927), 24–27); Bede, *HE* 3.28 (Colgrave and Mynors (1969), 314–15).

234 See p. 93 above.

235 Bede, *HE* 3.28 (Colgrave and Mynors (1969), 316–17).

236 Bede, *HE* 3.28 (Colgrave and Mynors (1969), 316–17).

237 Bede, *HE* 4.2 (Colgrave and Mynors (1969), 334–35); Stephen of Ripon, *VW* 15 (Colgrave (1927), 32–33).

238 Bede, *HE* 4.2 (Colgrave and Mynors (1969), 334–35), said that Theodore performed Chad's re-consecration, but it is unclear exactly what was involved. Stephen of Ripon, *VW* 15 (Colgrave (1927), 32, with note on p. 162, is equally vague in his description.

239 Bede, *HE* 4.1 (Colgrave and Mynors (1969), 328–29). In the *Historia abbatum*, written after AD 716, Bede said that only Ecgberht, king of Kent, was responsible for sending Wigheard to Rome: Bede, *Historia abbatum* 3 (Plummer (1896), i 366; Grocock and Wood (2013), 26–29).

240 Bede, *HE* 4.1 (Colgrave and Mynors (1969), 328–29): *missis pariter apostolico papae donariis et aureis atque argenteis uasis non paucis.* See discussion in Plummer (1896), ii 200–01.

241 Bede, *HE* 3.29 (Colgrave and Mynors (1969), 318–19).

father Eorconberht (AD 640–664).[242] As Kirby noted, the see of Canterbury at this time would have been confined to Kent and East Anglia.[243] Bede stated that 'Oswiu, although educated by the Irish [Gaels], clearly realized that the Roman Church was both catholic and apostolic'.[244] Bede signalled Oswiu's determined attitude and his rôle in instituting change in the Anglo-Saxon church. Unfortunately, Wigheard died of plague upon reaching Rome.[245] Although plans were not carried out as intended, Oswiu's efforts produced lasting, positive results.

Vitalian wrote to Oswiu apparently to ensure the loyalty of a powerful secular ruler in the north of Britain.[246] The letter praised Oswiu for his decision at Whitby and for his efforts at converting his subjects.[247] The pope said to Oswiu:[248]

> *Benedicta igitur gens, quae talem sapientissimum et Dei cultorem promeruit habere regem, quia non solum ipse Dei cultor extitit sed etiam omnes subiectos suos meditatur die ac nocte ad fidem catholicam atque apostolicam pro suae animae redemtione conuerti.*

> That race is indeed blessed which has been found worthy to have so wise a king and one who is a worshipper of God; for you not only worship God yourself but you also labour day and night to bring about the conversion of all your subjects to the catholic and apostolic faith and so save your own soul.

Previously Pope Gregory, in a letter (*c.* AD 601), had exhorted King Æthelberht of Kent to work for the conversion of his people[249] and now Vitalian urged the same in his letter to Oswiu. Vitalian sent relics of Pope Gregory to Oswiu by AD 668.[250] They are probably our earliest recognition of Gregory's cult in Anglo-Saxon Britain.[251] The pope was aware of Oswiu's efforts to convert his *imperium*, including the East Saxons and the Mercians.[252] Vitalian stated that 'we are not at present able to find a man who is entirely suitable and fitted to be your bishop, as you request in your letter. But as soon as a fit person is found, we will

---

242 Bede, *HE* 4.1 (Colgrave and Mynors (1969), 328–29).

243 Kirby (1992), 7.

244 Bede, *HE* 3.29 (Colgrave and Mynors (1969), 318–19): *intellexerat enim ueraciter Osuiu, quamuis educatus a Scottis, quia Romana esset catholica et apostolica ecclesia.*

245 Bede, *HE* 4.1 (Colgrave and Mynors (1969), 328–29).

246 Charles-Edwards (2000), 434, argued that this letter from the pope to Oswiu has implications for control over northern Britain and the islands 'to bring his power to bear on Iona in the interests of orthodoxy'.

247 Bede, *HE* 3.29 (Colgrave and Mynors (1969), 318–23).

248 Bede, *HE* 3.29 (Colgrave and Mynors (1969), 318–19).

249 Bede, *HE* 1.32 (Colgrave and Mynors (1969), 110–15).

250 Bede, *HE* 3.29 (Colgrave and Mynors (1969), 320–21). An excerpt from Oxford, Bodleian Library, Digby 63, 59v, sent by Pope Vitalian as part of this letter, urged Oswiu not to follow Victorius; Jones (1943), 102–03.

251 It can be argued that a cult of Pope Gregory began earlier in Ireland than in Anglo-Saxon England; see Ireland (2015a), 143–47.

252 For Sigeberht and the East Saxons, see p. 100; for the Mercians, see p. 90.

send him to your land'.[253] A significant outcome of Oswiu's request was Vitalian's choice of Theodore of Tarsus as archbishop, to be accompanied by Abbot Hadrian from North Africa. These two teachers, well trained in secular and divine literature and in Latin and Greek, established the school at Canterbury upon arrival c. AD 669.[254] On his journey to Britain Theodore stayed with Agilberht, who was now bishop of Paris. Ecgberht of Kent sent an envoy to Paris to accompany Theodore across the English Channel to Britain.[255]

Vitalian had asked Hadrian to accept the archbishopric, but he excused himself on the grounds of inability. He proposed Theodore in his place and Vitalian accepted on condition that Hadrian accompany Theodore to Britain because he knew the way through Gaul.[256] Hadrian was also to 'prevent Theodore from introducing into the church over which he presided any Greek customs which might be contrary to the true faith'.[257]

Theodore delayed his departure by four months while his hair grew so that he 'might receive the tonsure in the shape of a crown' because he wore a different tonsure.[258] Note that Vitalian's concerns about Theodore paralleled those debated at the 'synod': doctrine and tonsure. Kirby stated that the post-Whitby era 'inaugurated a new phase of redirection and re-organization under his [Theodore's] sole authority'.[259] But this 'redirection and re-organization' could not have happened without Oswiu's decision at Whitby and his request from Rome for an archbishop at Canterbury.

Oswiu died after an illness in AD 670, the second year after the arrival of Theodore.[260] Oswiu had become so devoted to orthodox customs that he intended, if he recovered from his illness, to visit Rome and end his life there among the holy places.[261] He had asked Wilfrid to act as his guide and had offered

---

253 Bede, HE 3.29 (Colgrave and Mynors (1969), 320–21): *Hominem denique, inquit, docibilem et in omnibus ornatum antistitem, secundum uestrorum scriptorum tenorem,* [...] *Profecto enim dum huiusmodi apta reppertaque persona fuerit, eum intructum ad uestram dirigemus patriam.*
254 In Bischoff and Lapidge (1994), there is no mention of Oswiu's rôle in establishing the school. Aldhelm studied at Canterbury probably c. AD 670–672, but the dates are not certain; Aldhelm, *Epistula ad Hadrianum* (ed. Rudolf Ehwald in MGH Auct. ant. 15), 478; trans. Lapidge and Herren (1979), 153–54); see Lapidge and Herren (1979), 8, 31, 137–38; Bischoff and Lapidge (1994), 60–61, 173, 180–81, 249, 268–69; Yorke (2010), 173–75.
255 Bede, HE 4.1 (Colgrave and Mynors (1969), 330–31).
256 Bede, HE 4.1 (Colgrave and Mynors (1969), 329–31).
257 Bede, HE 4.1 (Colgrave and Mynors (1969), 330–31): *et ut ei doctrinae cooperator existens diligenter adtenderet, ne quid ille contrarium ueritati fidei Graecorum more in ecclesiam cui praeesset introduceret.*
258 Bede, HE 4.1 (Colgrave and Mynors (1969), 330–31): *quo in coronam tondi posset.* For discussion of Theodore's original tonsure, see Bischoff and Lapidge (1994), 65.
259 Kirby (1992), 7.
260 Bede, HE 4.5 (Colgrave and Mynors (1969), 348–49).
261 Bede, HE 4.5 (Colgrave and Mynors (1969), 348–49). See Stancliffe (1983) for the context of other Anglo-Saxon kings desiring to make pilgrimages to Rome.

him substantial financial reward.[262] Oswiu's commitment to Rome was thorough. His decision at the 'synod', and subsequent correspondence with the pope, had guaranteed the orthodoxy of the Northumbrian Church.

Conclusions

The Easter controversy had many manifestations in the early medieval Christian world. It continued in the West until Rome had established its authority over the most important date in the Christian calendar. The issue was more fraught for Britons, Picts, and Gaels, than for the Anglo-Saxons, who had long-established traditions to overturn in order to integrate them comfortably into the evolving practices of Rome.

Many Anglo-Saxon peoples were still in the process of conversion when the issues came to a head at Whitby.[263] Their adoption of the new Christian dispensation in its latest Roman manifestation was natural for a recently converted people. The newly established Anglo-Saxon church was heavily reliant on outside influences for its evolution and development. Those influences came from 1) the Continent, specifically from Rome and Francia, the latter of which included a substantial Gaelic presence, 2) a predominantly orthodox presence in Ireland, and 3) a more conservative tradition based in Iona.

Abbess Hild and her community supported the Ionan party. Hild might have been expected to support the Wilfridians because of her baptism by Paulinus. Her life in religion, however, was marked by relationships with Ionan clerics and orthodox Gaels. Her pastoral methods suggest that Hild emulated the *modus vivendi* that she learned from Lindisfarne and Iona. Her opposition to Wilfrid, which lasted to the end of her life, ensured that when Wilfrid lost his see at York in AD 678 it was filled by members from her own community. Her stance at the 'synod', and during its aftermath, argues that no Anglo-Saxon cleric can claim credit for making the Northumbrian Church orthodox.[264]

---

262 Bede, *HE* 4.5 (Colgrave and Mynors (1969), 348–49): *si ab infirmitate saluaretur, etiam Romam uenire ibique ad loca sancta uitam finire disponeret, Uilfridumque episcopum ducem sibi itineris fieri promissa non parua pecuniarum donatione rogaret*. Oswiu's intention to remunerate Wilfrid well echoes other instances of Wilfrid's preoccupations with the acquisition of material wealth in contrast to those trained in, or sympathetic to, the Ionan tradition.

263 One only need recall Oswiu's rôle in the conversion of the pagan Mercians in the AD 650s (Bede, *HE* 3.21, 3.24 (Colgrave and Mynors (1969), 278–81, 288–95)) and Wilfrid's efforts converting the pagan South Saxons in the early AD 680s (Bede, *HE* 4.13 (Colgrave and Mynors (1969), 370–77)).

264 Bede, *HE* 4.2 (Colgrave and Mynors (1969), 334–35), described Wilfrid at one point as 'the first bishop of the English race to introduce the catholic way of life to the English churches' (*primus inter episcopos qui de Anglorum gente essent catholicum uiuendi morem ecclesiis Anglorum tradere didicit*). Stephen of Ripon, *VW* 47 (Colgrave (1927), 96–99), made a similar claim for Wilfrid. Technically, Bede may be right that only non-Anglo-Saxon bishops before Wilfrid were fully 'catholic', but both Bede and Stephen are exaggerating the claim for Wilfrid's contribution.

Oswiu, educated among the Gaels, determined Northumbria's orthodoxy by his decision at the 'synod'. His cross-cultural liaisons with a Briton, a Gael, and an Anglo-Saxon queen all produced kings and highlight his political and diplomatic acuity as overlord of a large *imperium*. His foundation of Gilling foreshadowed the contrast between Ionan and orthodox traditions. Wilfrid, from his wife's household, and Benedict Biscop, from his own retinue, became prominent representatives of Roman interests by the mid-AD 650s. Pope Vitalian praised Oswiu for choosing orthodoxy and for converting many of his subjects.[265] Oswiu admired Gaelic learning as reflected in the many Anglo-Saxons who sought free education among the Gaels during his reign and in *sapientes* of Cenél nÉogain, including his own son Aldfrith. His request to the pope brought Theodore and Hadrian to Canterbury where they established their school and consolidated orthodoxy in Britain beginning with the Council of Hertford (AD 672/3).[266] He intended a pilgrimage to Rome accompanied by a well remunerated Wilfrid, but succumbed to illness before the journey began.

Once Oswiu had committed to orthodoxy, all Northumbria followed. The Anglo-Saxon region with the most dynamic cultural influence and political power in the seventh and early eighth centuries ensured the future direction of its neighbours. Orthodoxy in Northumbria had been assured nearly a decade before the birth of Bede. After Oswiu's death two sons and a grandson succeeded to the Northumbrian throne: Ecgfrith (AD 670–685),[267] Aldfrith (AD 685–704),[268] and Osred (AD 705–716). These kings maintained the connection to Rome which allowed the archiepiscopate at Canterbury under Theodore (AD 668–690) and Beorhtwald (AD 692–731) to flourish and extend its influence throughout all of Anglo-Saxon Britain. Despite their commitments to orthodoxy, both Ecgfrith and Aldfrith had contentions with Wilfrid.[269] On the other hand, Wilfrid, while

---

265 In his discussion of Bede's reform agenda Higham (2013a) did not mention Pope Vitalian's letter to King Oswiu (*HE* 3.29 (Colgrave and Mynors (1969), 318–23)) although Bede quoted extensively from it.

266 Wormald (1992), 210; Cubitt (1995), 27–29, 31–33, 62–64, 82–83, 249–50, 261–62, 298–300, 319–20.

267 Higham (2013a), 493, in the context of Bede's reform agenda, argued that Bede viewed Ecgfrith as an *exemplum* of a bad king. However, Stephen of Ripon, *VW* 17 (Colgrave (1927), 34–37), referred to Ecgfrith as a *rex christianissimus* in the context of his patronage of Wilfrid. It would seem that claims made by Wilfrid *c.* AD 678 about the geographical extent of his authority (Bede, *HE* 5.19 (Colgrave and Mynors (1969), 524–25)) were based on the territories he anticipated that Ecgfrith would eventually control under his *imperium*; Pelteret (2011), 159–60. It is clear that Wilfrid, through Ecgfrith's conquests, was gaining territories formerly in Brittonic hands; Jones (1995). Wilfrid's claims included territories and peoples who had not yet adopted orthodox practices.

268 Bede stated, in his *Epistola ad Ecgbertum* 13 (ed. Plummer (1896), i 416; Grocock and Wood (2013), 148–51), that since the death of Aldfrith Anglo-Saxon monasteries had been in decline.

269 Goffart (1988), 289, noted that Stephen of Ripon portrayed Oswiu and his descendants who occupied the Northumbrian throne rather benignly, despite the contentions that arose with Wilfrid, especially in the cases of Ecgfrith and Aldfrith; see n. 80 above.

he lived, almost certainly controlled Osred.[270] Nevertheless, the commitment of Oswiu's descendants to orthodoxy encouraged the cultural flowering associated with the Northumbrian 'Golden Age'.

Bede claimed that the Gaelic-educated Ecgberht of Ráth Máelsigi had converted Iona to orthodoxy in AD 716 and brought that community to a 'more perfect way of life'.[271] But it can also be argued, from Bede's own evidence, that Gaelic-speaking King Oswiu, baptized and educated among the Gaels, through his rôle at the 'synod' of Whitby, brought Northumbria and, by extension, the entire Anglo-Saxon Church to the benefits of orthodoxy.

---

270 Stephen of Ripon, *VW* 59 (Colgrave (1927), 128–29), said that Osred, son of Aldfrith, became the adopted son of Bishop Wilfrid: *Osred, filius Aldfrithi regis, et sancto pontifici nostro filius adoptivus factus est.*

271 Bede, *HE* 5.22 (Colgrave and Mynors (1969), 554–55): *ad perfectam uiuendi normam.*

LEOFRANC HOLFORD-STREVENS

'If you find it, give thanks'

A Problematic Chapter of Bede's De temporum ratione

▼ **ABSTRACT** Chapter 47 of Bede's *De temporum ratione* is notorious for the difficulties caused by the account of the Northumbrian mission to Rome and Bede's irony at the expense of believers in the traditional Western date of 25 March AD 29 for the Crucifixion; but it also has a bearing on his interpretation of Dionysius Exiguus' date for the Nativity. I examine the chapter as a whole and propose solutions for the problems raised.

▼ **KEYWORDS** Bede, Dionysius Exiguus, Victorius of Aquitaine; Christmas, Nativity, Passion, Crucifixion, Easter; Northumbria, Rome; paschal candles

Introduction

The forty-seventh chapter of Bede's *De temporum ratione* has attracted no little attention from scholars for its ironic treatment of the mismatch between the supposed date of the Passion and Dionysius Exiguus' Easter tables;[1] however, it also has a bearing on the presumptive date of the Nativity, which is not entirely clear in Dionysius' exposition. What is still lacking is a continuous commentary. This want I here attempt to meet.[2]

---

1 See most recently Nothaft (2012), 80–88.
2 Since Charles W. Jones's text is easily accessible, having been published in Jones (1943), 265–68, and republished in CCSL 123B, 427–33, I forbear to quote it *in extenso*. Readers are also presumed to know Faith Wallis's annotated translation; Wallis (1999).

Pre-Carolingian Latin Computus and its Regional Contexts, ed. by Immo Warntjes, Tobit Loevenich, and Dáibhí Ó Cróinín, Studia Traditionis Theologiae, 54 (Turnhout: Brepols, 2023), pp. 121–140
BREPOLS ❦ PUBLISHERS   10.1484/M.STT-EB.5.133487

The epoch of Dionysius' incarnation era

Bede begins[3] by quoting Dionysius' decision to number the years of his table from the Incarnation rather than the coming to power of the persecutor Diocletian; he leaves the reader to perceive his implied snub to Victorius in preferring the *causa*, the condition precedent, of the Passion to the Passion itself. He then continues:[4]

> *Qui in primo suo circulo quingentesimum tricesimum secundum dominicae incarnationis annum in capite ponendo, manifeste docuit secundum sui circuli annum ipsum esse, quo eiusdem sacrosanctae incarnationis mysterium coepit.*

By putting year 532 of the Incarnation first, says Bede, Dionysius clearly indicated that the second year of the cycle was that in which the Incarnation itself took place. Obviously he means that it took place in what we call AD 1, not 533, but just as the Romans said 'this is the day' of such and such an event where we say, or may say, 'this is the anniversary',[5] so Bede treats 1 and 533 as the same year. Evidently he takes it for granted that Dionysius not only understood the principle of the 532-year cycle[6] despite displaying no knowledge of it in his writings,[7] but began his first 19-year cycle in year 532 of the Incarnation on that basis and not merely because that was the year next following 247 Diocletian, which concluded the Cyrillan table still current when he wrote.[8] He also takes it for granted that Dionysius not only began his Incarnation era in the second year of the cycle, which he can easily prove from the *Argumenta paschalia*,[9] but considered the Incarnation itself to have occurred in that year; as a result, the 533rd year of the Incarnation corresponds cyclically to the first.

Dionysius treats the date of the Incarnation as an uncontroversial fact, so little in need of demonstration that he does not bother to identify the year by any of the means available; as a result, not only can it not be determined from his text whether he had in mind the consulate of Cossus Cornelius Lentulus and L. Calpurnius Piso the Augur (our 1 BC) or C. Caesar and L. Aemilius Paullus (our AD 1), but even whether he had thought about the matter at all. Moderns who hear Christmas sermons, or read journalistic articles, asserting

---

3 Bede, *De temporum ratione* 47 (Jones (1943), 265 ll. 1–9 = CCSL 123B, 427 ll. 3–11).

4 Bede, *De temporum ratione* 47 (Jones (1943), 265 ll. 9–13 = CCSL 123B, 427–28 ll. 11–15).

5 Feeney (2007), 158–59.

6 As set out in Bede, *De temporum ratione* 47 (Jones (1943), 265 ll. 13–21 = CCSL 123B, 428 ll. 15–25).

7 Not only does Dionysius make no mention of the 532-year cycle: his assertion in the *Epistola ad Petronium* that *luna XIIII* falls on Saturday, 21 March, once in 95 years (ed. Krusch (1938), 65) requires this to happen five times in 475 years instead of four times in 532. Bede, like many modern writers, passes over this point. Dionysius is no expert computist; he can explain how to find the epact and the concurrent, but not define them; on his stumbling exposition of the nineteen-year cycle see Warntjes (2013), 50–51, 66.

8 Dionysius' own explanation in his *Epistola ad Petronium* (Krusch (1938), 64).

9 Bede, *De temporum ratione* 47 (Jones (1943), 266 ll. 30–35 = CCSL 123B, 429. ll. 36–42, from *Argumentum* 5 (ed. Krusch (1938), 76)).

that Our Saviour was born as many years ago as there are currently years in the Christian era must infer, if they think about it, that the Nativity took place, or at least is being said to have taken place, on 25 December 1 BC, 532 years before AD 532,[10] so that Christ was incarnated in the year before the first of the Incarnation, a paradox incompatible with Bede's language, which clearly points to year 533 ≡ 1 mod 532. The same moderns may therefore infer that Bede, like the Chronographer of AD 354,[11] set the Nativity in the consulate of Caesar and Paullus. We shall see, however, that matters are not so simple.

The relation between lunar and solar years in the decemnovenal cycle

There follows some rather strange language:[12]

> *Quia ergo* [since paschal characteristics repeat after 532 years] *secundo anno circuli quem primum Dionysius scripsit quingentesimus tricesimus tertius ab incarnatione domini completus est annus, ipse est nimirum iuxta concursus siderum ille in quo incarnari dignatus est.*

> Since it was in the second year of Dionysius' first cycle that the 533rd year from the Lord's Incarnation was completed, that must be, according to the matching orbits of the heavenly bodies, the year in which he deigned to be incarnated.

The focal position of *secundo anno* indicates that *ipse* refers to the second cyclical year rather than year 533 from the Incarnation; moreover, in the algorithms that follow it is always the characteristics of cycle 2 that govern the operations to be performed on the year-number AD, which I hereafter call by its French name *millésime*. But if one year is completed in another, they cannot be coextensive; had Bede simply wished to say that AD 533 was cycle 2, he could simply have said *secundus annus circuli quingentesimus tricesimus tertius ab Incarnatione est.* Instead, he appears to be saying that the solar year 533 was completed, that is to say terminated, in the second lunar year of the decemnovenal cycle as set out in Dionysius' letter to Bonifacius and Bonus, which runs from 6 April to 25 March.[13]

---

10 Modern astronomers simplify their calculations by numbering this year 0, just as one of Bruckner's symphonies in D flat is known as 'die Nullte', and at Oxford the week before Full Term is called Noughth Week; but in Bede's day the concept of zero did not exist in the West.

11 Divjak and Wischmeyer (2014), ii 410.

12 Bede, *De temporum ratione* 47 (Jones (1943), 265 ll. 21–24 = CCSL 123B, 428 ll. 25–29). All translations are my own, unless otherwise stated.

13 Dionysius, *Epistola ad Bonifatium et Bonum* (ed. Krusch (1938), 85): *Anno decennouenalis circuli secundo, lunaris XVIII, ab octauo Idus Aprilis usque in octauum Kalendas Aprilis, quia common* [recte: *communis*] *est, fiunt dies CCCLIIII* ('In the second year of the nineteen-year cycle, the eighteenth of the lunar, from 6 April to 25 March, since it is a common year, comes to 354 days').

If so, he is wrong, for the structure of Dionysius' *enucleata formula* requires the lunar year to end on *luna XIIII* in the *mensis novorum* of the solar year to which its paschal characteristics apply, with the absurd consequence that Easter falls at the beginning of the next lunar year; thus the second year of Dionysius' first decemnovenal cycle began on 6 April 532 and ended on 25 March 533, but the Easter indicated by its characteristics fell on 27 March in the third cyclical year, even though 533 is the second year in the table. In other words, it was not year 533 of the Incarnation that was completed in the second year of the cycle, but the second year of the cycle that was completed in 533. It is as if Bede, not looking at the letter to Boniface and Bonus but relying on common sense, had identified the second year of the cycle as that beginning with the new moon of the *mensis novorum* next after the solar new year, hence running from 12 March 533 to 28 February 534, in which case 533 was indeed completed in it.

Bede goes on to state unequivocally that the Incarnation took place in the second year of the decemnovenal cycle (the eighteenth of the lunar), with eleven epacts, five concurrents, and *luna XIIII* on 25 March, so that had the Pasch been celebrated on a Sunday it would have fallen on 27 March, *luna XVI*;[14] these are unmistakably the characteristics of what we call AD 1, though in *De temporum ratione* Bede does not yet, as he would in *Historia ecclesiastica*, retroject this reckoning before AD 532.[15]

As already noted, Bede now proves his point from Dionysius' algorithm (*Argumentum* 5)[16] for finding the place of the year in the decemnovenal cycle (what later would be called the Golden Number). The parameter of 1 added to the *millésime* before division by 19 indicates, so he declares, that one year of the cycle had already been completed at the time of the Incarnation (*significans illo incarnato unum circuli decemnouenalis annum iam fuisse completum*). In Dionysius' scheme the first year of the cycle ran from 17 April to the next 5 April, so that the year in which according to Bede, the Incarnation took place, being cycle 2, began on 6 April 1 BC and ended on 25 March AD 1. It looks as if Bede had previously forgotten, but now remembered, the counter-intuitive structure of the cycle, which in chapter 56 he would gloss over by saying that owing to Jewish law it began in the paschal month and ended there.[17]

This passage is the first of four demonstrations from the *argumenta paschalia*;[18] they do not require much comment, since the inferences may be confirmed by simple arithmetic, but it is worth dwelling for a moment, not on the algorithm for

---

14 Bede, *De temporum ratione* 47 (Jones (1943), 265–66 ll. 25–30 = CCSL 123B, 428–29 ll. 28–36).

15 e.g., Bede, *Historia ecclesiastica* 1.4 (ed. Plummer (1896), i 16; Colgrave and Mynors (1969), 24): *Anno ab incarnatione Domini centesimo quinquagesimo sexto*.

16 See n. 9.

17 Bede, *De temporum ratione* 56 (Jones (1943), 276 ll. 4–6 = CCSL 123B, 445 ll. 5–7). That sentence must not be misconstrued as stating that the Jewish year both began and ended in Nisan, which is not and never has been true, though months are regularly counted from it and formerly some regnal years as well; see now Thiele (1983).

18 Bede, *De temporum ratione* 47 (Jones (1943), 266 ll. 30–48 = CCSL 123B, 429–30 ll. 36–58).

finding the concurrent days in itself, but on the explanation given for adding the parameter 4:[19] *quia nimirum v erant concurrentes anno quo natus est Dominus* ('of course because there were five concurrents in the year when the Lord was born'). Here Bede speaks, not of the Incarnation, but of the Nativity; he had similarly conflated them 22 years earlier, in chapter 14 of *De temporibus*,[20] where too there were five concurrents in the year of the Lord's Nativity, and in which his variation of language proves that 'year from the Incarnation', 'year of the Lord', and 'year of the Nativity' denote exactly the same thing; over a century earlier, when Victor of Tunnuna and John of Biclarum had ended their chronicles with a combined Eusebian and Dionysian dating, it was the Nativity that they spoke of.[21] At some time after Bede, churchmen would decide that the Incarnation meant not the Nativity but the Annunciation on 25 March;[22] but this had not yet happened.

The year of the Passion

Bede now moves on from Incarnation to Crucifixion. As he understood Church teaching, Christ had been crucified after a little over 33 years of life on earth:[23]

> *Habet enim, ni fallor, ecclesiae fides Dominum in carne paulo plus quam xxxiii annos usque ad suae tempora passionis vixisse.*

> For unless I am mistaken the faith of the Church has it that the Lord lived in the flesh a little more than 33 years until the time of his Passion.

---

19 Bede, *De temporum ratione* 47 (Jones (1943), 266 ll. 46–47 = CCSL 123B, 429 ll. 55–56).

20 Bede, *De temporibus* 14 (ed. Jones (1943), 301 = CCSL 123B, 598–99).

21 Victor of Tunnuna, *Chronica* (ed. Theodor Mommsen in MGH Auct. ant. 11, 206): *Colliguntur omnes anni ab Adam primo homine usque ad natiuitate domini nostri Iesu Christi secundum carnem V̄CXCIX, a natiuitate uero domini nostri Iesu Christi secundum carnem, quae facta est XLIII Augusti Octauiani Caesaris imperii anno, usque in annum Iustini primum principis Romanorum, qui Iustiniano in imperio successit, anni DLXVII* ('Taken together, all the years from Adam the first human being to the birth of Our Lord Jesus Christ according to the flesh are 5199; from the birth of Our Lord Jesus Christ according to the flesh, which took place in the 43rd year of Augustus Octavianus Caesar, to the first year of Justin, emperor of the Romans, who succeeded Justinian as ruler, 567 years'). That, since Justin II in fact succeeded in AD 565, Victor's first Nativity year is 2 BC does not affect the matter. John of Biclarum, *Chronica* (ed. Theodor Mommsen in MGH Auct. ant. 11, 220) likewise reckons: *a natiuitate domini nostri Iesu Christi usque in annum VIII Mauricii principis Romanorum anni DXCII* ('from the birth of Our Lord Jesus Christ to the eighth year of Maurice, emperor of the Romans, 592 years'); again, he is in error, for Maurice became emperor on 13 August AD 582 and the Visigothic king Reccared I, with whose fourth year John equates 8 Maurice, succeeded in the spring of AD 586.

22 Owing to the uncertainties of Dionysian chronology, this could be either 25 March AD 1 (the *stilus Florentinus* also followed in post-Conquest England down to 1751) or 25 March 1 BC (the *calculus Pisanus*).

23 Bede, *De temporum ratione* 47 (Jones (1943), 266 ll. 50–53 = CCSL 123B, 430–31 ll. 60–63).

Although until fairly recent times there was some confusion between being so many years old and being in one's so-manieth year, Bede's language seems to defy all ambiguity, since he expounds the Church's faith as being that Jesus was baptized according to Luke 3:23 when thirty years old, which had commonly been interpreted as on his thirtieth birthday, and had then preached according to St John in his Gospel and Apocalypse, corroborated by Daniel, for three and a half years.[24]

The Fourth Gospel, as is well known, seems to speak of three different Passovers that Jesus attended (John 2:13, 6:4, 11:15); but Daniel prophesies persecution for a period variously stated as 'a time and times and half a time' (Daniel 7:25, 12:7), which, even though in the respective Aramaic and Hebrew 'times' is vocalized as plural and not dual, is commonly taken to mean three and a half years; as 2300 evening and morning sacrifices, making 1150 days (Daniel 8:14); as 1290 days (Daniel 12:11); and as 1335 days (Daniel 12:12). As Porphyry saw,[25] the reference is to Antiochus IV's suppression of the Temple cult, though Christians preferred to understand the reign of Antichrist.[26] In the Apocalypse, two witnesses shall prophesy for 1260 days (Revelation 11:3); the woman clothed with the sun is fed in the wilderness for the same period (Revelation 12:6), and again for 'a time, and times, and half a time' (Revelation 12:14). Bede in his commentary[27] refers these passages to Christ's mission.

The author of Daniel presumably intended lunar years based on an observed, not calculated, calendar;[28] if nevertheless we suppose the common year to contain 354 days, three and a half years come to 1239 days, increased to 1269 or 1299 by embolism. On the other hand, from 6 January (the traditional day of Jesus' baptism) in one year to 23 April (the latest Good Friday allowed by Dionysius' tables) three years later — a period that must include one and only one leap day — there are no more than 1204 days even if we count inclusively and (contrary to Matthew 4:17) incorporate in the mission the forty days and forty nights spent in the desert. Nevertheless, as Bede's subjunctives *fuerit baptizatus* and *praedicauerit* in our passage show, he was merely repeating what he understood to be established doctrine.

Bede confirms this assertion by stating that the Roman church inscribes its paschal candles with a year of the Passion 33 lower than the Dionysian year of the incarnation; when monks from Wearmouth–Jarrow were in Rome at Christmas AD 701, in the fourteenth indiction, they saw the Passion year on the candles in

---

24 Bede, *De temporum ratione* 47 (Jones (1943), 266 ll. 53–56 = CCSL 123B, 431 ll. 64–66).

25 Porphyry, Fragment 43.W.7 (ed. von Harnack (1916), 72). To be sure, from the profanation of the Temple to its cleansing was a round three years according to 1 Maccabees 1:54, 4:52.

26 Thus Jerome, *Commentariorum in Danielem libri III* 12.11 (ed. François Glorie in CCSL 75A, 942–43).

27 Bede, *Explanatio Apocalypseos* (ed. Roger Gryson in CCSL 121A, 369–71).

28 There is no warrant for postulating the sectarian pseudo-solar calendar of 364 days used in certain circles, which would make 1274 days, let alone the Egyptian *annus uagus* of 365 days, which would make 1277½.

the Pantheon given as 688.[29] Therefore, since according to the Western tradition Christ was crucified in his 34th year, and since the first year of the Incarnation held the same place in the 532-year paschal cycle as AD 533, the Crucifixion year held the same place as 566.[30]

As has long been recognized,[31] the brethren were in Rome to collect Pope Sergius' confirmation of their house's privileges; they therefore had no business to be dallying there at Christmas AD 701 over three months after Sergius' death and burial on 8 September, instead of taking their document back to Abbot Ceolfrið as soon as it was in their hands.[32] The Christmas must therefore be that of what we call AD 700, at the beginning of the Pope's fourteenth year and in the third of the Emperor Tiberius III. This had already been seen by Whiting:[33]

> At Christmas time in the fourteenth indiction, the Christmas of the year 700 as we should reckon it, though in Bede's reckoning it was 701, certain monks from the community were in Rome, and there procured from Pope Sergius a privilege for the protection of the monastery, similar to one which Pope Agatho had granted to Benedict Biscop.[34]

His reward was to be brushed aside by Jones, who did not notice the difficulty:[35]

> The event was Christmas, A.D. 701, not 700 as Professor Whiting avers (*Bede*, p. 11); for 668 + 33 = 701 (the date on Christmas) and 668 + 34 = 702 (the date on Easter). Hence Bede thinks of *annus indictionis xiv* as of January 1, 701, despite his doctrine below (Ch. XLVIII).[36] This is another indication of how thoroughly entrenched the January 1 New Year was.

In other words, seeing that in Felix of Squillace's table the indiction XIIII (by which the brethren may have found the year identified at Rome) corresponded to AD 701 (by which they would not), he had supposed it valid the

---

29 Bede, *De temporum ratione* 47 (Jones (1943), 266–67 ll. 56–69 = CCSL 123B, 431 ll. 68–77). For the Pantheon, otherwise known as Santa Maria Rotonda, see the gloss in Berlin, Staatsbibliothek Preußischer Kulturbesitz, Phillipps 1832, 46r, published by Jones in his note on Bede, *De temporum ratione* 47 (CCSL 123B, 431 l. 76): MARIAE: *Est ibi ecclesia rotunda sanctae Mariae et ibi uiderunt illos cereos* (I thank Immo Warntjes for an image of the page).

30 Bede, *De temporum ratione* 47 (Jones (1943), 266 ll. 65–71 = CCSL 123B, 431 ll. 79–82).

31 See Plummer (1896), ii 365 on Bede, *Historia abbatum* 15.

32 Even if, as Bede does not, we associate the young Hwætberht's Roman study leave with this occasion (Bede, *Historia abbatum* 18, ed. Grocock and Wood (2013), 66, cf. 59 n. 147), that in no way authorizes us to postulate a group presence so long after the mission's purpose had been fulfilled.

33 Whiting (1935), 11–12.

34 In his n. 1, Whiting cites 'De Temp. Rat. xlvii; H.A. xv; H.A. An. xx'; the latter two are Bede's *Historia abbatum* 15 (Grocock and Wood (2013), 58) and the anonymous *Historia abbatum* 20 (ed. Plummer (1896), i 394–95).

35 Jones (1943), 381.

36 Namely, that the indiction was reckoned from 24 September; Bede, *De temporum ratione* 48 (Jones (1943), 268 ll. 17–18 = CCSL 123B, 434 ll. 20–22).

whole year through;[37] an inference that Jones might also have drawn from the algorithm in chapter 14 of *De temporibus* for finding the Incarnation year from the indiction:[38] multiply the number of completed indiction cycles by 15 and add a parameter of 12, or as he puts it 12 regulars, *quia quarta indictione secundum Dionysium Dominus natus est* ('because according to Dionysius the Lord was born in the fourth indiction'). Dionysius says no such thing, either in his first *Argumentum paschale* or anywhere else;[39] but Bede has either found it in some such source as the chronicle of Mellitus cited by Cuppo,[40] *Anno uero natiuitatis Domini indictione IIII*, or perhaps more probably worked it out for himself from the corollary: 'to find the indiction from the year of the Lord, add 3 and divide by 15'.[41] In *De temporibus* one might argue that Bede had simply applied to the whole year the indiction of 1 January, as the Romans did the names of the consuls, but in *De temporum ratione* he must, according to Jones, have supposed that it truly was in force for all twelve months of the year AD.

But perhaps we should look a little deeper. In pre-Conquest England, and generally in Benedictine houses, it became the custom, once AD dating was established, to reckon the year from the putative winter solstice on 25 December, which doubled as the day of the Nativity; that *principium anni*, in fact, was already known to the Irish author of *De ratione conputandi*.[42] If we suppose that it had become the custom in Northumbria, then what to us is 25 December 1 BC was for Bede the eighth day of the January Kalends in the year of the Incarnation, which had eleven epacts on the eleventh before the April Kalends and five concurrents on the ninth, or as we should say 22 and 24 March, not preceding but following in AD 1, but already in the fourth indiction since the previous September; this falsifies our hypothesis that Bede, like the Chronographer of AD 354, set the Nativity in the consulate of Caesar and Paullus, on the day that we call 25 December AD 1, but allows him to set it at the start (if we may lend him our language) of his AD 1 even though it is still our 1 BC, *Lentulo et Pisone coss.* While his purely computistic year begins on 1 January, when historical fact bursts in he reckons from one week earlier. Likewise, the Christmas that the brethren spent in Rome was indeed that of 700 in our terms, not still but already in the fourteenth indiction, but beginning the year 701 in Bede's understanding, and theirs too, if like Willibrord they were dating their movements by the years of the paschal table. That the *millésime* was reckoned literally *ab incarnatione Domini* no

---

37 For Felix of Squillace as the continuator of Dionysius see Cuppo (2011).

38 Bede, *De temporibus* 14 (Jones (1943), 301 ll. 1–7 = CCSL 123B, 598–99 ll. 1–8).

39 Dionysius, *Argumentum* 1 (Krusch (1938), 75).

40 Cuppo (2011), 124.

41 Dionysius, *Argumentum* 2 (Krusch (1938), 75); cf. Bede, *De temporibus* 14 (Jones (1943), 301 ll. 7–8 = CCSL 123B, 599, ll. 8–10). For Dionysius all that mattered was the *millésime* and indiction current at Eastertide.

42 *De ratione conputandi* 45 (ed. Dáibhí Ó Cróinín in Walsh and Ó Cróinín (1988), 153–54). Immo Warntjes refers me to the Irish-influenced calendar in Zürich, Zentralbibliothek, Rhen. 30, 166v–169v (Nivelles, saec. VIII[in]), which begins on that day.

more affected the conception of the year as intrinsically beginning on 1 January than in Rome before 153 BC,[43] when the consuls entered office on various other dates (from 222 BC the March Ides), or indeed in later times when 1 January was called New Year's Day even if the *millésime* did not change on it.[44] Admittedly, Bede makes no statement to this effect, which contrasts with his specification in the next chapter for the beginning and end of the indiction year; but everyone in the monastery knew on what day the *millésime* changed, whereas in the West the indiction was no more than a frill, about whose origin Bede was completely misinformed.

Nevertheless, all is still not well. The inscription seen by the brethren in Rome on Christmas Day in what we call 700 and they called 701 on the Pantheon Easter candle — which of course was that prepared for the following Easter, not the already broken-up candle of 700 — read *a passione Domini nostri Iesu Christi anni sunt dclxviii*.[45] If as Bede says the number written on the candle is always 33 lower than that in Dionysius' table, then this was indeed the candle to be displayed at Easter in AD 701; but by the same token the implied date for the Passion was AD 33, which is still the year favoured by the Roman church, yet Bede makes it AD 34. In the manner of ancient authors, he has equated 'there are 688 years', that is to say elapsed since 33, with 'this is the 688th year', current from an epoch of 34; moreover, the wording of his self-correction, *his adde xxxiii vel potius xxxiiii, ut illum ipsum quo passus est Dominus attingere possis annum* ('to these add 33, or rather 34, so that you can reach the very year in which the Lord suffered'),[46] seems to indicate a belated realization that if Christ was born 532 years before Dionysius' year 533 as reckoned from Christmas (in our reckoning 1 BC, by Nativity dating AD 1), then if he had completed 33 years of age, he had done so on what we call 24 December AD 33, and the Passover at which he had been crucified must have been that of AD 34.

But the fact remains that the inscription on the candle indicates Crucifixion in AD 33, which *ex hypothesi* would set Christ's birth in our 2 BC, or in Nativity reckoning 1 BC, in the first year of the cycle, corresponding to AD 532. And that, understood not in relation to Dionysius' era however calculated but as Eusebius' 5199th year of the world, the 42nd year of Augustus, and the third year of the 194th Olympiad, was without a doubt what the Roman church intended; it was the traditional date, reproduced even by writers who thought they were using Dionysian dates,[47] and indeed by Bede himself in chapter 66 of *De temporum ratione*, though he gives the year of the world as 3952 and misstates the Olympiad

---

43 Michels (1967), 97–99.
44 I do not know whether Whiting's unexplained expression 'in Bede's reckoning' indicates an anticipation of this proposal; he is more concerned with sanctity than with computistics.
45 Bede, *De temporum ratione* 47 (Jones (1943), 267 ll. 64–65 = CCSL 123B, 431 l. 77).
46 Bede, *De temporum ratione* 47 (Jones (1943), 267 ll. 66–68 = CCSL 123B, 431 ll. 79–81).
47 See above, n. 21.

as the 193rd through the loss, at some prior stage, of a numeral-stroke.[48] But Bede, to put it kindly, was no Scaliger, to cleanse the Augean stables of inherited chronology; having brought Tiberius to the throne in the year of the world 3989, he calls his fifteenth year, when Jesus (so he says though Luke does not) was baptized, 3981, dates the Crucifixion to 3984, and begins Caligula's reign nine years later in 3993.[49]

Bede, we may be sure, simply did not recognize the inconsistency;[50] he had not mapped Dionysius' Incarnation years onto his own world years, nor yet, as he would do six years later, made them into a chronological grid that could be extended backwards as well as forwards;[51] in contrast to the *Historia ecclesiastica*, he never specifies any Incarnation year before 532. Nevertheless, the fact remains that he ought to have stated the year, one great paschal cycle later, at which we ought to be looking in Dionysius' table as not AD 566 but 565; yet fortunately for him no damage is done to his main argument, to which establishing the date of the Passion is subordinate.

The conflict with tradition

A Western tradition from the early third century had dated the Crucifixion to 25 March AD 29, the consulate of C. Fufius Geminus and L. Rubellius Geminus, so that the Resurrection took place on the 27th;[52] but that story was completely incompatible, not only with Dionysius' tables, which in AD 34 = 566 put Easter on the 28th (and in AD 33 = 565 on 5 April), but with the Church's date for the Passion. Those who still believed in it had to be disabused; and Bede sets about doing so, having raised the stakes by imposing the Synoptic chronology that made the Crucifixion *luna quinta decima* as opposed to the Fourth Gospel's *luna quarta decima*. He bids his reader:[53]

> *Et ideo circulis beati Dionysii apertis, si quingentesimum sexagesimum sextum ab incarnatione domini contingens annum, quartam decimam lunam in eo viiii kal. Apr. quinta feria repereris, et diem paschae dominicum vi kal. Apr. luna decima septima, age Deo gratias quia quod quaerebas, sicut ipse promisit, te invenire donavit. Nam quod dominus xv luna feria sexta crucem ascenderit, et una sabbatorum, id est die dominica, resurrexerit a mortuis, nulli licet dubitare catholico ne legi, quae per agnum paschalem decima quarta die primi mensis ad*

---

48 Bede, *De temporum ratione* 66 (CCSL 123B, 495, entry 268). For the short Vulgate-based world chronology used by Bede see Mc Carthy (2010); cf. Nothaft (2012), 82.

49 Bede, *De temporum ratione* 66 (CCSL 123B, 495–96, entries 270, 273, 274, 276).

50 See Nothaft (2012), 84–85.

51 See Bede, *Historia ecclesiastica* 1.2 (Plummer (1896), i 13; Colgrave and Mynors (1969), 20): *ab Vrbe condita sescentesimo nonagesimo tertio, ante uero incarnationis Dominicae tempus sexagesimo.*

52 See Nothaft (2012), 49–56.

53 Bede, *De temporum ratione* 47 (Jones (1943), 267, ll. 71–81 = CCSL 123B, 431–32, ll. 85–97).

vesperam immolari praecipit, pariter et evangelio, quod Dominum eadem vespera tentum a Iudaeis et mane sexta feria crucifixum ac sepultum, prima sabbati resurrexisse perhibet, videatur incredulus.

And therefore, open up the blessed Dionysius' cycles, and if with your finger on Incarnation year you find *luna quarta decima* on Thursday 24 March, and Easter on 27 March, being *luna septima decima*, give thanks to God that, as he promised, he allowed you to find what he promised. For no catholic may doubt that the Lord mounted the Cross on Friday, on the 15th day of the Moon, and rose from the dead on the first day of the week, that is on Sunday, lest he appear not to believe in the Law which stipulates that the Paschal lamb be sacrificed on the 14th day of the first month in the evening, nor in the Gospel which asserts that the Lord, taken captive by the Jews on that same evening and crucified in the morning, it being Friday, and buried, rose on the first day of the week.

Many doctors of the Church, he continues, have asserted that he was crucified on 25 March and rose on the 27th; but Theophilus of Caesarea (meaning the spurious synodal *Acta*[54]) had stated that he was handed over on the 22nd and rose on the 25th.[55] This was standard Eastern doctrine, entailing Passion in either AD 31, the year favoured at Constantinople, or 42, accepted at Alexandria.[56]

The original context, however, in the *Acta* is an argument against the exclusion of 22–24 March from the lawful dates for Easter. Bede's excerpt not only begins with that protest[57] but ends by licensing celebration from 22 March to 21 April;[58] the upper limit was uncontroversial except to followers of the *latercus* (which recognized no Easter before 26 March), but the lower, which had been found unworkable in the *Supputatio Romana* and was not even that of the *latercus* (23 April),[59] is utterly out of place in Bede's exposition, where it would seem to taint the very source he was using to cast doubt on the tradition of the 27 March Resurrection. According to Jones's apparatus one scribe adjusted the lower limit to the Victorian 24 April and two others to the Dionysian 25th,[60] but unless we

---

54 *Acta Synodi Caesareae* 3 (ed. Krusch (1880), 310); treated with scorn by pseudo-Byrhtferð (ed. Hervagius (1563), ii 156 = PL 90, 493D), on whom see Contreni (forthcoming).

55 Bede, *De temporum ratione* 47 (Jones (1943), 267–68 ll. 82–94 = CCSL 123B, 432 ll. 98–110).

56 See Mosshammer (2008), 49; Nothaft (2012), 56–68; Moreton (1998) explains Bede's citation by the discrepancy between visible and computed lunar age discussed in Bede, *De temporum ratione* 43 (Jones (1943), 257–60 = CCSL 123B, 412–18), and underlying Wilfrið's false date for the eclipse of AD 664 (Mc Carthy and Breen (1997), 24–30); but even that apart, he had to undermine belief in the Western tradition.

57 Bede, *De temporum ratione* 47 (Jones (1943), 267 ll. 87–90 = CCSL 123B, 432 ll. 104–08).

58 Bede, *De temporum ratione* 47 (Jones (1943), 267–68 ll. 87–90 = CCSL 123B, 432 ll. 108–10).

59 On the *latercus* see Mc Carthy (1993), correcting Mc Carthy and Ó Cróinín (1987–1988); Blackburn and Holford-Strevens (1999), 870–75; Warntjes (2007).

60 Bede, *De temporum ratione* 47 (Jones (1943), 268 = CCSL 123B, 432–33, the latter with corrupted apparatus). Several MSS of the *Acta* (which I am in the process of re-editing) also alter the lower limit to the 24th or 25th, contrary to the context.

will suppose that a later reader, going back to the source, inserted both *et impium non est* [...] *excludatur?*[61] and *Quomodo tres dies* [...] *observari* in the copy from which our extant manuscripts are derived, we must allow that Bede failed to prune his transcription, a rare lapse in his streamlined exposition. By contrast the following quotation, from the beginning of the *Acta*,[62] that in Gaul the Resurrection was always celebrated on 25 March irrespective of *feria*,[63] reinforces the point that the historical implication (though not of course the liturgical practice) should be taken seriously; in chapter 66 Bede inclines towards the corollary of Crucifixion on the 23rd.[64]

Bede ends chapter 47 by decreeing:[65]

> *Sin vero annum qualem quaerebas in loco quam putabas invenire non poteris, vel chronographorum incuriae vel tuae potius tarditati culpam adscribe, tantum diligentissime cavens ne chronicorum tempora defensando intemerabile legis vel evangelii testimonium videaris impugnare, dicendo Dominum Salvatorem vel xv aut xvi imperii Tiberii caesaris vel xxviiii aut xxx suae aetatis sacrosanctum crucis subisse mysterium, cum euangelia manifeste significent xv anno Tiberii praecursorem domini praedicare coepisse, ipsumque mox inter alios baptizasse Iesum incipientem iam fieri quasi xxx annorum.*

> However,[66] if you can't find such a year in the place you expected it, blame either the carelessness of the chronographers or your own slow wits, but don't whatever you do accept short chronologies that put the Crucifixion in the 15th or 16th year of Tiberius or the 29th or 30th of the Saviour's age, since the gospels clearly indicate that John the Baptist began to preach in the 15th year of Tiberius and in due course baptized Jesus, who was beginning to be about thirty.

These are indeed the data in Luke's gospel, not nearly as clear as we should like; but our concern here is not with what Luke meant, but with what the chronographers thought he meant. From their assertions that Augustus, having begun his reign in our 43 BC, was emperor for 56 years, it ought to follow that Tiberius' first year was AD 14, which actually was the year in which he succeeded his adoptive father, and consequently that his 15th and 16th were AD 28 and 29 respectively,

---

61 In Bede, *De temporum ratione* 47 (Jones (1943), 267 = CCSL 123B, 432), there should be a question-mark after *excludatur*, correctly supplied by Wallis (1999), 129; so already ps-Byrhtferð (see n. 54 above).

62 *Acta Synodi Caesareae* 1 (Krusch (1880), 307).

63 Bede, *De temporum ratione* 47 (Jones (1943), 268 ll. 92–94 = CCSL 123B, 433 ll. 111–12).

64 Bede, *De temporum ratione* 66 (CCSL 123B, 464 ll. 60–64): *Vnde merito creditur, si non uerior sententia uincit, quod beatus Theophilus* [...] *scripsit, eodem X Kalendarum Aprilium die Dominum fuisse crucifixum.* Crucifixion in AM 3984 = 18 Tiberius should point in the same direction, to 23 March AD 31; but see n. 74 below.

65 Bede, *De temporum ratione* 47 (Jones (1943), 268 ll. 94–102 = CCSL 123B, 433 ll. 113–23).

66 Bede's word is *sin*, 'if on the other hand', answering *si* at l. 71 = l. 85 (see above, at n. 53); this may suggest that at least the reference to Theophilus was added in a later stage of composition.

'IF YOU FIND IT, GIVE THANKS'   133

so that in two blows Bede would knock out first Victorius' Passion year,[67] and second the traditional AD 29. Moreover, if Jesus was born in 42 Augustus, then those two years will also be his 29th and 30th years of age. Hence it may seem attractive to suppose that 'the carelessness of the chronographers' means the error of dating the Passion to 28 March AD 28 or 27 March AD 29, and 'your slow wits' means the reader's failure to perceive that those dates were contradicted by Scripture; for in order to understand why they are, you need to know the relations between regnal years, Jesus' age, and Dionysius' tables. But if so, Bede has failed his own test, having slipped from the implied Dionysian date for the Nativity to the traditional 42 Augustus; in all probability it had not occurred to him that they were not the same thing. After all, if the correlations were as perspicuous to him as they are to us, why did he not state that Victorius, by putting the two Gemini in 15 Tiberius, had betrayed tradition without attaining truth? We cannot therefore be certain that when in chapter 66 he dated the Crucifixion to 18 Tiberius he equated this with AD 31, in which the Alexandrian computus of both Theophilus and Dionysius requires Easter to fall on *luna XV*, without regard to the chronology of the historical Passion; however great Bede's intellectual powers when he could give them free rein, when confronted with what he thought were authoritative data he could but take a pruning-knife to a jungle that needed a machete.[68]

In any case, his main target was the belief, so well entrenched that he proceeds by undermining in preference to frontal assault, that Christ was crucified on the eighth day, and therefore rose on the sixth day, before the April Kalends in the consulate of the two Gemini. That was not to be found in Victorius' tables, for having placed the two Gemini a year early through following a faulty copy of his compatriot Prosper's consul-list, he had to set Easter a day later, on the fifth day before the Kalends, or 28 March.[69] Moreover, as is shown in Table 1, he and Dionysius (or rather Dionysius as retrojected by Bede) have the same Easter dates, though not the same lunes, for every year from AD 28 to the last Pasch of Tiberius' reign in AD 36, and in none of those years does either put the feast on 27 March. Nor is that in the least surprising: at Alexandria, whose computus

---

67 The equation between AP 1 and AD 28 appears to have been made in the lost Easter table whose preface, dated to AD 699, was published from Bremen, Staats- und Universitätsbibliothek, msc 0046, 38r–v (St Gall, c. AD 900) by Warntjes (2010b). At pp. 269–70 Warntjes suggests that this text and table may have led to Bede's comments, and that the abridgement of chapter 47 in Leiden, Universiteitsbibliotheek, SCA 28, 29r–v (Flavigny, c. AD 816) may have been intended to counter Victorian doctrine. Philipp Nothaft, who drew this passage to his attention, refers me to two excerpts, one partly in Irish, from the same chapter in the Annals of Tigernach (ed. Stokes (1895), 409); that Tigernach himself was responsible appears from Mc Carthy (2008), 195–96. See the Appendix below.

68 Jerome's translation of Eusebius' *Chronicon* appears to put the Crucifixion in a. Abr. 2047 = Ol. 202.3 (ed. by Rudolf Helm in GCS 47), even though Phlegon of Tralles is cited as dating a solar eclipse (supposed to be that of the Passion) to Ol. 202.4 (ed. by Felix Jacoby in *FGrH*, iib, 257 F 13). By a crude equation of Olympic with consular years, these would be AD 31 and 32 respectively.

69 See MGH Auct. ant. 9, 351.

both Dionysius and (however inaccurately) Victorius were following, 25 March, or rather 29 Phamenoth, was not the Crucifixion but the Resurrection.

Table 1. Easter calculations for AD 28–36 and 42.

(*a*) Dionysian table for AD 560–568 and 574

		1	2	3	4	5	6	7	8
B.	DLX	VIII	VIIII	IIII	VII	VI Kal. Apr.	V Kal. Apr.	XV
	DLXI	VIIII	XX	V	VIII	XVII Kal. Mai.	XV Kal. Mai.	XVI
	DLXII	X	I	VI	VIIII	II Non. Apr.	V Id. Apr.	XVIIII
	DLXIII	XI	XII	VII	X	VIIII Kal. Apr.	VIII Kal. Apr.	XV
B.	DLXIIII	XII	XXIII	II	XI	II Id. Apr.	Id. Apr.	XV
	DLXV	XIII	IIII	III	XII	Kal. Apr.	Non. Apr.	XVIII
	DLXVI	XIIII	XV	IIII	XIII	XII Kal. Apr.	V Kal. Apr.	XXI
	DLXVII	XV	XXVI	V	XIIII	V Id. Apr.	IIII Id. Apr.	XV
B.	DLXVIII	I	VI	VII	XV	IIII Kal. Apr.	Kal. Apr.	XVII

	DLXXIIII	VII	XIIII	VII	II	XI Kal. Apr.	VIII Kal. Ap.	XVII

1 AD **2** indiction **3** epact 22 Mar **4** concurrent (weekday 24 March) **5** lunar cycle **6** Easter full moon **7** Easter Sunday **8** lunar age

(*b*) Victorian table for AP 1–9 and 15

	AP	CONSULS	WEEKDAY 1 JAN	EPACT 1 JAN	EASTER SUNDAY	LUNAR AGE
B.	I	duobus Geminis cssb.	d. V f.	XVIIII	V Kal. Apr.	XVI
	II	Vicinio et Longino	d. sabbato	XXX	XV Kal. Mai.	XVII
	III	Sulpicio et Sylla	d. dominica	XI	V Id. Apr.	XX
	IIII	Prisco et Vitellio	d. II f.	XXII	VIII Kal. Apr.	XVI
B.	V	Gallo et Noniano	d. III f.	III	Id. Apr.	XVI
	VI	Gallieno et Plautiano	d. V f.	XIIII	Nonas Apr.	XVIIII
	VII	Proculo et Nigrino	d. VI f.	XXV	V Kal. Apr.	XXII
	VIII	Iuliano et Asprenate	d. sabbato	VI	IIII Id. Apr.	XVI
B.	VIIII	Publicola et Nerua	d. dominica	XVII	Kal. Apr.	XVIII

XV	Vicinio et Cornelio	d. II f.	XXIII	VIII Kal. Apr.	XVII

To be sure, anyone who, possessing a more accurate list of consuls than that of Victorius, alone available in England, worked out that there were exactly four times 84 years between the consulate of the two Gemini and that of the Emperors Valentinian and Valens, or as we should say AD 29 and 365, would have found Easter on 27 March AD 29 in the old *Supputatio Romana*, but its last known outing had been in AD 501,[70] and it had never been employed by the English. Furthermore, the lunar age in that reckoning is 19, which suits neither Bede's Synoptic 17 nor the Johannine 16.[71] Rather, the tradition that Christ was crucified on 25 March (which Bede implicitly transfers from AD 29 to 34), having existed long before the *latercus*, had outlived it on the strength of assertions in various Latin authors from Tertullian onwards, and needed refutation.

Bede returns to the topic in chapter 61, where he claims to repeat the information (*ut supra memorauimus*, referring back to chapter 47), that some put the Resurrection on the 25th, others on the 27th, and others again on the 28th.[72] These dates, he continues, have computistic consequences:

RESURRECTION DATE	YEAR OF CYCLUS DECEMNOVENALIS	CONCURRENT	LUNA XIIII
25 March	5	7	22 March
27 March	13	5	24 March[73]
28 March	2	4	25 March

The work of finding the years in question he leaves to us. For the 25th his data indicate AD 42, when even in his day no-one in the West would have supposed Tiberius still to have been emperor or Pilate still in office. For the 27th they yield AD 12,[74] which he knew perfectly well to pre-date the reign of Tiberius, but which

---

70 Holford-Strevens (2011), 11–12.

71 See Mosshammer (2008), 211. It is the *latercus* that gave the desired date and lune, for (as Daniel Mc Carthy points out in the present volume) 'nat(iuitas) d(omi)ni', inserted in Padua, Biblioteca Antoniana, I 27, 77r (Verona?, saec. X^{in}) after the 52nd year of the cycle, seems to imply Crucifixion in cycle 52 + 33 = 85 ≡ 1 mod 84, on 25 March and *luna XIIII*, but since the *latercus* began in AD 354, the year would be AD 18 (= AD 354–336), with Nativity in 16 BC. (For the suggestion that Sulpicius Severus began his table with AD 354 as the year of St Martin's baptism see Warntjes (2007), 65 n. 103).

72 Bede, *De temporum ratione* 61 (Jones (1943), 283 ll. 54–57 = CCSL 123B, 452 ll. 61–64).

73 At Bede, *De temporum ratione* 61 (Jones (1943), 283 l. 60 = CCSL 123B, 452 l. 71), for *XI* read *IX*; correctly Noviomagus (1537), LXXIIr A in the margin (VIII in text); Wallis (1999), 147.

74 In Bede, *De temporum ratione* 61 (CCSL 123B, 452) Jones offers AD 31 or 50, which as he had observed at Jones (1943), 389 have respectively 7 and 3 concurrents, and therefore cannot present

was nevertheless afterwards adopted by Abbo of Fleury and Marianus Scottus,[75] who subordinated history to computistics. Contrary to *ut supra memorauimus*, only in this chapter does he mention 28 March, which as Easter on *luna XVII* will not be found from Dionysius' tables in the strict sense of those submitted to Bishop Petronius, nor even in their continuation by Felix of Squillace; having last occurred in AD 476, it did not return till AD 723, which corresponded in the pre-tabular great paschal cycle to AD 191.[76]

Yet for all this there remains the difficulty that Dionysius' tables fail to present a 17th lune on any credible date until 1 April AD 36, which (if the Synoptic chronology were correct and the tables matched the practice of first-century Judaea) would entail one of three things: that Jesus was born later than Dionysius implied, that he was not baptized until some years after John had started preaching, or that his mission lasted beyond three or even three and a half years; Bede cannot have been willing to assert any of these propositions or even, I suggest, to believe them. Yet even without that complication he was sawing off the branch on which he sat, for what were readers who fully accepted that the tradition was twaddle — what indeed were his pupils in the monastic school — supposed to think when they saw Bede apparently dating the Crucifixion to a year, namely AD 34, in which Easter was *luna XXI* yet insisting that it must have been *luna XVII*? Faith Wallis suggests three explanations:[77] that Bede had not noticed the contrariety; that he had, but employed irony to divert attention from it;[78] or that he considered Dionysius' inaccuracy as unimportant compared with the truth of the Gospel.

Of these suggestions, the first requires Bede to have focused so 'myopically', as Wallis puts it, on the solar date of Easter AD 34 that he overlooked the lunar date even while speaking of the two in the same breath:[79]

> si [...] quartam decimam lunam in eo VIIII Kalendarum Aprilium quinta feria repereris, et diem paschae dominicum VI Kalendarum Aprilium luna decima septima.

> if you find [...] the fourteenth lune in it [sc. AD 566] on 24 March, and Easter Sunday on 27 March on the seventeenth lune.

---

the desired date. In fact, as we have seen, AD 31 offers Easter on 25 March, but as *luna XV*, which will not suit Bede's present purpose, even if as a historian he was inclined to accept it.

75 On Abbo see Verbist (2010), 35–84; on Marianus Verbist (2010), 85–146, and Nothaft (2013).

76 Again, Jones on Bede, *De temporum ratione* 61 (CCSL 123B, 452) gives AD 20 and 39, but these had respectively 1 and 7 concurrents.

77 Wallis (1999), 338.

78 Irony had already been detected by pseudo-Byrhtferð (Hervagius (1563), ii 156 = PL 90, 492D): *Ironicè dicit hoc, dum nullo modo inuenitur* ('He says this ironically, since in no way is it found'); so too Jones (1943), 389; Pillonel-Wyrsch (2004), 314. Van der Hagen (1734), 305, working from the corrupt text of Noviomagus (1537), LXVII C, in which *apertis si* had been displaced by *apertissime*, confesses to bafflement.

79 Bede, *De temporum ratione* 47 (Jones (1943), 267 ll. 71–74 = CCSL 123B, 431–32 ll. 85–89).

The best one can say is that such a mistake is no more hair-raising than the solar date itself, which in AD 566, and therefore *ex hypothesi* in AD 34, was not *VI Kalendarum Aprilium* but *V*; granted that the greatest scholars occasionally make the wildest errors, such a notion is not to be entertained without evidence.

The second and third explanations are not mutually exclusive: if Bede did observe the conflict, he might well wish to throw readers off the scent and also regard it as unimportant in the scheme of human salvation. Cicero was not the only person in human history who knew how useful a relaxation of seriousness can be in distracting an audience from a fault in the argument; such diversion (in both senses) is at least as good as shouting or abusing the plaintiff's attorney. To be sure Bede is not writing a speech to be heard once and having swayed the vote to be read afterwards as a model of rhetorical technique; but in the circumstances he had to do the best he could. Moreover, for all his interest in the subject, he could hardly have disagreed that, again to quote Wallis, 'Chronology had no bearing on salvation and the order of the Church; the Paschal *computus* most definitely did'.[80] That was the view that Wilfrið, not indeed Bede's hero, had taken when he falsified the date of the Whitby eclipse;[81] and the upholding of this computus above all else had motivated the embarrassed attempt in chapter 43 to explain why the moon sometimes appears larger than calculation would suggest.[82]

The importance of the Synoptic dating

This overriding concern also explains Bede's insistence, both in chapter 47 and in chapter 61, on the Synoptic chronology for the Crucifixion. Even without straying from the Bible, one can find texts that support the Johannine dating to 14 Nisan: if Christ is the Lamb of God (John 1:29), and our Passover sacrificed for us (1 Corinthians 5:7), then the date on which the paschal lamb was sacrificed seems more appropriate, and so far as I know it has never been regarded by Rome as contrary to the Catholic faith; indeed, it had underlain the lunar limits not only of the *latercus*, but of Hippolytus, the *Supputatio Romana*, and Victorius' Latin dates, Good Friday being construed as representing the Crucifixion on 14 Nisan and Easter Day as the Resurrection on the 16th. If that principle were applied to the Synoptic chronology, the lunar limits would have to be 17–23; in fact, however, as Ceolfrið explained to King Nechtan,[83] the legitimate dates were understood as matching the seven days of unleavened bread, from the 15th to the 21st, so that the 14th, the day of Passover proper, was divorced from the historical Crucifixion and could perfectly well fall on Holy Saturday. On the one hand, therefore, if the chronology was not to be Johannine it had to be Synoptic; on

---

80 Wallis (1999), 338.
81 See above n. 56.
82 Bede, *De temporum ratione* 43 (Jones (1943), 257–60 = CCSL 123B, 412–18).
83 Bede, *Historia ecclesiastica* 5.21 (Plummer (1896), i 335; Colgrave and Mynors (1969), 536).

the other, Synoptic chronology did not sit well with Dionysian computistics. Bede therefore had to tread carefully, and he did: despite one reference to Crucifixion on *luna XV*, following arrest the previous evening on the day of the Jewish paschal sacrifice, the main emphasis is on the days of the week, which were not in the least controversial:[84]

> *Nam quod dominus xv luna feria sexta crucem ascenderit, et una sabbatorum, id est die dominica, resurrexerit a mortuis, nulli licet dubitare catholico, ne legi, quae per agnum paschalem decima quarta die primi mensis ad vesperam immolari praecipit, pariter et evangelio, quod dominum eadem vespera tentum a iudaeis et mane sexta feria crucifixum ac sepultum, prima sabbati resurrexisse perhibet, videatur incredulus.*

> For no catholic may doubt that the Lord mounted the Cross on Friday, on the 15th day of the Moon, and rose from the dead on the first day of the week, that is on Sunday, lest he appear not to believe in the Law, which stipulates that the Paschal lamb be sacrificed on the 14th day of the first month in the evening, nor in the Gospel, which asserts that the Lord, taken captive by the Jews on that same evening and crucified in the morning, it being Friday, and buried, rose on the first day of the week.

The Synoptic chronology has thus been smuggled in by sleight of hand alongside historical fact that all parties accepted. Again, at the end of chapter 61,[85] Bede warns us not to put the Resurrection on *luna XVI*, like some people (but *ut quidam* may also mean 'like a certain person', to wit Victorius), lest we incur not only inevitable damage to our calculation but the gravest danger to the Catholic faith; that really is a case of 'argument weak, shout'.

The explanation, I suggest, is this.[86] In Victorius' table the Easter of the Passion year, namely 28 March, fell on *luna XVI*, in accordance with St John's chronology; Bede, fighting Victorius tooth and nail, accordingly had to discredit St John, not of course by name. Wilfrið, out to destroy the *latercus*, had not scrupled to argue unrighteously in a righteous cause;[87] Bede, out to destroy Victorius, had to do likewise. He rose to the occasion.[88]

---

84 Bede, *De temporum ratione* 47 (Jones (1943), 267 ll. 76–81 = CCSL 123B, 432 ll. 90–97; Wallis (1999), 128–29).

85 Bede, *De temporum ratione* 61 (Jones (1943), 283 ll. 65–68 = CCSL 123B, 452 ll. 77–81).

86 Jones (1943), 389, invokes the Cologne Prologue, which few but Bede can even have known.

87 Holford-Strevens (2010), 156.

88 Jerome, *Epistula* 49.13–14 (ed. Isidor Hilberg in CSEL 54, 368–70) defends his use of sharp debating techniques to defeat, rather than instruct, Rufinus (though even he drew the line at distorting Scripture). Sometimes a saint's got to do what a saint's got to do.

'IF YOU FIND IT, GIVE THANKS' 139

Appendix

Philipp Nothaft has kindly drawn my attention to excerpts from *De temporum ratione* 47 in the Annals of Tigernach,[89] preserved in Oxford, Bodleian Library, Rawlinson B 502 and B 488 (for convenience below called A and B respectively), in the entries for AD 33 and 34.[90] The former runs (A, 10va; B, 3ra–b):

> *K.u. Anno .xuiii. Tiberii Cessaris Iesus | Christus crucifixus est anno xxxiii. ęta|tis*
> *suę cum semesse anni. uel xxx.iiii. ut Eusebio placet | qui xiiii. luna traditus*
> *est et .u. feria, .xu. autem luna et ui. feria passus .xuiiᵃ. autem luna die dominica*
> *resurrexit .ui. uel | .uiii. kł. apł.*

Tiberii Cessaris A: Tiberi Cesaris B | xxxiii. *om. B* | ętatis suę A: etatis sue B | semesse A: semessi B | ut Eusebio placet *above the line A* | traditus — autem luna *above the line A* | est *om. B* | .u. A: quinta B | passus est B | .xuiiᵃ A: .xuii B | die dominica A: dominica die B | resurexit B

'Kalends [of January] on Thursday. In the 18th year of Tiberius Caesar Jesus Christ was crucified in the 33rd year of his life with half a year, or the 34th as Eusebius thinks. He was handed over on the 14th lune, and on a Thursday; on the 15th lune, a Friday, he suffered [death], on the 17th lune, a Sunday, he rose again, on 27 or 25 March'.

After an account of Herodes Agrippa's imprisonment, the second extract follows (A, 10va–b; B, 3rb):

> *K.ui. Hóc anno .xix. ut alii aiunt Christus crucifixus est. Madat cethri bliadna*
> *trichat beite i n-áis Christ is for .xii. kl. ap̄ | xiiii. luna pascę. Madat tri .xxx. |*
> *col·leith immorro namma is for ochtkł ap̄ in cessad | 7 for uikł ind eiserge*
> *quod a multis auctoribus constat esse uulgatum. Hic est | numerus ab initio ind*
> *óigthathchuir co cesad Crist dlxui .xu. luna. crucifixus est .ui. feria uiiikł ap̄. Prima*
> *feria resurrexit hi sexkł. ap̄ hi sechtmaid dec escai Non sic autem in ciclo Dionissi*
> *inuenies.*

Madat — pascę *om. B* | Madat — eiserge A: Madat bliadna trichad co·leith nama is for .uiii.kł ap̄ ro·bat in cesat 7 for ui. kł. an eiserghe B | constat A: costat B | initio A: inicio B | óig thathchuir A: oigh athathchuir B | cesad A: cesadh B | dlxui.xu. A: dlxui .xu. B | luna A: bl'(iadna) B | Crucifixus *with capital A* | ap̄ *om. B* | hi sexkł. A: his | ex. kł. *with line-break* B | hi sechtmaid dec escai A: i sechtmad dh̄ [= dhec] esca B | Dionissi A: di|ósi B

---

89 The passages were edited by Stokes (1895), 409; however, I have examined the MSS in person. For Tigernach's responsibility see n. 61.

90 The years are identified in the usual Irish way by the feria of 1 January as *K.u.* and *K.ui.* respectively, which objectively fit those years; but we may also extrapolate those equivalences from the explicit statement that the preceding *K.i.* is AD 30 (*Ab incarnatione quoque .xxx.*) despite inaccurate statements of the Septuagintal and (in the margin of MS A) the Bedan years of the world.

'Kalends on Friday. In this year, the 19th as others say, Christ was crucified. If there are to be 34 years in Christ's age, the paschal fourteenth lune is on 21 March; but if only 33½, the Passion is on 25 March and the Resurrection on 27 March, which is well known to have been put into circulation by many authors. This is the number from the beginning of the great cycle till Christ's Passion, 566; on the 15th lune he was crucified, on Friday 25 March. On Sunday he rose again, on 27 March, on the 17th of the moon. But you will not find it thus in Dionysius' cycle'.

Poor Tigernach was out of his depth. 'Eusebius', meaning Jerome, does not say that Jesus was 34 at the time of the Crucifixion (not even Bede does so); indeed, he could not do so, since he placed the Nativity in Ol. 194.3 and the Crucifixion 32 years later in Ol. 202.3.[91] Bede's data for the Betrayal, Crucifixion, and Resurrection are followed, absurdly, by alternative dates for the Resurrection, both impossible, for if in a common year 1 January falls on a Thursday, as indeed it did in AD 33, neither 25 nor 27 March is a Sunday; they are respectively Wednesday and Friday. Nor indeed do the dates fit even a leap year, becoming Thursday and Saturday.

Under the following year, which must be AD 34, we are told that if Christ was 34, he was crucified on 21 March, *luna XIIII*. Again, the solar date is impossible in any year beginning on a Friday, whether common or bissextile (it will be respectively Sunday or Monday), even though in AD 34 = 566 Dionysius' tables make it *luna XIIII*. On the other hand, says Tigernach, if he was only 33½, he was crucified on 25 March and rose on the 27th, which was precisely the widespread error that Bede had combated; and the year would have to have been AD 29, which Tigernach passes over with nothing but a ferial ('Kui' *A*, 'K.ᵘⁱⁱⁱ.' *B*, equal and opposite errors for *K.uii.*), as indeed he does Victorius' Passion year (*K.u.*). He now jumps back to Bede's AD 566, confusingly or rather confusèdly described as 'the number from the beginning of the great cycle till the Passion of Christ', before repeating, this time as unqualified facts, the traditional data, and adding 'But you will not find it thus in Dionysius' cycle', which at least is unquestionably true whatever he meant by 'thus' and whatever inference he intended to be drawn. Yet his wrestlings with the chronological monster prove, no less than the efforts of later computists,[92] that the problem rather evaded than addressed by Bede could still disturb.

---

91 See above, n. 68.
92 See Verbist (2010); Nothaft (2012), 103–282.

IMMO WARNTJES

A Visigothic Computus of AD 722 (Leiden, Universiteitsbibliotheek, VMI 11, 26r–27r)

▼ **ABSTRACT** Leiden, Universiteitsbibliotheek, VMI 11 contains a short text (26r–27r) overlooked by scholars of early medieval computus. This short note demonstrates its Visigothic origin and AD 722 as the year of composition. The text should be classified as a computistical formulary similar to Dionysius Exiguus' *Argumenta*, but decidedly different in content and structure. It therefore bears witness to the independence of Iberian computistics from Rome, and more direct Alexandrian/Byzantine influence. This computus was written as a guide to the problem of updating the 95-year Alexandrian Easter tables from AD 627–721 to the subsequent period AD 722–816. There is no overlap with the contemporary Irish, Frankish, or Northumbrian (Bedan) tradition. This text is our prime witness for pre-Carolingian Visigothic computus, and will be the cornerstone for any subsequent study of the Visigothic approach to early medieval time-reckoning. The note is concluded by a transcription and liberal translation.

▼ **KEYWORDS** Visigothic computus; Alexandrian Easter calculation; Isidore of Seville; Dionysius Exiguus; *Laterculus Malalianus*

Pre-Carolingian Latin Computus and its Regional Contexts, ed. by Immo Warntjes, Tobit Loevenich, and Dáibhí Ó Cróinín, Studia Traditionis Theologiae, 54 (Turnhout: Brepols, 2023), pp. 141–158
BREPOLS ❧ PUBLISHERS   10.1484/M.STT-EB.5.133488

Introduction[*]

The manuscript Leiden, Universiteitsbibliotheek, VMI 11, is well-known to early medievalists for its transmission of the *Laterculus Malalianus*, one of only two extant copies of that work (the other being Vatican, Biblioteca Apostolica Vaticana, Pal. lat. 277; Rome?, saec. VIII[mid]?).[1] In the descriptions of the codex, reference to a 'Computus of 722' is frequently made,[2] but this text has escaped the notice of scholars of early medieval computus, the science of time-reckoning, one of the three essential pillars of early medieval education (alongside grammar and exegesis). The most industrious scholar of this field of research, Alfred Cordoliani, did not study it.[3] Charles W. Jones, the editor of Bede's works on time, did not include it in his list of works earlier than or contemporary with Bede († AD 735).[4] Curiously, Arno Borst was aware of this text's existence, but did not include it among his twenty foundational *Schriften zur Komputistik im Frankenreich, 721–818*.[5]

Any Christian educational text of such an early date, before the 'Carolingian Renaissance', certainly deserves a thorough investigation. This may be even more so the case for a text on computus. This discipline only emerged in the seventh century. The first few centuries of Christianity were marked by a fierce controversy over the date of Easter, the most important feast of this religion. This controversy reached its climax in the fifth century, epitomised by the debate between the Western and the Eastern churches around the middle of that century that can be reconstructed through the letter exchange of Pope Leo I († AD 461).[6] From the sixth century onwards, the Alexandrian system slowly became the dominant method of calculating Easter, a process facilitated in the Latin West by the translation work of the monk Dionysius Exiguus. Dionysius provided a 95-year Easter table for AD 532–626, of which every fourth year needed to be recalculated in order to update it to the subsequent 95-year period. For this task,

---

[*] I gratefully acknowledge that this research was facilitated by the Irish Research Council Laureate Programme.

1 These two manuscripts are described in Stevenson (1995a), 94–113, with a brief catalogue mention of the text that interests us here on p. 112; see also her characterization of this text in Stevenson (1995b), 204 n. 2. For Vatican, Biblioteca Apostolica Vaticana, Pal. lat. 277, see now Kautz (2016), 697–705.

2 *CLA* 10, 43 (no. 1586; https://elmss.nuigalway.ie/catalogue/317); Bischoff (1998–2017), i 80; de Meyier (1955), 246.

3 See the bibliography of Cordoliani's *oeuvre* in Warntjes and Ó Cróinín (2017), 40–42.

4 CCSL 123, XIII–XIV.

5 Borst (2006). Borst took note of the Computus of AD 722 only in an unpublished manuscript on the scientific writings of Hermann of Reichenau († AD 1054); see shortly Borst and Warntjes (2023), 145 n. 80.

6 The relevant letters are edited by Krusch (1880), 245–78. For the Easter controversy during the incumbency of Leo I, see Schmid (1907), 11–29; Jones (1943), 55–61; Declercq (2000), 77–82; Mosshammer (2017), 22–25.

Dionysius supplied algorithms for the data of each column of his Easter table.[7] When the monasteries became the centres of learning after the fall of Rome, Christian scholars relied on Easter tables, letters, and formularies (collections of algorithms) in their pursuit of understanding the methods of dating Easter. In the seventh century, this knowledge was formed into a discipline, called computus, which was soon expanded to include more exegetical and cosmological questions. The first textbooks of this new discipline were produced by Irish monks[8] and then Bede, whose works of AD 703 and 725 became standard school texts during the 'Carolingian Renaissance'.[9] After the adoption of the Alexandrian/Dionysiac reckoning, production of such works (formularies, textbooks, and shorter treatises) were often connected to the task of continuing existing Easter tables. The one translated by Dionysius expired in AD 626, its continuation in AD 721. Especially this later date led to considerable scribal activity that saw the production of the so-called Munich Computus in Ireland in AD 718/719, the Visigothic-influenced Prologue of AD 721 to an Easter table of AD 721–919, and Bede's *De temporum ratione* of AD 725 in Northumbria.[10] The text under discussion should be added to that list.

As important as its early date is its origin, which is undoubtedly Visigothic (and this may have been one of the reasons why Borst did not include it among his *Schriften zur Komputistik im Frankenreich*, though he never commented on the background of this text). This becomes immediately obvious from the first sentence:

> *Era inventa est a Iulio Caesare et dicta est eo quod orbis in moeniis publicis aes inferebat tributum, quia censitio facta est ante XXX et octo annis nativitatis Christi.*

> The era was invented by Julius Caesar and it is so called because he introduced throughout the world tribute in monetary form (*aes*) for official duties, because this taxing began thirty-eight years before the year of Christ's birth.

---

7 Dionysius Exiguus' computistica are edited by Krusch (1938), 59–86. Literature on this Easter reckoning is conveniently listed in Warntjes (2010), XXXIX n. 85.

8 The three pre-Bedan Irish textbooks are, in chronological order: *Computus Einsidlensis* of c. AD 700 (Einsiedeln, Stiftsbibliothek, 321 (647), 83–125; St Gall, c. AD 874 × 892, accessible online at: https://www.e-codices.unifr.ch/de/list/one/sbe/0321; an edition by Tobit Loevenich is near completion); the Munich Computus of AD 718/719 (ed. Warntjes (2010)); *De ratione conputandi* of the AD 720s (ed. by Dáibhí Ó Cróinín in Walsh and Ó Cróinín (1988), 99–213); for the chronological order of these three texts, see especially Warntjes (2010), CXXXIII–CLII, CXCI–CCI. For pre-Carolingian Irish computistics, see the overviews in Warntjes (2011a); Warntjes (2013); Warntjes (2016).

9 Bede's computistical works are edited by Charles W. Jones (1943); and then again by him in CCSL 123, 241–642; they are translated by Faith Wallis (1999); Kendall and Wallis (2010); see most recently, MacCarron (2020).

10 For the Munich Computus and Bede's *De temporum ratione*, see nn. 8–9; the Prologue of AD 721 was edited as *Prol. Aquit.* by Borst (2006), i 329–47; for its Visigothic background, though overstated, see Warntjes (2012), 78–79; Warntjes (2020a), 510–11.

The Hispanic era, a linear timeline starting in 38 BC, was extremely popular throughout the Iberian Peninsula but not beyond, and therefore is a strong indicator for Iberian/Visigothic origin of any text.[11] Much of the information here is actually taken from Isidore of Seville's *Etymologiae*, who defines the era thus:[12]

> *Aera singulorum annorum est constituta a Caesare Augusto, quando primum censu exagitato Romanum orbem descripsit. Dicta autem aera ex eo, quod omnis orbis aes reddere professus est reipublicae.*

> The era of individual years was established by Caesar Augustus when he first delineated the Roman world by exacting tax. An era was called aera because the whole world promised to pay money (*aes*) to the republic.

The time of composition is revealed through the immediately following sentence, converting the Hispanic era to AD:

> *Nam anno presenti incurriter a* (recte *incurrunt*) *DCCLX. Ex his subtrae XXXVIII, remanent DCCXX[X]II.*

> For in the present year there are 760. From these subtract 38, 722 remain.

The script is early Carolingian minuscule, probably written at the monastery of Weissenburg around AD 800;[13] this may be the reason why the Visigothic background has been overlooked, though other Visigothic features can be detected, like the Visigothic abbreviation for per (P)[14] and the subtractive numeral XL (X^L in Visigothic script)[15] that was more commonly noted additively as XXXX in the eighth and ninth centuries.

The text itself is rather short, occupying only 2 ½ pages (Leiden, Universiteitsbibliotheek, VMI 11, 26r–27r), but beautifully structured in a symmetrical way (cf. the breakdown in Table 1). The first half of the text starts with converting the Hispanic era into AD, followed by three calendrical formulae for a) the year in the 4-year bissextile cycle; b) the 'weekday that leads the year' (i.e. the weekday of 1 January, with the bissextile day inserted on 31 December rather than the following 24 February); and c) the epact (i.e. lunar age) of 31 December, before d) providing an algorithm for calculating the Julian calendar date and lunar age of Easter Sunday. The second half also commences with an algorithm for AD, but from a different variable, the indiction; this is also followed by three calendrical formulae, here for a) the indiction; b) the year in the *cyclus lunaris*; c) the year

---

11 For the Hispanic era, see Heller (1874); Vives (1938); Neugebauer (1981); Blackburn and Holford-Strevens (1999), 767.
12 Isidore, *Etymologiae* 5.36.4 (ed. Yarza Urquiola and Andrés Santos (2013), 123; trans. Throop (2005), no pagination, here slightly altered).
13 See n. 2 and Plates 1–3 in the Appendix.
14 Leiden, Universiteitsbibliotheek, VMI 11, 26v ll. 18, 34 (Plate 2 in the Appendix); 27r, ll. 11, 16, 18, 29 (Plate 3 in the Appendix). See Lindsay (1915), 496.
15 Leiden, Universiteitsbibliotheek, VMI 11, 26v, l. 4 (Plate 2 in the Appendix); 27r, ll. 5–6, 11 (Plate 3 in the Appendix).

in the *cyclus decemnovenalis*, before d) outlining an algorithm for the second most important moveable feast after Easter, the Julian calendar date and lunar age of the beginning of Lent. The text ends with the formula *Deo gratias*.

Table 1. Structure of the Visigothic Computus of AD 722.

FIRST HALF	SECOND HALF
1. Calculation of AD from Hispanic era	6. Calculation of AD from the indiction
2. Calculation of cyclic number in 4-year bissextile cycle from AD	7. Calculation of the indiction from AD
3. Calculation of the 'weekday that leads the year' (1 January, with the bissextile day on 31 December) from AD	8. Calculation of cyclic number in the *cyclus lunaris* from AD
4. Calculation of the epact (lunar age) of 31 December from AD	9. Calculation of the cyclic number in the *cyclus decemnovenalis* from AD
5. Calculation of the Julian calendar date and lunar age of Easter Sunday from the epact of 31 December (c. 4) and the 'weekday that leads the year' (c. 3)	10. Calculation of the Julian calendar date and lunar age of the beginning of Lent from the epact of 31 December (c. 4) and, here only implicitly, the 'weekday that leads the year' (c. 3)

This discussion of content makes it obvious that this work should be classified as a formulary. This genre has a continuous history since its introduction into the Latin West by Dionysius Exiguus, which can be well traced. Calendrical algorithms often included examples calibrated to the present year of the author, which were updated by later redactors to their time of writing. Dionysius had originally translated nine algorithms, with calculations for the year AD 525.[16] His friend and collaborator Cassiodorus updated these to AD 562.[17] The corpus was added to towards the end of the sixth century, and in AD 625, anticipating the expiry of Dionysius' original table, further algorithms were invented. By AD 675, this extended corpus had grown to sixteen argumenta and had reached the insular world.[18] When Willibrord moved to Francia for his 'Frisian mission', he brought

---

16 These are *Argumenta* 1 (§§ 1 and 2), 2, 3 (§ 1), 4 (§ 1), 5, 6, 8, 9 (§ 1) and 10 in Krusch (1938), 75–77.

17 Cassiodorus' Computus of AD 562 is edited by Lehmann (1912); for this text see Neugebauer (1982); Warntjes (2010a), 67–68.

18 The development of the Dionysiac corpus of argumenta between AD 525 and 675 is analysed in Warntjes (2010a).

with him an Easter table,[19] a calendar,[20] and another extended update of the Dionysiac corpus of argumenta datable to AD 689.[21] In the eighth century, these formularies then mushroomed and turned into large miscellanies of not always connected or cohesive material, at least not to the modern eye.

It would be a mistake, however, to locate the Computus of AD 722 in this Dionysiac tradition. Only four of the ten algorithms presented here also occur among the Dionysiac corpus, and for these four the computist of AD 722's terminology (especially *cyclus solis* for *cyclus decemnovenalis* that is indicative of Visigothic texts) and also the approach are sufficiently different to posit a similar source for our text and Dionysius' *Argumenta*, rather than to assume direct dependency of the former on the latter. The remaining six algorithms are fully independent of anything found in Dionysius' computistica and provide a unique insight into the terminology, concepts, and modes of calculation of pre-Carolingian Visigothic computistics. It is another key witness in the debate of Visigothic computistics developing independently of Dionysius and Rome.

Dionysius' formulary was intrinsically linked to his Easter table, as it only provided algorithms for calculating its data. Did the Computus of AD 722 serve a similar function, only for an Easter table with columns different to Dionysius'? As mentioned above, the date of composition would certainly speak in favour of this hypothesis: Alexandrian Easter tables covered 95 years and had to be updated to the following 95-year period by re-calculating every fourth year; Cyril of Alexandria's table was calibrated to the years AD 437–531; the following update (of which Dionysius' table was only one, Isidore's another) covered the years AD 532–626, the next AD 627–721. A computistical text composed in AD 722 (especially if written very early in that year, before the beginning of Lent) would therefore coincide perfectly with the fourth update, for the years AD 722–816. More conclusively, the manuscript evidence further corroborates this theory. Rome, Biblioteca Casanatense, 641, 1r–5v (Montecassino, AD 811/812) and its copy in Montecassino, Archivio della Badia, 3, pp. 1–11 (Montecassino, AD 874×892) preserve a Visigothic computus with dating clauses for Hispanic era 848 = AD 811.[22] It includes an Easter table starting with the subsequent

---

19 Willibrord's Easter table is preserved in Paris, Bibliothèque nationale de France, Lat. 10837 (https://gallica.bnf.fr/ark:/12148/btv1b6001113z.r=10837?rk=150215;2) and was composed in four successive stages: 1) AD 684–702: 44r; this single sheet Willibrord brought from Ireland to the continent; cf. Ó Cróinín (1984); 2) AD 703–721: 40v; 3) AD 722–759: 41r–v; 4) AD 760–797: 43r–v.

20 Paris, Bibliothèque nationale de France, Lat. 10837, 34v–40r (Echternach?, saec. VIII^in; see previous note); a facsimile edition of the calendar was produced by Wilson (1918).

21 London, British Library, Cotton Caligula A XV, 73r–80r (north-eastern France?, AD 743?; available online at: http://www.bl.uk/manuscripts/FullDisplay.aspx?ref=Cotton_MS_Caligula_A_XV); see Warntjes (2011).

22 This Computus of AD 811 is printed in *Bibliotheca Casinensis seu codicum manuscriptorum qui in tabulario Casinensi asservantur*, vol. 1 part 2 = 'Florilegium Casinense' (Montecassino 1874), 57–65, the Easter table at 63–64.

year AD 812 and ending in AD 840. The columns of this table are an almost exact match with the data calculated by the computist of AD 722: common and embolismic years, bissextile year (c. 2), Hispanic era (c. 1), AD (c. 1 and 6), indiction (c. 7), *cyclus decemnovenalis* (c. 9), epact on 31 December (c. 4), epact on 22 March, 'weekday that leads the year' (c. 3), Julian calendar date of the beginning of Lent (c. 10), Julian calendar date of the Easter full moon, Julian calendar date and lunar age of Easter Sunday (c. 5). This should be sufficient proof that the Computus of AD 722 was designed to accompany an Easter table containing exactly the data described in the text; this Easter table was later slightly expanded into the table found in the Computus of AD 811 (but omitting the *cyclus lunaris*). This does not make our text of AD 722 a 'prologue' to an Easter table, in the same way as Dionysius' *Argumenta* were not a prologue, a function rather served by his *Epistola ad Petronium*; but it certainly brings it into even closer context to the Visigothic-influenced Prologue (of AD 721) to an Alexandrian Easter table of AD 722–919 (*Prol. Aquit.*).[23]

The significance of this Computus of AD 722 for the study of early medieval Iberian computistics can hardly be overstated. Charles Jones had drawn attention to the importance of the Iberian Peninsula for the transmission of late antique computistical texts that became foundational in establishing computus in the early Middle Ages,[24] but he could only point to a few items that originated there.[25] Cordoliani tried to improve on that, especially by claiming the *Computus Cottonianus* of AD 689 for the Iberian peninsula.[26] But Joan Gómez Pallarès, in the most substantial study on medieval Visigothic computus to date, proved that this text was rather linked to the insular world.[27] His study highlighted the importance of two other manuscripts for early medieval Visigothic computus: León, Archivo de la Catedral, 8 (the famous Antiphonary of León; the section in question, 20r–27r, was written in León in the late AD 1060s) and Paris, Bibliothèque nationale de France, Nouv. acq. lat. 2169 (San Sebastián de Silos, AD 1072). These preserve two closely related computistical formularies, one with dating clauses for AD 806 (León, Archivo de la Catedral, 8), the other for AD 801 and 817 (Paris, Bibliothèque nationale de France, Nouv. acq. lat. 2169). The crucial question of the Visigothic contribution to the foundational period of computus, the sixth to eighth centuries, however, remained unanswered.

A fresh perspective was provided by the introduction of the early manuscript Paris, Bibliothèque nationale de France, Lat. 609 into the debate. I came across this codex when searching for seventh-century dating clauses in computistical manuscripts,[28] and at the same time Alden Mosshammer studied it for three

---

23 For *Prol. Aquit.* see n. 10 above.
24 Jones (1943), 74–77, 105–13.
25 Jones (1943), 34–54.
26 Cordoliani (1956a); Cordoliani (1956b); Cordoliani (1958).
27 Gómez Pallarès (1999), here especially 57–62, 93–109. See also Warntjes (2011), 179–81.
28 Warntjes (2012), 77–78; see now also Warntjes, (2020a), 509–10.

previously neglected short tracts and the *Prologue* attributed to Cyril.[29] It was known to Cordoliani, but possibly only second-hand;[30] he certainly did not study it in detail. This miscellany of computistical material, written in Visigothic script in AD 812 probably north of the Pyrenees, contains principally, if not exclusively, Iberian computistica. It consists of three layers, datable to AD 812 (the time of composition), AD 745, and AD 663. Therefore, these two oldest layers are prime witnesses to the question of pre-Carolingian Iberian computus. But as with other computistical miscellanies with various datable layers, it is very difficult to disentangle the strata and confidently ascribe each item to a specific time-period.[31]

The importance of the Computus of AD 722, therefore, lies in the fact that it contains, after Paris, Bibliothèque nationale de France, Lat. 609, the second oldest collection of Visigothic calendrical *argumenta*. More importantly, it is the oldest Visigothic formulary that survives in its original form, uncontaminated by later additions from other periods and, potentially, other regions.[32] Any study of early medieval Iberian/Visigothic computus must therefore take this text as its point of departure. As mentioned above, this formulary differs fundamentally from its Dionysiac cousin in terminology (like *canonici* for *regulares*; *cyclus solaris* for *cyclus decemnovenalis*), concepts (like *feria quae ducit annum* = weekday of 1 January, with the bissextile day on 31 December; *numerus ad lunae cursum* = epact on 31 December), and modes of calculation (especially for Easter Sunday and the beginning of Lent). It can provide the basis for the formulation of Visigothic computistical characteristics (or 'symptoms' in the terminology of Bischoff's famous article on Irish exegesis[33]), which will help identify Visigothic influence in the Carolingian world and beyond. I provide below a transcription and liberal translation. A critical edition with detailed commentary will follow in a monograph on early medieval Iberian computus co-authored by Alden Mosshammer and me.[34]

---

29 Alden Mosshammer drew attention to the manuscript in Mosshammer (2013), 64–67, and described it in more detail in Mosshammer (2017), 35–36. His edition of the three mentioned tracts (*Expositio bissexti, Quo tempore initium mundi, Ratio lunae*) will be published shortly, in the monograph mentioned in n. 34.

30 Cordoliani (1956a), 695; he appears to have taken his information here from Barlow (1950), 262.

31 A full-scale study of the computistica of Paris, Bibliothèque nationale de France, Lat. 609 and its various layers will appear shortly, in the monograph mentioned in n. 34.

32 Later examples of such Visigothic formularies are: AD 981 — Karlsruhe, Badische Landesbibliothek, 442, 89r; AD 1001 — Berlin, Staatsbibliothek Preußischer Kulturbesitz, Phillipps 1833, 61r–v (now ed. by Alfred Lohr in CCCM 300, 144–46), appropriately headed *Compotus Hispanorum secundum antiquam consuetudinem Romanorum*.

33 Bischoff (1954). For a critique of Bischoff's theory, see Stancliffe (1975); Gorman (1997); Gorman (2000); Wright (2000); Ó Cróinín (2000); Ó Cróinín (2001); Stansbury (2016).

34 Mosshammer and Warntjes (forthcoming).

A VISIGOTHIC COMPUTUS OF AD 722   149

Text

<…> = additions by editor
[…] = deletions by editor
(…) = comments by editor

<1. A.> *Era inventa est a Iulio Caesare et dicta era eo quod orbis in moeniis publicis aes inferebat tributum, quia censitio facta est ante XXX et octo annis nativitatis Christi.*

<B.> *Nam anno presenti incurriter a* (recte *incurrunt*) *DCCLX. Ex his subtrae XXXVIII, remanent DCCXX[X]II.*

<2.> *Hos partire per quartam partem pro ratione bissexti: quater C, CCCC; super-sunt CCCXXII; quater <L>XXX, CCCXX; supersunt II. Non est bissextus, sed secundus annus post bissextum. Nam in hoc sollititus esto, quando per quartam partem partiendo, unus aut duo vel tres remanserint, non est bissextum; quando vero nihil remanserit, scias in ipso anno esse bissextum.*

<3.> *Item ratio fer<i>ae:*
Si vis scire qualis dies vel feria tibi annum absque errore deducat, sumptis annis ab incarnatione domini, ut puta sicut incurrunt in presenti anno DCCXXII. His adice quartam annorum, per quam bissextum requisisti, id est a DCCXXII adde C, fiunt DCCCXXII; adde LXXX, fiunt DCCCCII. Adde canonicos sex, fiunt DCCCCVIII. Hos autem partire per septimam partem: septies C, DCC; supersunt CCVIII; septies XX, CXL; supersunt LXVIII; septies VIIII, LXIII; supersunt V. Qui V I feria, II feria, III feria, IIII feria et V feria, qui deducit annum.

<4.> *Item racio lune cursi:*
Si nosse vis aepactas, id est adiectiones lunares, sume annos ab incarnatione domini, qui in eo anno occurrunt, quo conpotare volueris, sicut in presenti anno DCCXXII. Hos parti per XVIII<I> partem: decem et nobies XXX, DLXX; supersunt CL<II>; decem et nobies octoni, CLII; superat nihil. VIII habebis in eo anno ad lunae cursu<m>. Hoc scito: quando per XVIIII partem nihil remanserit, primus annus cyclus solaris (i.e. *decemnovenalis*) *et octo sunt addendi in eo anno ad lunae cursum. Quando vero unum aut duo vel amplius usque ad decem et octo, quanti remanserint super XVIIII partem, tantos multiplicabis per XI partem et ut des* (recte *addes*) *semper octo. Ut puta, si remanserint per XVIIII partem de annis Domini decem, hos multiplicabis per XI partem: undecies X, CX; his adde VIII, fiunt C<X>VIII; hos partire per XXX partem et quod remanserit, ipsi sunt ad lunae cursum*

<5.> *Item ratio pascae:*
Si nosse vis perfecte pascham inquirere, sume aepactas, id est adiectiones lunares, quae incurrunt in eo anno, quando computare volueris, sicut sunt in presenti anno in era DCCLX ad lunae cursum VIII. His VIII adsumptis conputabis cum eis ab XI

Kalendas Aprilis usque in XXIII. Et dum perveneris ad XXIII, et inquirebis feriam et lunam secundum Hebreos. Ita in quacumque die occurrerit XIIII luna inquiras. Et si ipse XXmus tertius numerus in prima feria vel II feria aut reliquos dies ebdomade incurrerit, subsequenti die dominico nostram pascham sine errore <re>pperis.

Sicut sunt, ut supra diximus, in era DCCLX ad lunae cursum VIII. His adsumptis ita computabis: XI Kalendas Aprilis, X, VIIII, VIII, VII, VI, V, IIII, III, II, Kalendas, IIII Nonas, III Nonas, II Nonas, Nonas, quod sunt XXIII. Ita computabis: in Nonas Aprilis dies XCV; pro Nonas nihil remanent ipsi XCV; septies X, LXX; superant XXV; septies terni, XXI; remanent IIII. Qui IIII V feriam, VI feriam, Sabbatum et I feriam, quod fuit reposita.

Summa XCV ad lunae cursum VIII, quod fiunt CIII; ter XXX, XC; superant XIII; ter semis, I semis; et luna XIIII. A Nonas Aprilis, que incurrunt in die dominico, usque in supervenienti alio die dominico incurrunt feriae VIII. Et a Nonas Aprilis usque in pridia Idus computabis et nostrum pascham, sicut diximus.

Simul cum luna sine errore repperies. Hoc autem sollicite custodebis, ut si XXIII aut XXV aut XXVI aut XXVIII vel XXX ad lunae cursum fuerint usque in LIII computabis, et pascha sine errore repperies. Nam et in hoc sollititus eris: si antequam ipsum numerum, qui quinquagesimum tertium inpleas, ad XIIII Kalendas Maias perveneris, supra conputandum non transeas, sed XII[II] Kalendas Apriles revertens ipsum quinquaginta tres numerum conputando per inpleas et nullum errorem incurres.

<6.> Anni dominici:

Si nosse vis quotus est annus ab incarnatione domini, computa XLVII per XVmam partem: XV XL, DC; XVes VII, CV. Adde XII, fiunt DCCXVII. Adde et indictionem anni presentis, ut puta V, fiunt DCCXXII. Ipsi sunt anni ab incarnatione domini.

<7.> Si vis scire quota est indictio in quolibet anno ab annos domini, adde III et partim totum ipsum numerum per XVmam partem, et quod remanserint, ipsa est indictio ipsius anni.

Sicut est in presenti anno: anni domini incurrunt DCCXXII. His adice III, fiunt DCCXXV. Parti per XVmam partem: quindecies XL, ·DC; quindecies VIII, CXX; superant V. Ipsa est indictio presentis anni[s].

<8.> Racio cyclus lunaris:

Si nosse vis quotus est cyclus lunaris, qui decem et nobennali circulo continetur, sume annos ab incarnatione Domini, qui in eo anno, quo conputare volueris, incurrunt. His subtrae duo[, fiunt DCCXX]. Parti per XVIIII partem. Et quod remanserit, ipse est cyclus lunaris.

Sicuti est in presenti anno: anni domini incurrunt, sicut supra diximus, DCCXXII. His subtrae duo, fiunt DCCXX. Parti per XVIIII partem: decem et nobies XXX, DLXX; superant CL; decem et nobies septem, CXXXIII; superant decem VII; septimus dies (recte decimus) est cyclus lunaris in presenti anno.

<9.> *Si nosse vis quotus est cyclus solaris* (i.e. *decemnovenalis*) *ad* (recte *ab*) *annos domini, adice unum in anno, quando volueris, et parti per XVIIIImam partem, et quod remanserit, ipse est cyclus solaris* (i.e. *decemnovenalis*).
Sicuti est in presenti anno: anni domini, ut iam dictum est, incurrunt DCCXXII. His adice unum, fiunt DCCXXIII. Hos partire per XVIIIImam partem: XVIIIIes XXX, DLXX; superant CLIII; decem et novies VIII, CLII; superat unus; ipse est cyclus solaris (i.e. *decemnovenalis*). *[LX]*

<10.> *Ut scias inicium quadragesimae sine errore invenire, computa Kalendae Februariae, in quo die occurrunt, et adsume lunae cursum, qui currunt in ipso anno, in manibus. Et conputabis cum eis de illo die, in quo Kalendae Februariae fuerit, per ferias usquedum supra XX<X> numerum dies tibi dominicus incurrat* (corr. from *incurrunt*). *Et dum perveneris supra XXX ad diem dominicum iterum computabis. De ipsis Kalendis Febroariis per quotas usque ad ipsum numerum per quem ferias conputasti, et compotato ibi die dominico inicium quadragesimae computando ita sine errore celebrabis. Hoc tantum sollicitus esto, ut XXV aut XXVI vel XXVIII sive XXX ad lunae cursum occurrerint, non querebis diem dominicum super XXX, sed super LX compotando primum per ferias et postea per quotos, et ita sine errore initium quadragesimae invenies.*

Deo gratias.

Translation

(…) = additions or explanations

1. A. (Definition of the *era*:)
The era was invented by Julius Caesar and it is so called because he introduced throughout the world tribute in monetary form (*aes*) for official duties, because this taxing began 38 years before the year of Christ's birth.

B. (Relation between *era* and AD:)
For in the present year there are 760. From these subtract 38, 722 remain.

2. (Determining bissextile years:)
These divide by 4 for the calculation of the bissextile year: 4 × 100 = 400; 322 remain; 4 × 80 = 320; 2 remain. It is not a bissextile year, but the second year after the *bissextus*. For should it happen in this year, after division by 4, that 1 or 2 or 3 remain, it is not bissextile; if, however, nothing remains, you will know that a *bissextus* is in this very year.

3. The calculation of the weekday (that leads the year):

If you want to know, which day or rather weekday leads the year for you without mistake, add up the years from the incarnation of the Lord, as there are, e.g., 722 in the present year. To these add the fourth part of these years, through which you have found the *bissextus* (i.e. the 180 of 2), i.e. to 722 add 100, which makes 822; add 80, which makes 902. Add the standard parameter (*canonici*) 6, which makes 908. These divide by 7: 7 × 100 = 700; 208 remain; 7 × 20 = 140; 68 remain; 7 × 9 = 63; 5 remain. These 5 are Sunday, Monday, Tuesday, Wednesday, and Thursday, which leads the year.

4. The calculation of the course of the moon (i.e. the epacts of 31 December):

If you want to know the epacts, i.e. the lunar additions, sum up the years from the incarnation of the Lord, which occur in the year that you intend to analyse, like 722 in the present year. These divide by 19: 19 × 30 = 570; 152 remain; 19 × 8 = 152; nothing remains. You will have 8 as epact of 31 December (*ad lunae cursum*) in this year. Know this: if nothing remains after division by 19, it is the first year of the *cyclus decemnovenalis* and 8 is the epact of 31 December in this year. If, however, 1 or 2 or more up to 18, however many remain after division by 19, thus many you will multiply by 11 and always add to 8. For example, should 10 remain after dividing the year of the Lord by 19, you will multiply these by 11: 11 × 10 = 110; to these add 8, which make 118; these divide by 30 and what remains, that is the epact of 31 December.

5. The calculation of Easter:

If you want to know how to perfectly find Easter, sum up the epacts, i.e. the lunar additions, which occur in the year you want to analyse, like epact 8 on 31 December in the present year, era 760. After these 8 are summed up, add to these 8 the days from 22 March until you reach a sum of 23. And when you arrive at 23, you will find the weekday and the moon according to the Hebrews (i.e. the Easter full moon). Like this you should find on whatever weekday the Easter full moon falls. And if the 23rd number occurs on Sunday or Monday or the remaining weekdays, you will find our Easter, without mistake, on the following Sunday.

Like there is epact 8 on 31 December in era 760, as we said above. After these have been summed up, you will calculate in the following way: 22, 23, 24, 25, 26, 27, 28, 29, 30, 31 March, 1, 2, 3, 4, 5 April, which are 23 (in total, i.e. 8 + these 15 days). (The weekday) you will calculate like this: On 5 April, there are 95 days (from 1 January, inclusively); for 5 April, nothing of these 95 days remains (i.e. the count is inclusive); 7 × 10 = 70; 25 remain; 7 × 3 = 21; 4 remain. These 4 are Thursday, Friday, Saturday, Sunday (the count starts with Thursday because this is the weekday of 1 January in this year AD 722), which is restored (as the weekday of 5 April).

Add 95 to the epact 8 of 31 December, which makes 103; 3 × 30 = 90; 13 remain; 3 × ½ = 1 ½; thus it is *luna* 14. From 5 April, which falls on a Sunday, to the following Sunday, there are 8 days (counted inclusively). And you will count from 5 April to 12 April, our Easter, like we said.

Like this you will find (Easter) without mistake for all epacts. But this you will need to watch carefully: if the epact of 31 December is 23 or 25 or 26 or 28 or 30, you will have to count up to 53, and you will find Easter without mistake. In this you will have to be careful: If you reach 18 April through that very number, which you fill up to 53, through the above computation, you will not transgress this, but you will fill this number 53 in the computation by reverting to 21 March and you will encounter no problem (this is the case for epact 23, for which the Easter full moon falls on 21 March, and therefore this case cannot be calculated with the 23- or the 53-algorithm, which both start the count of days from 22 March).

6. The lordly years (i.e. AD):
If you want to know the how-manieth year it is from the incarnation of the Lord, multiply 47 by 15: 15 × 40 = 600; 15 × 7 = 105. Add 12, which makes 717. Add the indiction of the present year, e.g. 5, and this makes 722. These are the years form the incarnation of the Lord.

7. (The indiction:)
If you want to know the indiction in any given year from the years of the Lord, add 3 and divide the sum by 15; and the remainder is the indiction of said year.
As for the present year: There are 722 years of the Lord. To these add 3, which makes 725. Divide by 15: 15 × 40 = 600; 15 × 8 = 120; 5 remain. This is the indiction of the present year.

8. The calculation of the *cyclus lunaris*:
If you want to know the year of the *cyclus lunaris*, which is contained in the cycle of 19 years, add up the years from the incarnation of the Lord that occur in the very year you want to analyse. From these subtract 2. Divide by 19. What remains, that is the year of the *cyclus lunaris*.
As for the present year: There are 722 years of the Lord, as we said above. From these subtract 2, which makes 720. Divide by 19: 19 × 30 = 570; 150 remain; 19 × 7 = 133; 17 remain. The 17th is the year of the *cyclus lunaris* in the present year.

9. (The *cyclus decemnovenalis:*)
If you want to know the year of the *cyclus decemnovenalis* (here called 'solar cycle') from the years of the Lord, add 1 to the year you are interested in, and divide by 19, and what remains is the year of the *cyclus decemnovenalis*.
As for the present year: There are 722 years of the Lord, as already mentioned. To these add 1, which makes 723. These divide by 19: 19 × 30 = 570; 153 remain; 19 × 8 = 152; 1 remains; this is the year in the *cyclus decemnovenalis*.

10. (The calculation of the beginning of Lent:)

As you should know how to find the beginning of Lent without mistake, calculate the weekday of 1 February and sum up in your hands the epact of 31 December of the year in question. And you will count with the epact of 31 December in hand from 1 February and its weekday through the weekdays to when a Sunday occurs beyond the number 30. And while you move beyond 30, you will again count to a Sunday. And once you have counted from 1 February to said number (30) through the weekdays, wherever you locate a Sunday there, you will celebrate the beginning of Lent without mistake. Only this you will need to watch carefully: if the epact of 31 December is 25 or 26 or 28 or 30, you will not search for a Sunday above the number 30, but above the number 60 counting through the weekdays to the first (i.e. Sunday), and thus you will find the beginning of Lent without mistake.

Thanks be to God.

Facsimile

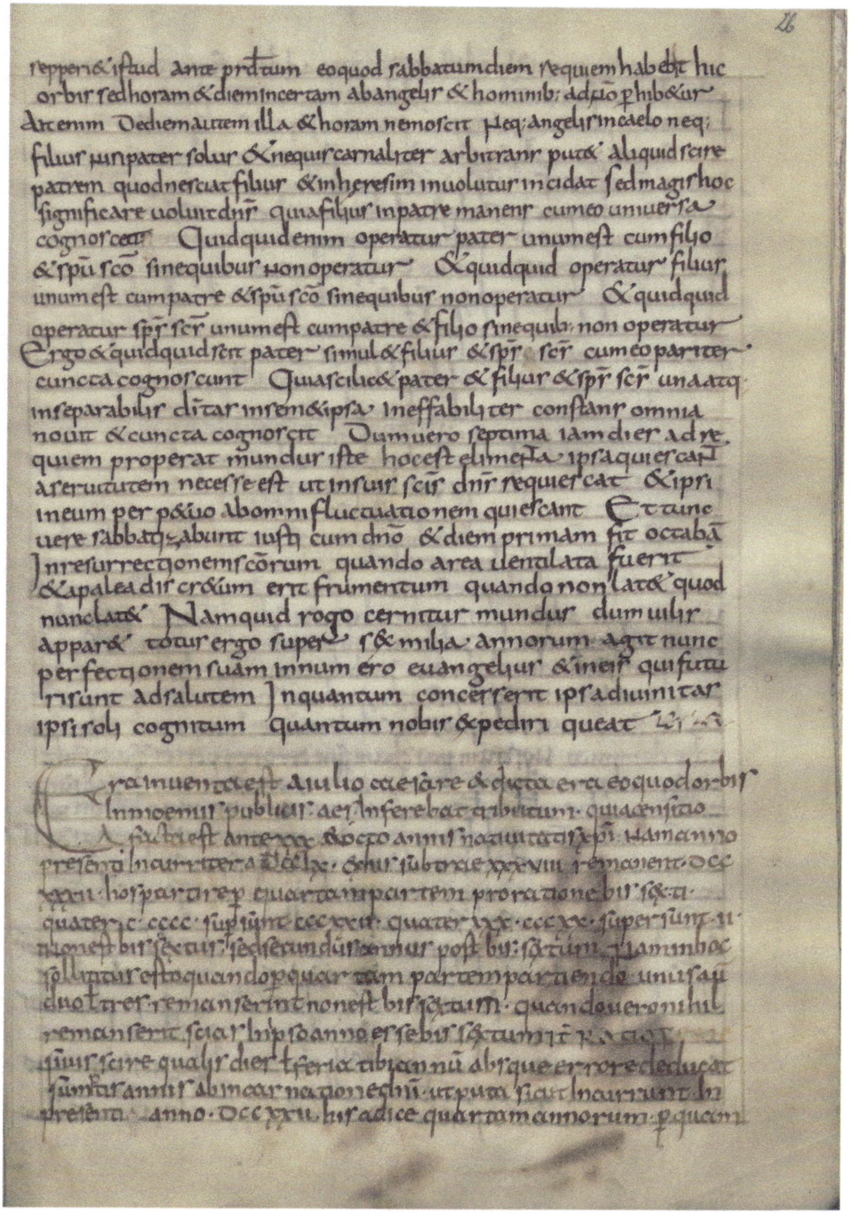

Plate 1. Leiden, Universiteitsbibliotheek, VMI 11, 26r.

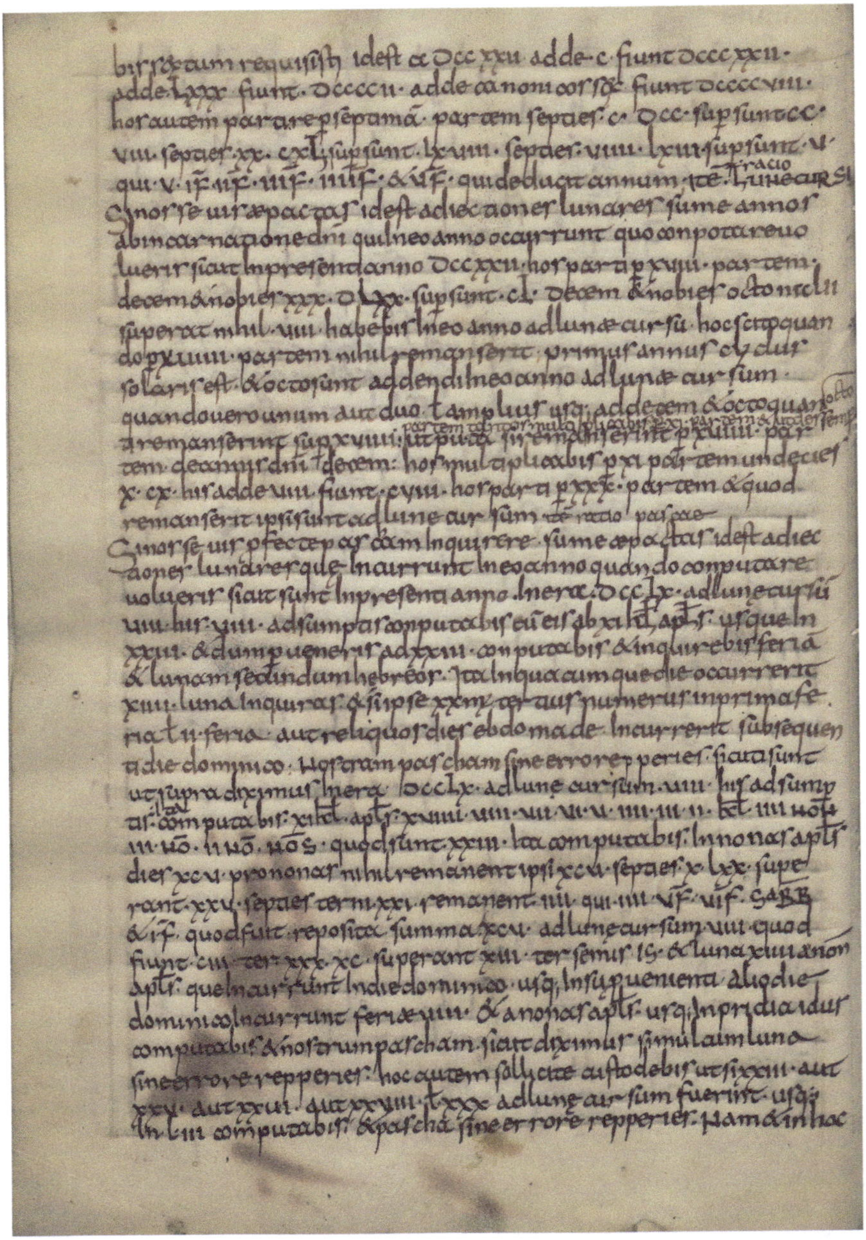

Plate 2. Leiden, Universiteitsbibliotheek, VMI 11, 26v.

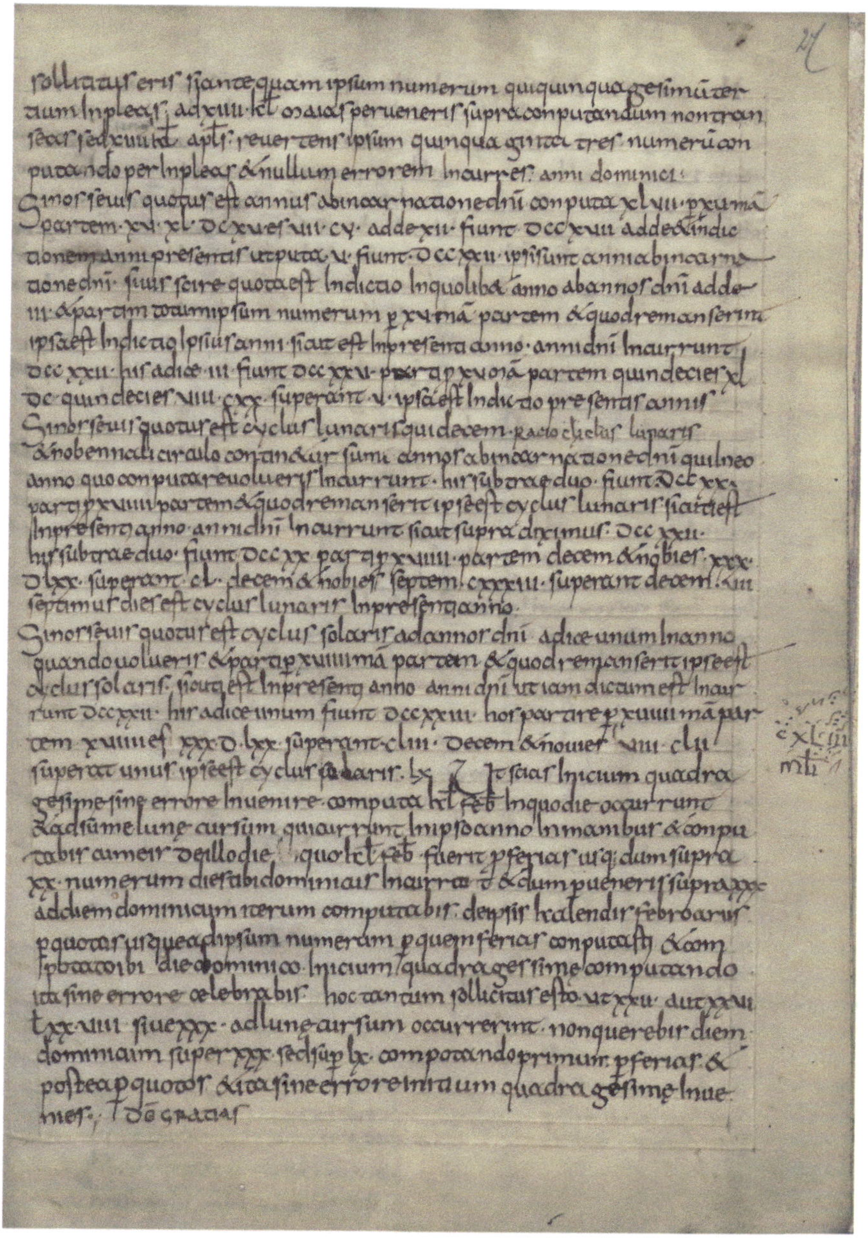

Plate 3. Leiden, Universiteitsbibliotheek, VMI 11, 27r.

DAVID HOWLETT

Irish Computistical Texts of the Seventh Century

Three Dating Passages

▼ **ABSTRACT** The essay considers six means by which two computists fixed the texts of three passages that date their work, supplying the foundation upon which literary compositions of hagiographers and poets were based as deeply as on the grammatical, syntactical, and rhetorical studies of the *triuium*.

▼ **KEYWORDS** Chiastic and parallel arrangement of diction, *clausulae*, *cursus*, arrangement *per cola et commata*, composition by calendrical phenomena, fixed interval, ratio, gematria, modular composition; error detection program, error correction program; *latercus*, *Liber Anatolii*, *De ratione paschali*, *Computus Oxoniensis* of AD 658, Munich Computus of AD 689, Sirmond Computus of AD 699.

Introduction

In recent years Immo Warntjes has drawn attention to two important Irish computistical texts: the Munich Computus with two passages dating to AD 689[1] and a prologue to the Easter Table of Victorius of Aquitaine, Bremen, Staats- und Universitätsbibliothek, msc 0046, composed in a Hiberno-Latin milieu in AD 699 and copied at St Gall about AD 900.[2] Here we shall consider six means by which these authors fixed and dated their compositions: chiastic arrangement of diction, incorporation of calendrical phenomena, composition by fixed interval, by ratio, by gematria, and modular composition. The first phenomenon they might have

---

1 Lapidge and Sharpe (1985), 702–04 (no. 336); Ó Corráin (2017), 692–94 (no. 551). Munich Computus 41, 62 (ed. Warntjes (2010), 140–41, 278–79).
2 Warntjes (2010b).

Pre-Carolingian Latin Computus and its Regional Contexts, ed. by Immo Warntjes, Tobit Loevenich, and Dáibhí Ó Cróinín, Studia Traditionis Theologiae, 54 (Turnhout: Brepols, 2023), pp. 159–176
BREPOLS ❦ PUBLISHERS   10.1484/M.STT-EB.5.133489

DAVID HOWLETT

learned from the Hebrew Old Testament and the Greek New Testament mediated through Jerome's *Biblia Vulgata*.[3] The second, third, and sixth they might have learned from the Late Latin translation of the Greek *Liber Anatolii De ratione paschali* by Anatolius bishop of Laodicea († AD 283).[4] The fourth and fifth they might have learned from any of four Hiberno-Latin computistic texts of the sixth and seventh centuries (*Disputatio Chori et Praetextati*, the note about Mo-Sinu maccu Min learning computus at Bangor, *Cummiani Epistola de controversia paschali*, *Computus Oxoniensis*)[5] or from any of more than twenty Cambro- and Hiberno-Latin literary texts from the fifth, sixth, and seventh centuries.[6]

The Munich Computus' first passage

Here follows text and translation of the first of the dating passages from the Munich Computus as presented in the edition:[7]

> *Annus plenus de bissextis in mille CCCCtisLX continetur. Bissexti totius libri Victorii CXXXIII. Ab initio mundi IIII anni de bissextis pleni sunt usque in preṣentem annum sub consulibus Bero et Bardoa.*

> A year full of bissextile days' is contained in 1460 (solar) years (365 × 4 = 1460 years). The bissextile days of the entire Victorian cycle (amount to) 133 (532/4 = 133 bissextile days). Four 'years full of bissextile days' (i.e. 4 × 1460 = 5840 years) have passed from the beginning of the world to the present year under the consuls Berus and Bardoa (i.e. AM 5889).

Let us restore the *e-caudata* of *preṣentem* to the Classical diphthong *ae*, write all numerals as words, arrange the text *per cola et commata* ('by clauses and phrases'), and mark rhythms of the *clausulae* with macrons and breves and rhythms of the *cursus* with acute and grave accents.[8]

---

3 Howlett (1995), 1–54; Howlett (1997), 1–100.

4 Anatolius, *De ratione paschali* is ed. by Mc Carthy and Breen (2003); for the phenomena mentioned in this text see Howlett (2008). For evidence that both *latercus* and *De ratione paschali* had arrived in Ireland between AD 410 and 425 see Mc Carthy (1993); Mc Carthy (2011).

5 Howlett (2010a), 266–79; the *Disputatio Chori et Praetextati* is now ed. by Holford-Strevens (2019).

6 Howlett (1995), 56–116, 138–213, 243–53; Howlett (1998a), 1–68; Howlett (2010a), 279–303; Howlett (forthcoming a); Howlett (forthcoming b).

7 Munich Computus 41 (Warntjes (2010), 140).

8 For accounts of composition *per cola et commata* and rhythmic composition in insular Latin see Howlett (1995), 21–29; Howlett (1997), 22–31; Howlett (1997a).

Annus plenus de bissextis in mille quadringentis sexaginta continetur	9	23	61
Bissexti totius libri Victorii centum triginta tres	7	18	45
Ab initio mundi quatuor anni de bissextis pleni sunt	9	19	44
usque in praesentem annum sub consulibus Bero et Bardoa	9	19	47
	34	79	197

3 sentences, 34 words, 79 syllables, 197 letters, 230 letters and spaces. Orthography, grammar, syntax, and rhythm are faultless.

Calendrical phenomena

From | *Bissexti totius libri Victorii* 2 to *usque in praesentem annum* | 3 there are 130 letters and spaces between words, coincident with the 'present year', the 130th of the Victorian cycle.

From *Annus plenus* | 1 to *usque in praesentem annum* | 3 there are 189 letters and spaces between words, the last two numbers coincident with the year AD 689.

Composition by fixed interval

There are 6 syllables before *bis|sextis* 1. The 6th word after *bissextis* | 1 is *bissexti* 2. Between *bissexti* | 2 and | *bissextis* 3 there are 12 words, and | *bissextis* 3 is the 12th word from the end.

There are 100 letters and spaces before | *centum* 2.

Composition by ratio[9]

The 34 words divide by *epitritus* or sesquitertian ratio 4:3 at 19 and 15, at *triginta* | *tres* 2.

The 14 words from | *quadringentis* 1 to *quatuor* | 2 divide by sesquitertian ratio 4:3 at 8 and 6, at | *triginta tres* 2.

Composition by gematria[10]

From the fifth century onward insular writers understood the traditions of gematria in Hebrew and Greek and Latin. Easily accessible examples from

---

9 For calculation on the ratios of Pythagorean, Platonic, and Boethian cosmic and music theory see Howlett (2005), 3 and references there cited.

10 For an account of gematria, the Hebrew alphanumeric system, see *Gesenius' Hebrew grammar* (ed. and trans. Kautzsch and Cowley (1910), 26). For knowledge among the Irish of the shapes and names of Hebrew letters see the seventh-century Old Irish text *Auraicept na n-éces* (ed. and trans. Calder

Antiquity survive in the Hebrew text of Judges 3:7–11, in the Greek text of Apocalypse 13:18, in the Latin text of Martianus Capella *De nuptiis Philologiae et Mercurii*, book II.[11] As there 100 letters and spaces from the beginning to *Victorii* | 2, coincident with the alphanumeric value in the twenty-three-letter Latin alphabet of VICTORII, 20 + 9 + 3 + 19 + 14 + 17 + 9 + 9 = 100,[12] we see two reasons for placement of *Victorii* | *centum.*

The Munich Computus' second passage

Here follows text and translation of the second of the dating passages from the Munich Computus as presented in the edition.[13]

> *Anni VDX faciunt annos saltus <decies> XXVIIII. Saltus in libro Victorii a principio mundi numerantur CCLXXXII <usque ad annum> sub Bero et Bardua consulibus.*

> 5510 years incorporate ten times 29 years of a *saltus* (since 5510 = 290 × 19). In the book of Victorius 282 *saltus* are counted from the beginning of the world to the year of the consuls Berus and Bardua.

Anni quinque mille quingenti decem faciunt annos saltus decies			
u͞ig͞inti no͞uem	11	26	66
Saltus in libro Victorii a principio mundi numerantur ducenti			
óc͞tog͞in͞ta d͞ŭo	11	29	65
usque ad annum sub Bero et B͞ard͞ŭa cons͞ŭl͞ibus	08	16	37
	30	71	168

3 lines, 30 words, 71 syllables, 168 letters, 197 letters and spaces. Orthography, grammar, syntax, and rhythm are faultless.

(1917), 86–87, 229–30). For early insular explanations of the Greek system see Bede, *De temporum ratione* 1 (ed. Charles W. Jones in CCSL 123, 272–73), and *Auraicept na n-éces* (Calder (1917), 231–32). For actual calculation of Greek values see the eighth-century Hiberno-Latin manuscript Milan, Biblioteca Ambrosiana, F 60 sup., 61rb. For examples in the Hebrew Old Testament, Judges 3:7–11, the Greek New Testament, Apocalypse 13:18, and Late Latin poetry see Howlett (1995), 29–32; Howlett (2005a), 30–31; Howlett (2013), 113. For a tenth-century Cambro-Latin quatrain that uses the Greek system see Howlett (2015), 233–50. For gematria in Irish poetry see Howlett (2011); Howlett (2011a). For gematria in Old Welsh and Old English poetry see Howlett (2005), 176–83, 224–25. For a fourteenth-century Anglo-Norman poem that illustrates gematria while discussing it see Howlett (2006b).

11 Howlett (2010a), 264–65; Howlett (2013), 112–13.

12 For play on the alphanumeric value of *Victorius* in another Insular Latin text see Howlett (2011b), 301.

13 Munich Computus 62 (Warntjes (2010), 278).

Calendrical phenomena

From | *Anni* 1 to | *usque ad annum* 3 there are 131 letters and spaces between words, one more than the 'present year', the 130th of the Victorian cycle.

Composition by fixed interval

The tenth syllable is the first of *decem* 1. From | *decem* 1 the tenth syllable is the first of *decies* 1. Between *decem* | 1 and | *uiginti nouem* 1 there are 29 letters and spaces between words.
Before *ducenti octoginta duo* | 2 29 syllables bring one to *uiginti nouem* | 1.

Composition by gematria

There are 100 letters and spaces from the beginning to the last of *Victorii* 2, coincident with the alphanumeric value of *Victorii*.

Although these two passages of AD 689 are much shorter than the Prologue of AD 699 to the Easter Table of Victorius of Aquitaine, the phenomena embedded in them that confirm explicit statements are identical. The shorter passages, less dense and less intricate in their composition, may have served as models for the longer later Prologue.

Prologue to the Easter table of Victorius

From the text of the Bremen manuscript we infer that the scribe did not completely understand what he was copying. The text as transmitted implies nonetheless that the author both understood the material he was discussing and knew how to express himself clearly, crisply, and, as we shall see, with astonishing complexity that confirms his text in multiple ways. Among indications that he was well instructed in Latin orthography, grammar, and syntax we note the unassimilated consonants in *conposuit* 2 and *adnectentes* 28.[14] From the internal evidence of *paschalem* 2, *paschalis* 4, and *pascha* 15, 21 we may correct *pascale* 30 to *paschale*. Let us remove from *sollempnitas* 4 the epenthetic *p*, as unlikely to have been written by a seventh-century Irishman.[15] For internal consistency let us normalize the flattened *e* of *cesaris* 19 and the *e-caudata* of *romę* 1, *dominicę* 5, 28, and *cęsaris* 20 and the first suspensions of *p'sens* 7, *p'te'rier'* 25, and *scl'i* 26 to the Classical

---

14 For unassimilated consonants in other seventh-century Hiberno-Latin compositions see Howlett (1996), 17; Howlett (1998b), 29, 41; Howlett (2006a), 35; Howlett (2008a), 162; Howlett (2010b), 137.
15 For avoidance of epenthetic *p* see also the Hiberno-Latin hymn *Recordemur iustitie / Audite pantes ta erga*, Lapidge and Sharpe (1985), 147 (no. 575); Ó Corráin (2017), 386 (no. 281), 455–58 (no. 341); Howlett (forthcoming b).

diphthong *ae*. Let us write all numerals as words. These minor changes from the manuscript restore a text faultless in orthography, grammar, syntax, and rhythm.

In the text that follows I have marked sentences with Roman numerals and lines arranged *per cola et commata* 'by clauses and phrases' with Arabic numerals, represented *litterae notabiliores* and punctuation marks of the manuscript with boldface, and marked the rhythms of the *clausulae* with macrons and breves and the rhythms of the *cursus* with acute and grave accents.

Text

I

Victorius natione Aquitanus inuitatus a sancto Hilario urbis Romae episcopo uel

> *ārchīdīăcŏno*

conposuit Paschalem recursum indagatiōnĕ caŭtissĭma

et pertendit annorum seriem usque ad annum quingentesimum trigésimūm sĕcŭndum .

recipiat Paschalis sollemnitas eundem mensem et diem eándemquĕ lūnam

qua primo Passionis ac Resurrectionis Dominicae ānno făcta est . 5

II

Quoniam igitur supramemoratus circulus ad sui principium atque originem reuersus

> *modo probabili reuolutiōnĕ dĕcŭrrit .*

cuius reuolutionis ac recursionis centesimus quadragesimus praesens nunc ánnŭs

> *pĕrăgĭtur*

núlli dúbium est

quod in fŭtŭro ānno .

hoc est centesimo quadrăgēsĭmo prĭmo 10

qui est a Passione Domini sexcentesimus septuagesimus tĕrtĭŭs ānnus .

ab Incarnatione uero sēptingēntēsĭmus .

per decimam tērtĭam indīctĭōnem

Kalendis Ianuarii quinta feria cum bisēxto lūna sēxta

Pascha tertio Idus Aprilis . luna decima septima Domino adiuŭantĕ

> *cĕlĕbrăbĭtur .* 15

III

In quo ab exordio mundi explentur anni quinque milia nōngenti ūnus .

ab initio quippe mundi usque ad diluuium duo milia ducenti quādrāgintā dūo .

a diluuio usque ad natiuitatem Abraham anni quinque milia septingenti quādrāgintā
  dūo

a natiuitate Abraham usque ad decimum quintum annum Tiberii Caesaris supputantur
  anni duo milia quádrāgintā quătŭor .

fiunt simul ab exordio mundi usque ad decimum quintum Tiberii Caesaris annum   20
  quinque milia ducénti uiḡinti ōcto .

porro a decimo quinto anno Tiberii et passione Xpisti usque in supradictum annum quo
  Paschă cĕlĕbrābĭtur

per decimam tertiam indictionem fiunt anni sexcenti séptuāḡintā tres .

fiunt ergo a principio mundi simul per eandem indictionem anni quinque milia nōngenti
  ūnus .

IIII

A quo anno initium sementes per centum annórum quī fŭtŭri sunt

omissis consulum nominibus quorum tempora iam dudūm prăetĕrĭerunt   25

annorum qui ab initio sáeculī decŭrrunt

continuatam sériem perdŭxĭmus

adnectentes ex latere annos Incarnationis siue Passiónis Domínicae

ut facílius ĕlŭcĕscat

quoto anno ab exordio mundi uel Incarnationis siue Passionis Domini Paschale festum
  celebrārĕ dĕbeāmus .   30

---

1 romę. epō. 2 cōposuit. 3 DXXXII. 4 sollēpnitas eodēm se & die evndēq, luñ qua. 5 dominicę.
6 adfui. 7 CXL. p'sens. 10 CLI. 11 qd'. DCLXXVI. 12 DCC. 13 p. XIII. 14 V. VI. 15 III. XVII.
16 V̄DCCCCI. 17 in | tio. ĪICCXLII. 18 V̄DCCCCXLII. 19 XV. cesaris. ĪIXLIIII. 20 XV. cęsaris.
V̄CCXXVIII. 21 XV. 22 XIII. DCLXXIIII. 23 V̄DCCCCI. 24 sumitis. C. 25 cōsulib;. p'te'rier'. 26 scl'i.
29 dominicę. 30 pascale.

Translation

I

Victorius by nation (or 'birth') an Aquitanian, invited by Saint Hilary, bishop or
     archdeacon of the city of Rome,
composed a recurring paschal cycle by a most cautious searching out,
and it extended through a series of years as far as the 532nd year;
the paschal solemnity should return to the same month and day and the same moon
on which it was performed in the first year of the Dominical Passion and
     Resurrection.   5

II

Since therefore the cycle called to mind above has run its course, having returned
     to its own beginning and origin just now in a revolution capable of proof
     (or 'in a revolution by a measure capable of proof'),
of which revolution and recurring cycle the present, 140th, year is now being run
     through,
it is doubtful to no one
that in the year that is going to be,
that is the 141st,   10
which is from the Passion of the Lord the 673rd year,
from the Incarnation, in truth, the 700th,
through the thirteenth indiction,
with the Kalends of January on the fifth day (i.e. Thursday), with a *bissextus* and
     luna sixth,
Easter will be celebrated, with the Lord helping, on the third of the Ides of April
     (i.e. 11 April), *luna* seventeenth.   15

III

In which (year) from the beginning of the world 5901 years are fulfilled,
from the beginning of the world as far as the flood 2242,
from the flood as far as the birth of Abraham 5742 years,
from the birth of Abraham as far as the fifteenth year of Tiberius Caesar 2044
     years are computed;

there are taken together from the beginning of the world as far as the fifteenth
 year of Tiberius 5228; 20
furthermore from the fifteenth year of Tiberius and from the Passion of Christ as
 far as the abovesaid year in which Easter will be celebrated
through the thirteenth indiction there are taken 673 years;
there are taken together therefore from the beginning of the world through the
 same indiction 5901 years.

IIII

From which year taking the beginning [and continuing] through a hundred years
 that are going to be,
with omitted names of consuls whose times have already passed, 25
we have extended a continued series
of years that are running from the beginning of the age,
attaching to it from the side the years of the Dominical Incarnation or Passion,
so that it may shine out more easily
in which year from the beginning of the world or of the Incarnation or of the
 Passion of the Lord we ought to celebrate the paschal feast. 30

Analysis

Our computist has composed a text faultless in orthography, grammar, syntax, and rhythm. Like the author of the two passages of the Munich computus he has made his prose rhythms fulfil the requirements of both Classical Latin *clausulae* and Late Latin *cursus*. But the length of this text has allowed our computist to do something else. He has composed thirty lines, of which all but three exhibit clausular endings. Of those three lines 11 exhibits a hexameter ending, line 8 a *cursus medius*, and line 28 a *cursus tardus*. The purpose is to demonstrate mastery of three distinct systems simultaneously, a phenomenon common in Insular Latin literature from the time of Gildas' *De excidio Brittanniae* (AD 540) and the *Disputatio Chori et Praetextati* (AD 600 or a little earlier).[16]

---

16 As above nn. 5 and 6. Other insular writers whose works exhibit this phenomenon include Ailerán of Clonard (+ AD 665), English diplomatists from AD 679 onward, Adomnán of Iona (AD 683–686 and 704), Anonymous of Lindisfarne (698), and Bede of Wearmouth-Jarrow (AD 720). For these authors see Howlett (1997), 90, 101, 104; Howlett (2010a), 294; Howlett (forthcoming b).

168 DAVID HOWLETT

Our computist's prose reads smoothly, with no trace of ambiguity, obscurity, or archness. But he has also infixed phenomena that confirm the authenticity and integrity of his text, a form of error-detection program to enable a reader to determine that he is reading exactly what the author wrote, and, if not, an error-correction program to enable a reader to restore exactly what the author wrote.

Chiastic and parallel arrangement of diction

Let us note our author's control over the arrangement of his text, first by his chiastic and parallel arrangement of diction (see schema, p. 165).

Note how much distinctive diction occurs and recurs only in this pattern. In another pattern the first line of sentence III ends *ab exordio mundi* [...] *anni quinque milia nongenti unus* 16, and the last line of sentence III ends *a principio mundi* [...] *anni quinque milia nongenti unus* 23. This accounts for more than 31% of the words of the entire composition.[17]

Calendrical phenomena

Let us note second calendrical phenomena infixed into the text.

The first sentence contains four clauses, coincident with the four seasons and the four years of a leap year cycle.

The first sentence also contains 354 letters and spaces between words, coincident with the number of days in a lunar year.[18]

The entire text is arranged in 30 lines, coincident with the number of days in a solar month.[19] It contains 276 words, coincident with the number of days in the nine months from the Annunciation, celebrated on 25 March, to the Nativity, celebrated on 25 December.[20]

Lines 14–15, which state the particulars of the date on which Easter will be celebrated, *Kalendis Ianuarii quinta feria cum bisexto luna sexta Pascha tertio Idus Aprilis luna decima septima*, contain 101 letters and spaces between words, coincident with the number of days from the Kalends of January to the third of the Ides of April, from 1 January to 11 April, 101 days.

From the account of the last year of the first cycle of 532 years, *annum quingentesimum trigesimum secundum* | 3, to the account of the 141st year of the second

---

17 For other examples of seventh-century Hiberno-Latin texts in which parallel and chiastic diction accounts for a large part of the whole see Howlett (2020), 107–24; Howlett (forthcoming a); Howlett (forthcoming b).

18 For other examples of this phenomenon in seventh-century Hiberno-Latin texts see Howlett (2017), 212–28; Holford-Strevens (2019), 78–80.

19 For other examples of this phenomenon in seventh-century Hiberno-Latin texts see Howlett (1996), 32–50.

20 For other examples see Howlett (1995a), 1–3; Howlett (1997), 294; Howlett (2000), 84, 89, 95, 160.

Schema. Chiastic and parallel arrangement of diction.

A	4	*Paschalis sollemnitas*
B1	4	*eandemque*
B2	5	*Passionis ... Dominicae*
B3	5	*anno*
B4	11	*a Passione Domini*
C	11	*sexcentesimus septuagesimus tertius*
D	11	*annus*
E	13	*per decimam tertiam indictionem*
F	15	*Pascha ... celebrabitur*
G1	16	*ab exordio mundi*
G2	19	*usque ad decimum quintum annum Tiberii Caesaris*
H	19	*supputantur*
I	19	*anni duo milia quadraginta quatuor*
H'	20	*fiunt simul*
G'1	20	*ab exordio mundi*
G'2	20	*usque ad decimum quintum Tiberii Caesaris annum*
G'2'	21	*a decimo quinto anno Tiberii*
F'	21	*Pascha celebrabitur*
E'	22	*per decimam tertiam indictionem*
D'	22	*anni*
C'	22	*sexcenti septuaginta tres*
B'1	23	*eandem*
B'2	29	*Passionis Dominicae*
B'3	30	*anno*
B'4	30	*Passionis Domini*
A'	30	*Paschale festum*

cycle, the 141st syllable is the first of *centesimo quadragesimo primo* 10.[21] From |
recursum 2 to | *ac recursionis* 7 there are 141 syllables.

Lines 9–12, which define the 141st year of the second cycle, *quod in futuro anno hoc est centesimo quadragesimo primo qui est a Passione Domini sexcentesimus septuagesimus tertius annus ab Incarnatione uero septingentesimus*, contain 141 letters.

From *per decimam tertiam indictionem* | 13 (note the coincidence of the line number with the number of the indiction) to | *simul per eandem indictionem* 23 there are 674 letters, one more than perfectly coincident with *a Passione Domini sexcentesimus septuagesimus tertius annus.*[22]

Composition by ratio

Let us note third composition by ratio. The twelve words of line 17 divide by duple ratio 2:1 at 8 and 4, at *duo* | and *duo* |.

The twenty-eight words of lines 18 and 19 divide into two equal parts in the fourteen words from | *duo* 18 to *duo* | 19.

The thirty lines of the text divide by extreme and mean ratio, 0.61803 and 0.38197, at 19 and 11, at the end of line 19, exactly at the end of the crux of the chiastic pattern, *anni duo milia quadraginta quatuor* |.

Dividing the 276 words by *hemiolus* or sesquialter ratio, 1½:1 or 3:2, the first and larger part of 166 words divides at 100 and 66, at the present, 140th, year, *centesimus quadragesimus* **praesens** | *nunc annus* 7; the second and smaller part of 110 words divides at 66 and 44, at the one hundred future years, *centum annorum qui* | *futuri* sunt 24.

Dividing again by diminution, by the same sesquialter ratio, 66 words divide at 40 and 26, in the first and larger part, at the *annus futurus* reckoned from the Passion and from the Incarnation, *sexcentesimus septuagesimus tertius annus ab* | *Incarnatione uero septingentesimus* 12, and in the second and smaller part at the *annus futurus* reckoned from the Passion, *anni* | *sexcenti septuaginta tres* 22.[23]

Composition by fixed interval

Let us note fourth composition by fixed interval, illustrating the values of words for numbers by their positions. In line 13 the third word is *tertiam*. From | *tertiam* 13 to *quinta* | 14 there are 5 words. After *quinta* | there are 5 words, or reckoned

---

21 For examples of play on the number 532 in other seventh-century Hiberno-Latin texts see Howlett (2010a), 268, 286.

22 For an account of actual equality, which must be exact, and merely apparent equality, which may be off by one or two, see the *Rhetorica ad Herennium* 4.20.27–28 as discussed in Howlett (1995), 23–26; Howlett (1997), 24–27.

23 For other examples of repeated diminution by the same ratio in Cambro- and Hiberno-Latin texts see Howlett (1995), 213–16; Howlett (2002), 90–91; Howlett (2010a), 309–10; Howlett (2013), Howlett (2005), 117; Howlett (2020), 116.

another way, from | *quinta* 14 to *sexta* | 14 there are 6 words. After *sexta* | 14 the seventh word is *septima* | 15.

In line 14 there are from *bi|sexto* to *sexta* | 6 syllables. From | *bisexto* to *sexta* | there are 18 letters and spaces between words, the sum of 2 × 6 + 6 or 18.

In line 15 the third syllable is the first of *tertio*. From | *tertio* 15 to | *decima* 15 there are 10 syllables. The seventh word of line 15 is *septima*.

10 words before the end of the crux of the chiasmus at line 19 bring one to *decimum* | 18. The fifteenth syllable of line 19 is *decimum* | *quintum*, and from *decimum* | to the end of the line there are 10 words. The fifteenth syllable of line 20 is the first of *decimum quintum*. Between *ad decimum quintum* | 19 and | *ad decimum quintum* 20 there are 15 words. From | *quintum* 20 to *quinque* | 20 there are 5 words, and the latter is the fifth word from the end. From | *ad decimum quintum* 20 to *a decimo quinto* | 21 there are 15 words.

There are 10 letters to *decimam* | 22.

From *decimam tertiam indictionem* | to the end of line 22 there are 13 syllables. From *per decimam tertiam indictionem* | 22 to *per eandem* | *indictionem* 23 there are 13 words.

From *quadraginta duo* | 17 to *quadraginta quatuor* | 19 there are 44 syllables.

From | *centesimus* 7 to | *centesimo* 10 there are 100 letters and spaces between words.

From | *septingentesimus* 12 to *nongenti unus* | 23 there are 901 letters and spaces between words.

Composition by gematria

Let us note fifth composition by gematria. Line 1 contains 129 letters and spaces between words, coincident with the alphanumeric value of the first word, VIC-TORIUS, 20 + 9 + 3 + 19 + 14 + 17 + 9 + 20 + 18 or 129.[24]

As the man who asked Victorius to produce the cycle was Hilarius, later bishop of the city of Rome, the first sentence contains after *Victorius* | 44 words, coincident with the alphanumeric value of ROMA, 17 + 14 + 12 + 1 or 44. Between *Victorius* | and | *Romae* there are 44 letters.[25]

From | *a diluuio usque ad natiuitatem Abraham* 18 to *Abraham* | 19 there are 42 syllables, and between *natiuitatem Abraham* | 18 and | *natiuitate Abraham* 19 there are 42 letters, coincident with the alphanumeric value of ABRAHAM, 1 + 2 + 17 + 1 + 8 + 1 + 12 or 42.[26]

---

24 As above n. 12.

25 For play on the alphanumeric value of *Roma* in another seventh-century Hiberno-Latin text see Howlett (2008a), 160–61.

26 For play on the alphanumeric value of Abraham in another seventh-century Hiberno-Latin text see Muirchú moccu Macthéni, *Vita sancti Patricii* 1.27 as discussed in Howlett (2006a), 30, 153, 159, 171.

From | *Pascha* 14 to *Pascha* | 21 there are 92 words, coincident with the alphanumeric value of PASCHA, 15 + 1 + 18 + 3 + 8 + 1 or 46, twice.[27]

Modular composition

Learning from the *Liber Anatolii De ratione paschali* insular writers from the fifth century onward incorporated into their texts modular composition, by which the number of one element in one part signalled in advance or confirmed in retrospect the number of another element in another part.[28] The first sentence contains four clauses, prefiguring the entire text of four sentences.

Conclusions

Each of the phenomena incorporated by our authors into their texts can be paralleled many times in other Insular Latin computistic texts. Each of the phenomena is simple, but in concert they are wondrously complex. Because our second author was writing about the 140th and 141st years of the second Victorian cycle he used the words *recursum* and *recursionis*, emphasizing the recurrent nature of the cycle, but an additional reason for using *recursum* for the *cursum* of his source is that he wanted the calendrical number 354 letters and spaces between words in the first sentence, in the first line of which he also wanted 129 letters and spaces between words to coincide with the alphanumeric value of the first word, the name *Victorius*, and also a unit of 44 letters (and in the sentence 44 words) to coincide with the alphanumeric value of *Roma*.

Recollect also that the crux of the chiasmus ends with a correct *clausula* and a correct *cursus* rhythm at the end of line 19, at which point the entire text divides by extreme and mean ratio, reckoned by the 30 lines. Moreover, the fifteenth syllable of line 19 is *decimum* | *quintum*, and the forty-fourth syllable of line 19 is the last of *quadraginta quatuor*. There is play on the word *decimum* ten words before the end of the crux and play on *decimum quintum* in the fifteenth syllable after the crux, and multiple play on *decimum quintum* before and after the crux.

Every phenomenon is discretely perfect, and all the phenomena function simultaneously without impeding any single phenomenon.

Our author's desire to coordinate the numbers of the Victorian and Dionysiac systems attests the independence and suppleness of his mind. His ability to

---

27 For examples of this phenomenon in a contemporary Hiberno-Latin computistic text see Howlett (2017), 225.

28 For other examples in insular Latin texts see Howlett (1998c); Howlett (2000), 1–5, 40–51, 76–102, 111–15, 131–42, 146–55, 185–87, 192; Howlett (2006a), 167–80; Howlett (2010a), 263–64; Howlett (2010c), 180; Howlett (2011b), 300–01.

coordinate the varied phenomena we have considered[29] while writing limpid rhythmical prose that neither descends into ambiguity, obscurity, or archness, nor calls attention to any of the infixed phenomena, attests his competence in both trivial and quadruvial arts, based upon grammar and computus respectively. By the standards of our day he seems a remarkable man. But given the number of other authors who unobtrusively packed vast amounts of information into tightly compressed yet easily comprehended texts, he may not have been, among Hiberno-Latin writers of the seventh century, unusual.

I suggested above that the two short passages that date the Munich Computus to AD 689 may have served as models for the more expansive Sirmond computus of AD 699, but both of these remarkable compositions fit neatly into two larger traditions, one of computistic texts and one of hagiographic texts informed by them. Let us remember seven Late Antique mathematicians: the first Christian scientist, Anatolius bishop of Laodicea (+ AD 283), the Latin translation of whose *Liber Anatolii De ratione paschali* was known to Rufinus of Aquileia by AD 402. Paulinus of Nola undertook to forward to Rufinus a question from the Romano-Gaul Sulpicius Severus, who knew both the *latercus* and *De ratione paschali* by AD 410. His 84-year cycle, by which insular churches calculated the date of Easter, arrived in Ireland between AD 410 and 425, even earlier than the papal deacon Palladius, who came from Celestine as first bishop of the Irish in AD 431.[30] In AD 457 Victorius Aquitanus published in Rome for the man who became Pope Hilary his 532-year cycle, which became the basis for the computus attributed by Cummian in his *Epistola de controuersia paschali* of AD 633 to *papa noster Patricius*.[31] Boethius published *De institutione arithmetica* before AD 525, and in AD 525 Dionysius Exiguus published his computus based upon Alexandrian principles and reckoned from the era of the Incarnation. By AD 600 or a little earlier the *Saturnalia* of Macrobius Ambrosius Theodosius, a fifth-century treatise for pagans about the Roman calendar, was abridged in southeastern Ireland as the *Disputatio Chori et Praetextati*. Isidore bishop of Seville died in AD 636, leaving his successor Braulio to publish his *Etymologiae* in AD 640, information from which source was incorporated into a computistic Hiberno-Latin poem about the Six Ages of the World that dates itself in three ways to AD 645.[32] As the last chapters of the Hiberno-Latin *Computus Oxoniensis*, that dates itself to AD 658, discuss Anatolius, Macrobius, Victorius, Dionysius, Boethius, and calculus,[33] it is beyond dispute that the Irish absorbed the teaching of all seven of these authorities during the fifth, sixth, and seventh centuries.

---

29 The phenomena considered here do not comprise an exhaustive analysis, but only a modest beginning of an attempt to recover an understanding of our authors' craftsmanship.

30 Above n. 4.

31 Mc Carthy (2017), 84–137.

32 Howlett (1996), 1–6.

33 Howlett (2010a), 271.

The first issue was creation of at least ten computistic texts:[34]

Anonymous	*ante*600	*Disputatio Chori et Praetextati*
Cummianus	633	*Epistola de controuersia paschali*
Mo-Cuoróc maccu Net Sémon	640	*Nonae Aprilis*
Circle of Cummianus	*post*640	*De ratione conputandi*
Anonymous	*post*640	Note about Mo-Sinu maccu Min, Mo-Cuoróc maccu Net Sémon, and the learning of computus at Bangor
Anonymous	645	*Versus de annis a principio, Deus a quo facta fuit huius mundi machina*
Anonymous	658	*Computus Oxoniensis*
Anonymous	689	Munich Computus
Anonymous	699	Sirmond Computus
Anonymous	*ante*700	*De ratione temporum*

Among insular scholars Sulpicius Seuerus was equally famous as the mathematician who devised about AD 410 the 84-year cycle by which insular churches calculated the date of Easter and as the hagiographer who published in AD 397 the *Vita sancti Martini* in three parts with two prefaces. When the insular Latin hagiographic tradition began, not later than the middle of the seventh century, a favoured pattern was three books with two prefaces. All of the extant hagiographers incorporated the computistic phenomena we have been considering here to fix and date their texts, as I shall show elsewhere:[35]

---

34 For texts and analyses see *Disputatio Chori et Praetextati* (Holford-Strevens (2019)); Cummianus, *De controversia paschali* (ed. and trans. Maura Walsh in Walsh and Ó Cróinín (1988), 56–97); *De ratione conputandi* (ed. Dáibhí Ó Cróinín in Walsh and Ó Cróinín (1988), 115–213); Howlett (2013), 113–15, 115–19; above n. 32; Howlett, (2010a), 268–79; above nn. 1–2; Howlett (2017), 212–28.

35 Howlett (forthcoming b). See Aileranus Sapiens, *Interpretatio mystica et moralis progenitorum Domini Iesu Christi* (ed. and trans. Breen (1995)); Howlett (1996), 6–20; Howlett (1998d); Howlett (2020); Howlett (2010a), 291–94, 294–97; Howlett (2015a); *Vitae sancti Cuthberti* (ed. and trans. Colgrave (1940)); Muirchú moccu Macthéni, *Vita sancti Patricii* (Howlett (2006a)); *Vita Gregorii* (ed. and trans. Colgrave (1968)); Adomnán, *Vita Columbae* (ed. and trans. Anderson and Anderson (1991)); Stephen of Ripon, *Vita Wilfridi* (ed. and trans. Colgrave (1927)); Bede, *Poemata* (ed. and trans. Lapidge (2019), 184–312); *Vita sancti Samsonis* (ed. and trans. Flobert (1997)); *Vita Ceolfridi* (ed. and trans. Grocock and Wood (2013), 77–120); Bede, *Historia ecclesiastica* (ed. and trans. Colgrave and Mynors (1969)); Howlett (1997a), 110–16; Howlett (1997), 179–93; Æthelwulf, *De abbatibus* (ed. and trans. Campbell (1967)).

Ailerán of Clonard	*ante*665	*Interpretatio mystica*
		Canon Euangeliorum
		Vita I sanctae Brigitae
Lutting of Lindisfarne	681	*Versus* in honour of his master Baeda
Adomnán of Iona	683–686	*De locis sanctis*
Cogitosus of Kildare	692–693	*Vita sanctae Brigitae*
Anonymous of Lindisfarne	698	*Vita sancti Cuthberhti*
Muirchú moccu Mactuéni	*ante*700	*Vita sancti Patricii*
Anonymous of Whitby	704	*Vita sancti Gregorii*
Adomnán of Iona	704	*Vita sancti Columbae*
Stephen of Ripon	712–720	*Vita sancti Uilfridi*
Bede of Wearmouth-Jarrow	720	*Vita sancti Cuthberhti*
	720	*Vita metrica sancti Cuthberhti*
Anonymous of Dol	722	*Vita sancti Samsonis*
Anonymous of Wearmouth-Jarrow	*ante*731	*Vita sanctissimi Ceolfridi abbatis*
Bede of Wearmouth-Jarrow	731	*Historia ecclesiastica gentis Anglorum*
Cuthbert of Wearmouth-Jarrow	735	*Epistola de obitu Baedae*
Aediluulf of Bywell	819	*De abbatibus*

A phenomenon of all these authors, noticed neither by modern editors nor by analysts nor commentators, is that every one of them composed Classical as distinct from Medieval Latin, every one of them wrote like a computist, and every one of them composed metrical *clausulae*, because they were obsessed with time, the measurement of which in alternation of long and short is best expressed by metrical composition. In the Munich Computus of AD 689 and the Sirmond Computus of AD 699 Immo Warntjes has presented the works of two acute minds that help us to perceive in new ways the coherent beauty of the thought of our ancestors.

JAMES T. PALMER

An Eighth-Century Irish Computus in Lombardy*

▼ **ABSTRACT** This essay examines the *Computus Amiatinus* (*CA*), a work written in Lombardy in AD 747 and preserved only in three eleventh-century manuscripts copied at the Badia Amiatina in southern Tuscany. Although its dating clause was first published in 1872, the work as a whole has not previously received full scholarly attention, partly because it was considered to be little more than a reworking of passages from Isidore of Seville's *Etymologiae*. On closer inspection, *CA* actually incorporates a distinctive early version of the Irish *De divisionibus temporum* (*DDT*) tradition that also gave rise to the Munich Computus of AD 718/19. It also contains cosmological and computistical material consistent with what one might expect from an early-eighth-century text based on insular learning and developed in Lombardy. The essay outlines key features of *CA* and its possible context, and argues that the author was motivated to reflect on the order and nature of time as they engaged with the belief that the world might end after 6000 years — a date they believed would fall a little over half a century after the date of composition. An appendix includes a preliminary edition and translation of the *DDT* section of *CA*.

▼ **KEYWORDS** *Computus Amiatinus* of AD 747, *De divisionibus temporum*, Munich Computus of AD 718/19; Irish computistics, Lombard computistics; Columbanus, Isidore of Seville; Bobbio; apocalyptic chronologies

---

* My thanks to Immo Warntjes, Jacopo Bisagni, and Tobit Loevenich for their comments and patience during the writing of this essay. Mistakes remain my own.

Pre-Carolingian Latin Computus and its Regional Contexts, ed. by Immo Warntjes, Tobit Loevenich, and Dáibhí Ó Cróinín, Studia Traditionis Theologiae, 54 (Turnhout: Brepols, 2023), pp. 177–200
BREPOLS ❧ PUBLISHERS   10.1484/M.STT-EB.5.133490

Introduction

Insular and continental computistical traditions from the early Middle Ages are deeply entwined. When Charles Jones identified the Sirmond Collection of texts known to Bede — subsequently identified by Dáibhí Ó Cróinín as an Irish compilation predominantly shaped by AD 658 — it was striking that the manuscript evidence was continental and, indeed, seemed to have acquired Frankish additions.[1] Evidence for the important Irish treatises *De ratione conputandi* (*DRC*), the *Computus Einsidlensis* (*CE*), the Munich Computus (*MC*), and indeed much of Bede, is almost exclusively continental too.[2] It is perhaps no surprise, therefore, to find many similarities between early insular texts and early computi from the Frankish and Lombard kingdoms in the eighth century. Indeed, confusion can easily arise over how to categorise some texts given the high levels of exchange, at least once one gets past texts with relatively secure origins. A significant challenge for scholars of computus in the coming generation will be to articulate more clearly what features might define the different cultural heritages of the texts we study.

The present article aims to contribute to the challenge outlined above through the analysis of a text that has not yet received much attention: the *Computus Amiatinus* of AD 747 (hereafter *CA*). It is, as we shall see, a text that displays a number of features that could be labelled classically Irish, and at the same time it is clearly a Lombard composition. It provides, in many ways, a clean slate for interpretation, as it has never been analysed for anything more than its dating clause and a couple of passages relevant to apocalyptic theology.[3] The dating clause at least provides a firm geographical and temporal marker, as the author notes 'from the nativity of Christ, which was the 42nd year of the empire of Octavian Caesar, up to the present year, the third year of Ratchis's reign in Italy and the sixth of the pontificate of Pope Zacharias of the City of Rome, the fifteenth indiction, there are 747 years'.[4] This note caught the eye of Ludwig Bethmann when he examined

---

1 Jones (1937); Ó Cróinín (1983b); Bisagni (2020), 18–19.

2 Wallis (1999), LXXXV–XCVI; Warntjes (2016), 178 n. 56.

3 Landes (1988), 169 n. 129. For a reassessment of Landes's argument, see now Warntjes (2019). There are some comments restricted to observations about apocalyptic content in Palmer (2013), 611. For a wider survey of late antique chronological notes in Italy, excluding the present example, see Krusch (1884), 101–15.

4 For the text, see Appendix: *CA* 15. The dating clause contains corruptions that requires some clarification. The year from the nativity is given as *DCCLV* in the manuscripts. Gorman (2002), 268, notes that this fits the later legendary foundation date of San Salvatore. Most of the other temporal markers, however, point towards the very end of AD 746 or, more likely, AD 747. The fifteenth indiction ran from September AD 746 to September AD 747. Ratchis became king no later than September AD 744 (Hartmann (1903), 155) so his third regnal year covered about the same window of time. Pope Zacharias became pope in December AD 741 (*Liber pontificalis* 91.18 (ed. Duchesne (1886–1892), i 421)), so his sixth year ran from December AD 746 to December AD 747. The note ends with the calculation of the years from the *annus praesens* to the 6000th year since Creation (AM) — a system of dating typically connected to the Eusebian calculation that the Nativity occurred

two manuscript witnesses, both in Florence, in 1854; and Theodor Mommsen subsequently published the dating clause in the conspectus of his 1892 edition of the *Liber genealogus* for the *Monumenta Germaniae Historica*.[5] Neither, it seems, saw anything more in the rest of the text than some borrowings from Isidore and Augustine.[6] Perhaps as a result of this initial assessment, few scholars followed up these references to provide a fuller analysis.

The manuscript tradition of *CA* is limited. The oldest witness is Florence, Biblioteca Medicea Laurenziana, Conv. Sopr. 364 (= **C**), written in a late Caroline minuscule most likely of the eleventh century from the Badia Amiatina.[7] The manuscript is dominated by a well-decorated copy of Isidore's *Etymologiae* (1r–106v) and Junillus' *Instituta* (107r–116r).[8] It is the better textual witness for the computus, but in some ways a second manuscript is more revealing about origins. Florence, Biblioteca Medicea Laurenziana, Plut. 20.54 (= **P**) was written a few years after **C**, also at the Badia Amiatina, and it contains almost exactly the same material, except that it does not have the *Etymologiae* but does have a tenth-century hybrid of the chronicles of Isidore and Bede extended to Otto I's conquest of Italy in AD 961 (at 30r–37r).[9] Although this copy of the computus contains more textual errors, it is useful because it contains some better readings in places and has other features that suggest it was copied from a witness to the text earlier than **C** rather than directly from **C**. Abbreviations in **P** but not in **C**, for instance, seem to confirm that this older, lost manuscript was written by a scribe trained in insular practices. These abbreviations include 7 for 'et', ÷ for 'est', vł for 'vel', i suspended over g for 'igitur', o suspended over v for 'vero', and ħ for 'haec'. The exemplar, like the text itself, points strongly to insular-continental intellectual circles.[10]

---

around AM 5200. The scribe of **P** (the sigla are explained p. 175) gives 53 years to complete the sixth millennium here, which again potentially fits AD 747 on the basis of the standard Eusebian calculation. A complication arises, however, as the text gives 5198 years from Creation to the Nativity, not 5200, which would mean the calculation in **P** is two years short (or four years short if one insisted on AD 745). The scribe of **C** gives 57 years to complete 6000 years, which would at least fit the Nativity in AM 5198 and an uncorrected *annus praesens* of 745 years from the Nativity; but given that the year AD does not fit with the indiction or the dates for Ratchis or Zacharias, the number in **C** is more likely a later effort to correct an inconsistency. Certainly in the mid-eighth century, use of AD and AM dates was sufficiently inconsistent that, if other indicators point towards a date, one should not put too much store in the stated year.

5 Bethmann (1874), 719 and 728; ed. Theodor Mommsen in MGH Auct. ant. 9, 158.

6 Bethmann (1874), 728.

7 Gorman (2002), 268.

8 On Junillus, see Maas (2003), which reproduces Kihn's edition of 1880 (which did use the Florence manuscripts). On the reception of the work, see Laistner (1947), 23–31.

9 The contents and date are summarised in Gorman (2002), 268. The manuscript is available online at: http://mss.bmlonline.it/?Collection=Plutei&search=Plut.20.54. The chronicle is *Supplementum* to *Regum Italiae et imperatorum catalogi* (ed. Georg Pertz in MGH SS 3, 873).

10 There is a third manuscript witness closely related to the other two, Cesena, Biblioteca Malatestiana, D.XXIV.1. According to Gorman (2002), 268, this was also produced in the Badia Amiatina in the late eleventh century and its contents closely match those of **C**. Unfortunately, I have been unable to

CA itself is made up of three distinct sections as follows:

1. A version of *De divisionibus temporum* (*DDT*) (**C** 116r; **P** 15r–v; this part is edited in the Appendix below) — a text with many known variants.[11] The first part concludes with the apocalyptic dating clause. It is followed by a short text on ten ways to assess history (**C** 116r–v; **P** 15v–16r). There is then a long section, starting as a dialogue, on the structure and meaning of world history and the harmony of numbers and elements (**C** 116v–118v; **P** 16r–18v).
2. Tables and comment on the structures and cycles of time (**C** 118v–119r; **P** 18v–19v).
3. A more strictly computistical section with tables, *argumenta*, and a long discussion of *bissexti* (**C** 119r–120r; **P** 19v–21r).

There is much here which is in keeping with Irish computistical learning. Many Irish treatises proceeded from divisions of time, through interest in nature, to more detailed concern for paschal reckonings. As we shall see, the Amiatian text also contains many affinities with the major Irish computi of the period (*DRC*, *CE*, and *MC*).[12] The inclusion of apocalyptic material, on the other hand, is more unusual. Despite Landes's arguments that time-reckoning and apocalypse were closely related, the two spheres of knowledge tended to be treated separately.[13] There were exceptions, notably the Sirmond dating clause of AD 658, the Victorian Prologue of AD 699, and the poem *Deus a quo facta fuit*, which all contain calculations looking ahead to the year AM 6000.[14] These texts were also insular in origin, so they stand as relevant context for understanding *CA*.

Irish learning and Lombardy

Before assessing *CA* in detail, it is important to sketch the backdrop of Irish learning and computus in Lombardy. Connections between Ireland and Lombardy had a long, strong history, following the foundation of Bobbio by Columbanus in the Trebbia river valley in *c*. AD 614.[15] Many manuscripts connected with

---

consult the manuscript for the present study. Significant material from *CA* was also incorporated into a *Ratio pascalis* in the late-ninth-century Lombard manuscript now Monza, Biblioteca Capitolare, e-14/127, 3r–16v (Bischoff (1998–2017), ii 214 (no. 2890)); this only came to light in the final stages of the present essay's production so it is not fully incorporated into the analysis.

11 Bisagni (2020), especially 25–34.

12 *De ratione conputandi* (*DRC*) (ed. Dáibhí Ó Cróinín in Walsh and Ó Cróinín (1988), 99–213); Munich Computus (*MC*) (ed. Warntjes (2010)). There is no edition of the *Computus Einsidlensis* yet but it is outlined in Warntjes (2005). An *editio princeps* is being prepared by Tobit Loevenich (TCD). It takes up pp. 82–125 of Einsiedeln, Stiftsbibliothek, 321 (647), available online http://www.e-codices.unifr.ch/en/searchresult/list/one/sbe/0321 (*CE* in the following).

13 Palmer (2011), 1319–20.

14 Ó Cróinín (1983b), 234; Warntjes (2010b); Warntjes (2019), 55–56.

15 Jonas of Bobbio, *Vita Columbani et eius socii* 1.30 (ed. Bruno Krusch in MGH SS rer. Germ. 37, 223).

AN EIGHTH-CENTURY IRISH COMPUTUS IN LOMBARDY 181

the monastery were written in insular scripts and suggest that it was a popular destination for Irish monks well into the eighth century.[16] In terms of computus, however, it is difficult to know exactly what practices were observed. Columbanus had used the 84-year *latercus* favoured in Ireland and had been criticised for it — not that one would know from the silence of his hagiographer, Jonas of Bobbio, on the matter.[17] We know that Jonas, writing in the middle of the seventh century, used the tables of Victorius of Aquitaine, in keeping with observance in the Frankish kingdoms and, indeed, areas of Ireland.[18] By that time the papacy, along with much of southern Italy and Spain, probably observed a non-Victorian Alexandrian Easter, but it remains surprisingly difficult to work out how quickly or forcibly Victorius was abandoned in Rome or elsewhere in the Italian peninsula.[19] At least one centre with Columbanian connections north of the Alps used a Victorian table, modified to remove double Easter dates, into the AD 720s.[20] This might suggest Bobbio did too if — if — one thought Columbanian houses maintained similar practices to each other. In northern Italy, Victorius' table was used by one centre for chronological purposes as late as AD 767.[21] If there was an

---

16 Duncan (2016), 221–22. On Bobbio's early library see Zironi (2004), especially the reconstruction at 159–65. Richter (2008) discusses many connections between Bobbio and Ireland.

17 Corning (2006), 24–30; Stancliffe (2018), 118–23; O'Hara and Wood (2017), 30.

18 Jonas of Bobbio, *Vita Iohannis abbatis Praef.* (ed. Bruno Krusch in MGH SS rer. Germ. 37, 326).

19 Palmer (2017), 145–47. Still useful for a review of the evidence for early Italian paschal observances is Krusch (1884), 101–15, and Schmid (1907), 38–80, although neither considered that there was much dispute after the sixth century.

20 This is the 'Computus of 727' or *Dial. Burg.* 16 (ed. Borst (2006), 368–72), preserved in Bern, Burgerbibliothek, 611 (possibly Bourges, 720s; *CLA* 7, 9 (no. 604)), with the Easter table on 96r, available online at: https://www.e-codices.unifr.ch/en/searchresult/list/one/bbb/0611. Notes forming a second partial table, at one time in the same Bourges compilation, can be found in Paris, Bibliothèque nationale de France, Lat. 10756, 66v–67r (available online at: https://gallica.bnf.fr/ark:/12148/btv1b52512740n.r=latin%2010756?rk=42918;4). On the manuscript see now Ganz (2019), 265–80.

21 London, British Library, Cotton Nero A II, 35v (Northern Italy, late eighth century; *CLA* 2, 20 (no. 186); Bischoff (1998–2017), ii 107 (no. 2421); available online at: http://www.bl.uk/manuscripts/Viewer.aspx?ref=cotton_ms_nero_a_ii_f035v): *Super sunt anni post passionem domini per ciclum Victuriae anni quingenti treginta et due. Ipsus expletus, hoc anno impleti sunt centum septuaginta et VIIII. Sunt in summa ab exordio mundi usque ad praesente tempore anni quinque milia nogenti XXVIII et remanent de sexto miliario anni LXXII, subtractus XL remanent XXXII* ('There are above, after the Passion of the Lord, 532 years by the Cycle of Victorius. This [cycle] having ended, and this year having finished, there are 179 [years]. There are in total from the beginning of the world up to the present time 5928 and there remain 72 years of 6000. Subtracting 40, there remain 32 [years]'). Levison (1946), 304, dated the text to AD 778 on the basis of the first statement, that the year is the 179th of the Victorian cycle (= AD 738), to which he added the 40 years indicated at the end. AD 778, however, does not leave 32 years until the completion of 6000 years but 21 on the standard correlation of AD and AM[II] dates. Subtracting 32 years from 6000 would take us to 5968 (= AD767), and subtracting 40 from that would give us 5928 (= AD 727) — the other year mentioned in the text. The text would seem, I would suggest, to bring together two dating clauses, one from AD 738, and one from AD 727 that was later updated to AD 767.

Easter dispute in Lombardy to rival those in Ireland, England, or even Francia, we do not know about it.

Reconstructing more specifics about knowledge of computus in eighth-century Italy is unsurprisingly challenging in this context. In 2006, Arno Borst argued that there were two insular-influenced computistical tracts from eighth-century Bobbio or its orbit: the *Dialogus de computo Langobardiae* of *c.* AD 750 and the *Quaestiones de computo Langobardiae* of *c.* AD 780.[22] A third of his texts, the Veronese *Libellus annalis* of AD 793, provides an end piece to understanding Lombard computistics in the century, and represents a coherent Dionysius-influenced computistical handbook.[23] His principal reason for connecting these texts with the Lombard kingdom was their presence in a manuscript from Verona of *c.* AD 800.[24] This is far from decisive as reasons go, not least given that much of the rest of the manuscript is taken up with texts that are not Lombard in origin, including Isidore of Seville, Bede, and an explicitly Frankish computus of AD 737.[25] Indeed, in the case of the *Dialogus*, Immo Warntjes has observed that the text would look entirely insular were it not for the last chapter on indictions — a chapter that is clearly an addition to the original text in the manuscript anyway.[26] Logically, of course, there is little to rule out composition within Italy in circles that included, or that were inspired by, Irish scholars. Either way, the evidence we have for computistical knowledge in eighth-century Lombardy suggests that it was very much in keeping with that elsewhere: it was built up from material which circulated from across Christendom and much of it was relatively generic.

Within the above context, *CA* provides an unusual point of reference. As the computistical text with the clearest statement of its early Lombard origins, we can use it to establish stronger foundations for understanding computus in eighth-century northern Italy.

Divisions of time

The beginning of *CA*, on the fourteen divisions of time, establishes some important points of contact. Variations of such texts were a major part of the insular and continental computistical repertoires, not least in the way it provided a rough organisational structure to treatises, moving from the shortest to the longest units.[27] Understanding the relationship between the different extant versions,

---

22 *Dial. Langob.* is ed. by Borst (2006), 424–61; *Quaest. Langob.* by Borst (2006), 509–26.

23 *Lib. ann.* is ed. by Borst (2006), 660–772.

24 Now Berlin, Staatsbibliothek Preußischer Kulturbesitz, Phillipps 1831.

25 For a detailed description of the manuscript see Rose (1893), 280–86. See also the misgivings in Bullough (2003), 360, aimed specifically at Borst's claim that the *Lib. ann.* of AD 793 in the same manuscript was composed in Verona.

26 Warntjes (2010), CLXXIV–CLXXIX.

27 Graff (2010), 112–42, esp. 117–25.

however, is work in progress.[28] Graff's study of 2010 provisionally identified a few variants connected to a long recension δ (or *Standard DDT* in Bisagni's more expansive 2020 study), itself defined on the basis of the manuscripts of the Sirmond Collection.[29] Some of that text may be a later interpolation or development as it elaborates on points well beyond what seems to be the initial scope of the work.[30] Indeed, Warntjes noted that the Sirmond *Standard DDT* could be understood in its later manuscript context as part of a composite work with capitula that include topics anachronistic within Irish computistics that early: the incarnation year, the indiction, the *cyclus lunaris*, the calculation of the lunar age and weekday of any given day of a year, the time of the day of the kindling of the moon, the length of moonlight per day, the rogation, and material on astronomy.[31] Graff also identified a shorter recension β that may be closer to an insular archetype in some readings but which presents its own challenges, notably with no chapters on the *saeculum*, *aetas* or *mundus* but with instead a number of astronomical chapters from Isidore not found in δ.[32] Many other versions — often shorter — either seem dependent on these textual families, include other interpolations, or like β lack the later chapters. Some, including the core δ family, include more than one definition of some units of time, as if the authors were comparing the different

---

28 Bisagni (2020), 21.

29 Graff's key witnesses to δ are Oxford, Bodleian Library, Bodley 309, 62v–73v (Vendôme, *c.* AD 1075) and Geneva, Bibliothèque de Genève, Lat. 50, 139r–148v (Massay, *c.* AD 825; available online at: https://www.e-codices.unifr.ch/en/searchresult/list/one/bge/lat0050), to which can be added the other two well-known witnesses Tours, Bibliothèque municipale, 334, 20r–27r (Tours, *c.* AD 819); Paris, Bibliothèque nationale de France, Lat. 16361, 248–279 (Tours, early eleventh century; available online at: https://gallica.bnf.fr/ark:/12148/btv1b9067149q); and, with some omissions, Vatican, Biblioteca Apostolica Vaticana, Ross. 247, 152v–170r (Monastier-sur-Gazeille, *c.* AD 1020; available online at: https://digi.vatlib.it/view/MSS_Ross.247). Karlsruhe, Badische Landesbibliothek, 442, 61r–83r (prov. Durlach, *c.* AD 1000; available online at: https://digital.blb-karlsruhe.de/id/2589900) represents a close but much interpolated relative of δ. Graff's overview of the key similarities of the recension is far from exhaustive but it is notable that these all share the same long introduction. See also Bisagni (2020), 21–26, in which he argues for including the *Sententiae in laude conputi* as part of δ.

30 Graff (2010), 122–23, considers these predated Bede; Bisagni (2020), 21, leaves open the possibility that some editing was Carolingian.

31 Warntjes (2010), XXVIII–XXIX n. 55; Bisagni (2020), 21.

32 Graff's key witnesses to β are Bern, Burgerbibliothek, 417, 47r–61v (near Fleury, *c.* AD 826) and Dijon, Bibliothèque municipale, 448, 29r–37v (Saint-Bénigne de Dijon, early eleventh century; available online at: http://patrimoine.bm-dijon.fr/pleade/functions/ead/attached/FR212316101_saintbenigne/FR212316101_saintbenigne_e0001851.pdf). To β can possibly be added the witness of Cologne, Diözesan- und Dombibliothek, 83-II, 37r–44r (Cologne, AD 805; available online at: https://digital.dombibliothek-koeln.de/handschriften), which ends at the point that the other witnesses — and indeed δ — include a story about St Pachomius. Graff also discusses Vatican, Biblioteca Apostolica Vaticana, Urb. lat. 290, 34v–41r (Sankt Nikolaus Brauweiler, late eleventh century; available online at: https://digi.vatlib.it/view/MSS_Urb.lat.290) as being closer to β textually with some contamination from δ — but the contamination mostly seems to be that its contents follow δ to include the chapters on the *aetas*, *saeculum*, and *mundus* but not the Isidorean astronomical chapters found at the end of β.

texts available. In such a context, it may be important that *DDT* in *CA* lacks the multiple definitions and the anachronisms. It may therefore represent one of the earliest versions of the tradition, perhaps to be placed between *CE*, when the smallest unit, the *atomus*, was not fully part of the *DDT* scheme, and MC, when it was.[33]

CA lists the divisions as follows:

the atom, the moment, the *punctum*, the hour, the *quadrans*, the day, the week, the month, the season, the year, the *saeculum*, the age, and the world era.[34]

Immediately this shows a connection with MC, which also opens with this same rare ordering, with the *saeculum* placed before the era.[35] (It may be worth noting now that early knowledge of MC in Italy is also suggested by a similar extract in the same manuscript as the allegedly Greek-influenced Easter table of AD 763).[36] Many of the definitions of units of time offered in *CA* are taken from Isidore or are common to Irish texts, for example in a definition of the minute being 'just like a minor moment, because that which fills up more, counts less'.[37] Further Irish features can be found in the definition of the year, where the comment on the diminutive *annuli* (= months) is related to one in *CE*;[38] the mistaken equation of *quadrans* (1/4) with the Greek *dodras* (3/4) is found in MC;[39] and the etymology of *saeculum* 'from the observation of six ages' (*sex etatibus colitur*) echoes a comment in the *Dial. Langob.* and, again, MC.[40] It may also be significant that *CA* is only the second text known after MC to define a moment as containing 15 atoms.[41] In sharing rare features with both *CE* and MC, neither of which

---

33 On the importance of the *atomus* in distinguishing phases of *DDT* see Bisagni (2020), 13–14, 28–35, for the tradition of expanded versions of *DDT*, which Bisagni labels *aucti*.

34 *CA* 1 in the Appendix below.

35 MC 1 (Warntjes (2010), 4). Compare *DDT* 2.1.1 (Bisagni (2020), 67; PL 90, 653). *Dial. Langob.* 3B (Borst (2006), 434–35) in contrast gives 12 divisions of time, dropping the atom, *tempus*, *aetas*, and *mundus*, but adding *cyclus*.

36 Vatican, Biblioteca Apostolica Vaticana, Vat. lat. 6018, 68r–v (Central Italy, early ninth century; available online at: https://digi.vatlib.it/view/MSS_Vat.lat.6018), although it gives 13 divisions of time as it omits *tempus* like *Dial. Langob.* (see previous note). The text quotes the definition of time from MC 1 (Warntjes (2010), 2–3): *Tempus est spatium tendens ab initio usque in fine* — closer than *Dial. Langob.* 1B (Borst (2006), 433): *Tempus proprie dicitur spatium extendens ab initio usque ad finem.* See also n. 41 below. For the connections with Byzantine traditions, see Chekin (1999), 18–20.

37 *CA* 4 in the Appendix below with textual parallels. The quotation is attributed to Isidore but is not found in any of his works, perhaps suggesting an Irish teacher of that name (Warntjes (2010), 14, commentary).

38 *CA* 12 in the Appendix below. Compare *CE*, 95.

39 MC 7 (Warntjes (2010), 18).

40 MC 43 (Warntjes (2010), 142); *Dial. Langob.* 3B (Borst (2006), 435).

41 MC 1 (Warntjes (2010), 6). The text in Vatican, Biblioteca Apostolica Vaticana, Vat. lat. 6018, 68r may also be a relative as it states *V addomi in momento* — the *V* surely a mistake for *XV*.

circulated particularly widely in Europe, it seems likely that the source material came out of the same intellectual milieu in early-eighth-century Ireland.[42]

The apocalyptic material at the end of *CA's DDT* adds a different dynamic to the collection. Countdowns to the Year 6000 were not uncommon in the seventh and eighth centuries, but explicit reference to the End in these texts were. Almost all of our examples come from sources using Victorius of Aquitaine and Isidore of Seville — possibly starting in Ireland — plus the chronicles of Fredegar.[43] These generally pre-date the use of AD-dates, making the reference in *CA's* dating clause something of a novelty.[44] *CA* goes on to explain that there are six world ages in imitation of the six days of creation, with a seventh age of rest in imitation of the seventh day. This is not in keeping with Augustine's popular view that the seventh age was something that ran concurrently with the sixth, and it strays close to the millenarianism he argued against in his old age.[45] *CA* preserved the standard warnings from the Gospels that only God would know exactly when the End would come (Matthew 24:36; cf. Mark 13:32 and Acts 1:7). Nevertheless, the author also followed an old strategy, also employed in the fourth-century Cologne Prologue, in which the totality of history was compared to the twelve hours of the day, with Christ born at the end of the eleventh hour.[46] (If 12 hours represented 6000 years then each hour represented 500 years, with Christ born in AM 5500). By doing this, the author gave the impression of more certainty about the time left to come than was usually acceptable. The shadow of the End hung over this discussion of time and one wonders, not just about the proximity of an Apocalyptic Year 6000, but also the anxiety caused by the circulation of Pseudo-Methodius' *Revelationes* at this time in Italy and Columbanian circles, which gave a narrative of the End Times that started with the Arab conquests of the seventh century 'in the seventh millennium.'[47]

The implications of the apocalyptic section are woven into the material that follows. The author draws various parallels between time, the body, and the world. Just as there are four elements, there are four humours and four seasons, all inexorably linked; and there are four principal rivers, and four cardinal points, just as the body has four cardinal points (head, feet, right and left). There are six

---

42 A final feature to note about *DDT* in *CA* is that this was almost certainly one of the sources used by the compiler of the Bobbio Computus (Milan, Biblioteca Ambrosiana, H 150 inf. — Burgundy, after AD 826/7; available online at: http://213.21.172.25/0b02da8280051be4) and a related *computus* of AD 826 (Paris, Bibliothèque nationale de France, Lat. 528, 72r–76r — St Denis, after AD 826; available online at: https://gallica.bnf.fr/ark:/12148/btv1b9078378q), which both contain sixteen divisions of time but which quote a number of the same or similar definitions (as will be apparent in the apparatus of the Appendix below).

43 A full list is provided in Warntjes (2019), 54–61.

44 Often AD dates were popularised alongside the revised AM[III] reckoning: Palmer (2011), 1320–21.

45 Augustine, *De civitate Dei* 20.7; 22.30 (ed. Bernhard Dombart and Alfons Kalb in CCSL 48–49, 709, 865–66). See Palmer (2013), 610–11; Palmer (2014), 45–46.

46 The Cologne Prologue is ed. as *Prologus paschae*, here c. 5, by Krusch (1880), 232.

47 Palmer (2014), 123–26. Pseudo-Methodius, *Revelationes* 10.6 (ed. Aerts and Kortekaas (1998), i 135).

186 JAMES T. PALMER

ages of man, just as there are six ages of the world, and no one knows when the world will end, just as no one knows when an old man will die. Human existence and time are symbolically linked and yet, at the same time, they are unpredictable beyond a certain point. This all pushes eschatological matters much further than one finds in the near-contemporary *Dial. Langob.*, for instance, which is more focused on the calendar.[48] But, perhaps importantly, the interest in comparing numerical patterns in this way has a strong Irish pedigree, best represented by the *Liber de numeris* which itself drew on a version of *DDT* and which may have originated in the circles connected to Virgil of Salzburg in the middle decades of the eighth century.[49]

CA continues with extensive consideration of the ordering of time and nature. It discusses, for example, how Octavian divided the world into three (Europe, Africa, and Asia), and how he introduced the indiction cycle — a comment which again suggests that this is a Lombard appropriation of Irish material since, as mentioned above, Irish computi were not much concerned with the indiction (**C** 117v; **P** 17r).[50] Threes are a common organising principle as the material unfolds. There are three cycles: of the moon, of the sun, and of days. The *mundus* is made of three parts: heaven, earth, and sea, each comprising three elements. While Bethmann thought that it was all 'meist aus Isidor', there are few direct parallels, and indeed some notable differences.[51] Isidore, for instance, says that the *mundus* is so named because it is in constant motion, *in motu*; CA, on the other hand, says that it is named from cleanliness, *munditia*, its original state before it was corrupted (**C** 117v; **P** 17v).[52] Both definitions, notably, are given in the δ recension of *DDT*, again suggesting a shared heritage.[53]

Next, the author outlines a standard theory about how the tides wax and wane in relation to the course of the moon (**C** 118r; **P** 18r). The author divides the tides between the *malina* and *lido*, both relatively unusual terms that mark the higher and lower average tides and which are used in the seventh-century Irish texts *De mirabilibus sacrae scripturae* and *De ordine creaturarum*.[54] CA outlines how

---

48 E.g. compare *Dial. Langob.* 7 (Borst (2006), 437).

49 McNally (1957), 51. The earliest manuscript is Colmar, Bibliothèque municipale, 43 (39), 60r–175v (Alsace region, provenance Murbach, late eighth century or early ninth; Bischoff (1998–2017), i 206 (no. 953)). For the manuscript transmission of and literature on the *Liber de numeris*, see now Ó Corráin (2017), 738–40 (no. 577). Another parallel is of course Isidore of Seville's *Liber numerorum* (ed. Guillaumin (2005)).

50 See Warntjes (2010), CLXXVI.

51 Bethmann (1874), 728. One clear borrowing is on **C** 118r; **P** 18v: *sol per se ipsum movetur, non cum caelo veritur, nam si fixus in caelo esset, omnes dies et noctes equalies existerent.* Compare Isidore, *Etymologiae* 3.50 (ed. Gasparotto and Guillaumin (2009), 115): *solem per se ipsum moveri, non cum mundo verti. Nam si fixus caelo maneret, omnes dies et noctes aequales existerent.*

52 Isidore, *Etymologiae* 13.1 (ed. Gasparotto (2004), 6). Cf. Lozovsky (2000), 104.

53 *DDT* 2.15.1–2 (Bisagni (2020), 104–05).

54 *De mirabilibus sacrae scripturae* 7 (PL 35, 2157–59); *De ordine creaturarum* 9.4–7 (ed. Díaz y Díaz (1972), 148–50). On the latter, see now Smyth (2011), 137–222, esp. 140–42 on the discussion of tides in the two texts.

the *malina* and *lido* each last seven days and nine hours, which added together make 14 days and 18 hours, and therefore per lunar month of 29 ½ days there are two *malinae* and two *lidones* — a statement which in fact agrees better with Bede in *De temporum ratione*[55] than any known Irish text (**C** 118r; **P** 18r). The author of *De ordine creaturarum* observed that the *malina* is in such agreement with the moon that the moon is always born in the middle of it. *CA* takes a similar position, by stating that a *malina* always begins on *luna XXVII* (*cum et enim vicesima septima luna fuerit tunc indubitanter prima mallina sit* — 'For when it was *luna XXVII*, it would undoubtedly be the first *malina*'). A *lido* is said to start on *luna XX* (although there is a corruption in the text to *vicesima v*), when it overcomes the *malina* which had begun on *luna XII*.[56] *CA* then takes a more idiosyncratic direction by linking the tides to winds and days of the week. If a *lido* should begin on a Thursday, for instance, *CA* suggests the wind will come from the south.

Natural philosophy lessons in *CA* end with discussion of the sun, with an unusual addition, which again might point towards origins in an Irish milieu. The author borrowed from Isidore's *Etymologiae* to outline the nature and cycle of the sun.[57] But Isidore had described the sun going under the earth (*sub terras*), imagining that it passed under a globe.[58] *CA* changes this so that the sun 'plunges itself into ocean, goes along an unknown subterranean passage, and again returns to the East' (*Oceano se intinxerit per incognitas subterras vias vadit et iterum ad orientem recurrit*; **C** 118r; **P** 18v; first part also in Monza, Biblioteca Capitolare, e-14/127, 12r). This is not necessarily a nod to the idea of antipodes, as there is no indication here of inhabited lands. The mystery of where the sun goes at night, on the other hand, might still have parallels in the Irish poetic cosmological speculation discussed by John Carey, in which it was imagined that the sun travelled under the sea and land.[59]

Computistical material in *CA*

After the divisions of time and nature, *CA* turns to computistical matters. Discussion opens with a typical section on the classification of the months in accordance with their calends, nones, and ides, common to many early medieval computi (**C** 118v; **P** 19r). Here, the notable feature is that the 'March Class' of months precedes the 'April Class', which again is typical of computi from the middle of

---

55 Bede, *De temporum ratione* 29 (ed. Charles W. Jones in CCSL 123B, 368–69).

56 Compare the table in *Lib. ann.* 51 (Borst (2006), 746–47), where the sequence of *malina* and *ledo* is reversed.

57 Isidore, *Etymologiae* 3.49–50 (Gasparotto and Guillaumin (2009), 113, 115).

58 Isidore, *Etymologiae* 3.34 (Gasparotto and Guillaumin (2009), 97).

59 Carey (1989), 1–10.

the eighth century in contrast to *CE* and *MC*.[60] The accompanying breakdown of months into their calends, nones, and ides is, on the other hand, classically Irish, and has direct parallels in both *MC* and *CE*.[61] It was, at the same time, so widespread a bit of text that it is hard to draw any conclusions about it other than *CA* was typical of its time.

Many of the rules for calculating Easter are entirely in keeping with early Dionysian orthodoxy.[62] It stipulated a 35-day window for Easter Day between 22 March and 25 April. The limits for *luna XIV* were 21 March to 18 April and Easter Day had to fall on the following Sunday. Yet the authorities cited by the author for some of the issues involved are certainly not standard. There are no references to the obvious champions of the Alexandrian reckoning, Cyril and Dionysius, who were cited for instance in the near-contemporary Frankish computus of AD 737 (*Dial. Neustr.*); nor, even, is the famous legend of the Council of Nicaea mentioned.[63] The only writer cited for defence of Alexandrian lunar paschal dates starting on *luna XV* is Victorius in one of two alleged quotations that do not correspond to extant Victorian texts. The second quotation even seems to derive from a comment on common and embolismic years from Dionysius' *Epistola ad Bonifatium et Bonum*, which might suggest some damage or corruption in the author's source material.[64] Twice Anatolius of Laodicea, whose work was most popular in Ireland, is cited. Neither time, however, does the citation correspond to any of his extant works, and indeed one of the quotations seems to be by Isidore.[65] This is perhaps again in keeping with early eighth-century computistics: the author knows some of the right technical details for the Alexandrian Easter, but the material has come to them in such a state that they did not know accurately

---

60 This feature of Irish computi is outlined in Warntjes (2010a), 80.

61 *CE*, 96–97; MC 28 (Warntjes (2010), 78).

62 The Dionysian computistical corpus is ed. by Krusch (1938), 59–86. On the technical dimensions, see Declercq (2002), 165–246. On the development of Dionysius' *Argumenta*, see Warntjes (2010a).

63 *Dial. Neustr.* 15C, 18, 19 (ed. Borst (2006), 396, 398, 402): Dionysius, Cyril, Cyril and Dionysius respectively. The perceived authority of the Council of Nicaea of AD 325 seems to have been popularised by Dionysius, *Epistola ad Petronium* (ed. Krusch (1938), 63), but there is no evidence that the council did issue a table: Duchesne (1880), 5–42.

64 **C** 119r; **P** 19v: *ut Victorius dicit, 'Embolismus annus est, qui communium annorum damna supplet'* — compare Dionysius, *Epistola ad Bonifatium et Bonum* (ed. Krusch (1938), 83): *Embolismorum autem ista ratio probatur existere, quod annorum communium videtur damna supplere*. There is a similar appropriation of the sentence in *CE*, 113: *Embolismus enim ergo superadditus interpretatur, id est annus damna enim communis inplet*. For the context in Irish teachings see Warntjes (2010), 244.

65 The first quotation is on **C** 119r; **P** 19v: *ut Anatolius dicit: annus solis per anfractus peractis CCCLXV diebus et quadrante ad eadem loca siderum redit ex quibus prius progressus est*. Cf. Isidore, *Etymologiae* 5.36.1 (ed. Yarza Urquiola and Andrés Santos (2013), 121). The computus in Karlsruhe, Badische Landesbibliothek, 442 (see n. 29), 71v attributes the quotation to Ambrosius. It is attributed to Augustine in MC 31 (Warntjes 2010), 88. The second Anatolius quotation is on **C** 120r; **P** 20v: *Nam sicut Anatolius dicit: luna quae in mense extinguitur illo reputatur non quod incipit*. Perhaps relatedly there is a third pseudo-Anatolian quotation in Monza, Biblioteca Capitolare, e-14/127, 15v–16r (but not **C** or **P**) on the Greek and Latin terms for the *saltus lunae*. For Anatolius, see Mc Carthy and Breen (2003).

who had written it.[66] More importantly: for a computist to appeal to the trusted authority of Victorius and Anatolius for Alexandrian authority suggests they were working in an insular-influenced environment no later than the first half of the eighth century, after which the authority of both authors was much diminished. This might give us more confidence in accepting the hypothesis that the whole text is from around AD 747, rather than being a much later confection that appropriates an earlier text at the beginning only.

The placing of the *saltus lunae* in *CA* reinforces the argument that we are dealing with an early, coherent composition. The three major Irish treatises proposed that the *saltus lunae* should be placed on 21 or 22 March, while Victorius proposed 17 November, and Bede and the Franks observed it on 24 November.[67] It is the Victorian date that is stated in *CA*, which suggests a reliance on Victorian computi for some technical detail (**C** 119r; **P** 19r). The list of epacts for January, given shortly beforehand in the text, is nevertheless the standard Dionysian-Bedan one, with the *saltus* placed in the nineteenth year. Again, such mild inconsistency in tradition is in keeping with other mid-eighth-century computi from the Frankish kingdom, as communities adopted new tables while still using older, outmoded texts for various points of detail.[68] Further reliance on Victorius is suggested by the dating of the Creation of the World to 25 March (**C** 119v; **P** 20r). This date is mentioned in the *Prologus Victorii* as it was standard in Roman and Greek chronological traditions, and indeed *CA* specifies that this tradition was *secundum Latinos*.[69] Insular reckonings, in contrast, dated Creation to 21 or 22 March, with Bede arguing instead for 18 March.[70] *CA* was evidently not compiled by someone bound by all the current parameters of insular thinking. All of this and the fact that no alternatives are discussed in the text, unlike in *CE*, *MC* or Bede, seems to confirm the impression that the assemblage was written in Lombardy itself and postdates the final major computistical debates in the insular and Frankish worlds, as it points only to consensus on controversial points, if only unsteadily.

CA is typical of early eighth-century computistical debates by concluding with a long section on the *bissextus*, a technical issue which exercised the Irish computists and Bede but fewer computists after *c*. AD 800. The author strongly defended a calculation based on a model that counts the 12 hours of daytime only, meaning that they reckoned an increment of 3 hours per year. Such a calculation is also contained in *DRC* and *Dial. Langob.*, perhaps again suggesting

---

66 See also Palmer (2011), 223–24, 234–35.

67 MC 62 (Warntjes (2010a), 278): 22 March; *CE*, 113, 123–24; *DRC* 112 (Walsh and Ó Cróinín (1988), 211). Although Bede placed the *saltus* in the November, he had sympathy for the March option: Bede, *De temporum ratione* 20 (CCSL 123B, 348).

68 Palmer (2011a), 222–23, 233, 241.

69 Victorius, *Prologus* 7 (ed. Krusch (1938), 23).

70 *DRC* 68 (Walsh and Ó Cróinín (1988), 177) and MC 44 (Warntjes (2010), 146): 21 March; *Dial. Langob.* 18B (Borst (2006), 449): 22 March; Bede, *De temporum ratione* 7 (CCSL 123B, 294): 18 March.

Irish-Lombard connections.[71] Indeed, it is supported in *CA* with inclusion, right at the end, of the pseudo-Dionysiac *Argumentum XVI*, a widely circulated text on the *bissextus*, which Warntjes suggests was written in Rath Melsigi *c.* AD 675.[72] In the Badia Amiatina text, the 12-hour argument is explicitly cited against scholars (who would ultimately include Bede) who argued in favour of a 6-hour increment per annum based on a 24-hour clock. The assumption of our computist is that night-time is governed by the moon and therefore is of no relevance to leap-year calculations. This needs to be understood alongside the statement earlier, in *DDT*, that the author accepted that a 'natural day' has 24 hours.[73] The computist placed the *bissextus* on 24 February, as most people did, with the common saying 'it is the sixth calends today and the sixth calends tomorrow' (*sexto kalendas hodie et vi kalendas cras*) — a phrase found also in *Dial. Langob.*, and in *CE* without commitment to that option.[74]

More distinctively, *CA* includes a novel version of the discovery of the bissextile increment by King Gignus of the Sabines (**C** 120r; **P** 20v). It is said that Gignus charted the course of the sun by making a mark on one of the four principal towers in the city on the solstice, 25 June. He noticed that after a year the sun did not return to the original mark, but rather lagged one quadrant behind. From this observation, the king knew to add four quadrants to every fourth year. The story is distinctive as most sources followed Macrobius in attributing the discovery to Caesar. A rare exception is the Irish MC, which gives a slightly different version in which Gignus discovered an 'overflow of light in nature' by observing the sun's passage through the Zodiac.[75] Despite the difference, it might be a further indication that *CA* and MC were distantly related. Further evidence that the story was known in Irish circles can be found in the *DDT Auctus* 1 (AD 754×797), where a comment closer to that in *CA* noted some people preferred the Gignus story.[76] The limited textual footprint of the Gignus legend

---

71 *DRC* 55–56 (Walsh and Ó Cróinín (1988), 166–68); *Dial. Langob.* 24 (Borst (2006), 457). See also Vatican, Biblioteca Apostolica Vaticana, Vat. lat. 6018 (see n. 36), 67v, in a section strongly influenced by Irish computistics. The issue of the different bissextile calculations based on a 12- or 24-hour day is discussed in Smyth (2017), with the key sources on the 12-hour day summarised at 236–46.

72 Warntjes (2010a), 92–94.

73 *CA* 8 in the Appendix below.

74 *Dial. Langob.* 24 (Borst (2006), 457); *CE*, 105; Laon, Bibliothèque municipale, 422 (see n. 76), 52r; Cologne, Diözesan- und Dombibliothek, 83-II (see n. 32), 26r; Angers, Bibliothèque municipale, 477 (461) (see n. 75), 20r. See also Geneva, Bibliothèque de Genève, Lat. 50 (see n. 29), 148v. On the principles see also MC 41 (Warntjes (2010), 130–31); *DRC* 57 (Walsh and Ó Cróinín (1988), 168–69); *De bissexto* (PL 101, 997C–D).

75 MC 41 (Warntjes (2010), 122). It is copied in the Angers Glosses in Angers, Bibliothèque municipale, 477 (461), 20r (Landévennec, late ninth century; available online at: https://bvmm.irht.cnrs.fr/mirador/index.php? manifest=https%3A%2F%2Fbvmm.irht.cnrs.fr%2Fiiif%2F1097%2Fmanifest). See Warntjes (2010), CV, with gloss itself printed on CLXXXVI.

76 Laon, Bibliothèque municipale, 422, 51v (Notre-Dame, Laon, first half of ninth century; Bischoff (1998–2017), ii 34 (no. 2114); available online at: https://bibliotheque-numerique.ville-laon.fr/

further strengthens the suggestion that CA as we have it is based on earlier insular texts.

Underlying the concern for the bissextile increment in CA is a desire to ensure the correct calculation of time. The consequences of failing to calculate leap years is carefully outlined, to show how natural time and artificial time would get out of sync. If year 1 starts on a Sunday, then in year 5 it should fall on a Friday if you had counted correctly, but you would have made it a Thursday if not. The placing of this discussion just after a declaration of ignorance about the timing of the coming Judgement may be significant because you would not want to generate unnecessary anxiety about time through basic miscalculation. Bede, too, warned about the confusion that would follow if one failed to calculate the leap year.[77] The reckoning of time was a complicated business and accuracy was important.[78]

Conclusion

CA deserves a place alongside the other computistical treatises of the seventh and eighth centuries as a significant witness to debates about nature as they unfolded across the Latin West. Despite only surviving in three high medieval manuscripts, there is plenty of evidence that CA belongs to this earlier period — not just in its dating clause, but throughout. It was composed by someone able to consult material that can be found in DRC, CE, and MC — treatises which did not circle widely but which do seem to have been written in the same milieu in the south of Ireland and some of which was available in Italy. Further sources and features reinforced the insular connections. At the same time, there are a number of features that suggest at least minor editorial developments made in Lombardy itself. The use of the work of Victorius of Aquitaine on a number of points may be telling here, especially where the text deviates from insular ideas on Creation and demonstrates interest in the origins of indictions. While the overall composition broadly reflects the growing Alexandrian (and Dionysian) consensus in Western Europe in the early eighth century, it also highlights the early uncertainty of authority that dogged the process. The computist could do little more than cite the names of authorities he knew — Victorius, Anatolius, and Isidore — while apparently not always having information that allowed him to identify his sources correctly. Local Latin traditions seeped into the mix as a result. Efforts to systematise computistical knowledge can be seen here but had to be pursued with more energy later in the century, as we see with the Lib. ann. of AD 793.

---

viewer/1471/?offset=43#page=114&viewer=picture&o=bookmark&n=0&q=) provides the fullest version. The abbreviated version in Cologne, Diözesan- und Dombibliothek, 83-II (see n. 32), 26r — which includes a dating clause to AD 797 on 26v — repeats only the sentence on Gignus.

77 Bede, De temporum ratione 38 (CCSL 123B, 400).
78 Palmer (2013), 615.

In the meantime, there was a tangible feeling that time itself was in a precarious position. What did time mean, when its end could come at any moment? Did the approaching Year 6000 mean anything more than the approach of an abstract number? What reassurance was there in the abstractions of time and nature when there was no agreement about how time itself could be understood? *CA* shows a lively attempt to understand the philosophy and theology of time at the same time as computus. It is unusual in doing so, despite widespread consideration of apocalypse and computus. Does this mean that the end weighed more heavily on the imagination in Northern Italy than elsewhere? The debate about Pseudo-Methodius' Revelation in the region might suggest so, but we cannot be sure. There is clearly more work to be done on understanding the diverse and vibrant intellectual culture in Lombardy in the eighth century.

APPENDIX: *De divisionibus temporum* in *CA*

Edition

I provide here an edition of the opening chapters of *CA* to make better available the unique version of *DDT* and provide context for the Lombard dating clause. The notes indicate variations between **C** and **P**, with some consideration of passages from a related *Ratio pascalis* from a ninth-century Lombard manuscript (Monza, Biblioteca Capitolare, e-14/127). I include some telling parallels with other texts where appropriate, which are not intended to be exhaustive. The swift and widespread cross-contamination of different versions of *DDT* make it hard to associate *CA* with any one tradition. To demonstrate the reliance on early Irish computi, I have included comparison with *CE*, *MC*, and *DRC*, as well as the Sirmond *Standard DDT* in its recensions δ (via Bisagni (2020), 57–105) and β (via Dijon, Bibliothèque municipale, 448). Because of the connection with the Gignus legend, I also include parallels with *DDT Auctus* 1. I include the Bobbio Computus and Vatican, Biblioteca Apostolica Vaticana, Reg. lat. 123 as two important examples of computi that compile excerpts from different *DDT* traditions. Finally, I have included Paris, Bibliothèque nationale de France, Lat. 528 as an example of the Carolingian *DDT Auctus* 3, as it contains some parallels to suggest it is a descendant of the same material used in *CA*.

<...> = additions by editor

(...) = comments by editor

\<1.\> *Divisiones temporum quattuordecim sunt: athomos, momentum, minutum, punctum, hora, quadrans, dies, ebdomada, mensis, tempus, annus, saeculum, etas, mundus.*[79]

Quindecim athomos in momentum.[80] *Quattuor momenta in minutum. Duo minuta*[81] *et medium punctum. Quattuor puncti in hora\<m\>. Tres hora in quadrante\<m\>. Quattuor quadrantes in diem. Septem dies in ebdomada\<m\>. Quattuor ebdomadae in mense\<m\>. Tres menses in tempus. Quattuor tempora in annum. Decem et novem annos in cyclo lunae. Quingenti trigenta duos annos in solis et lunae adunatum cyclum.*[82]

\<2.\> *Athomos Grecum nomen est, quod Latini*[83] *interpretantur indivisibile.*[84] *Omne enim quicquid dividi non potest, athomos dicitur.*[85]

Athomorum genera V sunt: athomos in re philosophiae; athomos in corpore; athomos in numero; athomos in tempore; athomos in oratione.[86]

Athomos in re philosophiae dicunt quasdam partes in mundo minutissimas, ut visui[87] *non pateant, nec sectiones recipiant. Huc illucque feruntur, sicut minutissimi pulveres qui effusi per tenebras solis radiis videntur.*[88]

---

79 See MC 1 (Warntjes (2010), 4), where the same sentence with the same rare ordering appears but introduced by the question *divisiones temporum quot sunt?*.

80 MC 1 (Warntjes (2010), 6).

81 minuti **P.**

82 Similar passages can be found in MC 1 (Warntjes (2010), 6); *Dial. Langob.* 3B, 4B (Borst (2006), 435–36). In these, it is certain that the structure should be 'in+acc.' as the smaller unit 'goes into' the larger, so I have emended *CA* accordingly where the scribes use 'in+abl.'. The use of 'in+abl.' with *in cyclo* unsettles the certainty of the correction, but it may be that the author or a scribe imagined the nineteen lines or section in a lunar table. To complicate matters, the version in Monza, Biblioteca Capitolare, e-14/127, 3r–v, unambiguously uses 'in+abl.' throughout and it cannot be determined if this represents the original text or a later attempt to standardise it.

83 Latine **C.**

84 Cf. MC 2 (Warntjes (2010), 8); Bobbio Computus 89 (PL 129, 1316A); Paris, Bibliothèque nationale de France, Lat. 528, 72r; Vatican, Biblioteca Apostolica Vaticana, Reg. lat. 123, 3v: *Atomus nomen Graecum est, quod interpretatur indivisibilis, nam atomon apud Graecos indivisum, vel indivisible interpretatur.*

85 Cf. Bobbio Computus 89 (PL 129, 1316A); Paris, Bibliothèque nationale de France, Lat. 528, 72r: *Omne enim quod in mundo est sive corporale, seu incorporale, quod dividi ac partiri non potest, atomus est.*

86 Cf. Bobbio Computus 89 (PL 129, 1316A); Paris, Bibliothèque nationale de France, Lat. 528, 72r; Vatican, Biblioteca Apostolica Vaticana, Reg. lat. 123, 3v: *Atomorum genera quinque sunt, id est atomus in re, atomus in corpore, atomus in oratione, atomus in numero, atomus in tempore.* The Sirmond *DDT* 2.2.5 (Bisagni (2020), 70, and Dijon, Bibliothèque municipale, 448, 31r) reverses *atomus in re* and *atomus in corpore*, relabelling the former *atomus in sole*. An explanation of the different label is given in *DDT Auctus* 1 (Laon, Bibliothèque municipale, 422, 37v only, as Cologne, Diözesan- und Dombibliothek, 83-II treats it differently).

87 sui **P.**

88 Cf. Dijon, Bibliothèque municipale, 448, 31r; Bobbio Computus 89 (PL 129, 1316A); Paris, Bibliothèque nationale de France, Lat. 528, 72r; Vatican, Biblioteca Apostolica Vaticana, Reg. lat. 123, 3v: *Sicut ait (dixit* in Reg. lat. 123; *diffinium dicens* in Dijon 448) *Isidorus: Atomos philosophi*

Athomos in corpore: ut frangis granum in mille partes. Millesima pars quae dividi non potest, athomos in corpore dicitur.[89]

Athomos in numero: ut soluitur mille in centum, centum in viginti, viginiti in decem, decem in quinque, quinque in duo, duo in unum. Unum quod dividi non potest, athomos in numero dicitur.[90]

*Athomos in tempore: ut soluitur mundus in aetates, aetates in annum, annus in tempore, tempora in menses, menses in ebdomdas, ebdomada in dies, diem in quadrans, quadrans in horas, hora in punctum, punctum in minutum, minutum in momentum, momentum in quindecim (15v **P**) partes. Quintadecima pars momenti quae dividi non potest, athomos in tempore dicitur.*[91]

Athomos in oratione: ut soluitur oratione sentencias, sententias in versus, versus in partes, partes in pedes, pedes in syllaba, syllaba in libro. Littera non habet in quo soluet inde athomos dicitur indivisible, quia non solui nec dividi potest.[92]

<**3.**> *Momentum, certus lectus solis est in caelo.*[93] *Momentum minutum atque angustissimum tempus, a motus siderum dictum,*[94] *est enim extremitas horae in brevibus intervallis, cum sol aliquid sibi cedit aut succedit.*[95]

---

dicunt quasdam partes in mundo minutissimas, ut visui non pateant, nec sectionem recipiant. Huc illucque feruntur sicut minutissimi pulveres, qui effusi per tenebras solis radiis videntur.

89 Cf. Bobbio Computus 89 (PL 129, 1316B; Milan, Biblioteca Ambrosiana, H 150 inf., 36r): *In corpore veluti cum partiris quamlibet partem lapidis in mille particulas, millesima pars quae partiri, vel dividi non potest, atomus in corpore dicitur, id est indivisibilis*; and Vatican, Biblioteca Apostolica Vaticana, Reg. lat. 123, 3v: *Athomus in corpore veluti si dividis quamlibet partem lapidis mille particulas. Millesima pars quae divide non potest, athomus in corpore dicitur.*

90 Cf. Bobbio Computus 89 (PL 129, 1316A); Paris, Bibliothèque nationale de France, Lat. 528, 72r; Vatican, Biblioteca Apostolica Vaticana, Reg. lat. 123, 4r: *Atomus in numero sicuti solvitur millias in M, M in C, C in XX, XX in X, X in V, V in II, II in I, I vero quod dividi, aut solvi non potest, atomus in numero dicitur.*

91 Cf. *DDT Auctus 1* (Laon, Bibliothèque municipale, 422, 57v), which omits the *mundus* and *aetas*, and divides moments into 12.

92 Cf. Bobbio Computus 89 (PL 129, 1316B); Paris, Bibliothèque nationale de France, Lat. 528, 72r: *Atomus in oratione, sicuti oratio in versus, in partes, in syllabas dividitur, ita syllaba in literas, litera autem dividi, vel solvi non potest, ideoque atomus a Latinis philosophis dicta est.* Vatican, Biblioteca Apostolica Vaticana, Reg. lat. 123, 3v–4r, offers a different definition.

93 *CE*, 86 and *DDT* 2.3 (Bisagni (2020), 71), spuriously attributed to Isidore in the latter. Cf. MC 3 (Warntjes (2010), 12).

94 iterum dictus **P** and **C**.

95 Cf. *DRC* 17 (Walsh and Ó Cróinín (1988), 126–27); *DDT* 2.3 (Bisagni (2020), 71); Dijon, Bibliothèque municipale, 448, 31r; *DDT Auctus 1* (Laon, Bibliothèque municipale, 422, 57v; Cologne, Diözesan- und Dombibliothek, 83-II, 20r); Bobbio Computus 96 (PL 129, 1318B); Paris, Bibliothèque nationale de France, Lat. 528, 72v: *Momentum minutum atque angustissimum tempus a motu siderum dictum* (the Sirmond DDT, Dijon 448 and *DDT Auctus 1* add *hic/hoc est a motu sol et lunae*): *est enim extremitas horae in brevibus intervallis, cum sol aliquid sibi cedit, atque succedit*; Monza, Biblioteca Capitolare, e-14/127, 13v: *Momentum minimum atque angustissimum tempus, a modum dierum dictum est, enim extremitas ore brebibus intervallis, cum sol aliquando cedit atque succedit.* The passage is derived from Isidore, *Etymologiae* 5.29.1–2 (Yarza Urquiola and Andrés Santos (2013), 87, 89), which is followed in: *CE*, 86; MC 3 (Warntjes (2010), 12); Bobbio Computus 35 (PL 129,

AN EIGHTH-CENTURY IRISH COMPUTUS IN LOMBARDY 195

\<4.> *Minutum ex minutis elementis dictum, velut minus momentum, quia minus numerat id quod maius implet.*[96]

\<5.> *Punctus a pungendo aciem oculorum, additis enim decem momentis ad presentiam lucis, solatium*[97] *oculorum inpingit.*[98]

\<6.> *Hora dicta est eo quod temperat articulos diei. Horam autem maris et hora\<s> vestimentorum dicimus.*[99]

\<7.> *Quadrans dicitur eo quod quartem partem diei appendit, quem Hebrei quodrantem, Graeci dodrantem, Latini quadrantem vocant.*[100]

\<8.> *Dies dicitur a dividendo lucem ac tenebras. Dies naturalis XXIIII horas. Artificialis vero XII tantum horas habere videtur. Divisiones diei naturalis duae sunt: diurnum et nocturnum. Partes diei tres sunt: mane, meridie, supprema. Mane ab hortu solis quattuor horas habet, meridies quaternas, et supprema quattuor tenere videtur.*[101]

1293C); and Vatican, Biblioteca Apostolica Vaticana, Reg. lat. 123, 4r. The addition of 'sol' may be derived from an effort to clarify that it is the motion of the sun that matters in this definition, as per the first sentence, as Isidore left the matter open and other texts starting with *CE* discussed different kinds of 'moment'.

96 Dijon, Bibliothèque municipale, 448, 31v; *DDT Auctus* 1 (Laon, Bibliothèque municipale, 422, 38v; Cologne, Diözesan- und Dombibliothek, 83-II, 21v); Bobbio Computus 96 (PL 129, 1319A); and Paris, Bibliothèque nationale de France, Lat. 528, 73r. Similar wording in MC 4 (Warntjes (2010), 14), *DRC* 18 (Walsh and Ó Cróinín (1988), 127), and Vatican, Biblioteca Apostolica Vaticana, Reg. lat. 123, 4v, and Sirmond *DDT* 2.4 (Bisagni (2020), 72). Cf. *CE*, 86. Often attributed to Isidore.

97 solatiam **P** and **C**.

98 Cf. Bobbio Computus 96 (PL 129, 1319A); Paris, Bibliothèque nationale de France, Lat. 528, 73r: *Punctum pungendo aciem oculorum dictum; tunc enim post hyemem, et brumalis frigoris caliginem adjunctis X momentis ab acie solis de luminis gratia oculos obtensos transactis frigoris nebulis acies solaris, quasi pungere, seu rutilare humanus visus videtur, et inde illud spatium temporis punctum nominator;* Vatican, Biblioteca Apostolica Vaticana, Reg. lat. 123, 4v: *Super pungendum acie oculorum quo sol oculos pungit, addito puncto super diem, et deinde transfertur admoram X momentorum quae sunt in puncto. Aliter punctus a pungendo quia philosophi horalogium pungebant et scirent quod puncta in unaquaque hora essent.* The first sentence is similar to MC 5 (Warntjes (2010), 14). See also *DDT Auctus* 1 (Laon, Bibliothèque municipale, 422, 38v; Cologne, Diözesan- und Dombibliothek, 83-II, 20v).

99 Cf. Bobbio Computus 96 (PL 129, 1319B); Paris, Bibliothèque nationale de France, Lat. 528, 73r: *Item hora dicta est quasi hora, eo quod temperat articulos diei. Horam autem maris, et horas vestimentorum dicimus.* The Sirmond *DDT* 2.6.2 (Bisagni (2020), 72) and Vatican, Biblioteca Apostolica Vaticana, Reg. lat. 123, 5r, provide only a much looser parallel here, being closer to *CE*, 88. See also MC 6 (Warntjes (2010), 16), which probably reflects the fuller original source material.

100 A misinterpretation of *CE*, 89, a version of which was transmitted to the MC 7 (Warntjes (2010), 18) and the Sirmond *DDT* 2.7 (Bisagni (2020), 73), Bobbio Computus 97 (PL 129, 1319C), and Paris, Bibliothèque nationale de France, Lat. 528, 73v, possibly via this version of *De divisionibus temporum*. The definition is attributed to Isidore in Vatican, Biblioteca Apostolica Vaticana, Reg. lat. 123, 5v.

101 Cf. Bobbio Computus 70 (PL 129, 1307B–D but corrected against Milan, Biblioteca Ambrosiana, H 150 inf., 27v–28r): *Dies dicta est a dividendo ad iacendo lucem a tenebris [...] Mane ab ortu solis usque ad horam quartam dicitur, quod ut quadrans artificialis. Meridies V, VI, VII, VIII, horam tenet.*

<9.> *Ebdomada apud Graecos et Latinos septem*[102] *dierum cursus agitur, apud Hebreos septem*[103] *anni sunt. Declarat hoc Danihel de LXX*[104] *ebdomatibus.*[105]

<10.> *Mensis a mensura*[106] *nomen accepit, quoniam scilicet omnis mensis lunaris dies XX et VIIII et dimidium in se mensurat.*[107]

<11.> *Tempus a temperamento nomen accepit, quia omne tempus tribus mensibus temperatur, vel quia natura unius cuiusque temporis ab alio temperatur.*[108] *Veris enim tempus calorem estatis, aestas auptuni humores, hiemps veris siccitatem temperat. Veris tempus dicitur, quoniam in eo omnia vernant et nascuntur.*[109] *Aestas ab estu dicta est, quia videlicet in eo tempore esti vis caloribus omnia aestuant et fervescunt.*[110] *Autumnus a tempestate vocatur, quoniam in ipso tempore folia arborum cadunt et omnia maturescunt.*[111] *Hiemps a deliberando*[112] *dictus <est>, quia in eo tempore omnia habitant et del<ib>erare videntur.*

<12.> *Annus dictus est quasi anus, id est circulus, inde et anuli mensis diminutive dicti sunt.*[113]

Supprema VIIIIa, X, XI, XII horam obtinere videtur. The Sirmond *DDT* 2.8.1–28 (Bisagni (2020), 73–78) is significantly more expansive.

102 sex **C**.

103 sex **C**.

104 declit **C** and **P**, corrected against MC 10 (Warntjes (2010), 34).

105 Cf. Sirmond *DDT* 2.9.1–2 (Bisagni (2020), 79); Dijon, Bibliothèque municipale, 448, 32r; *DDT Auctus* 1 (Laon, Bibliothèque municipale, 422, 44v; Cologne, Diözesan- und Dombibliothek, 83-II, 22r); Bobbio Computus 56 (PL 129, 1300C, corrected against Milan, Biblioteca Ambrosiana, H 150 inf., 21v–22r); Paris, Bibliothèque nationale de France, Lat. 528, 75r: *Ebomdada apud Graecos et Romanos VII dierum cursu peragitur. Apud Hebraeos autem VII anni sunt. Declarat hoc Daniel de LXX ebdomadibus.* Similar in MC 10 (Warntjes (2010), 34). The first part is from Isidore, *De natura rerum* 3.1 (ed. Fontaine (1960), 183).

106 MC 12 (Warntjes (2010), 44); *Dial. Burg.* 6A (Borst (2006), 357); *Dial. Lang.* 11A (Borst (2006), 441).

107 mensurat in se **P**. Compare Bobbio Computus 58 (PL 129, 1301D, corrected against Milan, Biblioteca Ambrosiana, H 150 inf., 22v): *XXVIIII diebus et semis mensuratur.*

108 cuiusque temperatur temporis ab alio **P**.

109 Cf. *DRC* 42 (Walsh and Ó Cróinín (1988), 150–51); MC 30 (Warntjes (2010), 86); and *Dial. Lang.* 2B (Borst (2006), 434).

110 Cf. *DRC* 43 (Walsh and Ó Cróinín (1988), 152): *Aestas ab estu dicitur, id est a calore.* Bobbio Computus 28 (PL 129, 1290C): *Aestas dicitur ab aestu, id est a calore, et aestas quasi usta, id est exusta et arida.*

111 **P** and **C** both end with *matriscunt*. Corrected against *DRC* 43 (Walsh and Ó Cróinín (1988), 152), Cologne, Diözesan- und Dombibliothek, 83-II, 23v, and Bobbio Computus 28 (PL 129, 1290C).

112 ad erando **P**.

113 Isidore, *De natura rerum* 6.2 (Fontaine (1960), 193): *Annum autem quasi anum dici quidam putant, id est circulum. Unde et annuli dicit sunt diminutive;* also, in *DRC* 44 (Walsh and Ó Cróinín (1988), 153) and *DDT Auctus* 1 (Laon, Bibliothèque municipale, 422, 50r; Cologne, Diözesan- und Dombibliothek, 83-II, 24r). *CE*, 95: *Annus dicitur quasi anus. Unde annuli diminutive dicti sunt, id*

AN EIGHTH-CENTURY IRISH COMPUTUS IN LOMBARDY   197

<13.> *Saeculum dictum est, quoniam sex aetatibus colitur, et est nomen conpositum ex vocabulo numeri, quod est sex, et nomen cultura, et haec compositio sensui intellectum ve<l> contradictum. Colitur enim saeculum ab initio usque in finem per volumina temporum quattuor, per dimensiones dierum sex et praesenas temporum vicissitudines necnon et per sex mundi aetates.*[114]

<14.> *Prima aetas ab initio usque ad diluvium. Secunda a diluvium usque ad Abraham. Tertia ab Abraham usque ad David. Quarta a David usque ad transmigrationem Babylonis.*[115] *Quinta a transmigratione Babilonis usque ad Christem. Sexta a Christo usque in consumationem saeculi, cuius finis incertam. A Christo usque in diem iudicii, quot anni venturi sunt, nullus hominum scit, nisi Deus solus,*[116] *ut ipsa veritas testatur. De die autem illa nemo scit, neque angli neque filius hominis nisi Deus solus. Scriptura dicit saeculi cursu<m> per sex milia constare.*

<15.> *A principio mundi quod est primi hominis initium usque ad adventum salvatoris nostri Ihesu Christi quod fuit quadragessimo secundo anno imperii Octaviani cesaris, in sexto miliario saeculi computantur anni circiter quinque milia centum nonaginta octa. A nativitate vero Ihesu Christi domini nostri que fuit XLII anno imperii Octaviani cesaris usque in presentem annum, id est tertio regni Ratchisi*[117] *in Italia, sexto pontificatus Zachariae pape urbis Romae, indictio XVa, sunt anni DCCXLV<II>.*[118] *Restant igitur de sexto miliario anni circiter LIII,*[119] *finitis igitur sex aetatibus, id est sex miliaribus saeculi terminus est. Si vero aliquid superstiterit extra saeculum sit.*

Translation

1. There are fourteen divisions of time: the atom, the moment, the minute, the *punctum*, the hour, the *quadrans*, the day, the week, the month, the season, the year, the *saeculum*, the age, and the world era. There are fifteen atoms in a moment. Four moments in a minute. Two and a half minutes in a *punctum*. Four *puncti* in

---

est menses. MC 31 (Warntjes (2010), 88): *Annus dictus est quasi circulus. Unde et annuli diminuti dicti sunt, qui sunt menses.*

114 Cf. MC 43 (Warntjes (2010), 142): *Seculum secus colendo dictum, vel sex et colo, quia sex aetates mundi continet. Et pro infinito numero ponitur; Dial. Lang.* 3B (Borst (2006), 435): *Seculum autem dicitur eo, quod copulat in se sex aetates mundi;* Sirmond *DDT* 2.14 (Bisagni (2020), 103): *Saeculum quid est? Nomen compositum hoc est ab illo nomine quod est sex et ab alio nomine quod est cultus. Inde saeculum dicitur a seno culto quia per sex aetates mundi vita humana colitur.*

115 Babilloniae **P**.

116 solus Deus **P**.

117 Racisi **P**.

118 Correction to *DCCXLVII* to bring the calculation in line with the indiction and calculation of years left in the sixth age.

119 LVII **C**.

an hour. Three hours in a *quadrans*. Four *quadrans* in a day. Seven days in a week. Four weeks in a month. Three months in a season. Four seasons in a year. 19 years in a lunar cycle. 532 years in a combined luni-solar cycle.

2. Atom is the Greek name for what the Latins interpret as indivisible. For anything that it is not possible to divide is called an atom.

There are five kinds of atoms: the atom of philosophical matters; the atom of an object; the atom of number; the atom of time; and the atom of speech.

They name the atom of philosophical matters those smallest parts in the world that seem neither to be evident nor which accept division. They are carried here and there, as if they seem to be the smallest pieces of dust cast through shadows by the rays of the sun.

The atom of an object: as if you smashed a grain into a thousand parts. The thousandth part, which is not possible to divide, is called the atom of an object.

The atom of number: as if a thousand was parted into a hundred, a hundred into twenty, twenty into ten, ten into five, five into two, two into one. The one that it is not possible to divide is called the atom of number.

The atom of time: as if the world age was parted by the age, the age by the year, the year by the season, the season by months, months by weeks, week by days, day by the *quadrans*, the *quadrans* by hours, the hour by the *punctum*, the *punctum* by the minute, the minute by the moment, the moment by fifteen parts. A fifteenth part of a moment that it is not possible to divide is called the atom of time.

The atom of speech: as if speech were parted into sentences, sentences by verses, verses by parts, parts by feet, feet by the syllable, the syllable by the book. A letter has nothing into which it can part, then it is called an indivisible atom, because it is possible neither to part nor divide it.

3. The moment is a certain position of the sun in the sky. The moment is the smallest and narrowest unit of time, so called from the motion of the stars, for it is the end of the hour in short intervals, when the sun to some extent both falls and advances.

4. The minute is called from the minute element, as if it were the minor moment, because that which fills up more counts less.

5. The *punctum* (is so called) from the penetrating of the pupil of the eye, for having added ten moments to the present light it strikes the solace of the eyes.

6. The hour is so-called because it combines the points of the day. We say 'the hour of the sea' and 'the hour of clothes'.

7. The *quadrans* is so-called because it weighs out a fourth part of the day, which the Hebrews call a 'quodrant', the Greeks a 'dodrans', and the Latins a 'quadrant'.

8. The day is so-called from the division of light and dark. The natural day is 24 hours. The artificial (day) seems to have 12 hours. There are two divisions of the natural day: the day and the night. There are three parts to the day: morning, midday, and the 'suprema' (when the sun sets). From the rising of the sun, morning has four hours, midday (has) four, and 'suprema' seems to have four.

9. The week according to the Greeks and Latins follows a course of seven days, or by the Hebrews there are seven years. Daniel explains this [in his tract] about the 70 weeks.

10. The month takes its name from measure, since of course all months measure in themselves 29 ½ lunar days.

11. The season takes its name from a combination (*temperamentum*), because each season is a combination of three months, or because the nature of one and each season is kept within limits by another. For the season of spring refrains from the heat of summer, summer from the moisture of autumn, winter from the dryness of spring. The season of spring is so called as everything in it blooms and is born. Summer is called from seething, because in that time everything boils and burns from the strength of the heat. Autumn is named from the storm, since in that time the leaves of the trees fall and everything ripens. Winter is called from deliberation, because in that time everything stays and seems to deliberate.

12. The year is named as if it were a ring, that is a circle, from which the months are called by the diminutive *annuli* (little rings).

13. The *saeculum* is named for the observation of six ages, and the name is made up from the word for the number, which is six, and the word 'observe', and this compound is understood by several meanings, both consistent with and contradictory to (the etymology). For the *saeculum* is observed from the beginning up to the end through four volumes of time, through the dimensions of the six days, and the present vicissitudes of times, and by the six ages.

14. The first age is from the beginning to the flood. The second from the flood up to Abraham. The third from Abraham up to David. The fourth from David up to the Babylonian migration. The fifth from the Babylonian migration up to Christ. The sixth from Christ up to the consummation of the cosmos, the end of which is uncertain. From Christ up to the day of Judgement, how many years there will be to come, no man knows, but God alone, as the Truth testifies: 'of that day no one knows, not the angels nor the son of man, but God alone' (Mark 13:32). Scripture says the course of the *saeculum* consists of 6000 (years).

15. From the beginning of the world — that is, from the beginning of the first man — up to the coming of our lord Jesus Christ, which was in the 42nd year of the reign of Octavian Caesar, in the sixth millennium of the world around 5198 years are reckoned to have passed. From the birth of our lord Jesus Christ, which was in the 42nd year of the reign of Octavian Caesar, up to the present year — which is the third of the reign of Ratchis in Italy, the sixth of Pope Zacharias in the city of Rome, 15th indiction — there are 747. And so there remain about 53 years of the sixth millennium, so completing the sixth of the ages — i.e. the *saeculum* will end after six thousand years. If anyone survives, they will be beyond the *saeculum*.

C. PHILIPP E. NOTHAFT

Victorian Survival in High Medieval Chronography

The Strange Case of the Angevin Paschal Chronicle

▼ **ABSTRACT** In spite of having fallen out of use during the eighth century, the Easter table of Victorius of Aquitaine was still being copied in the high medieval period, as witnessed by a famous computus codex from Trinity Abbey, Vendôme (Oxford, Bodleian Library, Bodley 309, 113r–120r; c. AD 1075) and by the Red Book of Saint-Florent de Saumur (Angers, Archives départementales de Maine-et-Loire, H 3715, 77r–94v; saec. XIII[1/2]). In contrast to earlier copies, these manuscripts have Victorius segue into the standard Easter table of Dionysius Exiguus, thereby implying that both tables share the same system of counting the years from Christ's Passion. It appears that this unusual arrangement enjoyed wider circulation as part of an extended paschal chronicle created in eleventh-century Angers, the existence of which sheds new light on high medieval attempts to revise the conventional chronology of Jesus Christ. It also reveals how the chronographic usefulness of Victorius' table outlived its application to the reckoning of Easter by several centuries.

▼ **KEYWORDS** Victorius of Aquitaine; Dionysius Exiguus; medieval chronicles; medieval annals; chronography; chronology of Jesus; date of crucifixion; Angers; *Annus Domini*

Pre-Carolingian Latin Computus and its Regional Contexts, ed. by Immo Warntjes, Tobit Loevenich, and Dáibhí Ó Cróinín, Studia Traditionis Theologiae, 54 (Turnhout: Brepols, 2023), pp. 201–222
BREPOLS ❧ PUBLISHERS   10.1484/M.STT-EB.5.133491

Introduction: why copy Victorius?[*]

At an unknown date in the year AD 457, Victorius of Aquitaine, a man renowned for his skill as an accurate calculator (*calculator scrupulosus*),[1] presented the papal archdeacon Hilarus (or Hilarius) with a new Easter table covering a cyclical period of 532 years (originally from AD 28 to 559). Hilarus had solicited Victorius' advice after repeated disputes with the Alexandrian patriarchate over the date of Easter had ended in a humiliating defeat for Pope Leo I.[2] The table Victorius produced in response to this request was designed to forestall this sort of outcome in the future, as it effectively adopted Alexandria's 19-year lunar cycle, albeit not without combining it with certain vestiges of Roman computistical tradition.[3] The reception of this new Easter cycle in Latin Christendom began in the second half of the fifth century and continued for roughly 300 years, finding its main temporary strongholds in Merovingian Gaul and on the British Isles. By AD 800, however, the competing Easter table of Dionysius Exiguus, which represented the Alexandrian computus in its unadulterated form, had established itself as the sole standard for Easter reckoning in Latin Christendom, rendering the earlier table of Victorius obsolete in practical terms.[4]

Of the handful of copies of the Victorian Easter table that are known to have survived the ensuing process of disposal and destruction, only three have been classified as integral, meaning that they represent the complete 532-year cycle together with the consular list Victorius used to identify individual years. The earliest of these comes from seventh-century Burgundy and hence from a time and place when Victorius' Easter reckoning would still have been in active use.[5] Things look different for an early-ninth century manuscript believed to have been written at Flavigny Abbey, whose Victorian table was copied at a time when its data no longer provided a safe basis for determining the dates of the mobile feast days. Its presence in a Carolingian manuscript may be explained with the

---

[*] I am heavily indebted to Immo Warntjes for his invaluable advice and assistance during the various stages of this article's formation.

1 This is the epithet used in Gennadius of Massilia, *De viris inlustribus* 87 (ed. Bernoulli (1895), 91).

2 On this background, see Holford-Strevens (2011), 6–11; Mosshammer (2017), 22–25.

3 The most recent edition of Hilarus' letter to Victorius, Victorius' prologue, and the Easter table itself is found in Krusch (1938), 16–52. On Hilarus' letter, see Krusch (1879). On the table, see Ideler (1825–1826), ii 275–85; Rühl (1897), 126–28; Mac Carthy (1901), LXXXIII–LXXXIX; Schwartz (1905), 72–80; Ginzel (1914), 245–47; Jones (1934), 409–13; (1943), 61–68; Pedersen (1983), 46–49; Ohashi (1999), 20–24; Wallis (1999), L–LIII; Declercq (2000), 82–95; Declercq (2002), 181–87; Blackburn and Holford-Strevens (1999), 793, 808–09; Holford-Strevens (2008), 192–96; Mosshammer (2008), 239–44; Mosshammer (2017), 25–27; Mc Carthy (2017), 111–15.

4 On Victorius' reception and role in early medieval Easter controversies, see Krusch (1884); Schmid (1907), 38–107; Poole (1918); Jones (1934); Jones (1943), 65–66; Ó Cróinín (2008), 257–58; Ohashi (1999); Ohashi (2005); Ohashi (2011); Palmer (2011); Palmer (2017); Dailey (2015); Cuppo (2017), and, most importantly, Warntjes (2015), 40–63.

5 Gotha, Forschungsbibliothek, Memb. I 75, 77v–106r (eastern France, saec. VIII[in]). See Krusch (1884a), who used this manuscript as the basis for his critical edition (n. 4 above).

antiquarian and chronological interests of its scribe, who placed the Dionysiac and Victorian tables side by side on facing pages, thereby facilitating their comparison.[6] Yet this still constitutes a relatively early case of survival compared to the third example sometimes mentioned in the literature, which was only copied at the start of the final quarter of the eleventh century, at the monastery of the Holy Trinity in Vendôme.[7] This manuscript, also known as the 'Sirmond computus' (henceforth: S), has played a significant role in modern research on early medieval Irish computistics and its 113r–120r have been described as containing 'the only Victorian Easter table known to have circulated in the British Isles'.[8] But why was it copied in the first place?

The Annals of Vendôme and Angers

As I hope to show in the present article, the answer to this question is hidden in the paschal annals that in S adorn not just the Victorian Easter table, but an extensive set of tables according to Dionysius Exiguus, which follow upon the former without any significant rupture or break. Interest in these annals was first shown by the historian André Duchesne (1584–1640), who made a copy of the entries for the years AD 678–1251, later to be edited by Philippe Labbé (1657).[9] Through undisclosed channels, S made its way from Vendôme into the possession of the French Jesuit scholar Jacques Sirmond (1559–1651), and later into the private book collection of the Oxford astronomer Edward Bernard (1638–1696), the relevant part of which was acquired by the Bodleian Library in 1698. The codex received the shelfmark Bodley 309 and appears to have been ignored for the next two hundred years until 1898, when Rose Graham announced its rediscovery and edited those parts of the paschal annals previously omitted by Labbé.[10]

At first approximation, the annals in S can be parsed into three main parts:[11] the first counts years from Christ's Passion rather than his incarnation and is, for the most part, a Roman-Byzantine imperial chronology up to the accession of

---

6 Leiden, Universiteitsbibliotheek, SCA 28, 3r–21r (Flavigny, c. AD 816). See Bischoff (1998–2017), ii 48 (no. 2180).

7 Oxford, Bodleian Library, Bodley 309, 113r–120r. See Halphen (1903), XXV–XXVI; Giordanengo (1998), 108, 119, 124; Peden (2003), XL–XLI; Borst (2006), 263.

8 Warntjes (2010), LXXXIV. See p 17 below for discussion. The expression 'Sirmond computus' or 'Sirmond manuscript' (after its former owner, Jacques Sirmond) was introduced into modern scholarship by Jones (1937); Jones (1943), 105–13, whose studies gave rise to the term 'Sirmond group' to designate the shared lineage of various manuscripts containing late antique and early medieval insular computus texts. For more recent discussions, see Ó Cróinín (1983b); Ó Cróinín (2003a); Wallis (1999), LXXII–LXXIX; Springsfeld (2002), 68–80; Graff (2010), 113–16, 137–38; Warntjes (2010b), 256–59, 266, 275; Warntjes (2016), 172–73; Mosshammer (2017), 38–39.

9 Labbé (1657), 283–91.

10 Graham (1898). A more comprehensive edition, covering the years AD 678 to 1347, appears in Halphen (1903), 50–79.

11 See on this point Halphen (1903), XXVIII–XXX, XLVII–XLVIII; Lecouteux (2008), 239–45.

Leo III in what is given as the year 690. A second layer runs from AD 678 to 965 (inclusive) and offers dates that are recognizably dependent on the common *Annus Domini* era of Dionysius Exiguus. This is mostly a history of the Carolingian dynasty (starting with Pepin the Middle) and the West Frankish kingdom, which is followed after AD 965 by a series of entries that are mainly concerned with the diocese of Angers and county of Anjou. From AD 1075 onwards, the events begin to be contemporary with the hands recording them, a great variety of which appear in the manuscript margins. These continuations come to an end in AD 1347, with the final entry relating to the Battle of Crécy (AD 1346) and its aftermath.

Of the three parts just mentioned, only the last one, stretching from AD 1075 to 1347, is exclusive to the manuscript from Trinity Abbey, whereas earlier entries are paralleled in two further witnesses. One of these is a twelfth-century bifolium (henceforth: *V*) offering a compact presentation of the annals to AD 1075 known from *S*, but with an independent continuation reaching up to the year 1106. Confusingly, the entries after AD 965 are out of sequence, with some appearing at the bottom of 10v and the remainder on 9r, in no strict chronological order.[12] The other witness is a cartulary known as the *Codex rubeus* or Red Book of the abbey of Saint-Florent de Saumur (henceforth: *A*), which contains annals by a single thirteenth-century hand covering the years 1 to 1236.[13] In addition, there is some considerable overlap between the sources just mentioned and several monastic annals from Angers, including those of Saint-Aubin (AD 929 to 1212) and an obituary from Saint-Serge (AD 768 to 1138). According to a hypothesis developed by Louis Halphen, who edited these sources in 1903, and more recently confirmed by Stéphane Lecouteux, the archetype for the material shared between them was a composite chronicle produced in the eleventh century at the cathedral of Saint-Maurice d'Angers and once extant in London, British Library, Cotton Otho B III, which was almost completely destroyed when the Cotton Library went up in flames in 1731. Lecouteux calls this chronicle the *Recueil initial de Saint-Maurice d'Angers*, attributing the portion from AD 966 to 1075 to the local archdeacon and schoolmaster Rainaldus (Renaud).[14]

According to the seventeenth-century catalogue entry for the Cotton manuscript in question, the earlier part of the hypothetical Angers chronicle

---

12 Vatican, Biblioteca Apostolica Vaticana, Reg. lat. 980, 9r–10v (saec. XII; available online at: https://digi.vatlib.it/view/MSS_Reg.lat.980). See Halphen (1903), XXXII–XXXIII, 80–90; Lecouteux (2008), 251–52.

13 Angers, Archives départementales de Maine-et-Loire, H 3715, 77r–94v (Saint-Florent de Saumur, saec. XIII; available online at: http://bvmm.irht.cnrs.fr/resultRecherche/resultRecherche.php?COMPOSITION_ID=12133). See Halphen (1903), XXXVII–XXXIX, 111–26; Lecouteux (2008), 257.

14 Halphen (1903), XXXIII, XXXIX–XLIX; Lecouteux (2008). See also Lecouteux (2009), on the likely originator of the copy and continuation in *S*.

stretched from 'Emperor Octavian [Augustus] to the year of Christ 966'.[15] This would seem to agree with the annals in *A*, where the first year on 77r is identified as the year of Christ's birth and equated with the 42nd year of Augustus, whose years are then counted in sequence. Yet the other two witnesses mentioned earlier, manuscripts *S* and *V*, go back in time as far as the reign of Ptolemy VIII Euergetes, which began in the first year of the 159th Olympiad (= 144/143 BC). Lecouteux's reaction to this discrepancy is to connect the annals in *S* and *A* to the *Recueil initial de Saint-Maurice d'Angers* via separate branches of transmission. According to his stemma, *A* derives from the *Recueil* via a direct route, whereas *S* and *V* go back to a lost intermediary containing a chronologically expanded but verbally tauter version of the work.[16] Lecouteux refers to this hypothetical intermediary as a *Tableau de comput intermédiaire*, in line with the fact that *S* places its annals in the margins of the Easter tables of Victorius and Dionysius Exiguus.[17] What his stemma ignores, however, is that virtually the same arrangement is also present in *A*,[18] which would suggest either that this tabular format already characterized the archetype or that *A* derives from the same intermediary as *S*. That the Easter tables found in these two manuscripts cannot have been drawn up independently from each other is abundantly clear from their idiosyncratic context and construction, which I shall analyse in what follows. Together with the chronographic matter that precedes them and the annals that adorn their margins, these tables constitute what I shall refer to as the Angevin Paschal Chronicle,[19] the redactional history of which must remain subject to further investigation. For the moment, it is worth underlining that the latest known copy of the Victorian Easter table appears not in *S*, but in the Red Book of Saint-Florent de Saumur (*A*), which was only assembled in the thirteenth century.

A Victorian-Dionysiac paschal chronicle

Chronographic preludes

Although the paschal chronicles in *S* and *A* are based on one and the same set of chronological premises and layout ideas, their content differs in enough ways to rule out the possibility that the tables in *A* were copied directly from those in the

---

15 Smith (1696), 69: *Chronica Frodoardi, Monachi S. Albani, ab Octaviano Imperatore, ad annum Ch. 966*. The reference to the *Chronica Frodoardi* is deconstructed by Lecouteux (2008), 233–39.

16 Lecouteux (2008), 234 n. 23, 252, 261.

17 Lecouteux (2008), 261. The layout and layout changes were first described by Halphen (1903), XXVI–XXVIII, who, however, does not identify the Easter tables involved.

18 See already Halphen (1903), XXXVII–XXXVIII.

19 In referring to the work as a 'paschal chronicle', I follow the terminology suggested by Burgess and Kulikowski (2013a), 1–62; Burgess and Kulikowski (2013b), who make a strong case against the term 'Easter annals'.

earlier manuscript *S*. The divergences are particularly strong when it comes to the preliminary matter or chronographic prelude to the tables, which in the case of *A* is somewhat difficult to define. On 75r–76r, we find a rudimentary chronicle from the creation of the world to the reign of Ptolemy I Soter († 282 BC), but instead of continuing further down towards the reigns of Cleopatra, Julius Caesar, and Augustus, the verso-side of folio 76 was left blank and later filled with unrelated notes. Given the quick pace of the previous chronicle, this one page would have probably been enough to fill the chronological gap that was left open between Ptolemy I at the bottom of 76r and the chronographic note in the first line of 77r, which commemorates the birth of Jesus Christ on 25 December in the 42nd year of Octavian Augustus, the third year of the 194th Olympiad, the 752nd year since the foundation of Rome, and the second year of the 15-year indictional cycle.[20]

The same note appears in *S* on 112v (see Plate 1a), but the preceding three-and-a-half page long chronographic prelude has no parallel in *A*. It begins extremely abruptly at the head of 111r with year 28 of the reign of Ptolemy VI Philometor, who is not mentioned by name, but only represented by the corresponding years of his regnal era and the Olympic era (Ol. 157.1 = 152/1 BC), each of which appears in a separate column.[21] The column for the regnal era of Ptolemy VI counts up to year 35 (Ol. 158.4) and then re-starts with the years of Ptolemy VIII Euergetes, who is also the first ruler mentioned in *V* (9v). For the chronological skeleton of regnal years and Olympic years as well as for the chronographic entries that start on 111v, the prelude to the Victorian table in *S* clearly depends on the chronicle of Eusebius of Caesarea, the difference being that the latter features the reigns of different kingdoms and nations in parallel columns, whereas the excerptor in *S* counted years only for the Ptolemaic dynasty of Egypt. He continued to do so up to year 2 of Cleopatra VII, after which he switched to the Roman regnal years of Julius Caesar and Augustus, following the examples of Prosper of Aquitaine, Isidore of Seville, and the Venerable Bede.[22]

In manuscripts *A*, *S*, and *V*, Christ's birth in the 42nd year of Augustus inaugurates a count of years *a nativitate Domini*, which receives its own column.

---

20 *A*, 77r: *Nativitas domini nostri Ihesu Christi secundum carnem VIII kal. Ianuarii, Olympiadis CXC^{me} IIIIe, anno tertio, anno ab urbe condita D° CCLII, Indictione II*. This is worth comparing with the corresponding note in Bede, *Chronica maiora* s.a. 3952 (ed. Theodor Mommsen in MGH Auct. ant. 13, 281–82). The year 752 from the foundation of the city stems from Orosius, *Historia adversum paganos* 6.22.1, 7.3.1 (ed. Arnaud-Lindet (1990–1991), ii 234, iii 20).

21 The astonishingly abrupt start of this section raises the suspicion that earlier pages might have gone missing, yet the quiring of *S* shows no traces of such a loss. The pages that immediately precede the chronographic section contain Victorius of Aquitaine's prologue to the *Cursus paschalis* (108rb–110va), which is followed by an unrelated series of computistical *argumenta* and a brief text concerning the legend of the 12 'golden Fridays', of the type discussed in Ivanov (2011); Ivanov (2012). *S*, 110vb: *Isti sunt XII dies Veneris de quibus ego, Clemens Romanus pontifex, inveni in canonibus et in actibus Apostolorum* [...] *XII ante natale domini*.

22 See Prosper of Aquitaine, *Chronicon* § 316 (ed. Theodor Mommmsen in MGH Auct. ant. 9, 404); Isidore of Seville, *Chronica* 1.232, 2.232^a (ed. José Carlos Martín in CCSL 112, 110–11); Bede, *Chronica maiora* s.a. 3925 (MGH Auct. ant. 13, 280).

A and *S* also have a parallel column that counts the years of the 15-year indictional cycle, starting with number 2 in the year of the nativity. Another count featured in *A* and *S* is that of the years from the foundation of Rome (years a.u.c. = *ab urbe condita*), which are noted for every fourth year in the left margin. In *A*, their first appearance is next to year 3 = 44 Augustus, which is equal to 754 a.u.c. The chronographic section in *S* extends the count backwards to the year 710 a.u.c. = Ol. 184.1 = 44/43 BC (112r) and has it run in parallel with the years of the Olympic era.[23] There are no traces of this Olympic count in *A*, whose world chronicle on 75r–76r does not number the years continuously, but imitates the model of Isidore and Bede in providing summary entries for the 'reigns' of individual patriarchs or kings, with the end-point of these reigns being expressed as years from the creation of the world. Chronologically speaking, these entries are clearly dependent on Isidore's *Chronica maiora*, which just like *A* has the reign of Ptolemy I end in *Annus Mundi* or AM 4913.[24] A sign of continuity between 76r and the chronographic material on 77r comes in the form of annotations for the final years of Christ's life, which claim that his crucifixion in the 18th year of Tiberius occurred 5228 years after the creation of Adam and 2044 years after the birth of Abraham. This agrees perfectly with Isidore's chronology, where Abraham's birth is assigned to AM 3184 and the crucifixion to AM 5228, exactly 2044 years later. An Isidoran origin is likely, moreover, for an isolated note appearing in both *S* (120r; see Plate 2b) and *V* (10r), which tells us that there were 5197 years from the creation of the world to the advent of Jesus Christ (*Ab origine mundi in adventum domini nostri Ihesu Christi anni .V.CXCVII*). This is just one year higher than the 5196 years one can infer from Isidore's chronicle and may therefore constitute a faint echo of the world chronicle preserved in *A*.[25]

All three manuscripts equate the 32nd year of Christ's life with the 17th year of Tiberius and follow this up with the year of his death. In *S* and *A*, the latter coincides with the initial year of the Victorian Easter table, which is preceded by a note identifying it as the year of the 'crucifixion of Christ, when the two Gemini were consuls'.[26] Their first names, Rufius and Rubellius (correct: C. Fufius and L. Rubellius) are supplied by the first line of the Victorian table, which is well known for incorporating a list of annual consuls (see Plate 1b). Since this list is also referred to at the corresponding place in *V* (9v), followed by the ferial and lunar date for 1 January in the Victorian *Annus Passionis*, one may safely conclude that the annals in this manuscript were excerpted from an exemplar of the same

---

23 There are also two earlier, isolated occurrences in Ol. 169.1 = 104/3 BC = 650 a.u.c. (*S*, 111v) and Ol. 181.3 = 54/53 BC = 700 a.u.c. (*S*, 112r). The Olympic era is dropped after the entry for Ol. 194.1 (= 4/3 BC), after which only the a.u.c. count is carried forward (*S*, 112v; see Plate 1a).

24 Isidore of Seville, *Chronica* 1.196; 2.196 (CCSL 112, 96–97).

25 For the relevant entries, see Isidore of Seville, *Chronica* 1.31, 1.235–38; 2.31, 2.235–39 (CCSL 112, 28–29, 112–15).

26 *S*, 113r: *Crucifixio Christi consulibus duobus Geminis*. The scribe of *A* (77r) turned *Crucifixio* into *Circumcisio*.

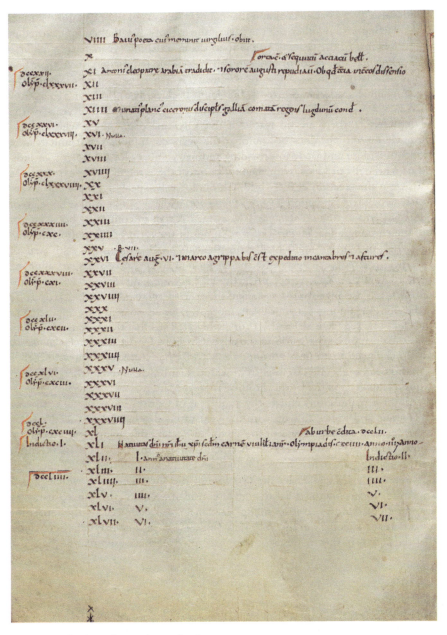

Plate 1a. Oxford, Bodleian Library, Bodley 309, 112v.

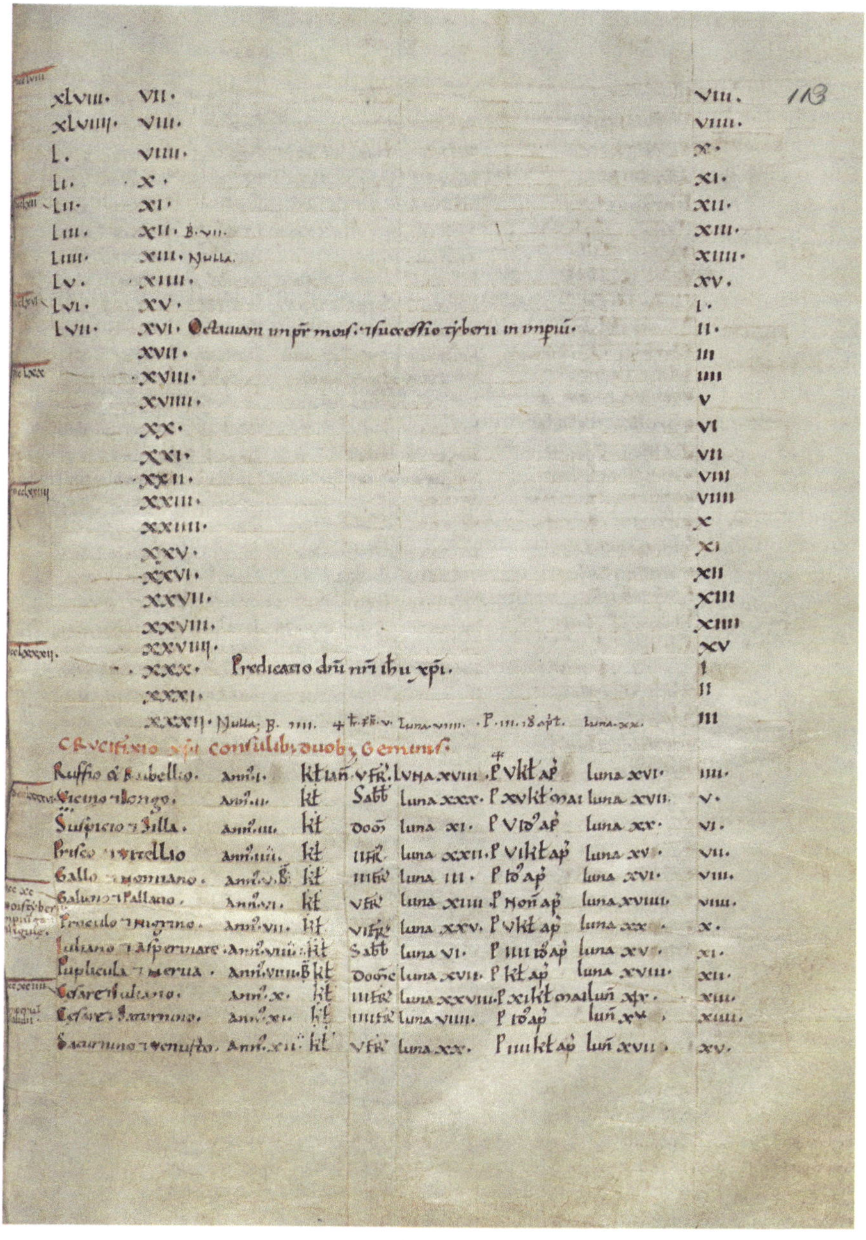

Plate 1b. Oxford, Bodleian Library, Bodley 309, 113r.

tabular paschal chronicle that is preserved in *S* and *A*.[27] If the chronographic prelude to this work and the start of the Victorian table are read together, as was presumably intended, this leads to the conclusion that Christ died in the 33rd year from his birth (counting inclusively), in what would have been the 18th year of Tiberius. This is entirely in line with the Chronicle of Eusebius, who assigned Christ's birth to 42 Augustus = Ol. 194.3 and recorded his death for 18 Tiberius = Ol. 202.3, 32 years later.[28] If these Olympic dates are taken at face value, Jesus would have been born at the end of 2 BC and died in AD 32, whereas C. Fufius and L. Rubellius Geminus were consuls in AD 29.

The discrepancy is easily explained if we bear in mind that Eusebius, in his chronicle and other writings from his pen, upheld a 'long' chronology for Jesus's life, which counted three years between Christ's baptism in the 15th year of Tiberius (Luke 3:1, 23) and his crucifixion in the 18th year of Tiberius.[29] Such a three-year chronology could be defended by reference to the number of Passovers mentioned in the Gospel of John (2:13; 5:1; 6:4; 11:55), but it was not the prevailing view in the Latin West at the time when Victorius of Aquitaine constructed his Easter cycle, which was embedded in a clearly mapped out chronological framework running from the creation to the present. The immediate source for this framework was the chronicle of Victorius' compatriot Prosper of Aquitaine, the last version of which dates from AD 455.[30] Although essentially an epitome and continuation of Eusebius's chronicle and hence dependent on the latter's chronology, Prosper's chronicle also reinstated a Latin tradition associating Christ's Passion with the consulate of the two Gemini in the 15th year of the reign of Tiberius = AD 29.[31] He thereby shortened the life of Jesus by approximately three years, collapsing the year of Jesus's baptism and the year of his crucifixion

---

27 *V*, 9v: *Crucifixio Christi consulibus Geminis. Rufio et Rubellio. Ex hinc bini consules fuerunt usque ad CCCC.LI* [!] *annum. Annus I a passione Domini, bissextus, Kal. Ian. V feria luna XVIIII.*

28 Eusebius (trans. Jerome), *Chronicon* (ed. by Rudolf Helm in GCS 47, 169, 174).

29 Eusebius (trans. Jerome), *Chronicon* (GCS 47, 174); Eusebius (trans. Rufinus), *Historia ecclesiastica* 1.10 (ed. Theodor Mommsen in GCS 9.1, 72–77); Eusebius, *Demonstratio Evangelica* 8.2.107 (ed. Ivar A. Heikel in GCS 23, 389). For a comprehensive treatment of the chronology of Christ's public ministry, with ample references to patristic sources, see Ogg (1940). See, in addition, Richard (1951), 28–32; Strobel (1977), 104–09; Mosshammer (2008), 337–38.

30 On Prosper's chronicle, see Muhlberger (1990), 48–135; Humphries (1996).

31 See, e.g., (pseudo-)Tertullian, *Adversus Iudaeos* 8.18 (ed. Emil Kroymann in CCSL 2, 1363); Lactantius, *Divinae institutiones* 4.10 (ed. Heck and Wlosok (2005–2011), ii 341, ll. 4–5); Lactantius, *De mortibus persecutorum* 1.2 (ed. Samuel Brandt and Georg Laubmann in CSEL 27.2, 173–74); Augustine, *De civitate Dei* 18.54 (ed. Bernhard Dombart and Alfons Kalb in CCSL 48, 655); *Chronographus anni CCCLIIII* (ed. Theodor Mommsen in MGH Auct. ant. 9, 57, 73); *Computatio anni CCCCLII* (ed. Theodor Mommsen in MGH Auct. ant. 9, 153); *Consularia Italica* (ed. Theodor Mommsen in MGH Auct. ant. 9, 281); *Consularia Constantinopolitana* (ed. Burgess (1993), 227); *Prologus paschae* (ed. Krusch (1880), 228, 230, 232); *Computus Carthaginiensis* (ed. Krusch (1880), 289–90). For further references and discussion, see Ogg (1940), 105–11; Richard (1951), 32–42; Lazzarato (1952), 349–423; Loi (1971).

into one.[32] In addition to contracting the period of Jesus's public ministry, Prosper made the year of his death the starting point of a count of years since the Passion, which he supplemented with the names of the consuls leading up to the present consulate of Valentinian III and Anthemius. This was the year AD 455, but by labelling it the 428th year since the Passion, Prosper gave the false impression that the consulate of the Gemini had already taken place in AD 28 — an error attributable to the use of a corrupt consular list. Victorius ended up adapting his Easter table to this faulty chronology and hence took the year of the Passion to be the one with the computistical data of AD 28, with Easter Sunday on 28 March (*luna* 16).[33]

The Victorian table

The Easter table that begins with the date just mentioned reproduces in nearly all details the layout of Victorius' original composition. From left to right its columns are devoted to (a) the years a.u.c. (in four-year intervals); (b) the names of the consuls for each year; (c) the years numbered sequentially from Christ's Passion in the first year of the table; (d) the ferial on 1 January; (e) the lunar age on 1 January; (f) the date of Easter Sunday; (g) the lunar age on Easter Sunday; (h) the indiction. The only two elements foreign to the Victorian table are the flanking columns for the a.u.c.-era and indiction, which are continuations from the chronographic prelude. In MS S, these two extraneous year-counts are relegated to the inner (indiction) and outer (a.u.c.) margin of each page. MS A differs conspicuously by leaving ample space to the right, which is used for chronographic entries and for a column counting the years of the Roman emperors. There is no trace of this column in S, where chronography is reduced to a handful of imperial accession dates entered into the few remaining spaces between the a.u.c.-dates in the outer margin.

A subtler sign that the Victorian table incorporated into the Angevin paschal chronicle was tinkered with is the displacement of the *saltus lunae*, which appears already to have characterized the shared archetype of S and A. Victorius of Aquitaine followed standard practice in applying the *saltus* in the final year of each 19-year cycle, but he also chose to begin his version of the cycle in the year of creation (5201 BC), forcing him to start his count in the seventh year of

---

32 Prosper of Aquitaine, *Chronicon* § 388 (MGH Auct. ant. 9, 409–10): *Quidam ferunt anno XVIII Tiberii Jesum Christum passum, et argumentum huius rei ex evangelio adsumunt Iohannis, in quo post XV annum Tiberii Caesaris triennio dominus praedicasse intellegatur. sed quia usitatior traditio habet dominum nostrum XV anno Tiberii Caesaris duobus Geminis consulibus crucifixum, nos sine praeiudicio alterius opinionis successiones sequentium consulum a supra scriptis consulibus ordinemur.* This passage is quoted verbatim ahead of the prologue to Victorius' *Cursus paschalis* in S, 108rb, to which is added the apt reminder: *Hanc traditionem sequitur victorius.*

33 See Victorius of Aquitaine, *Prologus* 8–9 (ed. Krusch (1938), 23–25), and the remarks in Mosshammer (2008), 12–13. Declercq (2000), 46, incorrectly ascribes the shift to Victorius himself.

the standard Alexandrian cycle. At the head of his table, he placed the year of Christ's Passion (AD 28), which was the fourth year of this newfangled 19-year cycle, explaining why the first *saltus* in Victorius' table appears between years 16 and 17.[34] S and A change the position of the *saltus* by putting it between the first and second year of the table (or, what is the same, between the fourth and fifth year of the cycle), as implied by the way the epact or lunar age on 1 January in four consecutive years is lowered from 16, 27, 8, 19 to 15, 26, 7, 18 — consistently so in A, whereas S reverts back to the original sequence after *Annus Passionis* = AP 435 (epact 15).[35] The lunar age of Easter Sunday, as it is shown in a parallel column in S and A, is not only unaffected by this lowering of the epact, but it is raised by one in certain years, in particularly those with an epact of 26 (formerly 27). This, as Immo Warntjes has shown, is likely to reflect a seventh-century 'reform' of the Victorian cycle, which was aimed at securing a lawful 'Latin' (as opposed to 'Greek') Easter date for each of its 532 years.[36]

The resulting inconsistency between two columns in Victorius' table appears to have been noticed in the case of the entry for AP 1, which places Easter Sunday, and hence the Resurrection of Christ, on 28 March and assigns to this date a lunar age of 16. This lunar age would require an epact of 19 rather than 18, which may explain why AP 1 is the only instance in A where the epact of the fourth year of the Victorius' 19-year cycle is not lowered in the aforementioned way. That this was also the reading in the lost archetype is indicated by the fact that the same epact of 19 is reported for the year of the Passion in manuscript V (9v), whose exemplar apparently still came in a tabular format. Things look different in S, where the epact of the head year is 18, which by implication would have placed Easter Sunday on *luna* 15 and the preceding Good Friday on *luna* 13. This, of course, would have contradicted the Gospel accounts of Jesus's last days, which imply that the crucifixion occurred either on the 14th day (Gospel of John) or the 15th day (Synoptic Gospels) of the Jewish lunar month, so it is no surprise that the scribe of S left the lunar age on Easter Sunday unchanged. Early medieval Latin computists tended to prefer the synoptic crucifixion date on *luna* 15,[37] which probably explains why the two earliest complete copies of Victorius's table increase the lunar age of Easter Sunday in the first year from *luna* 16 to *luna* 17.[38]

---

34 Mosshammer (2008), 241–42.
35 This was already noted for S by Holford-Strevens (2008), 193 n. 53. Cf. Warntjes (2010), LXXXV n. 230.
36 Warntjes (2020), 658–66.
37 See Theophilus of Alexandria, *Prologus* 8 (ed. Mosshammer (2017), 70–71); Proterius of Alexandria, *Epistola ad Leonem papam* 3 (ed. Krusch (1880), 272); Bede, *De temporum ratione* 47, 61 (ed. Charles W. Jones in CCSL 123B, 432, 452); Wiesenbach (1986), 69–72; Declercq (2000), 15–17.
38 Gotha, Forschungsbibliothek, Memb. I 75, 77v; Leiden, Universiteitsbibliotheek, SCA 28, 3r. It seems important to note that *luna* 17 would have been the correct lunar age on 28 March, if AD 28 had gone without a lunar bissextile day. This seems to be the thought behind *De ratione conputandi* 86 (ed. Walsh and Ó Cróinín (1988), 194): *Sciendum nobis quoque quod .xvi. luna apud Latinos causa bissexti in die resurrectionis fuit. Nisi enim bissextus, .xvii. luna esset.*

Another noteworthy feature of the Victorian table in *S* and *A* is its consistent avoidance of double-dates, which were a well-attested hallmark of the original composition. In nearly all cases where Victorius offered the pope a choice between a 'Greek' and a 'Latin' date of Easter, usually by placing the latter in the margins, the two manuscripts only display the Latin date with its extraordinarily high lunar age of 22.[39] Earlier attestations of this practice include the ninth-century manuscript Leiden, Universiteitsbibliotheek, SCA 28, 3r–21r, which happens to be connected to *S* in being a member of the so-called Sirmond group. According to a hypothesis advanced by Immo Warntjes, the habit of listing only one possible date — and the Latin one at that — originated as a reaction on the part of Irish computists to the criticism of St Columbanus, who famously complained about the inconclusiveness of the Victorian table.[40] In support of the view that the Victorian table preserved in *S* itself goes back to an seventh-century Irish exemplar, Warntjes has called attention to an anonymous computus of AD 689, which followed Victorian principles and only survives as an earlier textual layer in the Munich Computus of AD 718/19. A passage from this layer renders the consuls of the year AD 157 as *Bero et Bardua* instead of *Verus II et Bradua*,[41] which is conspicuously similar to the reading in the table contained in *S*: *Ivro et Bardua* (115r; *A*, 79r: *Auro et Bardua*).[42] Another case in point is the treatise *De mirabilibus sacrae scripturae*, written by an southern Irish author in AD 654, which renders the consul names Aviola and Pansa (AD 119) as *Alia et Sparsa*. This again bears a resemblance to the readings found in *S* (114v) and *A* (78v): *Aulia et Parsa*.[43]

The hypothesis of a seventh-century Irish ancestor is attractive in light of a series of short chronological notes best preserved in *S* (95v–95*bisr*), which refer to the Victorian AP 631 as the 'Easter' of Suibne mac Commáin. From this, it has been plausibly inferred that the collection of computus texts characteristic of the 'Sirmond group' went through an important redactional stage in AD 658 in southern Ireland (east Munster), where the mentioned Suibne was a nobleman.[44] It is obviously tempting to suppose that the Victorian table in *S* must have arrived at Vendôme via the very same route as some of the computus texts that appear earlier in the same codex. Yet the parallel testimonies of *A* and *V*, which suggest

---

39 The small handful of exceptions include years AP 201, 204, 504, where the original main date is retained and the Latin alternative ignored.
40 See Columbanus, *Epistula* 2.7 (ed. Walker (1957), 18–19), and the remarks in Warntjes (2010), LXXXIV–LXXXV n. 228; Warntjes (2015), 86–87; Palmer (2011), 214.
41 Munich Computus 41, 62 (ed. Warntjes (2010), 140, 278).
42 Warntjes (2010), LVII–LVIII (n. 139), LXXX–LXXXII.
43 *De mirabilibus sacrae scripturae* 2.4 (PL 35, 2175–76). See Krusch (1884), 159; Ó Cróinín (1983b), 239; Warntjes (2010), LXXVIII–LXXIX n. 209; Warntjes (2015), 50–52.
44 Ó Cróinín (1983a), 82–83; Ó Cróinín (1983b), 233–38; Ó Cróinín (1989), 15–19; Ó Cróinín (2003a); Smyth (1987), 95–101; Warntjes (2010), LXXIII, LXXX.

The merger

The Victorian Easter tables in *S* and *A* both finish on AP 531 and hence one year earlier than would normally be expected. In place of AP 532 (= AD 559), the Angevin paschal chronicle puts the start of the Easter table of Dionysius Exiguus, which in *A* extends until the third year of the 42nd 19-year cycle, or AD 1313 (84r–94v), well after the last annalistic entry for 1236 (93v).[45] MS *S* continues the sequence of Dionysiac 19-year cycles even further, to 1421 (120r–131v), whereas the accompanying annals already end in 1347. By omitting the final year of the standard Victorian table and replacing it with the first year of the Dionysiac one, the redactor of the Angevin paschal chronicle created the illusion of a seamless transition between the two tables, as year 532 follows upon year 531. In reality, these tables use two completely different eras, with Dionysius' *Anni Domini* beginning 27 years earlier than Victorius' *Anni Passionis*.

The resulting mismatch becomes manifest from a look at the column for the 15-year indictional count, which sets in with the year of Christ's birth in the chronographic prelude and links all three parts of the paschal chronicle. For the year of Christ's Passion, the indiction is shown as 4, despite the fact that Victorius' AP 1 was the same as AD 28, which began in the first year of the indictional cycle. Likewise, the final year of the modified Victorian table is AP 531, which is equivalent to AD 558 and should have had indictional year 6 assigned to it. The number instead found in the margin of *S* (120r; see Plate 2b) is 9, which would have been correct for AD 531.[46] The obvious conclusion to draw from this is that the indictions trailing the Victorian table were purposefully projected backwards from the Dionysiac table, whose standard layout involves a column for the indiction to the right of the *Anni Domini*. A reverse case are the years from the foundation of Rome, which originated in the chronographic prelude and continue to show up in the margins of every fourth year of the Easter table even after the transition from Victorius to Dionysius. In *S*, they finally stop after 1346 a.u.c., which is placed next to year 563.[47] The gap of 1346 − 563 = 783 years makes

---

45 In *A* (94v), the final year is written as *M.CCCXII*, owing to omissions and duplications of years in the previous cycles.

46 In *A* (84r), the final five years of the Victorian table go without an indictional column, but from the previous sequence ending in year 526 it follows that year 531 would have had the indiction 10, just like the following year 532 at the start of the Dionysiac table. The scribal error responsible for this discrepancy occurs on 80r, where year 224 = indiction 2, is followed by 225 = indiction 4.

47 In *A*, the count only ends in 1526 a.u.c. on 86v, which is erroneously assigned to year 739 as the result of numerous foregoing scribal errors and displacements. The column for imperial regnal years, which runs up to AD 713 (the 27th year of Constantine V), is likewise heavily marred by errors.

chronological sense only if 563 is interpreted in accordance with the Victorian AP era. In the prelude, Christ's birth is dated to 752 a.u.c. and followed by another 31 years *a nativitate*, such that the year of the Passion is preceded by a total of 783 years since the foundation of Rome.

The third and perhaps most significant indicator of a fundamental and intended continuity between the two Easter tables is the lack of any disruption in the annalistic entries contained in their margins, which appear with greater frequency in *A*, but are chronologically far more reliable in *S*. It has already been mentioned that the Victorian table in *S* barely contains any annotations beyond the accession years of Roman emperors. One of the few exceptions is the *Dormitio sancti Nicholai* recorded for the year 317 (*S*, 117r). Since St Nicholas's traditional date of death is 6 December AD 343, it would appear that the year intended was the Victorian AP 317, which is equivalent to AD 344. The same use of AP dating accounts for all imperial accession years recorded in the Victorian part of the Angevin paschal chronicle. For example, the start of the reign of Justin I (AD 518–527) is entered next to year 490 (119v; see Plate 2a), which neatly follows from the intervals recorded in what appears to have been the chronicler's chief source, Bede's *Chronica maiora*. According to Bede, the crucifixion happened in AM 3984, while Justin I ended his 8-year rule in AM 4480.[48] It follows that the first year of Justin's reign overlapped with AM 4473, which is year 490 on an inclusive count from the crucifixion.

Remarkably, this sequence of (East) Roman emperors dated according to *Anni Passionis* continues without interruption in the margins of the Dionysiac Easter tables, although the individual dates often deviate from Bede by a few years. The antepenultimate emperor mentioned here is Anastasius II (AD 713–715), whose name appears next to year 685 (122r). Bede places the end of his 3-year reign in AM 4670, thereby implying that the accession took place in year 685 as counted from the Passion of Christ (4670 – 2 – 3983 = 685).[49] In *S*, Anastasius is followed by Theodosius III in year 688 and, finally, by Leo III in 690, who is also the last Byzantine emperor to make an appearance in Bede's *Chronica*.[50] According to Bede, Leo was nine years into his rule in AM 4680, from which it follows that his accession took place in the 689th year from the Passion (4680 – 8 – 3983 = 689).[51] The slight discrepancy is easily explained by the fact that Bede only allocated one year to the rule of Leo's predecessor Theodosius III, whereas the Angevin paschal chronicle counts two.

---

48 Bede, *Chronica maiora* s.a. 3984, 4480 (MGH Auct. ant. 13, 283, 306).
49 Bede, *Chronica maiora* s.a. 4670 (MGH Auct. ant. 13, 318).
50 MS *A* takes the imperial chronology further to Constantine V (see n. 47 above).
51 Bede, *Chronica maiora* s.a. 4680 (MGH Auct. ant. 13, 320).

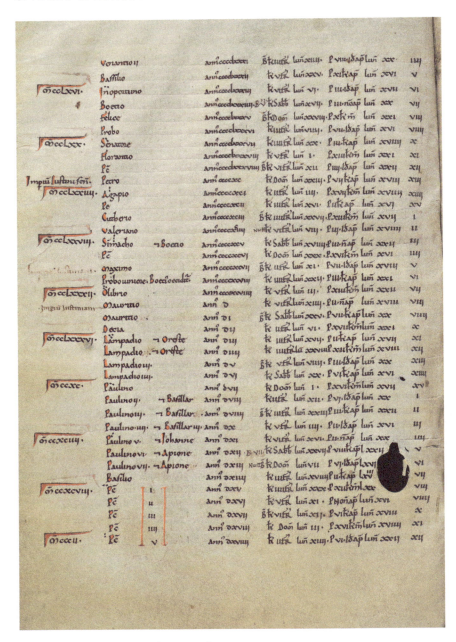

Plate 2a. Oxford, Bodleian Library, Bodley 309, 119v.

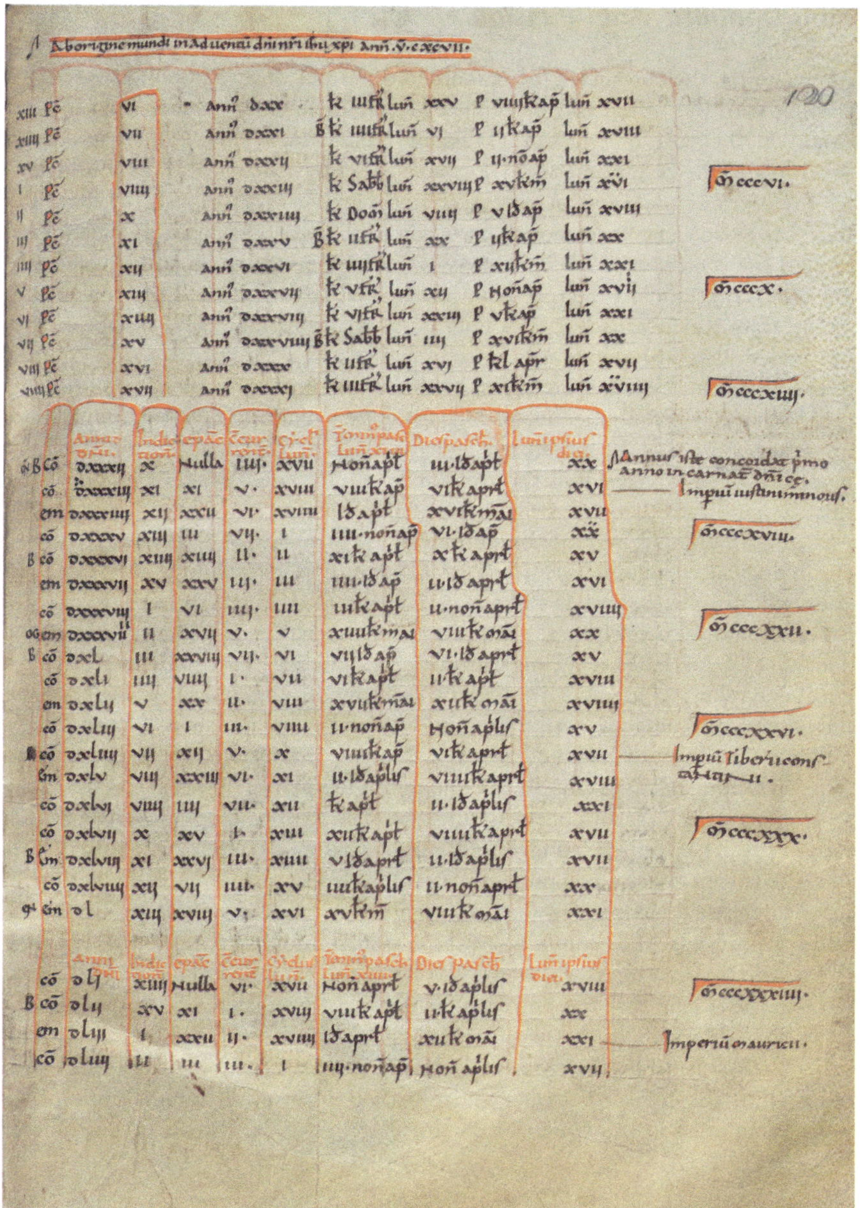

Plate 2b. Oxford, Bodleian Library, Bodley 309, 120r.

Anni Domini = Anni Passionis

After Leo III, the chronicle's focus shifts to the rulers of the Carolingian dynasty, starting with the *principatus* of Pepin of Herstal, which is here claimed to have begun in the year 678 (*S*, 122r). Pepin's *obit* date in 714 (122v) is correct according to the common era of Dionysius Exiguus, which is also the foundation for the entries that follow. A note accompanying year 533 in *V* (10r) identifies this year as one that corresponds cyclically to the year of the Lord's incarnation (*Annus iste concordat primo anno incarnationis Domini*), which would appear to presuppose a standard interpretation of the first year in Dionysius' table as the 532nd from the incarnation. This note is absent from *A*, but it also appears in *S* (120r; see Plate 2b), where it is placed next to 532, rather than 533. In contrast to the other entries found on this page, the scribe did not connect the note to its year with a horizontal line, but prefaced it with a sign linking it to another note in the top margin of the same page, which is the one that mentions the advent of Jesus Christ 5197 years after the creation.[52] While the evidence is inconclusive, this may indicate that the assignment of this note to AD 533, as found in *V*, was not an original part of the chronicle. As a matter of fact, the alternative chronological viewpoint, according to which the years in Dionysius's table are counted from the Passion, is still assumed in a note that accompanies year 968 in *S* (125v) and *A* (90r). It marks the 1000th year since Christ's birth (*Mille anni a nativitate Christi*), thus reflecting the 32-year gap between the nativity year in the chronographic prelude and the start of Victorius' Easter table.[53] Louis Halphen purposefully excluded this note from his editions of the annals of Trinity Abbey, Vendôme, and Saint-Florent de Saumur, stating in a footnote that it rested on an 'interprétation fausse du tableau de comput' on the part of the scribe.[54] According to Halphen, the paschal chronicle must be seen as involving an abrupt switch ('saut brusque') from counting years from the Passion of Christ to counting years in accordance with the common era, a switch that coincides with the change in historiographical focus after 690.[55] This suggests that the scribe responsible for the entry mentioning *Mille anni a nativitate Christi* committed a mistake in ignoring this switch and treating years AD as years AP in the case at hand.

Now, it is true that the entries after 690 have been derived almost without exception from sources that use AD-dating, which makes Halphen's thesis look superficially plausible. Yet to see this as a sign of a chronological gear change is to fail to distinguish between the recording of an event for the appropriate years of an era and the *interpretation* this era is given by the scribe or redactor

---

52 See p. 203 above.

53 The same basic idea was expressed by writing *DC* next to year 568 (*S*, 120v) and *DCCCC* next to year 868 (*S*, 125v). In *A*, the entry commemorating the millennium since Christ's birth is displaced towards the year 969 (90r). It reads *Mille anni a nativitate Christi, locis demones apparuerunt.*

54 Halphen (1903), 58 n. 2; see also 116 n. 6.

55 Halphen (1903), XXIX; see also XXXVIII–XXXIX.

involved. With this distinction in mind, it becomes possible to discern in the Angevin paschal chronicle an effort to (re-)define the Dionysiac or common era as being based on the number of years since the Passion of Christ and to apply this to all the years recorded in the table, not just those up to the year 690. This thesis of a conscious reinterpretation of the AD era recevies some support from the existence of a text on the *Ratio sphere Dionysii de circulo magno pasche*, which is extant in at least two manuscripts.[56] The author of this text, who apparently worked in the first half of the twelfth century, was adamant that the *Annus Domini* count established by Dionysius Exiguus had really been meant to refer back to the year of Christ's Passion. According to his argument, the latter had occurred on 25 March AD 1, whereas the Lord's nativity had taken place 33 years and 3 months earlier, on 25 December 34 BC. Accordingly, it was the number of years since Christ's Passion in AD 1 that one could find inscribed annually on Easter candles, which recorded this number,

> so that we may always keep in mind that his suffering liberated us from being held in bondage by the Devil and from the punishments of hell, knowing that if we join in with his suffering, we will also [join] the Resurrection. And this is the reason why we have to number the years of Christ not from the nativity, as some mistakenly believe, but from the Passion.[57]

This theological point aside, there can be little doubt that the author's stance was motivated at least in part by a desire to make the chronology of Jesus's life fit with the data provided by the conventional lunar and solar cycles. According to a widely held patristic assumption Jesus died on Friday, 25 March, which as the Gospels implied to have coincided with either the 14th or the 15th day of the paschal lunation. For followers of the Dionysiac Easter table and incarnation era, this created a major embarrassment, since the desired combination of calendrical data presented itself neither in AD 29 nor in AD 34, the likely Passion year according to the long chronology of Jesus' life, nor in any of the years in between.[58] It did, however, appear in AD 1, where 25 March was both a Friday and *luna* 14, thus conforming to the Johannine chronology of the crucifixion. While other computists aware of this problem — famous names among them include Abbo of Fleury († AD 1004), Marianus Scottus († AD 1082), and Gerland (*fl.* AD 1093)

---

56 Milan, Biblioteca Ambrosiana, Z 70 sup., 8v–10v (saec. XII); Vatican, Biblioteca Apostolica Vaticana, Vat. lat. 1548, 68r–69r (Italy; saec. XII). See Cuppo (2017), 140–46, 177–81, who discusses and transcribes the text on the basis of the latter manuscript but mistakenly places it in the context of early medieval debates. A new edition and analysis of the *Ratio sphere Dionysii de circulo magno pasche*, by Immo Warntjes and myself, is currently in preparation.

57 Vatican, Biblioteca Apostolica Vaticana, Vat. lat. 1548, 68r: *Ideo hii numeri temporis passionis Christi notati scribuntur in cereo paschali, ut semper recordemur nos illius passione liberatos esse de servitute diaboli et a penis inferni, scientes quia si socii passionis eius fuerimus, simul et resurrectionis erimus. Atque ideo non a nativitate, ut quidam oberrantes estimant, sed a passione annos Christi numerare debemus.* The translation is mine.

58 See on this point Nothaft (2012), 75–80; Warntjes (2015), 72–77.

— shifted the Passion of Christ to less remote years such as AD 12 and AD 42,[59] the choice of AD 1 was attractive for the way it allowed for the *Annus Domini* era, which by the eleventh century had become ubiquitous in both historiography and charter-dating, to be reinterpreted rather than discarded outright.[60]

A prominent exponent of the latter approach is the chronicler Heimo of Bamberg, whose *De decursu temporum* (AD 1135) recast universal history on the basis of the assumption that Jesus was born in 33 BC and died on 25 March AD 1.[61] Traces of such conscious re-framing of Dionysius's *Annus Domini* appear even outside theological or chronographic literature, as seen from a number of eleventh-century French charters that speak of the year *a Passione domini* despite their evident reliance on the common era.[62] The same practice is attested in far-flung Antioch, where Stephen of Pisa translated 'Alī ibn al-'Abbās al-Majūsī's Complete Book of the Medical Art. Colophons of different parts of the translation refer to the year 1127 *a passione Salvatoris*, but the ferial data provided as well as the external chronology of the text reveal this to be AD 1127.[63] At the end of the twelfth century, Gervase of Canterbury still noted that some referred to the years of the common era as *anni Passionis*.[64] More relevant, given the geographical context of the Angevin paschal chronicle, may be an inscription from Trinity Church, Angers, which commemorates the death of a priest named Guet Cavoafus on 26 December *anno a Passione Domini M. LXXXIIII*, although it is unclear whether this is an instance of a renamed common era or a case where year 1084 from the Passion was intended to correspond to 1084 + 33 = AD 1117.[65]

In light of these various parallels, it seems far from implausible that the count of years from the Passion implicit in the Angevin paschal chronicle was originally inspired by the same computistical and theological issues that agitated the anonymous author of the *Ratio sphere Dionysii*. What remains difficult to discern, however, is whether this chronicle started out in the tabular format we find in *S* and *A* or whether it was turned into a fully-fledged paschal chronicle only at a later stage in its redactional history. In principle, creating such a paschal chronicle would have required no more than a concatenation of several Dionysiac Easter tables, whose data were known to repeat every 532 years. The redactor

---

59 Medieval reactions to this problem are discussed in Wiesenbach (1986), 63–112; Verbist (2010); Nothaft (2012), 103–12; Nothaft (2012a); Nothaft (2013).

60 This attraction was still felt by the English Benedictine monk Walter Odington, who in his *Summa de etate mundi* of *c.* AD 1310 wondered aloud if the Church might have erred in linking the common era of years AD to Christ's incarnation rather than his Passion. See Nothaft (2016), 194–95.

61 Heimo's work is edited in Weikmann (2004) and discussed in Verbist (2010), 251–339; Nothaft (2012), 109–11.

62 See the examples mentioned in Giry (1894), 90.

63 See Burnett (2000), 67–69, and the examples cited in Haskins (1924), 133–34.

64 Gervase of Canterbury, *Chronica* (ed. Stubbs (1879), 90): *Annos enim quos quidam dicunt Incarnationis, alii Nativitatis, alii aetatis Domini, alii vero Passionis, hos ego in subsequentibus annos Gratiae dicam.*

65 Barbier de Montault (1888), 33–34.

responsible for the tabular format of the Angevin paschal chronicle evidently followed a different thought process and found it preferable to bridge the gap between the year of the Passion and the original start of the Dionysiac Easter table in AD 532 with the help of an old Victorian table, which had long fallen out of computistical use.[66] It is unclear what motivated this choice, although one point in favour of Victorius may have been the fact that his work expressly signposted year 1 as the year of the Passion, assigning to it the consulate of the two Gemini, who were widely reported in earlier Latin sources to have been the consuls in the year of the crucifixion.[67] This may have made the Victorian table look a good deal more attractive than the Dionysiac one, which came without such information and where the Passion (in AD 1) would have had to be assigned to the second, rather than the first year of the table.

If the creator of the Angevin paschal chronicle viewed the Victorian table as a list of historical consular and Easter dates more so than as a computistical tool, this would also explain why he remained oblivious or indifferent to the lack of compatibility between the tables he fused together. It has already been mentioned that the reinterpretation of Dionysius' era as one referring to the Passion had initially been motivated by the fact that AD 1 placed Good Friday on 25 March, *luna* 14, which was deemed an acceptable combination of data. The first year of Victorius' table, by contrast, placed Good Friday on 26 March, *luna* 14. That this table failed to cohere with the table that came after it was also revealed by the rhythm of the 532-year cycle, which dictated that AP 1 in Victorius' table should have contained the same set of data as the year 533, which in the Angevin paschal chronicle corresponds to the second year of the Dionysiac table. A later annotator of the tables in S made precisely this sort of point, by scribbling the following parameters next to the last year of the chronographic prelude (113r; see Plate 1b):

No epact (*Nulla*) — bissextile year (*B*) — concurrent: 4 (*IIII*) — ferial on 1 January: 5 (*feria V*) — lunar age on 1 January: 9 (*luna VIIII*) — Easter on 11 April, *luna* 20 (*P. III id. aprilis, luna XX*).

In doing so, he identified the year before the Passion as the first year of the Dionysiac Easter table, or as 1 BC.[68]

---

66 It is generally assumed that the Victorian table fell out of favour during the eighth century (see the literature cited in n. 4 above), although Mc Carthy (1994a), 65, has argued for its use among Ulster annalists until the year 1000.

67 See n. 31 above.

68 The same annotator signalled a *concordia cycli solaris et decemnovenalis* for the year Ol. 183.2 = 708 a.u.c. of the Eusebian excerpt (112r) and for year 456 of the Victorian table (119r), which are 532 years apart and both marked as bissextile years with a concurrent of 7 (*B. VII*) and an epact of 30 = 0 (*Nulla*). It may be that this was intended to be the situation in the year of the world's creation, since Bede placed the first day of the *hexaëmeron* on 18 March, necessitating a concurrent of 7. See Bede, *De temporum ratione* 6, 66 (CCSL 123, 293–94, 464).

Conclusion

Although much about the genesis of the Angevin paschal chronicle remains in the dark, it is possible to form an overall picture of its structure and purpose. It turns out that by joining the Victorian and Dionysiac Easter tables at the transition from AP 531 to AD 532, the redactor in charge sought to create an extensive chronographic canvas stretching from Antiquity to the present day, which was held together by a continuous count of years starting from the year of Christ's Passion. While this merger rendered the chronicle incoherent from a strictly computistical point of view, it also underscored the special utility of Victorius' Easter table, which — unlike that of Dionysius Exiguus — anchored the calculation of Easter in a plausible chronological framework. That the provision of this framework made for an attractive feature can be seen from the way the chronographic elements of Victorius' work, in particular his world era (from 5201 BC) and crucifixion year (AD 28), appear in early medieval sources independently of the table itself and even outlived its use in some quarters.[69] Masako Ohashi has detected such signs of Victorian resilience even in the manuscript tradition of Bede's *Chronica minora*, whose end date appears to have been altered to match the *Annus Passionis* of AD 28.[70] The use of Victorius' consular chronology by the eleventh-century redactor of the Angevin paschal chronicle may be taken as further confirmation that Easter tables were viewed not just as devices for locating mobile feast days in the present, but also as tools for reconstructing the past. It is precisely this chronographic purpose that explains why Victorius of Aquitaine's table was still being copied in the thirteenth century (MS *A*), more than 700 years after its creation.

---

69 See, e.g., *Continuationes Chronicarum Fredegarii* 16 (ed. Bruno Krusch in MGH SS rer. Merov. 2, 176), and the further examples cited in Krusch (1884), 133–34, 139, 166; Krusch (1885), 89–91; Cordoliani (1955a), 167, 186; Cordoliani (1955b), 313; Springsfeld (2010), 222; Warntjes (2010b), 264–68; Palmer (2011), 231–33, 239.

70 Ohashi (2003); Ohashi (2010).

Bibliography

Abels, R. (1983) 'The Council of Whitby: a study in early Anglo-Saxon politics,' *Journal of British Studies* 23, 1–25.

Aerts, W. J. and G. A. A. Kortekaas (1998) *Die Apokalypse des Pseudo-Methodius. Die ältesten griechischen und lateinischen Übersetzungen*, 2 vols, Louvain.

Aher, E. (2020) *Bede and the cosmos: theology and nature in the eighth century*, Abingdon.

Allott, S. (1974) *Alcuin of York c. A.D. 732 to 804 – his life and letters*, York.

Anderson, A. O. and M. O. Anderson (1991) *Adomnán's Life of Columba*, Oxford.

Arnaud-Lindet, M.-P. (1990–1991) *Orose: Histoires (contre les païens)*, 3 vols, Paris.

Barbier de Montault, X. (1888) 'Les croix de plomb placées dans les tombeaux en manière de Pitacium,' *Bulletin de la société archéologique et historique du Limousin* 36, 23–59.

Barlow, C. W. (1950) *Martini Bracarensis opera omnia*, New Haven.

Bauer, N. (1996) 'Abbess Hilda of Whitby: all Britain was lit by her splendor,' in M. Schmitt and L. Kulzer, *Medieval women monastics: wisdom's wellsprings*, Collegeville, 13–31.

Becker, M. and J.-M. Kötter (2016) *Prosper Tiro, Chronik / Laterculus regum Vandalorum et Alanorum*, Paderborn.

Bergmann, W. (2011) 'Dicuils Osterfestalgorithmus im Liber de astronomia,' in Warntjes and Ó Cróinín (2011), 242–87.

Bernoulli, C. A. (1895) *Hieronymus und Gennadius: De viris inlustribus*, Freiburg.

Bethmann, L. (1874) 'Dr. Ludwig Bethmann's Nachrichten über die von ihm für die Monumenta Germaniae Historica benutzten Sammlungen von Handschriften und Urkunden Italiens, aus dem Jahre 1854,' *Archiv der Gesellschaft für ältere deutsche Geschichtskunde* 12, 201–426, 474–758.

Bhreathnach, E. (2001) 'The genealogies of Leinster as a source for local cults,' in J. Carey, M. Herbert, and P. Ó Riain, *Studies in Irish hagiography: saints and scholars*, Dublin, 250–67.

Billett, J. D. (2013) 'Wilfrid and music,' in Higham (2013), 163–85.

Bisagni, J. (2020) *From atoms to the cosmos: the Irish tradition of the divisions of time in the Middle Ages*, Cambridge.

Bischoff, B. (1954) 'Wendepunkte in der Geschichte der lateinischen Exegese im Frühmittelalter,' *Sacris Eruditi* 6, 189–281; rev. ed. in B. Bischoff, *Mittelalterliche Studien. Ausgewählte Aufsätze zur Literatur und Schriftkunde*, 3 vols, Stuttgart 1966–1981, i 205–73.

— (1998–2017) *Katalog der festländischen Handschriften des neunten Jahrhunderts*, 4 vols, Wiesbaden.

Bischoff, B. and M. Lapidge (1994) *Biblical commentaries from the Canterbury school of Theodore and Hadrian*, Cambridge.

Blackburn, B. J. and L. A. Holford-Strevens (1999) *The Oxford companion to the year*, Oxford.

Borst, A. (1998) *Die karolingische Kalenderreform*, Hannover.

— (2001) *Der karolingische Reichskalender und seine Überlieferung bis ins 12. Jahrhundert*, 3 vols, Hannover.

— (2004) *Der Streit um den karolingischen Kalender*, Hannover.

— (2006) *Schriften zur Komputistik im Frankenreich von 721 bis 818*, 3 vols, Hannover.

Borst, A. and I. Warntjes (2023), *Hermann der Lahme, Schriften zur Zeitrechnung, mit Vorläufern und Bearbeitern*, Wiesbaden.

Breen, A. (1995) *Interpretatio mystica et moralis progenitorum Domini Iesu Christi*, Dublin.

Bromwich, R. (1978) *Trioedd Ynys Prydein: the Welsh Triads*, 2nd ed., Cardiff.

Brooks, D. (2014) *Prosper's chronicle: a critical edition and translation of the edition of 445*, Master thesis, University of Ottawa, available at: https://ruor.uottawa.ca/bitstream/10393/31820/1/Brooks_Deanna_2014_thesis.pdf.

Brooks, N. (2006) 'From British to English Christianity,' in C. E. Karkov and N. Howe, *Conversion and colonization in Anglo-Saxon England*, Tempe, 1–30.

Bullough, D. A. (2003) *Alcuin: achievement and reputation*, Leiden.

Burgess, R. W. (1993) *The Chronicle of Hydatius and the Consularia Constantinopolitana, two contemporary accounts of the final years of the Roman Empire*, Oxford.

— (2000) '"Non duo Antonini sed duo Augusti": the consuls of 161 and the origins and traditions of the Latin consular fasti of the Roman Empire,' *Zeitschrift für Papyrologie und Epigraphik* 132, 259–90.

Burgess, R. W. and M. Kulikowski (2013a) *Mosaics of time: the Latin chronicle traditions from the first century BC to the sixth century AD, vol. 1: a historical introduction to the chronicle genre from its origins to the high Middle Ages*, Turnhout.

— (2013b) 'Medieval historiographical terminology: the meaning of the word *annales*,' *The Medieval Chronicle* 8, 165–92.

Burnett, C. (2000) 'Antioch as a link between Arabic and Latin culture in the twelfth and thirteenth centuries,' in I. Draelants, A. Tihon, and B. van den Abeele, *Occident et Proche-Orient: contacts scientifiques au temps des Croisades*, Turnhout, 1–78.

Butler, B. (2011) 'Doctor of souls, doctor of the body: Whitby *Vita Gregorii* and its exegetical context,' in E. Mullins and D. Scully, *Listen, o isles, unto me: studies in medieval word and image in honour of Jennifer O'Reilly*, Cork, 168–80.

Byrne, F. J. (2001) *Irish kings and high-kings*, 2nd ed., Dublin.

Calder, G. (1917) *Auraicept na n-éces: the scholars' primer*, Edinburgh; repr. Dublin 1995.

Campbell, A. (1967) *Æthelwulf De abbatibus*, Oxford.

Campbell, J., (1987) 'The debt of the early English church to Ireland,' in P. Ní Chatháin and M. Richter, *Irland und Christenheit: Bibelstudien und Mission*, Stuttgart, 332–46.

Carey, J. (1989) 'Ireland and the antipodes: the heterodoxy of Virgil of Salzburg,' *Speculum* 64, 1–10.

Charles-Edwards, T. M. (2000) *Early Christian Ireland*, Cambridge.

— (2013) *Wales and the Britons 350–1064*, Oxford.

Chekin, L. S. (1999) 'Easter tables and the pseudo-Isidorean Vatican map,' *Imago Mundi* 51, 13–23.

Clancy, T. O. and G. Márkus (1995) *Iona: the earliest poetry of a Celtic monastery*, Edinburgh.

Colgrave, B. (1927) *The Life of Bishop Wilfrid by Eddius Stephanus*, Cambridge.

— (1940) *Two Lives of Saint Cuthbert: a Life by an anonymous monk of Lindisfarne and Bede's prose Life*, Cambridge.

— (1968) *The earliest Life of Gregory the Great, by an anonymous monk of Whitby*, Cambridge.

Colgrave, B. and R. A. B. Mynors (1969) *Bede's Ecclesiastical history of the English people*, Oxford.

Contreni, J. J. (forthcoming) 'A first look at ninth-century glosses on Bede's *De temporum ratione*'.

Cordoliani, A. (1955a) 'Les manuscripts de comput ecclésiastique de l'Abbaye de Saint Gall du VIIIe au XIIe siècle,' *Zeitschrift für schweizerische Kirchengeschichte* 49, 161–200.

— (1955b) 'L'évolution du comput ecclésiastique à Saint Gall du VIIIe au XIe siècle,' *Zeitschrift für schweizerische Kirchengeschichte* 49, 288–323.

— (1956a) 'Textes de comput espagnol du VIe siècle: encore le problème des traités de comput de Martín de Braga,' *Revista de archivos, bibliotecas y museos* 62, 685–97.

— (1956b) 'Textos de computo espagnol del siglo VI: El "Prologus Cyrilli",' *Hispania sacra* 9, 127–39.

— (1958) 'Textes de comput espangnol du VIIe siècle: Le computus cottonianus,' *Hispania sacra* 11, 125–36.

Corning, C. (2000) 'The baptism of Edwin, king of Northumbria: a new analysis of the British tradition,' *Northern History* 36, 5–15.

— (2006) *The Celtic and Roman traditions: conflict and consensus in the early medieval church*, New York.

Cramer, A. W. (1826) *De fragmentis nonnullis vetustarum membranarum narratio*, Kiel.

Cross, F. L. and E. A. Livingstone (1974) *The Oxford dictionary of the Christian church*, 2nd ed., Oxford.

Cubitt, C. (1989) 'Wilfrid's "Usurping Bishops": episcopal elections in Anglo-Saxon England, c. 600–c. 800,' *Northern History* 25, 18–38.

— (1995) *Anglo-Saxon church councils c. 650–c. 850*, London and New York.

— (2013) 'Appendix 2: the chronology of Stephen's Life of Wilfrid,' in Higham (2013), 334–47.

Cuppo, L. (2011) 'Felix of Squillace and the Dionysiac computus I: Bobbio and Northern Italy (MS Ambrosiana H 150 inf.),' in Warntjes and Ó Cróinín (2011), 120–36.

— (2017) 'Felix of Squillace and the Dionysiac computus II: Rome, Gaul, and the Insular World,' in Warntjes and Ó Cróinín (2017), 138–81.

Dailey, E. T. (2015) 'To choose one Easter from three: Oswiu's decision and the Northumbrian synod of AD 664,' *Peritia* 26, 47–64.

Declercq, G. (2000) *Anno Domini: the origins of the Christian era*, Turnhout.

— (2002) 'Dionysius Exiguus and the introduction of the Christian era,' *Sacris Erudiri* 41, 165–246.

de Meyier, K. A. (1955) *Codices Vossiani Graeci et miscellanei*, Leiden.

de Rossi, G. B. (1861) *Inscriptiones christianae urbis Romae septimo saeculo antiquiores*, vol. 1, Rome.

Díaz y Díaz, M. C. (1972) *Liber de ordine creaturarum: un anónimo Irlandés del siglo VII*, Santiago de Compostela.

Divjak, J. and W. Wischmeyer (2014) *Das Kalenderhandbuch von 354 — Der Chronograph des Filocalus*, Vienna.

Duchesne, L. (1880) 'La question de la pâque au concile de Nicée,' *Revue des questions historiques* 28, 5–42.

— (1886–1892) *Le liber pontificalis. Texte, introduction et commentaire*, 2 vols, Paris.

Dumville, D. (1997) *Councils and synods of the Gaelic early and central Middle Ages*, Cambridge.

Duncan, E. (2016) 'The Irish and their books,' in R. Flechner and S. Meeder, *The Irish in early medieval Europe: identity, culture and religion*, London, 214–30.

Englisch, B. (2011) 'Ostern zwischen Arianismus und Katholizismus: zur Komputistik in den Reichen der Westgoten im 6. und 7. Jh.,' in Warntjes and Ó Cróinín (2011), 76–109.

— (2017) 'Osterfest und Weltchronistik in den westgotischen Reichen,' in Warntjes and Ó Cróinín (2017), 182–211.

Etchingham, C. (1999) *Church organisation in Ireland A.D. 650 to 1000*, Maynooth.

Evans, D. S. (1965) *Buched Dewi*, Cardiff.

Fanning, S. (1991) 'Bede, Imperium, and the Bretwaldas,' *Speculum* 66, 1–26.

Feeney, D. (2007) *Caesar's calendar: ancient time and the beginnings of history*, Berkeley.

Fell, C. E. (1981) 'Hild, abbess of Streonæshalch,' in H. Bekker-Nielsen, *Hagiography and medieval literature: a symposium*, Odense, 76–99.

Flobert, P. (1997) *La Vie ancienne de Saint Samson de Dol*, Paris.

Fontaine, J. (1960) *Isidore de Séville: Traité de la nature*, Bordeaux.

Fouracre, P. (2008) 'Forgetting and remembering Dagobert II: the English connection,' in P. Fouracre and D. Ganz, *Frankland: the Franks and the world of the early Middle Ages: essays in honour of Dame Jinty Nelson*, Manchester, 70–89.

— (2013) 'Wilfrid on the Continent,' in Higham (2013), 186–99.

Gabriele, M. and J. T. Palmer (2019), *Apocalypse and reform from Late Antiquity to the Middle Ages*, London.

Ganz, D. (2019) 'In the circle of the bishop of Bourges: Bern 611 and late Merovingian culture,' in S. Esders et al., *East and West in the early Middle Ages: the Merovingian kingdom in mediterranean perspective*, Cambridge, 265–80.

Gasparotto, G. (2004) *Isidoro di Siviglia, Etimologie, Libro XIII: De mundo et partibus*, Paris.

Gasparotto, G. and J.-Y. Guillaumin (2009) *Isidore de Séville: Étymologies Livre III: De mathematica*, Paris.

Ginzel, F. K. (1914) *Handbuch der mathematischen und technischen Chronologie: Das Zeitrechnungswesen der Völker*, vol. 3, Leipzig.

Giordanengo, G. (1998) 'La bibliothèque de Geoffroy de Vendôme (1093–1132),' *Cahiers de civilisation médiévale* 14, 105–25.

Giry, A. (1894) *Manuel de diplomatique*, Paris.

Goffart, W. (1988) *The narrators of barbarian history (A.D. 550–800)*, Notre Dame.

Gorman, M. (1997) 'A critique of Bischoff's theory of Irish exegesis: the commentary on Genesis in Munich Clm 6302 (Wendepunkte 2),' *Journal of Medieval Latin* 7, 178–233.

— (2000) 'The myth of Hiberno-Latin exegesis,' *Revue bénédictine* 110, 42–85; repr. in M. Gorman, *The study of the Bible in the early Middle Ages*, Florence 2007, 232–75.

— (2002) 'Manuscripts books at Monte Amiata in the eleventh century,' *Scriptoria* 56, 225–93.

Gómez Pallarès, J. (1999) *Studia chronologica: estudios sobre manuscritos latinos de cómputo*, Madrid.

Graff, E. (2010) 'The recension of two Sirmond texts: *Disputatio Morini* and *De divisionibus temporum*,' in Warntjes and Ó Cróinín (2010), 112–42.

Graham, R. (1898) 'The Annals of the Monastery of the Holy Trinity at Vendôme,' *English Historical Review* 13, 695–700.

Grocock, C. and I. N. Wood (2013) *Abbots of Wearmouth and Jarrow*, Oxford.

Gruffydd, R. G. (1978) 'Canu Cadwallon ap Cadfan,' in R. Bromwich and R. B. Roberts, *Astudiaethau ar yr Hengerdd: studies in Old Welsh poetry – A presentation volume to Sir Idris Foster on his retirement*, Cardiff, 25–43.

Guillaumin, J.-Y. (2005) *Isidore de Séville: Le livre de nombres*, Paris.

Gunn, V. (2009) *Bede's Historiae: genre, rhetoric, and the construction of Anglo-Saxon church history*, Woodbridge.

Hänel, G. (1837) 'Zu A. G. Crameri, Narratio de fragmentis vetustatum membranarum,' *Kritische Jahrbücher für deutsche Rechtswissenschaft* 1, 756–60.

Halphen, L. (1903) *Recueil d'Annales Angevines et Vendômoises*, Paris.

Hammer, C. (2011–2012) 'Holy entrepreneur: Agilbert, a Merovingian bishop between Ireland, England and Francia,' *Peritia* 22–23, 53–82.

Hartmann, L. M. (1903) *Geschichte Italiens im Mittelalter, vol. 2.2: Die Loslösung Italiens vom Oriente*, Gotha.

Haskins, C. H. (1924) *Studies in the history of mediaeval science*, Cambridge.

Heck, E. and A. Wlosok (2005–2011) *L. Caelius Firmianus Lactantius: Divinarum institutionum libri septem*, 4 vols, Munich and Berlin.

Heller, J. (1874) 'Ueber den Ursprung der sogenannten spanischen Aera,' *Historische Zeitschrift* 31, 13–32.

Herbert, M. (1988) *Iona, Kells, and Derry: the history and hagiography of the monastic familia of Columba*, Oxford.

Herren, M. (1998) 'Scholarly contacts between the Irish and the southern English in the seventh century,' *Peritia* 12, 24–53.

— (2015) 'The "Papal letters to the Irish" cited by Bede: how did he get them?,' in E. Purcell et al., *Clerics, kings and Vikings: essays on medieval Ireland in honour of Donnchadh Ó Corráin*, Dublin, 3–10.

Hervagius, J. (1563) *Opera Bedae Venerabilis presbyteri, Anglosaxonis*, 8 vols, Basel.

Higham, N. J. (2006) *(Re-)Reading Bede: the Ecclesiastical History in context*, London and New York.

— (2013) *Wilfrid: abbot, bishop, saint*, Donington.

228 BIBLIOGRAPHY

— (2013a) 'Bede's agenda in book IV of the "Ecclesiastical History of the English People":
a tricky matter of advising the king,' *Journal of Ecclesiastical History* 64, 476–93.

— (2013b) 'Wilfrid and Bede's Historia,' in Higham (2013), 54–66.

— (2015) *Ecgfrith: king of the Northumbrians, high king of Britain*, Donington.

Holford-Strevens, L. A. (2008) 'Paschal lunar calendars up to Bede,' *Peritia* 20, 165–208.

— (2010) 'Marital discord in Northumbria: Lent and Easter,' in Warntjes and Ó Cróinín
(2010), 143–58.

— (2011) 'Church politics and the computus: from Milan to the ends of the Earth,' in
Warntjes and Ó Cróinín (2011), 1–20.

— (2019) *The Disputatio Chori et Praetextati: the Roman calendar for beginners*, Turnhout.

Hollis, S. (1992) *Anglo-Saxon women and the church: sharing a common fate*, Woodbridge.

Howlett, D. (1995) *The Celtic Latin tradition of biblical style*, Dublin.

— (1995a) 'Five experiments in textual reconstruction and analysis,' *Peritia* 9, 1–50.

— (1996) 'Seven studies in seventh-century texts,' *Peritia* 10, 1–70.

— (1997) *British books in biblical style*, Dublin.

— (1997a) 'Insular Latin writers' rhythms,' *Peritia* 11, 53–116.

— (1998a) *Cambro-Latin compositions: their competence and craftsmanship*, Dublin.

— (1998b) 'Insular acrostics, Celtic Latin colophons,' *Cambrian Medieval Celtic Studies* 38,
27–44.

— (1998c) '*Synodus prima Sancti Patricii*: an exercise in textual reconstruction,' *Peritia* 12,
238–53.

— (1998d) '*Vita I Sanctae Brigitae*,' *Peritia* 12, 1–23.

— (2000) *Caledonian craftsmanship: the Scottish Latin tradition*, Dublin.

— (2002) 'A miracle of Maedóc,' *Peritia* 16, 85–93.

— (2003–2004) 'Early Insular Latin poetry,' *Peritia* 17–18, 61–109.

— (2005) *Insular inscriptions*, Dublin.

— (2005a) 'Collectanea pseudo-Bedae,' *Peritia* 19, 30–43.

— (2006a) *Muirchú moccu Macthéni's Vita Sancti Patricii – Life of Saint Patrick*, Dublin.

— (2006b) 'Gematria, number, and name in Anglo-Norman,' *French Studies Bulletin* 27,
90–92.

— (2008) 'On the new edition of Anatolius' *De ratione paschali*,' *Peritia* 20, 135–53.

— (2008a) 'Wilbrord's autobiographical note and the *Versus Sybillae de iudicio Dei*,' *Peritia*
20, 154–64.

— (2010a) 'Computus in Hiberno-Latin literature,' in Warntjes and Ó Cróinín (2010),
259–323.

— (2010b) '*Versus cuiusdam Scotti de alphabeto*,' *Peritia* 21, 136–50.

— (2010c) 'Architecture, music, and time in Wulfstan's Verse,' in M. Henig and N. Ramsay,
*Intersections: the archaeology and history of Christianity in England, 400–1200: papers in
honour of Martin Biddle and Birthe Kjølbye-Biddle*, Oxford, 179–99.

— (2011) 'Gematria in Irish verse,' *Peritia* 22–23, 177–81.

— (2011a) 'The Old-Irish hymn "Brigit be bithmaith",' *Peritia* 22–23, 182–87.

— (2011b) 'Computus in the works of Victorius of Aquitaine and Abbo of Fleury and
Ramsey,' in Warntjes and Ó Cróinín (2011), 288–324.

— (2013) 'Music and the stars in early Irish compositions,' in M. Kelly and C. Doherty, *Music and the stars: mathematics in medieval Ireland*, Dublin, 111–28.

— (2015) 'Two Irish jokes,' in Moran and Warntjes (2015), 225–64.

— (2015a) 'Synaesthesia in early Irish compositions,' in Y. Dureau, *Synesthésie et transposition d'art dans la littérature et les arts de l'Angleterre Élisabéthaine*, Paris, 237–48.

— (2017) 'An addition to the Hiberno-Latin canon: *De ratione temporum*,' in Warntjes and Ó Cróinín (2017), 212–28.

— (2020) 'Lutting, Bede, and the Hiberno-Latin tradition,' *Peritia* 31, 107–24.

— (forthcoming a) 'Hilarius Hibernensis: poet and exegete'.

— (forthcoming b) 'Computus and modular composition in insular hagiography'.

Humphries, M. (1996) 'Chronicle and chronology: Prosper of Aquitaine, his methods and the development of early medieval chronography,' *Early Medieval Europe* 5, 155–75.

Hunter Blair, P. (1970) *The world of Bede*, Cambridge.

— (1985) 'Whitby as a centre of learning in the seventh century,' in M. Lapidge and H. Gneuss, *Learning and literature in Anglo-Saxon England: studies presented to Peter Clemoes*, Cambridge, 3–32.

Ideler, L. (1825–1826) *Handbuch der mathematischen und technischen Chronologie*, 2 vols, Berlin.

Ireland, C. (1991a) 'Aldfrith of Northumbria and the Irish genealogies,' *Celtica* 22, 64–78.

— (1991b) 'Some analogues of the Old English *Seafarer* from Hiberno-Latin sources,' *Neuphilologische Mitteilungen* 92, 1–14; repr. in J. Wooding, *The Otherworld Voyage in Early Irish literature: an anthology of criticism*, Dublin 2000, 143–56.

— (1996) 'Aldfrith of Northumbria and the learning of a *sapiens*,' in K. A. Klar, E. E. Sweetser, and C. Thomas, *A Celtic Florilegium: studies in memory of Brendan O Hehir*, Lawrence, 63–77.

— (1999) *Old Irish wisdom attributed to Aldfrith of Northumbria: an edition of Bríathra Flainn Fhína maic Ossu*, Tempe.

— (2005) 'The poets Cædmon and Colmán mac Lénéni: the Anglo-Saxon layman and the Irish professional,' in J. F. Nagy and L. E. Jones, *Heroic poets and poetic heroes in Celtic traditions: a Festschrift for Patrick K. Ford*, Dublin, 172–82.

— (2015a) 'Some Irish characteristics of the Whitby Life of Gregory the Great,' in Moran and Warntjes (2015), Turnhout, 139–78.

— (2015b) 'Where was King Aldfrith of Northumbria educated? An exploration of seventh-century insular learning,' *Traditio* 70, 29–73.

— (2016a) 'What constitutes the learning of a *sapiens*? The case of Cenn Fáelad,' *Peritia* 27, 63–78.

— (2016b) 'Vernacular poets in Bede and Muirchú: a comparative study of early insular cultural histories,' *Traditio* 71, 33–61.

— (2020) 'Lutting of Lindisfarne and the earliest recorded use of Dionysiac *Anno Domini* dating in Northumbria,' *Peritia* 31, 147–63.

Ivanov, S. (2011) 'The legend of the twelve golden Fridays in the Western manuscripts. Part I: Latin,' in N. N. Kazansky, *Colloquia Classica et Indogermanica V: studies in classical philology and Indo-European languages*, St Petersburg, 561–72.

— (2012) 'Dos versiones de *La leyenda de los 12 viernes* encontradas en los manuscritos de las bibliotecas españolas,' *Revista de literatura medieval* 24, 293–98.

Jackson, K. (1963) 'Angles and Britons in Northumbria and Cumbria,' in H. Lewis, *Angles and Britons*, Cardiff, 60–84.

James, E. (1984) 'Bede and the tonsure question,' *Peritia* 3, 85–98.

James, N. E. (1993) 'Leo the Great and Prosper of Aquitaine: a fifth century pope and his adviser,' *Journal of Theological Studies*, NS 44, 554–84.

Johnston, E. (2013) *Literacy and identity in early medieval Ireland*, Woodbridge.

Jones, C. W. (1934) 'The Victorian and Dionysiac paschal tables in the West,' *Speculum* 9, 408–21.

— (1937) 'The "lost" Sirmond manuscript of Bede's computus,' *English Historical Review* 52, 204–19; repr. in C. W. Jones, *Bede, the schools and the computus*, ed. by W. M. Stevens, Aldershot 1994, article X (without the crucial final pages).

— (1939) *Bedae pseudepigrapha: scientific writings falsely attributed to Bede*, Ithaca.

— (1943) *Bedae opera de temporibus*, Cambridge.

Jones, G. R. J. (1995) 'Some donations to bishop Wilfrid in Northern England,' *Northern History* 31, 22–38.

Kautz, M. (2016) *Bibliothek und Skriptorium des ehemaligen Klosters Lorsch: Katalog der erhaltenen Handschriften*, 2 vols, Wiesbaden.

Kautzsch, E. and A. E. Cowley (1910) *Gesenius' Hebrew Grammar*, 2nd ed., Oxford; repr. 1985.

Kendall, C. B. and F. Wallis (2010) *Bede: On the nature of things and on times*, Liverpool.

Kihn, H. (1880) *Theodor von Mopsuestia und Junilius Africanus als Exegeten: Nebst einer kritischen Textausgabe von des letzteren Instituta regularia divinae legis*, Freiburg.

Kirby, D. P. (1983) 'Bede, Eddius Stephanus and the "Life of Wilfrid",' *English Historical Review* 98, 101–14.

— (1991) *The earliest English kings*, London.

— (1992) *Bede's Historia ecclesiastica gentis Anglorum: its contemporary setting*, Jarrow.

Koch, J. (1997) *The Gododdin of Aneirin: text and context from Dark-Age North Britain*, Cardiff.

— (2003) *The Celtic heroic age: literary sources for ancient Celtic Europe and early Ireland and Wales*, Aberystwyth.

Krusch, B. (1879) 'Die Briefe des Hilarus und Victorius,' *Neues Archiv der Gesellschaft für ältere deutsche Geschichtskunde* 4, 169–72.

— (1880) *Studien zur christlich-mittelalterlichen Chronologie: Der 84jährige Ostercyclus und seine Quellen*, Leipzig.

— (1884) 'Die Einführung des griechischen Paschalritus im Abendlande,' *Neues Archiv der Gesellschaft für ältere deutsche Geschichtskunde* 9, 99–169.

— (1884a) 'Über eine Handschrift des Victurius,' *Neues Archiv der Gesellschaft für ältere deutsche Geschichtskunde* 9, 269–81.

— (1885) 'Chronologisches aus Handschriften,' *Neues Archiv der Gesellschaft für ältere deutsche Geschichtskunde* 10, 81–94.

— (1933) 'Neue Bruchstücke der Zeitzer Ostertafel vom Jahre 447,' *Sitzungsberichte der Preußischen Akademie der Wissenschaften, Jahrgang 1933, phil.-hist. Klasse*, 982–97.

— (1938) 'Studien zur christlich-mittelalterlichen Chronologie: Die Entstehung unserer heutigen Zeitrechnung,' *Abhandlungen der Preußischen Akademie der Wissenschaften, Jahrgang 1937, phil.-hist. Klasse, Nr. 8*, Berlin.

Labbé, P. (1657) *Novae Bibliothecae Manuscriptorum Librorum*, vol. 1, Paris.

Lacey, B. (2006) *Cenél Conaill and the Donegal kingdoms AD 500–800*, Dublin.

Laistner, M. L. W. (1947) 'Antiochene exegesis in Western Europe during the Middle Ages,' *Harvard Theological Review* 40, 19–31.

Landes, R. (1988) 'Lest the millennium be fulfilled: apocalyptic expectations and the pattern of Western chronography 100–800 CE,' in W. Verbeke, D. Verhelst, and A. Welkenhuysen, *The use and abuse of eschatology in the Middle Ages*, Leuven, 137–211.

Lapidge, M. (2007) 'The career of Aldhelm,' *Anglo-Saxon England* 36, 15–69.

— (2010) 'Aldhelm and the "Epinal-Erfurt Glossary",' in K. Barker and N. Brooks, *Aldhelm and Sherborne: essays to celebrate the founding of the bishopric*, Oxford, 129–63.

— (2019) *Bede's Latin poetry*, Oxford.

Lapidge, M. and M. Herren (1979) *Aldhelm: the prose works*, Ipswich.

Lapidge, M. and R. Sharpe (1985) *A bibliography of Celtic-Latin literature: 400–1200*, Dublin.

Lazzarato, D. (1952) *Chronologia Christi seu Discordantium fontium concordantia ad juris normam*, Naples.

Lecouteux, S. (2008) 'L'archétype et le *stemma* des Annales Angevines et Vendômoises,' *Revue d'histoire des textes, ns* 3, 229–61.

— (2009) 'L'abbé Geoffroy de Vendôme (1093–1132), initiateur des Annales de Vendôme?,' *Cahiers de civilisation médiévale* 52, 37–43.

Lees, C. A. and G. R. Overing (1994) 'Birthing bishops and fathering poets: Bede, Hild, and the relations of cultural production,' *Exemplaria* 6, 35–65.

Lehmann, P. (1912) 'Cassiodorstudien I,' *Philologus* 71, 278–99; repr. in P. Lehmann, *Erforschung des Mittelalters: Ausgewählte Abhandlungen und Aufsätze*, 5 vols, Stuttgart 1941–1962, ii 38–55.

Lehner, H.-C. (2021) *The end(s) of time(s): apocalypticism, messianism, and utopianism through the ages*, Leiden.

Lejbowicz, M. (2010) 'Les Pâques baptismales d'Augustin d'Hippone, une étape contournée dans l'unification des practiques computistes latines,' in Warntjes and Ó Cróinín (2010), 1–39.

Levison, W. (1946) *England and the Continent in the eighth century*, Oxford.

Lindsay, W. (1911) *Isidori Hispalensis episcopi etymologiarum sive originum libri XX*, 2 vols, Oxford.

— (1915) *Notae latinae: an account of abbreviation in Latin MSS. of the early minuscule period (c. 700–850)*, Cambridge.

Lohr, A. and C. P. E. Nothaft (2019) *Robert Grosseteste's Compotus*, Oxford.

Loi, V. (1971) 'Il 25 Marzo data pasquale e la cronologia giovannea della passione in età patristica,' *Ephemerides Liturgicae* 85, 48–69.

López, F. J. Á. (2013) 'The Rule of St Benedict in England at the time of Wilfrid,' in Higham (2013), 40–53.

Lot, F. (1934) *Nennius et l'Historia Brittonum*, Paris.

Lozovsky, N. (2000) *'The Earth is our book': geographical knowledge in the Latin West ca. 400–1000*, Ann Arbor.

Maas, M. (2003) *Exegesis and empire in the early Byzantine Mediterranean: Junillus Africanus and the Instituta regularia divinae legis*, Tübingen.

Mac Airt, S. and G. Mac Niocaill (1983) *The Annals of Ulster (to A.D. 1131)*, Dublin.

Mac Carthy, B. (1901) *Annals of Ulster, vol. 4: introduction and index*, Dublin.

MacCarron, M. (2020) *Bede and time: computus, theology and history in the early medieval world*, London.

Mayr-Harting, H. (1991) *The coming of Christianity to Anglo-Saxon England*, 3rd ed., London.

Mc Carthy, D. P. (1993) 'Easter principles and a lunar cycle used by fifth-century Christian communities in the British Isles,' *Journal for the History of Astronomy* 24, 204–24.

— (1994) 'The origin of the *latercus* paschal cycle of the insular Celtic churches,' *Cambrian Medieval Celtic Studies* 28, 25–49.

— (1994a) 'The chronological apparatus of the Annals of Ulster AD 431–1131,' *Peritia* 8, 47–79.

— (1996) 'The lunar and paschal tables of *De ratione paschali* attributed to Anatolius of Laodicea,' *Archive for History of Exact Sciences* 49, 285–320.

— (2003) 'On the shape of the Insular tonsure,' *Celtica* 24, 140–67.

— (2005) 'Irish chronicles and their chronology,' https://www.scss.tcd.ie/misc/kronos/chronology/synchronisms/annals-chron.htm.

— (2008) *The Irish Annals: their genesis, evolution and history*, Dublin.

— (2010) 'Bede's primary source for the Vulgate chronology in his chronicles in *De temporibus* and *De temporum ratione*,' in Warntjes and Ó Cróinín (2010), 159–89.

— (2011) 'On the arrival of the *latercus* in Ireland,' in Warntjes and Ó Cróinín (2011), 48–75.

— (2012) 'The harmonization of the lunar year with the Julian calendar by Anatolius, bishop of Laodicea,' in J. Ben-Dov, W. Horrowitz, and J. M. Steele, *Living the lunar calendar*, Oxford, 245–57.

— (2017) 'The paschal cycle of St Patrick,' in Warntjes and Ó Cróinín (2017), 94–137.

— (2022) 'Sulpicius Severus's construction of his 84-year paschal table,' *Peritia* 33 (2022), 139–58.

Mc Carthy, D. P. and A. Breen (1997) 'Astronomical observations in the Irish Annals and their motivations,' *Peritia* 11, 1–43.

— (2003) *The ante-Nicene Christian Pasch: De ratione paschali – the paschal tract of Anatolius, bishop of Laodicea*, Dublin.

Mc Carthy, D. P. and D. Ó Cróinín (1987–1988) 'The "lost" Irish 84-year Easter table recovered,' *Peritia* 6–7, 225–42.

McClure, J. (1984) 'Bede and the Life of Ceolfrid,' *Peritia* 3, 71–84.

McNally, R. (1957) *Der irische Liber de numeris. Eine Quellenanalyse des pseudo-isidorischen Liber de numeris*, Munich.

Michels, A. K. (1967) *The calendar of the Roman Republic*, Princeton.

Miller, M. (1979) 'The dates of Deira,' *Anglo-Saxon England* 8, 35–61.

Moisl, H. (1983) 'The Bernician royal dynasty and the Irish in the seventh century,' *Peritia* 2, 103–26.

Moisl, H. and S. Hamann (2002) 'A Frankish aristocrat at the battle of Mag Roth,' in M. Richter and J.-M. Picard, *Ogma: essays in Celtic studies in honour of Próinséas Ní Chatháin*, Dublin, 36–47.

Mommsen, T. (1850) 'Über den Chronographen vom J. 354,' *Abhandlungen der Königlich-Sächsischen Gesellschaft der Wissenschaften, phil.-hist. Cl.* 1, 547–693.

— (1863) 'Zeitzer Ostertafel vom Jahre 447,' *Abhandlungen der Königlichen Akademie der Wissenschaften zu Berlin, Jahrgang 1862, phil.-hist. Klasse*, 537–66.

Monge Allen, E. (2017) 'Metamorphosis of Eoin Bruinne: constructing John the Apostle in medieval Ireland,' *Études celtiques* 43, 207–23.

Moran, P. and I. Warntjes (2015) *Early medieval Ireland and Europe: chronology, contacts, scholarship – a Festschrift for Dáibhí Ó Cróinín*, Turnhout.

Moreton, J. (1998) 'Doubts about the calendar: Bede and the eclipse of 664,' *Isis* 89, 50–65.

Morris, J. (1980) *Nennius: British History and the Welsh Annals*, London.

Mosshammer, A. A. (1984) *Georgii Syncelli Ecloga chronographica*, Leipzig.

— (2008) *The Easter computus and the origins of the Christian era*, Oxford.

— (2013) 'The Praefatio (Prologus) Sancti Cyrilli de Paschate and the 437-year (not 418!) paschal list attributed to Theophilus,' *Vigilae Christianae* 67, 49–78.

— (2017) *The prologues on Easter of Theophilus of Alexandria and [Cyril]*, Oxford.

Mosshammer, A. A. and I. Warntjes (forthcoming) *Early medieval Iberian computus: studies and texts*.

Muhlberger, S. (1990) *The fifth-century chroniclers: Prosper, Hydatius and the Gallic Chronicler of 452*, Leeds.

Muratori, L. A. (1697–1713) *Anecdota, quae ex Ambrosianae bibliothecae codicibus nunc primum eruit, notis, ac disquisitionibus auget Ludovicus Antonius Muratorius*, 4 vols, Milan and Padua.

Neugebauer, O. E. (1981) 'On the "Spanish era",' *Chiron* 11, 371–80.

— (1982) 'On the computus paschalis of "Cassiodorus",' *Centaurus* 25, 292–302.

Ní Dhonnchadha, M. (1982) 'The guarantor list of *Cáin Adomnáin*, 697,' *Peritia* 1, 178–215.

Noris, E. (1691) *Annus et epochae Syromacedonum in vetustis urbium Syriae nummis praesertim Mediceis expositae; additis Fastis consularibus anonymi omnium optimis; accesserunt nuper Dissertationes de paschali Latinorum cyclo annorum LXXXIV ac Ravennate annorum XCV*, Florence.

Nothaft, C. P. E. (2012) *Dating the Passion: the life of Jesus and the emergence of scientific chronology (200–1600)*, Leiden.

— (2012a) 'Nicholas Trevet and the chronology of the Crucifixion,' *The Mediaeval Journal* 2, 55–76.

— (2013) 'An eleventh-century chronologer at work: Marianus Scottus and the quest for the missing twenty-two years,' *Speculum* 88, 457–82.

— (2016) 'Walter Odington's *De etate mundi* and the pursuit of a scientific chronology in medieval England,' *Journal of the History of Ideas* 77, 183–201.

— (2017) *Walcher of Malver, De lunationibus and De dracone: study, edition, translation, and commentary*, Turnhout.

— (2018) *Scandalous error: calendar reform and calendrical astronomy in medieval Europe*, New York.

Noviomagus, J. (1537) *Bedae presbyteri Anglosaxonis [...] opuscula cumplura* [sic] *de temporum ratione [...]*, Cologne.

O'Brien, M. A. (1962) *Corpus genealogiarum Hiberniae*, vol. 1, Dublin.

Ó Carragáin, É. and A. Thacker (2013) 'Wilfrid in Rome,' in Higham (2013), 212–30.

O'Connell, D. J. (1936) 'Easter cycles in the early Irish church,' *Journal of the Royal Society of Antiquaries of Ireland* 66, 67–106.

Ó Corráin, D. (2017) *Clavis litterarum Hibernensium*, 3 vols, Turnhout.

Ó Cróinín, D. (1982a) 'Mo Sinu maccu Min and the computus at Bangor,' *Peritia* 1, 281–95; repr. in Ó Cróinín (2003), 35–47.

— (1982b) 'Pride and prejudice,' *Peritia* 1, 352–62.

— (1983a) 'Early Irish annals from Easter tables: a case restated,' *Peritia* 2, 74–86; repr. in Ó Cróinín (2003), 76–86.

— (1983b) 'The Irish provenance of Bede's computus,' *Peritia* 2, 229–47; repr. in Ó Cróinín (2003), 173–90.

— (1984) 'Rath Melsigi, Willibrord, and the earliest Echternach manuscripts,' *Peritia* 3, 17–49; repr. in Ó Cróinín (2003), 145–72.

— (1985) '"New heresy for old": Pelagianism in Ireland and the papal letter of 640,' *Speculum* 60, 505–16; repr. in Ó Cróinín (2003), 87–98.

— (1987) 'Merovingian politics and insular calligraphy: the historical background to the Book of Durrow and related manuscripts,' in M. Ryan, *Ireland and insular art: AD 500–1200*, Dublin, 40–43.

— (1989) 'The date, provenance and earliest use of the works of Virgilius Maro Grammaticus,' in G. Bernt, F. Rädle and G. Silagi, *Tradition und Wertung: Festschrift für Franz Brunhölzl zum 65. Geburtstag*, Sigmaringen, 13–22.

— (1995) *Early medieval Ireland 400–1200*, London.

— (2000) 'Bischoff's "Wendepunkte" fifty years on,' *Revue bénédictine* 110, 204–37.

— (2001) 'A new seventh-century Irish commentary on Genesis,' *Sacris Erudiri* 40, 231–65.

— (2003) *Early Irish history and chronology*, Dublin.

— (2003a) 'Bede's Irish computus,' in Ó Cróinín (2003), 201–12.

— (2008) 'Dionysius Exiguus in the classroom,' in J. W. Dauben et al., *Mathematics celestial and terrestrial: Festschrift für Menso Folkers zum 65. Geburtstag*, Stuttgart, 253–74.

— (2010) 'The continuity of Irish computistical tradition,' in Warntjes and Ó Cróinín (2010), 324–47.

O'Donnell, D. P. (2005) *Cædmon's Hymn: a multi-media study, edition and archive*, Cambridge.

Ogg, G. (1940) *The chronology of the public ministry of Jesus*, Cambridge.

Ohashi, M. (1999) *The impact of the paschal controversy: computus, exegesis and church history in early Britain and Ireland*, unpubl. Ph.D. thesis, Nanzan University, Nagoya.

— (2003) 'Sexta aetas continet annos praeteritos DCCVIIII (Bede, De temporibus, 22): a scribal error?,' in G. Jaritz and G. Moreno-Riaño, *Time and eternity: the medieval discourse*, Turnhout, 55–61.

— (2005) 'Theory and history: an interpretation of the paschal controversy in Bede's *Historia Ecclesiastica*,' in S. Lebecq, M. Perrin, and O. Szerwiniack, *Bede le Venerable entre tradition et postérité*, Villeneuve d'Ascq, 177–85.

— (2010) 'The *Annus Domini* and the *sexta aetas*: problems in the transmission of Bede's *De temporibus*,' in Warntjes and Ó Cróinín (2010), 190–203.

— (2011) 'The Easter table of Victorius of Aquitaine in early medieval England,' in Warntjes and Ó Cróinín (2011), 137–49.

O'Hara, A. and I. Wood (2017) *Jonas of Bobbio: Life of Columbanus, Life of John of Réome, and Life of Vedast*, Liverpool.

Orschel, V. (2001) 'Mag nÉo na Sacsan: an English colony in Ireland in the seventh and eighth centuries,' *Peritia* 15, 81–107.

Ortenberg, V. (1999) 'The Anglo-Saxon church and the papacy,' in C. H. Lawrence, *The English church and the papacy in the Middle Ages*, Stroud, 29–62.

Orton, F. (2003) 'Rethinking the Ruthwell and Bewcastle monuments: some strictures on similarity; some questions of history,' in C. E. Karkov and F. Orton, *Theorizing Anglo-Saxon stone sculpture*, Morgantown, 65–92.

Overgaauw, E. (2009) 'Auseinandersetzung um den Ostertermin: die Berliner und Zeitzer Fragmente der Zeitzer Ostertafel,' in F.-J. Stewing, *Handschriften und frühe Drucke aus der Zeitzer Stiftsbibliothek*, Petersberg, 14–17.

Overgaauw, E. and F.-J. Stewing (2005) *Die Zeitzer Ostertafel aus dem Jahre 447*, Petersberg.

Palmer, J. T. (2011) 'Calculating time and the end of time in the Carolingian world, c. 740–c. 820,' *English Historical Review* 126, 1307–31.

— (2011a) 'Computus after the paschal controversy of 740,' in Warntjes and Ó Cróinín (2011), 213–41.

— (2013) 'The ordering of time,' in V. Wieser et al., *Abendländische Apokalyptik. Kompendium zur Genealogie der Endzeit*, Berlin, 605–18.

— (2014) *The apocalypse in the early Middle Ages*, Cambridge.

— (2017) 'The adoption of the Dionysian Easter in the Frankish kingdoms (c. 670–c. 800),' *Peritia* 28, 135–54.

Peden, A. M. (2003) *Abbo of Fleury and Ramsey: commentary on the Calculus of Victorius of Aquitaine*, Oxford.

Pedersen, O. (1983) 'The ecclesiastical calendar and the life of the church,' in G. V. Coyne, M. A. Hoskin, and O. Pedersen, *Gregorian reform of the calendar*, Vatican, 17–74.

Pelteret, D. A. E. (1998) 'Saint Wilfrid: tribal bishop, civic bishop or Germanic lord?,' in J. Hill and M. Swan, *The community, the family and the saint: patterns of power in early medieval Europe*, Turnhout, 159–80.

— (2011) 'The issue of apostolic authority at the synod of Whitby,' in Warntjes and Ó Cróinín (2011), 150–72.

— (2011–2012) 'Diplomatic elements in Willibrord's autobiography,' *Peritia* 22–23, 1–14.

BIBLIOGRAPHY

Picard, J.-M. (1991) 'Church and politics in the seventh century: the Irish exile of king Dagobert II,' in J.-M. Picard, *Ireland and Northern France AD 600–850*, Blackrock, 27–52.

Pillonel-Wyrsch, R.-P. (2004) *Le calcul de la date de Pâques au Moyen Âge: analyse et commentaire sur 'De temporum ratione' de Bède*, Fribourg.

Plummer, C. (1896) *Venerabilis Baedae opera historica*, 2 vols, Oxford.

Poole, R. L. (1918) 'The earliest use of the Easter cycle of Dionysius,' *English Historical Review* 33, 57–62.

Richard, M. (1951) 'Comput et chronographie chez saint Hippolyte (II),' *Mélanges de science religieuse* 8, 19–50.

Richardson, E. C. (1896) *Gennadius: Liber de viris inlustribus*, Leipzig.

Richter, M. (1999) *Ireland and her neighbours in the seventh century*, Dublin.

— (2008) *Bobbio in the early Middle Ages: the abiding legacy of Columbanus*, Dublin.

Rose, V. (1893) *Verzeichnis der lateinischen Handschriften der Königlichen Bibliothek zu Berlin*, Berlin.

Rowland, J. (1990) *Early Welsh saga poetry: a study and edition of the Englynion*, Cambridge.

Rühl, F. (1897) *Chronologie des Mittelalters und der Neuzeit*, Berlin.

Schmid, J. (1907) *Die Osterfestberechnung in der abendländischen Kirche vom I. Allgemeinen Konzil zu Nicäa bis zum Ende des VIII. Jahrhunderts*, Freiburg.

Schwartz, E. (1905) *Christliche und jüdische Ostertafeln*, Berlin.

Sharpe, R. (1995) *Adomnán of Iona: Life of St Columba*, London.

Sims-Williams, P. (1990) *Religion and literature in western England 600–800*, Cambridge.

Smith, T. (1696) *Catalogus librorum manuscriptorum Bibliothecae Cottonianae*, Oxford.

Smyth, A. P. (1984) *Warlords and holy men: Scotland AD 80–1000*, Edinburgh.

Smyth, M. (1987) 'Isidore of Seville and early Irish cosmography,' *Cambrian Medieval Celtic Studies* 14, 69–102.

— (2011) 'The seventh-century Hiberno-Latin treatise *Liber de ordine creaturarum*: a translation,' *Journal of Medieval Latin* 21, 137–222.

— (2017) 'Once in four: the leap year in early medieval thought,' in Warntjes and Ó Cróinín (2017), 229–64.

Springsfeld, K. (2002) *Alkuins Einfluß auf die Komputistik zur Zeit Karls des Großen*, Stuttgart.

— (2010) 'Eine Beschreibung der Handschrift St Gallen, Stiftsbibliothek, 225,' in Warntjes and Ó Cróinín (2010), 204–37.

Stancliffe, C. (1975) 'Early "Irish" biblical exegesis,' in E. A. Livingstone, *Studia Patristica XII. Papers presented to the Sixth International Conference on Patristic Studies held in Oxford, 1971*, Berlin, 361–70.

— (1983) 'Kings who opted out,' in P. Wormald, D. Bullough, and R. Collins, *Ideal and reality in Frankish and Anglo-Saxon society: studies presented to J. M. Wallace-Hadrill*, Oxford, 154–76.

— (2010) '"Charity with peace": Adomnán and the Easter question,' in J. M. Wooding, *Adomnán of Iona: theologian, lawmaker, peacemaker*, Dublin, 51–68.

— (2012) 'Disputed episcopacy: Bede, Acca, and the relationship between Stephen's Life of St Wilfrid and the early prose Lives of St Cuthbert,' *Anglo-Saxon England* 41, 7–39.

— (2013) 'Dating Wilfrid's death and Stephen's Life,' in Higham (2013), 17–26.

— (2018) 'Columbanus and shunning: the Irish peregrinus between Gildas, Gaul, and Gregory,' in A. O'Hara, *Columbanus and the peoples of the post-Roman Empire*, Oxford, 113–42.

Stancliffe, C. and E. Cambridge (1995) *Oswald: Northumbrian king to European saint*, Stamford.

Stansbury, M. (2016) 'Irish biblical exegesis,' in R. Flechner and S. M. Meeder, *The Irish in early medieval Europe: identity, culture and religion*, New York, 116–30.

Stevens, W. (2018) *Rhetoric and reckoning in the ninth century: the vademecum of Walahfrid Strabo*, Turnhout.

Stevenson, J. (1995a) *The 'Laterculus Malalianus' and the school of Archbishop Theodore*, Cambridge; repr. 2007.

— (1995b) 'Theodore and the Laterculus Malalianus,' in M. Lapidge, *Archbishop Theodore: commemorative studies on his life and influence*, Cambridge, 204–21.

Stokes, W. (1895) 'The Annals of Tigernach: first fragment,' *Revue celtique* 16, 374–419; repr. in W. Stokes, *The Annals of Tigernach*, 2 vols, Felinfach 1993.

— (1896) 'The Annals of Tigernach: third fragment,' *Revue Celtique* 17, 119–263; repr. in W. Stokes, *The Annals of Tigernach*, 2 vols, Felinfach 1993.

Story, J. (2005) 'The Frankish Annals of Lindisfarne and Kent,' *Anglo-Saxon England* 34, 59–109.

Strobel, A. (1977) *Ursprung und Geschichte des frühchristlichen Osterkalenders*, Berlin.

— (1984) *Texte zur Geschichte des frühchristlichen Osterkalenders*, Münster.

Stubbs, W. (1879) *The historical works of Gervase of Canterbury*, vol. 1, London.

Swanton, M. J. (2000) *The Anglo-Saxon chronicles*, London.

Thacker, A. (1983) 'Bede's ideal of reform,' in P. Wormald, D. Bullough, and R. Collins, *Ideal and reality in Frankish and Anglo-Saxon society: studies presented to J.M. Wallace-Hadrill*, Oxford, 130–53.

Thiele, E. R. (1983) *The mysterious numbers of the Hebrew kings*, 3rd ed., Grand Rapids.

Throop, P. (2005) *Isidore of Seville's Etymologies*, 2 vols, Charlotte.

Tyler, D. J. (2007) 'Early Mercia and the Britons,' in N. Higham, *Britons in Anglo-Saxon England*, Woodbridge, 91–101.

van der Hagen, J. (1733) *Observationes in Prosperi Aquitani chronicon integrum ejusque LXXXIV annorum cyclum, et in anonymi cyclum LXXXIV annorum a Muratorio editum, nec non in anonymi laterculum paschalem centum annorum a Bucherio editum*, Amsterdam.

— (1734) *Observationes in veterum patrum et pontificum prologos et epistolas paschales aliosque antiquos de ratione paschali scriptores. Accedit dissertatio de cyclo lunari Dionysii et Bedae*, Amsterdam.

Verbist, P. (2010) *Duelling with the past: medieval authors and the problem of the Christian era (c. 990–1135)*, Turnhout.

Vives, J. (1938) 'Über Ursprung und Verbreitung der spanischen Ära,' *Historisches Jahrbuch* 58, 97–108.

von Harnack, A. (1916) 'Porphyrius, "Gegen die Christen", 15 Bücher: Zeugnisse, Fragmente und Referate,' *Abhandlungen der Königlich Preussischen Akademie der Wissenschaften, Jahrgang 1916, phil.-hist. Klasse, Nr. 1*, Leipzig.

Walker, G. S. M. (1957) *Sancti Columbani opera*, Dublin; repr. 1997.

Wallace-Hadrill, J. M. (1975) 'Bede and Plummer,' in J. M. Wallace-Hadrill, *Early medieval history: collected essays*, Oxford, 76–95; and in G. Bonner, *Famulus Christi: essays in commemoration of the thirteenth centenary of the birth of the Venerable Bede*, London 1976, 366–85.

— (1988) *Bede's Ecclesiastical History of the English People: a historical commentary*, Oxford.

Wallis, F. (1999) *Bede: The reckoning of time*, Liverpool; repr. 2004.

Walsh, M. and D. Ó Cróinín (1988) *Cummian's letter De controversia paschali and the De ratione conputandi*, Toronto.

Ward, B. (1993) '"To my dearest sister": Bede and the educated woman,' in L. Smith and J. H. M. Taylor, *Women, the book and the godly*, Cambridge, 105–11.

Warntjes, I. (2005) 'A newly discovered Irish computus: *Computus Einsidlensis*,' *Peritia* 19, 61–64.

— (2007) 'The Munich Computus and the 84 (14)-year Easter reckoning,' *Proceedings of the Royal Irish Academy* 107 C, 31–85.

— (2010) *The Munich Computus: text and translation. Irish computistics between Isidore of Seville and the Venerable Bede and its reception in Carolingian times*, Stuttgart.

— (2010a) 'The Argumenta of Dionysius Exiguus and their early recensions,' in Warntjes and Ó Cróinín (2010), 40–111.

— (2010b) 'A newly discovered prologue of AD 699 to the Easter table of Victorius of Aquitaine in an unknown Sirmond manuscript,' *Peritia* 21, 255–84.

— (2011) 'The Computus Cottonianus of AD 689: a computistical formulary written for Willibrord's Frisian mission,' in Warntjes and Ó Cróinín (2011), 173–212.

— (2011a) 'Irische Komputistik zwischen Isidor von Sevilla und Beda Venerabilis: Ursprung, karolingische Rezeption und Forschungsperspektiven,' *Viator* 42, 1–31.

— (2012) 'Köln als naturwissenschaftliches Zentrum in der Karolingerzeit: Die frühmittelalterliche Kölner Schule und der Beginn der fränkischen Komputistik,' in H. Finger and H. Horst, *Mittelalterliche Handschriften der Kölner Dombibliothek: Viertes Symposium der Diözesan- und Dombibliothek Köln zu den Dom-Manuskripten (26. bis 27. November 2010)*, Cologne, 41–96.

— (2013) 'Seventh-century Ireland: the cradle of medieval science?,' in M. Kelly and C. Doherty, *Music and the stars: mathematics in medieval Ireland*, Dublin, 44–72.

— (2015) 'Victorius vs Dionysius: the Irish Easter controversy of AD 689,' in Moran and Warntjes (2015), 33–117.

— (2016) 'Computus as scientific thought in Ireland and the early medieval West,' in R. Flechner and S. Meeder, *The Irish in early medieval Europe: identity, culture and religion*, London, 158–78.

— (2017) 'Introduction: state of research on late antique and early medieval computus,' in Warntjes and Ó Cróinín (2017), 1–42.

— (2019) 'The final countdown and the reform of the liturgical calendar in the early Middle Ages,' in Gabriele and Palmer (2019), 51–75.

— (2020) 'AD 672 – the apex of apocalyptic thought in the early medieval Latin West?,' in Wieser et al. (2020), ii 642–73.

— (2020a) 'Isidore of Seville and the formation of medieval computus,' in A. Fear and J. Wood, *A companion to Isidore of Seville*, Leiden, 457–523.

Warntjes, I. and D. Ó Cróinín (2010) *Computus and its cultural context in the Latin West, AD 300–1200*, Turnhout.

— (2011) *The Easter controversy of Late Antiquity and the early Middle Ages*, Turnhout.

— (2017) *Late antique calendrical thought and its reception in the early Middle Ages*, Turnhout.

Weikmann, H. M. (2004) *Heimo von Bamberg: De decursu temporum*, Hannover.

Whitelock, D. (1972) 'The pre-Viking age church in East Anglia,' *Anglo-Saxon England* 1, 1–22.

Whiting, C. E. (1935) 'The life of the Venerable Bede,' in A. H. Thompson, *Bede: his life, times, and writings*, Oxford, 1–38.

Wiesenbach, J. (1986) *Sigebert von Gembloux: Liber decennalis*, Weimar.

Wieser, V. et al. (2020) *Cultures of eschatology*, 2 vols, Berlin.

Williams, I. (1978) *Canu Llywarch Hen*, Cardiff.

Wilson, H. A. (1918) *The calendar of St Willibrord*, London; repr. Woodbridge 1998.

Wood, I. N. (1990) 'Ripon, Francia and the Franks Casket in the early Middle Ages,' *Northern History* 26, 1–19.

— (1995) 'Northumbrians and Franks in the age of Wilfrid,' *Northern History* 31, 10–21.

— (2003) 'Ruthwell: contextual searches,' in C. E. Karkov and F. Orton, *Theorizing Anglo-Saxon stone sculpture*, Morgantown, 104–30.

— (2013) 'The continental journeys of Wilfrid and Biscop,' in Higham (2013), 200–11.

— (2016) 'The Irish in England and on the Continent in the seventh century: part II,' *Peritia* 27, 189–214.

Wormald, P. (1992) 'The Venerable Bede and the "Church of the English",' in Geoffrey Rowell, *The English religious tradition and the genius of Anglicanism*, Wantage, 13–32; repr. in Wormald (2006), 207–28.

— (1993) 'St Hilda, saint and scholar (614–680),' in J. Mellanby, *The St Hilda's College centenary symposium*, Oxford, 93–103; repr. in Wormald (2006), 267–76.

— (2006) *The times of Bede: studies in early English Christian society and its historian*, ed. by S. Baxter, Malden.

Wright, C. W. (2000) 'Bischoff's theory of Irish exegesis and the Genesis commentary in Munich Clm 6302: a critique of a critique,' *Journal of Medieval Latin* 10, 115–75.

Yarza Urquiola, V. and F. J. Andrés Santos (2013) *Isidoro de Sevilla: Etimologías, Libro V: De legibus – De temporibus*, Paris.

Yorke, B. (1990) *Kings and kingdoms of early Anglo-Saxon England*, London.

— (2010) 'Aldhelm's Irish and British connections,' in K. Barker and N. Brooks, *Aldhelm and Sherborne: essays to celebrate the founding of the bishopric*, Oxford, 164–80.

Zironi, A. (2004) *Il monastero longobardo di Bobbio: crocevia di uomini, manoscritti e culture*, Spoleto.

Index of Biblical Citations

Judges:
3:7–11: 162

Esther:
2:9: 95

Daniel:
7:25: 126
8:14: 126
12:7: 126
12:11: 126
12:12: 126

Matthew:
4:17: 126
24:36: 185

Mark:
13:32: 185, 199

Luke:
3:1: 210
3:23: 126, 130, 132, 210

John: 212
1:29: 137
2:13: 126, 210
5:1: 210
6:4: 126, 210
11:15: 126
11:55: 210

Acts:
1:7: 185

Apocalpyse:
11:3: 126
12:6: 126
12:14: 126
13:18: 162

Index of Sources

Abbo of Fleury: 15, 135, 219

Acta synodi Caesareae: 16, 131
1: 132
3: 131

Adomnán of Iona: 91, 110, 167
De locis sanctis: 175
Vita Columbae: 174–75

Æthelwulf:
De abbatibus: 174–75

Ailerán of Clonard: 167
Interpretatio mystica: 174–75
Canon Evangeliorum: 175
Vita I sanctae Brigitae: 175

Alcuin:
Epistola ad monachos Mugensis ecclesiae:
103

pseudo-Alcuin:
De bissexto: 190

Aldhelm: 110
Epistula ad Hadrianum: 117
Epistula ad Wilfridi abbates: 108

Anatolius Latinus:
De ratione paschali: 70, 82, 91, 160, 172–
73, 188–89, 191

Annales Cambriae:
626: 90, 94, 112

Annals of Tigernach: 110, 133, 139–40

Annals of Ulster: 221
660: 102, 110
663: 92

Augustine: 14, 79, 179, 188
De civitate Dei:
18.54: 210
20.7: 185
22.30: 185

Auraicept na n-Éces: 161–62

Bede: 12–13, 15–16, 88, 91, 141, 167,
178, 182–83, 189–90
De temporibus: 15, 142–43, 178
14: 125, 128
22 (*Chronica minora*): 92, 222
De temporum ratione: 15–16, 121–40,
142–43, 178
1: 162
6: 221
7: 189
20: 189
29: 187
38: 191
43: 131, 137
47: 122–27, 129–33, 136–38, 212
48: 127
56: 124
61: 135–38, 212
66 (*Chronica maiora*): 92, 130, 132, 139,
179, 206–07, 215, 221–22

Epistola ad Ecgbertum:

13: 119

Explanatio Apocalypseos: 126

Historia abbatum:

1: 111

2: 95

3: 115

15: 127

18: 127

Historia ecclesiastica gentis Anglorum: 87–120, 174–75

1.2: 130

1.4: 124

1.29: 106

1.32: 116

2.5: 93, 110

2.9: 89

2.12: 89, 98, 106

2.13: 89

2.14: 110

2.15: 107

2.16: 101

2.20: 90, 94, 101–02, 107, 111

3.1: 89, 109

3.3: 91–92, 109

3.4: 95, 112

3.6: 111

3.7: 100

3.13: 99

3.14: 93, 95, 97, 110–11

3.15: 89, 101, 112

3.19: 106–07

3.20: 108

3.21: 94, 118

3.22: 104

3.23: 104

3.24: 92–93, 107, 111, 118

3.25: 88, 90, 93–96, 100–02, 104, 107, 109–11, 113–14

3.26: 89, 96, 102–04, 114–15

3.27: 92, 96, 98, 103, 110

3.28: 92, 96–97, 101, 109, 111, 115

3.29: 115–17, 119

3.30: 92

3.32: 92

4: 91

4.1: 92, 115–17

4.2: 105, 115, 118

4.3: 104

4.4: 102–03, 114

4.5: 117–18

4.12: 99, 105

4.13: 99, 118

4.23: 89, 105–07

4.24: 105

4.26: 108, 112

5.2–6: 105

5.2: 106

5.3: 105

5.8: 105

5.10: 98

5.15: 91

5.19: 97, 119

5.21: 91, 137

5.22: 91, 120

5.23: 105–06

5.24: 94, 97, 105

Poemata: 174

Vita Cuthberhti: 175

Vita metrica sancti Cuthberhti: 175

7: 96

Bobbio Computus (= Milan, Biblioteca Ambrosiana, H 150 inf., 5r–110v): 185, 192

28: 196

35: 194

56: 196

58: 196

70: 195

89: 193–94

96: 194–95

97: 195

Boethius: 161

De institutione arithmetica: 173

INDEX OF SOURCES

Cáin Adomnáin (*Lex Innocentium*): 88

Cassiodorus:
Computus of AD 562: 145

Chronica Frodoardi: 205

Chronograph of AD 354 (also *Romana supputatio* 354 = RS-354): 20–21, 24, 26–28, 39, 45, 51–52, 55–56, 58–59, 61–62, 67, 69, 77–84, 123, 128, 210

Cogitosus of Kildare:
Vita sanctae Brigitae: 175

Cologne Prologue (*Prologus paschae*): 138, 185, 210
5: 185

Columbanus: 98, 100, 107, 180–81, 185
Epistulae:
2.7: 213

pseudo-Columbanus:
De saltu lunae: 16

Computatio of AD 452: 210

Computus Amiatinus (CA): 177–200
1: 184
4: 184
8: 190
12: 184
15: 178
see also Florence, Biblioteca Medicea Laurenziana, Conv. Sopr. 364 (siglum C); Florence, Biblioteca Medicea Laurenziana, Plut. 20.54 (siglum P)

Computus Carthaginiensis of AD 455: 14, 22, 51, 210

Computus Cottonianus of AD 689 (= London, British Library, Cotton Caligula A XV, 73r–80r): 147

Computus Einsidlensis: 12, 143, 178, 180, 184, 187–92, 194–96
see also Einsiedeln, Stiftsbibliothek, 321 (647)

Computus Hibernicus Parisinus of AD 754: 12

Computus Hispanorum secundum antiquam consuetudinem Romanorum (= Berlin, Staatsbibliothek Preußischer Kulturbesitz, Phillipps 1833, 61r–v): 148

Consularia Constantinopolitana: see *Descriptio consulum*

Consularia Italica: 210

Continuationes Chronicarum Fredegarii:
16: 222

Cummian:
De controversia paschali: 91, 160, 173–74

Cuthbert of Wearmouth-Jarrow:
Epistola de obitu Baedae: 175

De divisionibus temporum: 12, 178, 180, 183–86, 190, 192–200

De mirabilibus sacrae scripturae:
7: 186
2.4: 213

De ordine creaturarum:
9.5–7: 186–87

INDEX OF SOURCES 245

De ratione conputandi: 128, 143, 174, 178,
180, 191–92
17: 194
18: 195
42: 196
43: 196
44: 196
45: 128
55–56: 190
57: 190
68: 189
86: 212
112: 189

De ratione temporum (Annus solis): 174

Descriptio consulum: 35, 42–46, 210

Deus a quo facta fuit: 174, 180

Dial. Burg. of AD 727:
6A: 196
16: 181

Dial. Langob. of c.AD 750: 182
1B: 184
2B: 196
3B: 184, 193, 197
4B: 193
7: 186
11A: 196
18B: 189
24: 189–90

Dial. Neustr. of AD 737:
15C: 188
18: 188
19: 188

Dicuil:
Liber de astronomia / De cursu solis
lunaeque: 12

Disputatio Chori et Praetextati: 12, 160,
167, 173–74
see also: Macrobius: *Saturnalia*

Dionysius Exiguus: 15, 16, 84, 91–92, 96,
121–26, 129–31, 133–37, 140, 142–
43, 145–46, 148, 172–73, 182, 188–
89, 191, 202–05, 214–13, 218–22
Argumenta: 122, 124, 128, 141, 143, 145–
47, 188, 190
Epistola ad Bonifatium et Bonum: 122–26,
143, 188
Epistola ad Petronium (Prologus): 122,
143, 147, 188

pseudo-Dionysius: 145
Argumentum XVI: 190

Epistola Paschasini: 52–57, 79, 81, 85, 142
1: 53, 55, 635
2: 55–56, 80

Epistola Proterii (ad Leonem papam):
3: 212
12: 53

Eusebius of Caesarea:
Chronicon: 45, 79, 125, 129, 133, 139–40,
178–79, 206, 210, 221
Historia ecclesiastica:
1.10: 210
5.24: 70
7.32: 70
Demonstratio Evangelica:
8.2.107: 210

Fasti Vindobonensis: 45–50

Felix of Squillace: 127–28, 136

Frankish Annals of Lindisfarne and Kent:
658: 102

INDEX OF SOURCES

Fredegar: 185
see also *Continuationes Chronicarum Fredegarii*

Gennadius of Marseille:
De viris illustribus: 81
87: 202
89: 81

Gerland the Computist: 219

Gervase of Canterbuy:
Chronica: 220

Gildas:
De excidio Brittaniae: 167

Gregory the Great: 97, 116
Liber regulae pastoris: 108

Heimo of Bamberg: 15
De decursu temporum: 220

Hermann of Reichenau: 12, 16, 142

Hilarus: 78, 81, 164, 171
Epistola ad Victorium: 18, 58, 84, 202

Hippolytus: 52, 67, 69, 81, 84, 137

Historia abbatum:
20: 127

Historia Brittonum:
57: 89, 94, 112
63: 90, 94, 106, 112

Isidore: 146, 182, 184–85, 191, 194–95
Chronica:
1.31: 207
1.196: 207
1.232: 206
1.235–38: 207
2.31: 207

2.196: 207
2.232: 206
2.235–39: 207
De natura rerum:
3.1: 196
6.2: 196
Etymologiae: 173, 177, 179, 183
3.34: 187
3.49: 187
3.50: 186–87
5.29.1–2: 194
5.36.1: 188
5.36.4: 144
13.1: 186
Liber numerorum: 186

pseudo-Isidore: 184, 194–95
Liber de numeris: 186

Jerome:
Chronicon: see Eusebius: *Chronicon*
Commentariorum in Danielem Libri III:
12.11: 126
Epistolae:
49.13–14: 138

John of Biclarum:
Chronica: 125

Jonas of Bobbio:
Vita Columbani et eius socii:
1.30: 180
Vita Iohannis abbatis:
Praef.: 181

Lactantius:
De mortibus persecutorum:
1.2: 210
Divinae institutiones:
4.10: 210

Laterculus Malalianus: 142

Latercus (= Padua, Biblioteca Antoniana,
 I 27, 76r–77v): 14, 22, 82, 88, 91,
 102, 104, 109, 131, 135, 137–38, 160,
 173, 181

Leo I: 14–15, 18, 20, 26, 52, 54–59, 63,
 79–85, 142, 202
Epistola ad Marcianum: 52, 81, 142
1: 59
2: 56–57, 69–70
Epistola ad Paschasinum of AD 451: 52–
 53, 142
4: 56

Lib. ann. of AD 793: 182, 191
51: 187

Liber de numeris: see pseudo-Isidore

Liber genealogus: 179

Liber pontificalis:
91.18: 178

Lutting of Lindisfarne:
Versus in honour of his master Bede: 175

Macrobius:
Saturnalia: 11–12, 173, 190
see also: *Disputatio Chori et Praetextati*:

Marianus Scotus (Máel Brigte): 16, 135,
 219

Martianus Capella:
De nuptiis Philologiae et Mercurii
2: 162

Munich Computus: 22, 143, 159–63,
 173–75, 178, 180, 184, 188–91, 213
1: 184, 193
2: 193
3: 194
4: 195

5: 195
6: 195
7: 184, 195
10: 196
12: 196
28: 188
30: 196
31: 188, 197
41: 159, 160–62, 190, 213
43: 184, 197
44: 189
62: 159, 162–63, 189, 213

Muirchú moccu Macthéni:
Vita sancti Patricii: 174–75
1.27: 171

Nonae Aprilis: 174

Notker of St Gall: 12, 16

Orosius:
Historia adversum paganos: 206

Paschasinus of Lilybaeum: see *Epistola
 Paschasini*

Recueil initial de Saint-Maurice d'Angers:
 204–05

Peterborough Chronicle (Anglo-Saxon
 Chronicle, manuscript E)
617: 89
685: 105

Phlegon of Tralles: 133

Porphyr:
Fragment 43.W.7: 126

Prol. Aquit of AD 721: 143, 147

Prologus Cyrili: 148

INDEX OF SOURCES

Prologus paschae: see Cologne Prologue

Prologus Theophili:
8: 212

Prosper of Aquitaine: 14, 19–20, 79–84
Chronicon: 42–46, 75–80, 133, 210–11
316: 206
383–85: 81
388: 211
390: 80
1352: 56, 80
1396: 81

Proterius of Alexandria: see *Epistola Proterii*

pseudo-Methodius: 192
Revelationes:
10.6: 185

Quaest. Langob. of c.AD 780: 182

Quintus Iulius Hilarianus: 14

Ratio pascalis: 180, 192

Ratio sphere Dionysii de circulo magno pasche: 219–20
see also Milan, Biblioteca Ambrosiana, Z 70 sup., 8r–10v; Vatican, Biblioteca Apostolica Vaticana, Vat. lat. 1548, 68r–69r

Red Book of Saint-Florent de Saumur (*Codex rubeus*): see Angers, Archives départementales de Maine-et-Loire, H 3715

Rhetorica ad Herennium:
4.20.27–28: 170

Robert Grossesteste:
Computus: 12

Romana Supputatio 354 (= RS 354): see Chronograph of AD 354

Rufinus of Aquileia: 138, 173
see also Eusebius: *Historia ecclesiastica*

Rhygyfarch ap Sulien:
Vita Sancti David (*Buched Dewi*):
90, 112

Stephen of Pisa ('Alī ibn al-'Abās al-Majūsī):
Complete Book of the Medical Art: 220

Stephen of Ripon: 88
Vita Wilfridi: 90, 104, 174–75
Praef.: 96
1: 95
2: 95
3: 97
8: 96
10: 95, 100–01, 103, 113–14
11: 96, 115
12: 96–97, 101, 115
14: 97
15: 115
17: 119
24: 97
25: 97
26: 99
28: 98
29: 97
33: 98
45: 97
47: 98, 102, 118
50: 97
54: 97, 108
55: 97
58: 97
59: 120

Suetonius: 45

Sulpicius Severus: 14, 27, 70, 82, 91, 135, 173–74
Vita sancti Martini: 174

Supputatio Romana: 17–85, 135, 137
see also Chronograph of AD 354;
Cologne Prologue

Tertullian: 135
Adversus Iudaeos:
8.18: 210

Theophilus of Alexandria: 27, 34, 38, 52, 56–57, 59, 62, 69, 78–79, 81, 132–33
see also *Prologus Theophili*

Trioedd Ynys Prydein (Welsh Triads): 26W.30–32: 90

Victor of Tunnuna:
Chronica: 125

Victorian Prologue of AD 699
(= Bremen, Staats- und
Universtitätsbibliothek, msc 0046,
38r–v): 133, 163–75, 180

Victorius of Aquitaine: 14, 18, 25, 62–63, 77–79, 81, 84, 91, 96, 116, 122, 138, 171–72, 181, 185, 188, 191, 201–06, 210–14
Cyclus: 14, 18, 45–46, 49, 58–59, 78–79, 84, 131, 133–35, 137–38, 140, 160–64, 166, 171–73, 181, 202–03, 207, 210–15, 218, 221–22
Epistola ad Hilarum (Prologus): 105, 189, 202, 206
3: 61
4: 34, 59, 62, 67, 78
5: 59, 62, 78

6: 33
7: 81, 189
8–9: 211
12: 78

Visigothic Computus of AD 722
(= Leiden, Universiteitsbibliothek,
VMI 11, 26r–27v): 16, 141–57

Visigothic Computus of AD 811
(= Rome, Biblioteca Casanatense,
641, 1r–5v / Montecassino, Archivo
della Badia, 3, 1–11): 146–47

Vita Ceolfridi: 174–75
2: 111

Vita Cuthberti: 96, 174–75
Prol.: 96
4.1: 96

Vita Gregorii: 107, 174–75
12–19: 105
16: 89

Vita sancti Samsonis: 174–75

Walcher of Malvern: 12

Walter Odington:
Summa de etate mundi: 220

Willibrord:
Calendar (= Paris, Bibliothèque
nationale de France, Lat. 10837, 34v–
40r): 99, 146

Zeitz paschal table of AD 447
(= RS-447): 14, 17–85

Index of Manuscripts

Angers, Archives départementales de
   Maine-et-Loire, H 3715 (siglum A):
   205–07, 210–12, 220–22
75r–76r: 206–07
76r: 206
76v: 206
77r: 206–07
77r–94v: 201
78v: 213
79r: 213
84r: 214
84r–94v: 214
86v: 214–13
90r: 218
93v: 214
94v: 214

Angers, Bibliothèque municipale, 477
   (461):
20r: 190

Berlin, Staatsbibliothek Preußischer
   Kulturbesitz, Lat. qu. 298 (siglum B):
1r–4v [Reconstruction of original codex:
   1=4; 2=5; 3=10; 4=15]: 17–21, 23,
   25–27, 29–31, 38, 84–85
1r–v (=4r–v): 61
1r (=4r): 35, 44, 62–63
1v (=4v): 36, 45
2r–v (=5r–v): 61
2r (=5r): 37
2v (=5v): 38
3r–v (=10r–v): 32, 45, 61
3r (=10r): 40
3v (=10v): 41
4r–v (=15r–v): 32, 45, 61

4r (=15r): 42, 45
4v (=15v): 43

Berlin, Staatsbibliothek Preußischer
   Kulturbesitz, Phillipps 1831: 182

Berlin, Staatsbibliothek Preußischer
   Kulturbesitz, Phillipps 1832:

46r: 127

Berlin, Staatsbibliothek Preußischer
   Kulturbesitz, Phillipps 1833:

61r–v (= *Computus Hispanorum
   secundum antiquam consuetudinem
   Romanorum*): 148

Bern, Burgerbibliothek, 417:
47r–61v: 183

Bern, Burgerbibliothek, 611:
96r: 181

Bremen, Staats- und
   Universtitätsbibliothek, msc 0046:
   159, 163
38r–v (= Victorian Prologue of AD 699):
   133

Cesena, Biblioteca Malatestiana,
   D.XXIV.1: 179

Colmar, Bibliothèque municipale, 43
   (39):
60r–175v (= *Liber de numeris*): 186

INDEX OF MANUSCRIPTS 251

Cologne, Diözesan- und Dombibliothek,
83-II: 193
20r: 194
20v: 195
21v: 195
22r: 196
23v: 196
24r: 196
26r: 190–91
37r–44r: 183

Dijon, Bibliothèque municipale, 448: 192
29r–37v: 183
31r: 193–94
31v: 195
32r: 196

Einsiedeln, Stiftsbibliothek, 321 (647):
83–125 (= *Computus Einsidlensis*): 143,
180

Florence, Biblioteca Medicea
Laurenziana, Conv. Sopr. 364
(siglum C): 179–80, 192–97
1r–106v: 179
107r–116r: 179
116r: 180
116r–v: 180
116v: 180
117v: 186
118r: 186–87
118v–119r: 180
119r: 188–89
119r–120r: 180
119v: 189
120r: 188, 190
see also *Computus Amiatinus* (*CA*)

Florence, Biblioteca Medicea
Laurenziana, Plut. 20.54 (siglum P):
192–97
15r: 193–94
15v: 194–95

15r–v: 180
15v–16r: 180
16r–18v: 180
17r: 186
17v: 186
18r: 186–87
18v: 186–87
18v–19v: 180
19r: 187, 189
19v: 188
19v–21r: 180
20r: 189
20v: 188, 190
30r–37r: 179
see also *Computus Amiatinus* (*CA*)

Geneva, Bibliothèque de Genève,
Lat. 50:
139r–148v: 183
148v: 190

Gotha, Forschungsbibliothek, Memb.
I 75:
77v: 212
77v–106r: 202

Karlsruhe, Badische Landesbibliothek,
442:
61r–83r: 183
71v: 188
89r: 148

Laon, Bibliothèque municipale, 422:
37v: 193
38v: 195
44v: 196
50r: 196
51v: 189
52r: 189
57v: 194

INDEX OF MANUSCRIPTS

Leiden, Universiteitsbibliotheek,
SCA 28:
3r: 212
3r–21r: 203, 213
29r–v: 133

Leiden, Universiteitsbibliotheek,
VMI 11: 142
26r–27r: 141, 144
26r: 155
26v: 144, 156
27r: 144, 147
see also Visigothic Computus of AD 722

León, Archivo de la Catedral, 8: 147

London, British Library, Cotton Caligula
A XV:
73r–80r (= *Computus Cottonianus* of
AD 689): 146

London, British Library, Cotton Nero
A II:
35v: 181

London, British Library, Cotton Otho
B III: 204

Milan, Biblioteca Ambrosiana, F 60 sup.:
61rb: 162

Milan, Biblioteca Ambrosiana, H 150
inf.: 185
21v–22r: 196
22v: 196
27v–28r: 195
36r: 194
135v–137v: 51–52, 55
see also Bobbio Computus; *Supputatio
Romana*

Milan, Biblioteca Ambrosiana, Z 70 sup.:
8v–10v (= *Ratio sphere Dionysii de circulo
magno pasche*): 219

Montecassino, Archivo della Badia, 3:
1–11 (= Visigothic Computus of
AD 811): 146

Monza, Biblioteca Capitolare, 3-14/127:
192
3r–v: 193
3r–16v: 180
12r: 187
13v: 194
15v–16r: 188

Oxford, Bodleian Library, Bodley 309
(siglum S): 205, 211–12, 220, 222
62r–v: 160, 173–74
62v–73v: 183
95v–95bisr: 213
108rb–110va: 206
110vb: 206
111r: 206
111v: 207
112r: 207, 221
112v: 206–08
113r: 207, 209–13, 221
113r–120r: 201, 203–04, 207
114v: 213
115r: 213
117r: 215
119r: 221
119v: 215–16
120r: 207, 214, 217–18
120r–131v: 214
122r: 215, 218
122v: 218
125v: 218

Oxford, Bodleian Library, Digby 63:
59v: 116

Oxford, Bodleian Library, Rawlison
B 488:
3ra–b: 139

INDEX OF MANUSCRIPTS 253

Oxford, Bodleian Library, Rawlison
   B 502:
10va: 139

Padua, Biblioteca Antoniana, I 27:
76r–77v: 27, 61, 82
77r: 135
see also *Latercus*

Paris, Bibliothèque nationale de France,
   Lat. 528: 192
72r: 193–94
72r–76r: 185
72v: 194
73r: 195
73v: 195
75r: 196

Paris, Bibliothèque nationale de France,
   Lat. 609: 147–48

Paris, Bibliothèque nationale de France,
   Lat. 10837:
34v–40r: 99, 146
40v: 146
41r–v: 146
43r–v: 146
44r: 146

Paris, Bibliothèque nationale de France,
   Lat. 10756:
66v–67r: 181

Paris, Bibliothèque nationale de France,
   Lat. 16361:
248–279: 183

Paris, Bibliothèque nationale de France,
   Nouv. acq. lat. 2169: 147

Rome, Biblioteca Casanatense, 641:
1r–5v (= Visigothic Computus of
   AD 811): 146

St Gall, Stiftsbibliothek, 878: 12

Tours, Bibliothèque municipale, 334:
20r–27r: 183

Vatican, Biblioteca Apostolica Vaticana,
   Pal. lat. 277: 142

Vatican, Biblioteca Apostolica Vaticana,
   Reg. lat. 123: 192
3v: 193–94
3v–4r: 194
4r: 194–95
4v: 195
5r: 195
5v: 195

Vatican, Biblioteca Apostolica Vaticana,
   Reg. lat. 980: 213
9r–10v: 204–05
9v: 206–07, 210, 212
10r: 207, 218

Vatican, Biblioteca Apostolica Vaticana,
   Reg. lat. 2077: 22
79r–81r: 51–52, 55
see also *Supputatio Romana*

Vatican, Biblioteca Apostolica Vaticana,
   Ross. 247:
152v–170r: 183

Vatican, Biblioteca Apostolica Vaticana,
   Urb. lat. 290:
34v–41r: 183

Vatican, Biblioteca Apostolica Vaticana,
   Vat. lat. 1548
68r–69r (= *Ratio sphere Dionysii de circulo
   magno pasche*): 219

INDEX OF MANUSCRIPTS

Vatican, Biblioteca Apostolica Vaticana,
Vat. lat. 6018:

67v: 190
68r: 184
68r–v: 184

Zeitz, Stiftsbibliothek, fol. 33 (Zeitz
bifolia): see Berlin, Staatsbibliothek
Preußischer Kulturbesitz, Lat.
qu. 298 (siglum B)

Zeitz, Stiftsbibliothek, fols 3, 6
(siglum Z):

3r–v, 6r–v: 25–26, 28–29, 31–33, 84–85
3r: 33, 43, 62
3v: 34, 44, 62
6r: 39
6v: 39

Zürich, Zentralbibliothek, Rhen. 30:
166v–169v: 128